HALFORD LUCCOCK TREASURY

Christmas Gift - 1963 Bill Stark

HALFORD LUCCOCK TREASURY

Edited by

Robert E. Luccock

ABINGDON PRESS *new york nashville*

HALFORD LUCCOCK TREASURY

Library of Congress Catalog Card Number: 63-11378

SET UP, PRINTED, AND BOUND BY THE PARTHENON PRESS, AT NASHVILLE, TENNESSEE, UNITED STATES OF AMERICA

Special acknowledgment is made to the following who have granted permission for the reprinting of copyrighted material:

ABINGDON PRESS for the selections by Halford E. Luccock from *Christianity and the Individual,* copyright 1937 by Whitmore & Smith; *The East Window,* copyright 1925 by Halford E. Luccock; *Fares, Please!* copyright 1916 by Halford E. Luccock; *The Haunted House,* copyright 1923 by Halford E. Luccock; *In the Minister's Workshop,* copyright 1944 by Whitmore & Stone; *The Interpreter's Bible,* Vol. 7, copyright 1951 by Pierce & Smith; *Preaching Values in New Translations of the New Testament,* copyright renewal by Halford E. Luccock; *Preaching Values in the Old Testament in the Modern Translations,* copyright renewal 1961 by Halford E. Luccock; *Skylines,* copyright 1923 by Halford E. Luccock; and *Studies in the Parables of Jesus,* copyright 1917 by Halford E. Luccock.

ASSOCIATION PRESS for selection by Halford E. Luccock from *What Religion Means to Me,* edited by Kirby Page.

BOARD OF EDUCATION OF THE METHODIST CHURCH for selections by Halford E. Luccock from *Protestantism,* edited by William K. Anderson.

THE CHRISTIAN CENTURY FOUNDATION for selections by Halford E. Luccock from *The Christian Century* and from *The Pulpit.*

COMMISSION ON PROMOTION AND CULTIVATION OF THE METHODIST CHURCH for selection from *Endless Line of Splendor* by Halford E. Luccock.

DAVID C. COOK PUBLISHING COMPANY for selections by Halford E. Luccock from *New Century Leader.*

CROZER QUARTERLY for "The Reality of Christian Experience" by Halford E. Luccock (October, 1937), vol. XIV, no. 4, pp. 287-96. Copyright, 1937, by Crozer Theological Seminary.

DODD, MEAD & COMPANY and McCLELLAND & STEWART, LTD. for quotation from "The Great Lover" by Rupert Brooke. Reprinted by permission from *The Collected Poems of Rupert Brooke.* Copyright, 1915, by Dodd, Mead & Company. 1943, by Edward Marsh.

DOUBLEDAY & COMPANY for "Whoops! It's Christmas" by Halford E. Luccock. Copyright © Abbott Laboratories, 1959, from *Abbott Christmas Book.* Reprinted by permission.

E. P. DUTTON & COMPANY, INC. for quotation from *The Writer in America* by Van Wyck Brooks; E. P. Dutton & Company, Inc. and J. M. DENT & SONS, LTD. for quotations from "The Wild Knight" by G. K. Chesterton from *The Wild Knight and Other Poems* and from "The House of Christmas" by G. K. Chesterton.

NORMA MILLAY ELLIS for poems by Edna St. Vincent Millay, from *Collected Poems,* Harper & Brothers. Copyright 1927-1928-1934, by Edna St. Vincent Millay; renewed 1955-1962, by Norma Millay Ellis. Used by permission.

SAMUEL FRENCH, INC. for quotation from "A Prayer" by John Drinkwater.

GENERAL COMMISSION ON CHAPLAINS AND ARMED FORCES PERSONNEL for selection by Halford E. Luccock from *The Chaplain.*

HARCOURT, BRACE & WORLD, INC. for quotation from "Soul's Liberty" by Anna Wickham from *The Contemplative Quarry.*

HARPER & ROW, PUBLISHERS, INC. for selections by Halford E. Luccock from *Acts of the Apostles,* vols. I and II; *The Best of Dick Sheppard; Communicating the Gospel; Contemporary American Literature; Marching Off the Map; More Preaching Values in the Epistles of Paul; Preaching Values in the Epistles of Paul; Unfinished Business;* for "Do as I Tell You" by Genevieve Taggard from *Not Mine to Follow;* and for quotation from *The Bible: A New Translation* by James Moffatt. Copyright 1954 by James Moffatt. Reprinted by permission.

HARVARD UNIVERSITY PRESS for quotation from "The Sheep Meadow" by Christopher Morley from *Spirit Level and Other Poems.*

HOLIDAY for quotation from article by James A. Michener. Reprinted by special permission, copyright 1952, by The Curtis Publishing Company.

HOLT, RINEHART & WINSTON, INC. for "To Realize the Quality of Immortality" by Sarah N. Cleghorn, from *Fellow Captains* by Sarah N. Cleghorn and Dorothy Canfield Fisher. Copyright 1916 by Holt, Rinehart & Winston, Inc. Copyright renewed 1944 by Sarah N. Cleghorn and Dorothy Canfield Fisher. Reprinted by permission.

HOUGHTON MIFFLIN COMPANY for quotation from *The Heart of Emerson's Journals* by Bliss Perry, and from *The Grand Alliance* by Winston Churchill.

DR. HOWARD HUNTER for quotation from poem by Strickland Gillilan.

THE HUTCHINSON PUBLISHING GROUP for quotation from *Adonais* by Dorothy Hewlett.

J. B. LIPPINCOTT COMPANY for "No Coaching" by Christopher Morley from *Streamlines*. Copyright 1933, 1934, 1935, 1936 by Christopher Morley. And for quotation from *The Ironing Board* by Christopher Morley.

THE LITERARY TRUSTEES OF WALTER DE LA MARE and THE SOCIETY OF AUTHORS for quotation from "The Listeners" by Walter de la Mare.

LITTLE, BROWN & COMPANY for quotations from poems by Emily Dickinson from *The Complete Poems of Emily Dickinson,* edited by Thomas H. Johnson.

THE MACMILLAN COMPANY for selections from *American Mirror* by Halford E. Luccock. Copyright 1940 by The Macmillan Company. For quotation from *The Trial of Jesus* by John Masefield. For quotation from "Niagara" by Vachel Lindsay. Copyright 1917 by The Macmillan Company, copyright 1945 by Elizabeth C. Lindsay. For quotation from "Foreign Missions in Battle Array" by Vachel Lindsay. Copyright 1913 by The Macmillan Company. And for quotation from "Places" by Sara Teasdale. Reprinted with permission.

NEW YORK HERALD TRIBUNE for quotation from book review by Marion Sturges-Jones.

NEW YORK TIMES for quotation from book review by James McBride.

W. W. NORTON & COMPANY, INC. and GEORGE ALLEN & UNWIN, LTD. for quotation from *Policy for the West* by Barbara Ward.

OXFORD UNIVERSITY PRESS for selections from *Like a Mighty Army* by Halford E. Luccock. Copyright © 1954, Oxford University Press. And *Living Without Gloves* by Halford E. Luccock. Copyright © 1957, Oxford University Press. Oxford University Press and FABER AND FABER, LTD. for quotation from "Bar Room Matins" by Louis MacNeice from *Eight-five Poems*. Copyright 1959, Louis MacNeice. Reprinted by permission.

A. D. PETERS for quotations from *Rain Upon Godshill* by J. B. Priestly.

THE PRESBYTERIAN OUTLOOK for quotation from "Rise Up, O Men of God" by William Merrill.

THE PULPIT DIGEST PUBLISHING COMPANY for selections by Halford E. Luccock from *Pulpit Digest.*

FLEMING H. REVELL COMPANY for selections from *Five Minute Shop Talks* by Halford E. Luccock.

THE SATURDAY REVIEW and MARGARET CULKIN BANNING for quotation from "Changing Moral Standards in Fiction" by Margaret Culkin Banning.

SIMON AND SCHUSTER, INC. for quotation from *The Renaissance* by Will Durant.

THE VIKING PRESS, INC. for "The Veteran": From *Enough Rope* by Dorothy Parker. Copyright 1926, 1953 by Dorothy Parker. For "Interior": From *The Portable Dorothy Parker.* Copyright 1928, 1955 by Dorothy Parker. For "Lone Dog": From *Songs to Save a Soul* by Irene Rutherford McLeod. Reprinted by permission.

A. P. WATT & SON, MRS. GEORGE BAMBRIDGE, and MACMILLAN AND COMPANY, LTD. for quotations from "If" and "Tomlinson" by Rudyard Kipling.

THE WORLD PUBLISHING COMPANY for quotation from *Shakespeare Without Tears* by Margaret Webster. Reprinted by permission.

Introduction

I HAVE NEVER MET A PERSON WHO DID NOT LIKE HAL LUCCOCK. LIKE ANY man, he was sometimes criticized for his statements or for the positions he took, but I never knew anyone who had any personal animosity toward him. The goodwill he held toward all men was obvious, and one knew immediately that here was a man who loved people. The surface slickness that passes in our time for making friends and influencing people was quite foreign to his nature. He was genuinely and deeply concerned about individuals. Several generations of students will bear witness to this central truth about him.

I start with this trait of his character because there were so many other fine things which came from it. There is no more important mark of a Christian than the possession of this concern; it is the gift of Christ to all who have been captured by his spirit. Halford Luccock was interested in people before he had met them personally. He did me a much appreciated favor before I knew him, so that the first time we met we started on a basis of solid friendship.

He could write a letter refusing an invitation which was so gracious and enthusiastic about life in general that it was almost as good as having him say yes. I wrote to him in 1947—give or take a year or two—inviting him to be the preacher for the Nebraska Annual Conference which was meeting in my church in Lincoln. I felt so good after reading his reply that it was several minutes before it dawned upon me that he had said no. He always gave the impression that it was the greatest compliment in the world to be invited and that only major demands would have prevented his accepting.

I never knew a man with such a "homiletical mind." I mean that he could see ideas for sermons all around him and his gift for gathering effective illustrations was astounding. In the same letter he wrote to me refusing the invitation to be conference preacher he added a little paragraph, almost as an afterthought. He had noted, he said, that I was pastor of Saint Paul Methodist Church. Had I ever preached a sermon on what a church ought to be if it were worthy of the name Saint Paul? No, I never had and with a ninetieth anniversary just around the corner too!

He found a sharp insight in a cartoon, in a sign board, in a chance phrase. Hardly ever did he give the impression of reaching for it. You had the feeling that the word was there just waiting for a preacher with eyes to see. He wove the illustration into his text as if it were inevitable, and I never had the sense of a patch-work job in the finished product. I think that everything must have spoken to Luccock with religious overtones, for like the One he served, parables were a natural part of his speech.

It must have been a temptation for this man to become a preacher who would heal the people lightly. With his gifts of entertainment he could have charmed any congregation with surface observations. Hal Luccock was a prophet, however, and he spoke without fear against social evils. No one was ever in doubt as to whose side he was on and what conviction he held. When some of the brethren were running for cover, he was one who faced the storm. Because he was not impressed by a man's wealth or social status, he was not influenced by power or popularity in a cause. In all his long teaching career at Yale, we knew we had a prophet on the faculty.

His writings are voluminous and full of light. I remember reading his *Preaching Values in New Translations of the New Testament* and his *In the Minister's Workshop* when I was a young preacher. They gave me inspiration and encouragement, as did all his books. From my own experience I feel sure that hundreds of young preachers have sat at his feet through his writing, and they will all join me in calling his name blessed.

Halford Luccock was at home in the world. Everything was grist to his preaching mill because the world was the creation of God. He took his materials from literature and from the so-called secular writings. He knew about sports, drama, novels. His language was simple and understandable so that the plain man heard him gladly. He was at his best when he sounded off on the vocabularies of theology, the jargon of ecumenicity, or the feverish phrases of church promotional offices. The various fads which plague religious thinking never made an impression on his style or his thought. I am impressed with the unity of Luccock's life and teaching, which reveals a continual grasp of fundamentals in both the subject matter and the techniques of his profession.

The last few years of his life found me the lucky participant in a three-way correspondence with Dr. Luccock and Emory Bucke. Whoever wrote put a piece of carbon paper in the typewriter so that one fellow received an original and the other a carbon copy. The letters were always marked *Personal* because they were utterly frank, and they were better than an hour on the analyst's couch. Hal spoke his mind about Yale lectures, publishers, bishops, and church machinery. He commented on contemporary trends which displeased him, and now and then he would explode. It was wonderful. His typing was so bad that I could hardly make it out, and I told him once that he was the only friend I ever had whose letters were hardly legible even when typewritten.

Now those letters have stopped coming, and I miss them more than I know how to say. It always lifted up my heart to know that Halford Luccock was around somewhere. Gradually it has come to me that he is still around somewhere, and I am comforted. If you knew him, this book will bring him back into your study. If you never knew him, it will be the next best thing to hearing him coming along the hall singing an old hymn, slightly off key.

GERALD H. KENNEDY
Bishop, The Methodist Church
Los Angeles Area

Foreword

In one of his letters to The Christian Century, Simeon Stylites left solemn warning to any who might attempt writing his biography or memoirs: "No Boswell, Please!"

> On the basis of several recent books of recollections about this person and the other, I have unanimously concluded that a Boswell, gathering up for public view all one's occasional inanities and idiocies, either before or after one's death, is an unmixed calamity. One of the great joys of total obscurity is that there will be no danger of the recordings of a Boswell. Boswell may have been all right for Sam'l Johnson. But a Boswell can ruin almost anyone else if he is diligent enough. . . . So I say roughly, "No Boswell, please!"

In this Simeon Stylites spoke unerringly for Halford Luccock.

My father's real biography is written in the lives of those whom he loved and to whom he ministered as pastor and prophet, teacher and friend. He was both a voluminous letter writer and a noted conversationalist. Yet the remembrance of these he would roughly rule out of any "summing up" in complete favor of the faithful work of his own lifetime devotion to the ministry of writing. This treasury is a gathering together of some of that work.

From his twenty-seven books, more than six hundred letters of Simeon Stylites, one thousand *Springboards for Sermons,* and other published articles and church-school lesson commentaries, as well as from unpublished sermons and his own card file, the material for this anthology has been selected. The over-all plan of the book grew from the recognition of the several kinds of writing which he did—sermons, homiletics, exposition, commentary. Within each classification attempt was made to find writing that is most characteristic of his style and skill, his faith and concern. He frequently remarked that in the field of theology his amateur standing had never been questioned. Be that as it may, we find in his writings no "system" or fully ordered statement of faith. No effort has been made to impose such on the selections here included. He knew himself to be primarily a preacher, a teacher, a commentator whose peculiar gift it was to see and interpret the truth of the gospel in ways that arrested the mind, aroused the imagination, and appealed to the will of those to whom he spoke. The selections in this treasury are those which seem to the editor to represent Halford Luccock at his best. Effort has been made to bring together in one place a sampling of those writings by which he would be most clearly recognized and most widely remembered.

I am grateful for the help of Robert Wright of Abingdon Press in organizing the material to be included in this book and especially for his editorial assistance with Sections III and IV.

The book is a treasury, not a thesis. Accordingly I have felt no constraint to include either a little of everything that Luccock wrote or to have his entire thought represented. Guiding the whole editorial process was the hope and purpose to produce a book in which the reader might find the witness of Luccock's faith, the essence of his teaching, the demonstration of his preaching, the challenge of his mind, the flavor of his spirit, the concerns of his heart.

ROBERT E. LUCCOCK

Contents

Bibliography of Halford E. Luccock

Fares Please	The Abingdon Press	1916
Midweek Service WITH WARREN F. COOK	Methodist Book Concern	1916
Five Minute Shop Talks	Fleming H. Revell Company	1916
Studies in the Parables of Jesus	Abingdon Press	1917
Christian Crusade for World Democracy WITH S. EARL TAYLOR	Methodist Book Concern	1918
New Map of the World	Methodist Book Concern	1919
Skylines	The Abingdon Press	1923
The Haunted House	The Abingdon Press	1923
The East Window	The Abingdon Press	1925
The Story of Methodism WITH PAUL HUTCHINSON AND ROBERT W. GOODLOE	Abingdon Press	1926
Preaching Values in New Translations of the New Testament	Abingdon Press	1928
Jesus and the American Mind	The Abingdon Press	1930
Preaching Values in the Old Testament	Abingdon Press	1933
Contemporary American Literature and Religion	Willett, Clark & Company	1934
Christian Faith and Economic Change	The Abingdon Press	1936
Christianity and the Individual in a World of Crowds	Cokesbury Press	1937
The Acts of the Apostles in Present Day Preaching Vol. I.	Willett, Clark & Company	1938
The Acts of the Apostles in Present Day Preaching Vol. II.	Willett, Clark & Company	1939

American Mirror	The Macmillan Company	1940
In the Minister's Workshop	Abingdon Press	1944
Endless Line of Splendor ILLUSTRATIONS BY LYND WARD	The Advance	1950
The Interpreter's Bible, Exposition of the Gospel of Mark	Abingdon Press	1951
Marching off the Map	Harper & Row, Publishers	1952
Communicating the Gospel (LYMAN BEECHER LECTURES)	Harper & Row, Publishers	1954
The First Fine Careless Rapture	National Council of Churches	1954
Like a Mighty Army	Oxford University Press	1954
Unfinished Business	Harper & Row, Publishers	1956
Living Without Gloves	Oxford University Press	1957
Preaching Values in the Epistles of Paul Vol. I.	Harper & Row, Publishers	1959
Out of This World	Tidings	1959
365 Windows	Abingdon Press	1960
Never Forget to Live	Abingdon Press	1961
More Preaching Values in the Letters of Paul	Harper & Row, Publishers	1961

EDITOR

The Questing Spirit WITH FRANCES BRENTANO	Coward-McCann, Inc.	1947
The Best of Dick Sheppard (H. R. L. SHEPPARD)	Harper & Brothers	1951

I

Testament of Faith and Experience

Halford Luccock never wrote a systematic credo. To read any sizable portion of his life work is to be in no doubt as to his convictions. But he never summarized them. There remain two essays, however, which gather up the main certitudes within which he lived and moved and to which his ministry bore witness. His testament to "The Reality of Christian Experience," given originally in a symposium at Crozer Seminary in 1937, may be taken as the testament of his whole life. The essay on "Religion as Social Passion" appeared in a collection entitled *What Religion Means to Me*. Luccock's religion was a prophet's passion for social justice within the demands of the Hebrew-Christian ethic. The essay summarizes remarkably well his lifelong concerns and the predominant devotions of his ministry. The brief excerpt from the address given to the New York East Conference of The Methodist Church on the fiftieth anniversary of his ordination contains testimony to the joys of the ministry and his conviction that in Jesus Christ is the gospel for our age.

I

Testament of Faith and Experience

Halford Luccock never wrote a systematic credo. To read any sizable portion of his life work is to be in no doubt as to his convictions, but he never summarized them. There remain two essays, however, which gather up the main certitudes within which he lived and moved and to which his ministry bore witness. His statement on "The Reality of Christian Experience," given originally in a symposium at Drew Seminary in 1957, may be taken as the testament of his whole life. The essay on "Religion as Social Passion" appeared in a collection entitled *What Religion Means to Me*. Luccock's religion was a prophet's passion for social justice within the demands of the Hebrew-Christian ethic. The essay summarizes remarkably well his lifelong concerns and the predominant devotion of his ministry. The brief excerpt from the address given to the New York East Conference of The Methodist Church on the fiftieth anniversary of his ordination contains testimony to the joys of the ministry and his conviction that in Jesus Christ is the gospel for our age.

1

The Reality of Christian Experience

I WOULD LIKE AT THE VERY BEGINNING TO USE AS A GRACE, THE LINES OF Henry van Dyke's hymn, "The sea is great, our boats are small." Particularly this little rowboat that is now setting out.

May I bring into sight two affirmations, neither of them to be sketched in, but to be a part of the backdrop of our thinking. They are complementary and in conflict, and the tension between them adds to the complexity of our time.

First, *this is not a time when it is easy to believe in God.* It is not easy for this generation to find such signs of his presence in the world as would make an obvious basis for religious experience. You may ask, "When was such a time?" I suppose the true answer is, "Never." Yet certainly our time has peculiar obstacles, intensified in unique ways. There is no need to recall them in detail. We say it over often like a painful rosary. The international collapse, the economic disaster, the questioning of moral standards, the wide feeling of the impotence of the church, all make for many the still small voice seem very still indeed. It is too grim a mood to be dissipated by any performance of neat little arguments, no matter how agile they may be.

Second, *the conviction of God's reality, of the genuineness of contact with God, is measurelessly important for human life.* That is an axiom for Christian thinking, but a forgotten one over large areas of life. We have been told endlessly that religion is an illusion necessary to the adolescence of the race but now that we have grown up we should put away childish things. A close look at our world makes it evident that that is like saying, "Now that we have become men we must put away childish things, like water and food." Dostoievsky's word, "The man who bows down to nothing cannot bear the burden of himself," interprets a great deal of experience in our present world. Some of the tragedies of our industrial life are those of people having to work in an atmosphere, in mines and tunnels, to which man's nature is not adapted, in devitalized air from which oxygen has been withdrawn. Multitudes are demonstrating today that when that same thing is done spiritually, life shrinks and collapses.

With those two things then, the difficulty and necessity of religious experience, as part of the scenery, let us consider some remembrances with which to start. There is a profound word on this whole matter from Coleridge, "Make any truth too definite and you make it too small." Coming at the time that it did, when men were felt to be living in a tight, cosy, closed system of a physical world, that statement was an intuitive recognition of the dynamic quality of the universe. It was akin to Bergson's protest a century later against "frozen conceptualism," that is taking living, flowing, dynamic, many-sided experience and crowding it into rigid rationalistic pigeonholes and freezing it there. The history of physics for a generation furnishes a striking comment on Coleridge's "making truth too definite." Matter has dissolved into equations. The old universe had a greater fall than Humpty Dumpty. The too definite proved too small also in economics. Under the hurricane of the war and the worldwide depression, the eternal word once delivered to the classical economist is gone with the wind. And the too definite in religion, as laid down both by those outside and inside, is too small for a living flow of experience. John Buchan writes of Archbishop Laud, "He brought the mind of a college pedant to the broad and spacious life of England." Too often we have allowed ourselves to be browbeaten by those who brought the mind of a pedant, with its ludicrously definite measures of scientific knowledge, to the breadth and spaciousness of the response of the whole personality to the whole of life, which is included in what we call religious experience.

Let us say just a brief preliminary word about the *instruments* of religious experience. They are more like the antennae of a radio, or the sensitivity of a magnetic needle, than they are like a grocer's scales for weighing sugar, or a chemist's tube, or a logician's syllogisms. The reality of religious experience does not depend on a geometrical proof of God. When we speak, as a theologian does, of the "stinging coerciveness" of Jesus, it is not logical compulsion of proof which is meant. There is none. There may be an A, B, C in religion. There is no Q. E. D. The surrender of faith to God is not at all like the acceptance of the conclusion of an argument. It is rather the beginning of an adventure. We cannot even define that to which faith is committed in adventure. For as the French saying goes, "God defined is God finished." God analyzed is God dead. There is real insight in the reply of a school child asked to write on the subject, "The funniest thing I ever saw." He wrote, "The funniest thing I ever saw was too funny for words." Right! So the mind says, "The greatest thing I ever saw is too great for words." It breaks through language and escapes. Religious experience is a venture of personality in response to an eliciting environment. There lies the zest of life and the very essence of religion. There is a very true word of Christopher Morley in a little poem called "No Coaching":

I went to the theatre
With the author of the successful play.
He insisted on explaining everything;
Told me what to watch;
The details of directions,
The errors of the property man,
The foibles of the star.
He anticipated all my surprises
And ruined the evening.
Never again! And mark you,
The greatest author of all
Made no such mistake.

The highest expressions of religion have been recognitions that "God made no such mistake." Religion is choice, risk, test. "I do not ask to see the distant scene." "Though he slay me, yet will I trust him." "My God, why hast thou forsaken me?" "Faith is the assurance of things hoped for."

The instruments of religious experience and of Christian experience are all the endowments of the mind and spirit. The person who insists that religious experience is an illusion unless it can be proved with the scientific instruments of knowledge is not only inadequate but impertinent. He is exactly like a man trying to get a flower show over the radio. Color and perfume are a bit beyond the range of a loudspeaker, no matter how many tubes the set may have. But they are none the less real on that account. The color and perfume of experience are beyond capture by quantitative measurement. This is true in all walks of life. Often, however, we allow ourselves to be overborne in religion and sink into the depths of an inferiority complex when someone comes along, like a bully swinging a club, and tells us that religious experience cannot be proved by astronomy, chemistry, or psychology. We forget that the scientific bully could not prove half of what he knows, and the best half, that which he stakes his life on, with those same instruments. He may come out of his laboratory and heaven pity him if he tries to know his friends by the same infallible proofs of scientific dissection! He knows them in more accurate and adequate ways—through intuition, through faith, and sympathy. Professor Eddington has drawn a conclusive picture of this. He says, "The materialist who is convinced that all phenomena arise from electrons, and quanta and the like, controlled by mathematical formulæ must presumably hold the belief that his wife is a rather elaborate differential equation; but he is probably tactful enough not to obtrude this opinion in domestic life." He brings to that realm more fitting ways of knowing. To come to that great undertaking, "to know God, whom to know aright is life eternal," with any hope of achievement we must use the means adequate, observation of life and information, and testimony, of course, but also, experiment and discovery, insight and inference.

Let us briefly examine four lines of march for our thinking.

I

First, the reality of Christian experience is found in the way in which Jesus meets our nature. Christian experience is one form of religious experience and some of the weight of evidence for its reality comes from the testimony of religious experience in general. The testimony, in brief, is an amplification of Augustine's, "Thou hast formed us for thyself." The testimony of the eternal outreach of man tends toward the affirmation that the capacity for God is as much a part of man's nature as his adaptation to anything in his environment, the sight to objects, the hearing to sound, the lungs to air. Up and down through all the nooks and corners of the calendar and out through all the spread of the earth, we meet it, in varying forms of one unending search. Religion persists in spite of all the solemn and conclusive burial services held over it, because it meets this ineradicable need with which man started on his human journey and of which he becomes more conscious the farther he goes.

It is not any more imported into man by imagination or manipulation than is sex or hunger. It is there. It is there even when one gives up formal religious belief. Witness the testimony of Katherine Mansfield, in a casual letter, "God is now gone for all of us. Yet we must believe. And not only that, we must carry our weakness and our sin and our devilishness to somebody." Notice the musts, "we must believe; we must carry our weakness." Through these words it is the human race speaking.

It is both a belief in a spiritual power outside the seen universe with which fellowship is possible and a belief in the outward validity of the compulsions on conduct which are inwardly felt. Now, of course, one can call that aspect of man's nature "the great illusion." But one does not speak the last word in that easy phrase, for when anyone says it he subscribes to the strangest violation of the procedure of nature that could be imagined, a nature where organisms adapt themselves to reality in their environment. Georgia Harkness has written, "a deep-seated, long-persisting human quest is more likely to be organically related to reality than that which is inconsequential and temporary." Religion is, of course, personal, but not on that account necessarily subjective. The weight of the history of religion points to religion as a response to something dependable and eternal. Boutroux has called it "the response to the Beyond which is within," or as Dean W. R. Matthews has amended that to "the Beyond which is akin." This latter phrase finds an echo in the classic passage from William James in which he declares that his reading the lives of religious people had so strengthened his faith in God's living presence that he was unable to "pooh-pooh" it away and found in himself a "germ of something similar which makes response." "The Beyond which is akin"; "a germ of something similar which makes response"!

That experience of men in general can be paralleled by the individual who cares to test it in his own life. Let one begin with something he is sure of, some way of life that is seen as everlastingly right. Let him live up to that and follow it faithfully and persistently. He will come to feel that the voice calling him along that path is not simply his own voice, and that purity, honesty, and love which call are neither mere whims nor habits but have their source in reality.

Jesus meets our nature in a manner unique and permanently compelling. At the place where he does meet human needs there is the seat of authority in religion. May I try the aid of a homely, visual illustration? In the old-fashioned electric arc light there was a carbon coming down from above and one coming up from beneath. When the current was turned on, a flame leaped across the gulf between them. That may be not too inaccurate a picture of the instinctive human response to Jesus. There is the message and person of Jesus coming down, as it were, from the world of eternal reality and man's need reaching up, and a flame leaps across. Jesus lays an imperative on human life whenever he gets a chance to confront it. In moments of high visibility, when we get real glimpses both of what we ought to be and what we might be, Jesus puts a compulsion on us.

The finest words for that compulsion, I think, are to be found in *King Lear.* In one scene the banished Duke of Kent returns in disguise to take service with King Lear, and this dialogue takes place:

LEAR: What wouldst thou?
KENT: Service.
LEAR: Who wouldst thou serve?
KENT: You.
LEAR: Dost thou know me, fellow?
KENT: No sir, but you have that in your countenance which I would fain call master.

Those last words may well stand for the response made to Jesus by uncounted millions.

I have been greatly interested many times to see that same pull of authority, not only when one exposes himself to the figure of Jesus, but whenever people catch a glimpse of the spirit of Jesus as they have seen it in human life. It comes from the most unexpected places. One of the most striking of those places is that which I have found in one of the roughest, toughest books that I have ever read in my life, *The Way of a Transgressor.* It records about twenty years of the roving journeys of a cynical newspaper reporter over postwar Europe, where he met the leading figures of Europe and had very little real confidence in any one of them. In a wholly unintended manner he takes off his hat in reverence before just two people, Lord Irwin, the Governor-General of India, and George Lansbury, the leader of the Labor Party at that time in England. It occurred to me that they were the only two desperate Christians he ever met in his life. When, from his background and his experience he came up close to some life through which there could stream out the radiance of Jesus, he too said, "There is that in thy countenance which I would fain call master."

Jesus meets our nature at central points. He meets it in that dim borderland where our reach exceeds our grasp. Our inability to find fulfillment in material things as other creatures of earth do fits in, is mortised in, as it were, to Jesus' revelation of the great Other, the God in whom our fragments are complete. Our dissatisfaction with ourselves, our inescapable sense of missing the mark, fits in with Jesus' own demonstration, not merely of the life we are meant for, but of the possibility of forgiveness and a life made over. Our experience of the strange self-defeating quality of selfishness fits into Jesus' call to fulfillment in service.

In that fit there is the quality of an undebatable compulsion. We can trace in the Christian experience of the first century how that compulsion grew to take in wider meaning and how it grows today. The disciples began with a very simple fact. Here was a person, a fact in their daily experience. They responded to that. He said, "Follow me," and they followed him. But they could not keep their eyes on that person; he had a way of turning them back on themselves. They were faced, not merely with an attractive person, but by an uncomfortable moral challenge. "He that is not with me is against me." Later this moral fact and challenge could be explained only as a spiritual fact. Jesus came to represent the reality of God.

Something like that still goes on. Jesus as a person, a fact of history, cannot be shoved out of the way by the crowding of twenty centuries. He is a moral challenge, deeply disturbing because deeply compelling, so compelling that it carries the overtones of a cosmic voice, a source in the ultimate reality in the universe.

Does this sound more like personal confession than argument? The only effective persuasion in the realm of experience has been confession. Paul, when given a chance to defend the faith, always slides into autobiography. Christianity is invitation rather than debate. To those who try it, Jesus' way of life becomes its own evidence. That movement of the disciple's experience may be ours. If we are honest with life, that is, if we face life honestly and sincerely, and are willing to learn what it has to teach, we do become aware of one who speaks to us through duty and love —not something but Someone.

It is very evident that the chief instrument for such experience is not hard thinking, it is living. It is not those who think hardest and longest, but those who live fullest and deepest who travel the path to assurance of reality. If we want to verify religion we must first choose it. Commitment of self to an experiment with a way of living leads to experience.

II

Second, consider one particular aspect of the reality of Christian experience, the experience of things so worthful that they cannot be accounted for by any naturalistic explanation. An irreducible part of religious experience is the experience of values. Here is something with more than an instrumental usefulness, with an inherent worth in itself, such as truth, beauty, goodness. We did not make them. They wield command over us. What do they say to us?

One of the best stories connected with the Grand Canyon is that of the man who on first seeing it, paid it the tribute of reverent silence, and then exclaimed, "My, something must have happened here!" Quite probably! It was a bit obvious that an Indian did not drive a rude plow along the ground and thus create that vast chasm. A cause sufficient to produce the result is necessary. The thing is too big, too awe-inspiring for any trivial explanation. Those very words may well describe the feeling men have had times without number when looking at another sort of awe-inspiring wonder, the presence in human lives of the morally big, awe-inspiring manifestation of fidelity, honor, courage, magnanimity, or sacrifice. "Something must have happened here!" Something great enough to produce the effect. "O we're sunk enough here, God knows." There is evil as well as good, pigmy smallness as well as moral stature. Yet along the common highways there is greatness passing by. We have seen it and admitted its right to command. The fruits of the spirit, love, joy, peace, long-suffering, kindness, goodness, faithfulness, meekness, self-control, these are not hothouse products, rare as an orchid. They grow in the open, in all seasons, in the plainest backyards. To meet them, to manifest them, to feel their coerciveness, is to have a religious experience, for they carry overtones of an unseen spiritual environment in which they have their source.

This recognition of values is not to be confused with a romantic sense of the goodness of human nature which makes for self-sufficiency and is an archenemy of religious experience. In a very deep sense we can find God only when we have lost trust in ourselves. Such experience of values is not the confident humanism which was so disastrous a mark of the prewar mentality of the world. It is the recognition of the qualities of acts which need a cause great enough to account for them and to account for their undebatable command over us. On this point it is historically true that the recognition of moral values always moves toward religion, or, as one philosopher says, "morality trembles on the brink of religion," that moral consciousness finds its support in an affirmation that its judgments of value issue from a reality outside of itself.

One illustration of this concerns the highest values the race has ever experienced. I made a sentimental pilgrimage last summer to South

Kensington Museum in London to look up some of my ancestors. They were your ancestors, too, so you have no cause to feel superior. I went to see the skulls of some of the First Families, the Neanderthal man and the Java man. I was looking for one in particular, the Galilee man whose skull was dug up in Galilee. I was interested in him through the remark about him in Dr. Fosdick's *Pilgrimage to Palestine,* contrasting the Galilee man with the man of Galilee. I did not find the skull. It is too precious to expose to public view. Also, not all the bones are present. But I did find a plaster cast. As one looks at that low slanting forehead (he was the original low-brow), the question comes, How did humanity ever get up the long climb from the Galilee man to the man of Galilee? Is it not as reasonable, to use the language of understatement, to ascribe the supreme manifestation of spirit to a spirit akin to it in the universe, as to ascribe it to the accidental stirrings of some vast mud pie?

That is only a dramatic form of the compulsion laid upon us to seek the vindication of our highest moral values, which life needs both for its zest and significance, in their origin in a creator and preserver of values. As R. H. Strachan puts it in one sentence, "In every compelling vision of truth, beauty or goodness, we hear a voice saying 'Have I been so long among you and you have not known me?' " Duty, truth, and love compel men because they are rooted in the structure of the universe. Deep calls to deep. When we yield to them we are not merely following an idea of our own, not merely entertaining an idea of any kind, but are surrendering ourselves to an absolute demand, reaching out for a soul akin to us at the heart of the universe. The good which stirs men must be a part of a larger good, as real as granite or a star. That pull on man is not fiction but everyday reality. Recently at a college in a discussion group a student said to me with a fine, courteous air, "I hope you won't mind if I say that religion is all moonshine." I said, "No, I wouldn't mind it at all." After a bit I added, "But I'd like to thank you for that word, 'moonshine.' " I felt like the character in the trial scene in *The Merchant of Venice* who keeps dancing around the room exclaiming, "Oh wise young man, I thank thee for that word." I asked the student, "Have you ever been in Panama?" He said, "No, but what has Panama got to do with religion?" I said, "There's a lot of moonshine in Panama." I asked if he had ever seen a twenty-two-foot tide come in, such as there is in Panama. If one has never seen a twenty-two-foot tide come in he has missed something worth watching. There is an unbelievable lift of billions of tons of water, and what is doing it? Moonshine—the pull of another world, an unseen but resistless force! Religion is unseen and real like moonshine in its measureless lift to life.

III

There is another aspect of religious experience which I am confident will be more and more convincing in the years to come. It is the social validation of Christianity. The passing parade of life and history make clear that Jesus was everlastingly right in his reading of life. Some of the most effective arguments for Christianity are not being spun out of the brains of theologians, but are being shaped by events, by events of contemporary history. This demonstration brings daily testimony to the truth that other foundation can no man lay for lasting security, economic welfare, and peace than that which is laid in Christ Jesus. We are members one of another. And when that essential unity is denied the society which denies it starts on the road to disaster.

We have been given for generations the conventional picture of Jesus as a gentle, mildly idiotic sentimentalist, a figure for poetry and art, unfitted for any contact with the rough realities of the world. That picture is steadily changing for anyone not deaf, dumb, and blind. Jesus is emerging as the sternest realist who ever injected hard truth into a world ruled by illusion. The sentimentalist at the Versailles Peace Conference was not Jesus. The sentimentalists were the romantic fools who imagined it possible to build security and peace on a basis of hate and revenge.

Gilbert Stuart, who painted so many portraits of George Washington that one wonders how either of them ever had time for anything else, once looked at Talleyrand the French statesman, when he was in America, and made the remark, "If that man is not a scoundrel God does not write a legible hand." God writes a legible hand. Sometimes he writes on a human face. Sometimes, as in our own United States at the present time, he writes very legibly on the face of the land. The succession of dust storms and floods, drought and erosion of the soil, is legible writing to the effect that whatever a man or a nation sows that shall it also reap. When for generations we have abused and exploited the land, slaughtering the forests and skinning the topsoil, we pay for it in disaster. Such calamities are not, as our blasphemous phrase goes, "acts of God." They are acts of man, of man's greed.

God writes a legible hand in the economic and international world. Jesus does not come into our world like a Rip Van Winkle, antiquated, and alien in speech and garb. He comes with the only way of life which will stand in our interdependent world, a way based on mutuality and common welfare. In religious terms which are true in every realm it is a way of love and brotherhood. Jesus stands in our world as the stone which is the head of the corner, "and whoever shall fall on this stone shall be broken."

IV

The effective apologetics of the future will not be argument so much as demonstration. It will be the creation of a world, a way of common living together, in which it will be possible and natural for men to believe in God.

We cannot separate social effort for a Christlike world from the subject of the reality of religious experience. Religion can never be genuinely experienced in a social vacuum. We cannot say, "Go to now, I will have a religious experience." The experience of doing God's will in the concrete setting of today's life and need is an inseparable part of the consciousness of God. If God is love, the only adequate means of fellowship with such a God is by the practice of love.

The book of Acts gives an eternally valid picture of this. When the early Christian group actually practiced love within the terms of their situation, when they "had all things in common," there resulted a glow of abounding life.

As it was in the beginning, it is now, and ever shall be.

—THE CROZER QUARTERLY

2

Religion as Social Passion

"The First Fine Careless Rapture"

That's the wise thrush; he sings each song twice
over,
Lest you should think he never could recapture
The first fine careless rapture!
—ROBERT BROWNING

A MUCH WORN QUOTATION, NO DOUBT. YET IT WOULD BE HARD TO THINK of anything closer to the center of that much discussed question, Can religion demonstrate its moral power in this generation?

Whether Christianity can be adequate to the moral leadership of our civilization today and tomorrow depends on whether it can recapture that "first, fine, careless rapture" of its earliest days, for that is the thing so conspicuously missing over large areas of church life today. The churches have numbers, wealth, position, efficiency of many sorts, but anything resembling New Testament rapture and the divine carelessness from which it came is almost as hard to find as lost youth.

There is not much hope of recovering that mood and the power which it generated without knowing rather clearly where it came from.

One of the most striking differences between a large section of the church today and the Christian fellowship pictured in the New Testament is that the New Testament Church was *fighting something.* All through the New Testament, particularly in the latter part of it, when the shadow of persecution and martyrdom began to fall on the little Christian group, there is an oppressive sense of a desperate conflict, a fight to the death with malignant and powerful forces of evil. One of the suggestive translations which Professor Goodspeed has made of Paul's words is: "We struggle against the ruling spirits of this dark age." The church in the New Testament never thought of itself as being in a rest camp; it was obviously on a battle line. Some of the characteristic marks of the life reflected in the New Testament are due precisely to the experience of relentless battle with the ruling and malignant forces of evil in the world. In that life of the early Church we find an exhilaration of spirit, an intensity of fellowship, a moral energy that we can still feel in the New Testament like the throbbing of a great dynamo. There is a buoyancy and an unhesitating faith. All these combined to make that Christianity a tremendous moral power.

The vitality of first century Christianity was a product and a fruit of certain attitudes and actions. It was not a thing by itself. The rapid beating of a person's heart is the result of exertion. One cannot say, "Go to now, I will have my heart beat fast." Our hearts beat fast only when we do something to make them beat fast. In a very true sense the quick beating of the heart of the New Testament church was in part a product of a life and death struggle with monstrous forces of evil, during which the church often looked closely into the bright face of danger.

The supreme instance of this truth is found in the book of Revelation. That book is a dark forest, but it is lighted by many bivouac fires. There can be no question but that we find in Revelation two things—first, a terrific battle with the evil order in the world roundabout, and second, the most intense and joyful fellowship, the most heightened exhilaration made up of faith and courage, of which literature preserves any record. It is contended here that the union of these two things is not accidental. They depend upon one another. They are always found together. If we are to recover the vitality and rapture of the New Testament experience we must recover the New Testament fight.

The most vivid picture of this is found in the imagery of the Beast in the book of Revelation. It is a tradition that the passages about the beast have been the happy hunting grounds of biblical literalists and fanatics who have fastened the most weird and fantastic interpretations on that much-interpreted animal. Yet the imagery is very simple. It was readily understood by those to whom the book was addressed. The Beast was Rome; it was a succession of emperors, "a wild beast with ten horns and seven heads rising out of the sea."

The Christian fellowship was locked in deadly conflict with the great exploiting power of its time, that cruel, well-nigh omnipotent power which devoured and mangled the lives of men. The Christians were never deluded into thinking that they could make an easy compromise with such an evil power. They did not compliment it. They heaped upon it the ugliest and most shameful names of human speech. They did not attempt to shake hands with it in a hail-fellow-well-met jocular manner. That came later in the days of Constantine, and then the glory departed and the Church accepted the manacles of slavery.

The point which we are emphasizing here is that a large part of that intensity and vividness of spiritual experience and power manifested in the New Testament came because those Christians were fighting the Beast. There is always a special blessing—an intensity and richness which comes to those who fight the Beast. By the Beast we do not mean a constituted authority. The Christian struggle in the first three centuries was not against government as such. It was against that crushing, mangling force which spoiled and destroyed life. The equivalent of the Beast in our day is that brute force animated by the motive of profit, whether it is in the war system, which gorges itself on flesh and blood, or in a rampant industrialism which fattens on the same human diet.

Whoever fights the Beast has a special blessing. The blessing which the Church must get if it is to recover and maintain its allurement and power is that which comes to those who wage a thoroughgoing battle with the exploiting powers of evil in our time. The truth that there is such a blessing can be discovered in any company of people who have set themselves to battle desperately for what they consider their liberty, or to right what they consider injury. Take the average socialist and Communist group, for instance. Disagree as we may with their goals, with their motives, or with their methods, we cannot but admit that in such a struggling fellowship when the battle is on there is an intensity and vividness of life which puts the average Christian congregation to shame. To go from an average Sunday-evening church service, where a small company of people are decorously and drowsily going through a routine, into a protest meeting of working men, is like going from a cemetery to a three-alarm fire. The difference is largely because the protesting group has the blessing of an intensified life which is the reward of the fighter. The sluggish group in the church is not fighting anything particularly. The other group, in its own consciousness at least, is not only fighting for itself but for the world's future.

The future of Christianity depends on our recovery of that sense of the vivid reality of religion. That in turn depends on our facing and fighting in an uncalculating, reckless spirit the master iniquities of our age, which deny by their very existence the gospel of Jesus. The New Testament experience is lacking because over such wide areas in our church life there is so little fight. Ecclesiastical life has consisted so much, as Canon Woods has said, "in the uninspiring spectacle of a docile and mild-mannered gentleman trying to persuade a docile company of people to be still more docile." So many of our churches do not know that there is any fight going on. They are like the lady in London, over a hundred years old, who went through all the years of the Great War with Zeppelins dropping bombs over her very head without knowing a single thing about it. Her family, not wishing to distress her unnecessarily, kept her in entire ignorance that a war was going on.

The weakness of the church today is that people who ought to be fighting forces, struggling against social wrongs, are not so much fighters as they are dear old ladies in snowy white caps sitting in rocking chairs not knowing that there is any fight going on. One of the chief differences in the church of our age and that of the book of Revelation is that instead of fighting the Beast we stroke it and pet it and say, "Nice pussy!" We compliment it on its fur and feel flattered when it lifts a paw to shake hands with us in response to some address of salutation.

Often ministers and churches stultify themselves in their pious approval of pirates of the industrial world. They take positions quite incompatible with the implications of their gospel. If anyone thinks this last statement is exaggerated, let him read the eulogy delivered by a prominent minister at a memorial service held in Washington in honor of the late Judge Gary, in which it was solemnly declared by this representative of Christ that what America needed most was more men like this man. If that eulogy had been intended to cover merely the fine personal record of a high moral standard of private conduct it would have been quite fitting. But it was spread out as a tribute to the social accomplishments of the man—a man who led to the last ditch the fight for the twelve-hour day and the seven-day week, who stood for squeezing the life and soul out of men for the sake of biggest profits!

A long time ago Ralph Waldo Emerson said keenly that the real object of worship of many Christians of his day was represented by the best diagonal line which could be drawn between Abbott Lawrence and Jesus Christ. Abbott Lawrence was probably the most conspicuous industrial baron of his time. He embodied those sacred qualities of New England shrewdness and the ability to make two dollars grow where only one grew before. Our worship today still moves along the same kind of diagonal lines. Some people draw their diagonal line between Napoleon and Jesus Christ and accept the best resulting compromise that comes out. Others favor the diagonal line which represents the compromise effected between the far more potent financial King and the peasant of Galilee.

By this process we bleach all the color out of Jesus. Our life and words lack sting. The anticlimax which is the inevitable doom following such diagonal manipulations is very keenly described with unconscious satire in an entry in the Journal of Samuel Pepys: "A good sermon of Mr. Gifford at our church upon 'Seek ye first the kingdom of heaven.' A very excellent and persuasive, a good and moral sermon. *He showed like a wise man that righteousness is a surer moral way of being rich than sin.*" O lovely gospel!

On this entry Robert Louis Stevenson comments:

> It is thus that the respectable people desire their great hearts to address them, telling in mild accents how you may make the best of both worlds and be a moral hero without courage, kindness, or troublesome reflections and thus the Gospel, cleared of eastern metaphor, becomes a model of worldly prudence and a handy book for Pepys and the successful merchant.

Is not one of the major reasons for the absorption of so many ministers and churches in the petty and fussy details of ecclesiasticism the fact that there is no headlong fighting going on between them and the entrenched evils of the social order? Consequently, the first, fine, careless rapture is gone, so they take up a preoccupation with ecclesiasticism as a compensation or a defense mechanism. Thus the Church of St. Peter becomes the Church of St. Vitus, a fearful degeneration in which the headlong impetuosity of a prophet and fighter is replaced by the insignificant ups and downs of a parochial merry-go-round.

The heart of the matter—and nothing in the world affects more vitally the future of religion—is that so easily the church can become involved in the established order of things in the social and economic world, that it finds any kind of effective protest against the evils of that system increasingly difficult. It is not because the church has made any conscious surrender of its principles, but by a very natural and insidious process it depends so on wealth and the established order for its support that it becomes part of the very thing it should struggle against.

Sometimes it seems as though the churches have read their New Testament in this way, "A new commandment I give unto thee, *Thou shalt not upset the apple cart.*" These words fairly express the unconscious fears and timidities of many a congregation. It expresses the sense of a never-forgotten obligation to refrain from collision with current economic traditions and practices and with financial powers behind those practices.

Sometimes the elevation of this commandment to a place of first importance is due merely to an affinity on the part of many in the church for the good, the true, the beautiful, and the prosperous!

Sometimes, however, the bonds which unite the church to the powers that be in the economic world are of a firmer nature. The church must go on. Its overhead runs twenty-four hours a day, and each year seems to see an increase in the amount of overhead that must be kept running. The underlying philosophy is not very different from that piece of distilled prudence, "Don't bite the hand that feeds you." There is nothing so crude or simple as a deliberate betrayal of the gospel or cowardice in its presentation. The situation is far more complex and subtle and complicated than that.

But like the pressure of the atmosphere of fifteen pounds to the square inch on all of us, there is the ever-present pressure of the ruling ideas of the masters of the economic and business world and the situation of the church itself. That situation is complicated in thousands of instances by the fact that the church has given large hostages to the business world to further a building program. Millions of dollars of mortgages are held over churches. There are unpaid pledges of other millions of dollars. It is not to be wondered at that the first concern of a large number of trustees and other officials is for carrying through their venture successfully.

Hence, there is a very strong feeling to this effect: "There is no use of us or our minister being quixotic. We can very well postpone playing on some notes of the Christian gospel until a more convenient season. Prudence is the better part of valor. *Don't upset the apple cart.*"

We do not believe that anyone has yet seriously estimated the consequences of the prodigious exploits in church building in the last few years. Hundreds of millions of dollars expended in the erection of church buildings undoubtedly represents spiritual assets; it also represents appalling spiritual liabilities.

The result is often such an increase in prudence that the church's lips are sealed even in the presence of glaring wrong. The result is an ironical anticlimax of having built a magnificent place in which to say something and then having nothing to say. What shall it profit a church to gain a whole world of Gothic arches and stained-glass windows and lose its own voice? We do not believe the day is far distant when many Christian congregations, rather than have the soul crushed out of them by an unbearable weight of "overhead," will walk out into the streets as in older days, where, under the blue sky with no overhead but the face of God Almighty, they will be able to proclaim the unhindered word of God to this generation. Many a congregation would do well to lose a half-finished church building by leaving it half finished if that were necessary to save its own soul. It might lose a first mortgage but it would find a second blessing.

The churches so often lose this second blessing because they scatter their efforts in minor conflicts, sometimes judiciously chosen because they are so minor and remote from the main issues of life. They choose their opponents carefully and cautiously. It is possible to make a great bluster and parade of audacity when we are assaulting something that can't hit back or something which will arouse no one's ire or defense. Mr. E. W. Howe, the Kansas journalist and author, says that he has learned in forty years of newspaper experience that the only safe thing to attack is the man-eating shark! That expresses the platform of some doughty warriors exactly—"Down with the man-eating shark!" They pick out some "safe" demon to attack, from which there can be no "comeback" from the allies of the poor demon because it has no allies.

One thing seems sure, we will never recapture for our time the splendor of an apostolic fervor, the buoyant intensity of a fearless faith, the glory of being in an indiscreet and headlong conflict, *until we break the subservience of the church to the state.* We have made it our boast in America that the church has been entirely separated from the state. Often that is an empty boast, for while it is true formally the actual fact is that the state has dominated the church, especially when it needed the church to be its tool to work out the nationalistic purposes of the state. This has meant that the church pushed aside temporarily the dominance of the ideals of Jesus. There is no question but that in recent years that subservience of the church to the state has increased in America and every successive attempt at the regimentation of the minds of the people of the United States, forcing them to walk in a mental lockstep, tends to increase that subservience.

If the church is to find a rebirth of apostolic vitality it must snap the chains which bind it to the wheels of government—cost what that may. It was a great word which the Dartmouth College seniors put into their report on the curriculum a few years ago. They expressed resentment at the shaping of the curriculum to meet the needs of big business enterprises which require an increasing stream of young men to be fed into their hoppers with certain preparation already made. The Dartmouth seniors said, "The college must not be made the bellhop of business." By the same token, the church must not be made the bellhop either of business or of governments. The church should not hop to bells. The church should ring them.

The sequence of events to which this paper has striven to draw attention has never failed in Christian history. Wherever there has been a struggle against the great exploiting powers of injustice which measure men in terms of profits, which use them as a means and not as an end, there has always inevitably followed such an enrichment of life and an intense reality of spiritual experience that has not appeared at any other time. The blessing reserved to those who fight the Beast has never been withheld from the fighters. If the church at large today could only believe that it would throw itself recklessly and with a genuinely careless rapture into the struggle for a Christian social order and a deadly conflict with all that impedes it, no matter how respectable, or how hallowed by tradition. It would soon have such a warmth of fellowship at its hearth that multitudes would be drawn by an irresistible power.

—WHAT RELIGION MEANS TO ME

3

Semi-Centennial Address

THE FEW WORDS WHICH I DID HAVE FOR THESE FEW MINUTES OUGHT TO BE sung. That is not a threat, but an announcement of fact. So fear not, but if I did sing I could raise quite a Te Deum. For I have nothing but a song of thanksgiving, gratitude that I have had a part in the service of the church, and thanksgiving for the amazing gifts of friendships in this Conference, unearned and undeserved, but pressed down full measure, shaken together and running over.

I suppose the supreme test of the satisfaction of the life of anyone is whether he would do it again. I thank God I can say about the ministry loudly enough to be heard across the Brooklyn Bridge, "I would do it again!" I would like to begin again. The years ahead are going to be difficult ones; new difficulties are appearing every year. We can say to young recruits to the ministry, "Look down, look down, that lonesome road before you travel on." It will be hard, but it need not be a "lonesome road." You will not travel alone.

I have been deeply moved in recent months by an overwhelming feeling of the fitness of our gospel for our time. The words of an old Christmas carol or hymn come to me as a striking picture of that fitness. It is the hymn beginning, "Good Christian men, rejoice." You remember it.

> Good Christian men, rejoice
> With heart and soul and voice;
> Now ye hear of endless bliss;
> Jesus Christ was born for this!

We can look out at the bewildering and terrifying conditions in our world today and say, "Jesus Christ was born for this." Of course, Christ was born for the needs of every age. "Jesus Christ the same, yesterday, today and forever."

1. We are in a growingly impersonal world, and Jesus Christ was born

for this. In him we have a personal gospel for an impersonal world. The effect on many people of the conditions of our world is as though a fleet of steam rollers had run over them, squeezing all the individuality out of them. One of the big themes of psychology today is that of man's "lost identity." In our gospel man's "lost identity" is found, "Beloved, now are we the sons of God."

2. In these days of personal tension and breakdown, we have a gospel of people made whole. Jesus Christ was born for this day of "fighting within and fears without." A psychiatrist said to me not long ago, "Did you ever hear of Foxe's *Book of Martyrs?*" "I have a copy," I told him, "printed in the 1500's." "Does it have any pictures in it?" "It has pictures," I said, "that will make your hair curl." "I'd like to see it," he said. "A woman told me the other day she felt just like the pictures in Foxe's *Book of Martyrs*, in which a man had a horse tied to each hand and one to each foot, and the horses were all pulling in different directions. She said she was being pulled to pieces."

There are many people in these days who are being "pulled to pieces" by various forces in our hurried, anxious lives. For such a time as this, we are the messengers of One in "whom all things hang together." We "are complete in him." Again, it is a day when the world is on the dizzy edge of disaster. Jesus Christ was born for this particular need of salvation. Our first concern must be, not to get to the moon before Russia does, but to get to the earth before it is blown to bits. There is no other name whereby the world may be saved from destruction but that of Christ.

I have remembered all my life a word spoken by a retired minister to me at the time of my ordination as elder. The Conference was held at Middletown, Connecticut, and the presiding bishop, David H. Moore, made an address to the incoming class; it was wonderfully eloquent and wonderfully long. The candidates stood there trembling for a long time. He finally reached an eloquent climax. He shouted, "Now go out and work your head off!" As I went falteringly down the aisle, a retired minister—we called them "superannuates" in those dark days—called me over to him and whispered something in my ear that I have never forgotten. He said, "The Bishop told you to work your head off. Don't you do it. You may need it sometime!" I have needed it a good many times. We all need it all the time. To all young ministers we can say heartily, "Don't work your head off. Save it for the high task of preaching the word, as part of a whole varied program of church life and work."

—New York East Conference

II

Preacher

Of the eighteen sermons in the collection which follows eight have not previously been published. In some cases the key idea has appeared as a sermon springboard, but the full sermon development comes to print for the first time here. Seven other sermons are reprinted from volumes now out of print. The sermons were chosen to reflect the wide range of this preacher's view and the broad concerns of his pulpit ministry. He makes clear the social reference of the gospel even while he preaches to the individual who must respond to the gospel in faith. The sermons are broadly representative of his preaching: The resurrection was central to his Christian conviction; the gospel lays upon us the constraint of Christian social responsibility. These particular sermons were chosen because they contain some of the rich harvest of his homiletical eye, processed through his imagination and delivered out of the impulse of his faith.

"Thanksgiving, Religion, and Patriotism" was delivered on the Sunday before Thanksgiving in 1949 in the Unitarian Church of Germantown where as a visiting preacher during more than twenty years he preached nearly a hundred and fifty sermons. This one reflects the national and world situation at the time. But even as controversies in the churches to which Paul wrote provoked some of the apostle's most important communication, Christian truth which has remained though the subject of the controversy has long since faded, so the issues of that particular Thanksgiving season inspired a sermon that is not dated though the issues have taken on new shape. "News From a Graveyard," reprinted here from *Marching Off the Map,* was preached among other places at the Easter Dawn-Service broadcast nationwide from Radio City Music Hall in New York in 1945.

1

The Proof of Our Faith

The disciples . . . found it as he had told them.
(Mark 14:16.)

This is just an accidental detail in a narrative. As Jesus came up to Jerusalem, he evidently had what might be called today an "underground"—some dependable friends with whom he and his disciples might make contact and from whom they might get help. There is no moral or spiritual meaning of any sort in the simple statement.

Yet, as Horace Bushnell has said, the gospel is a gift to the imagination. As we bring our imagination up to these words, they spread out into all the nooks and corners of the map and the calendar. We do no violence to historical truth when we see in these words the interpretation of the experience of a great number of people, in all the centuries and all over the earth, who, like the disciples back in Jerusalem, took seriously what Jesus told them. They *have* gone out into life and found it as he told them. They *have* found that his reading of life was valid, that his assurance of what would happen has worked out as he told them it would. On that assurance rests part, at least, of Jesus' claim to the allegiance and following of men.

But many will say, and have said for centuries, "That is not true! Life does not work out as Jesus said. The facts are against it." Someone remarked of the arid philosophical mind of Herbert Spenser that his only conception of tragedy was "the murder of a beautiful theory by a gang of brutal facts." Many have a similar feeling today, that our world's gang of brutal facts—and it is a large and brutal gang, all right—has murdered the beautiful theories of Jesus. It is a natural feeling. Eve Curie expressed it vividly when, during World War II, after visiting Jerusalem she looked back at the towers of Zion. She recalls that she felt like saying, "Ah,

Jesus, so powerful and yet so powerless! You told us to be kind and forgiving, and yet for twenty solid centuries, wretched, incorrigible men have gone on being merciless, full of violence and hatred. Religious men and atheists alike have lived and ruled in a non-Christian way, and look at us now! We've never been in a worse mess!"

Yet, for the most part, such denials of Jesus' affirmations about life have come from people who have never really listened to what he said. He never said that life would be easy. He said plainly, "In the world you have tribulation." "You will be dragged before governors and kings . . . you will be hated by all for my sake." He said, "Follow me!" But the one thing in the world he seemed to be afraid of was getting followers under misunderstandings. He spoke of the costs of following him with a frankness which has never been matched by any leader of men.

No False Promises

Now the gospel *is* in a real sense a Cinderella story. It is a "success story" to this extent, that "the very stone which the builders rejected has become the head of the corner." Jesus was rejected by the religious leaders of his time, by the teachers, by the political figures, by the economic rulers. His truth in a real way has become the head of the corner in each of the realms which rejected him. But the gospel is not a Horatio Alger "success story." It is no Hollywood Class B romance. If it had been merely a success story, telling people how to get through life in passive peace and poise, if it had had at its center no cross, it would have been buried centuries ago in the rubble of the ancient world. For it would have had nothing to say to a world in the midst of tragedy or to an individual in disaster.

In regard to this truth it should be clearly seen that the most vicious attacks on Christianity in our day are not coming from open enemies or disbelievers, but from those superficial interpreters who have warped and mangled the gospel with a cross at its center into a set of six easy lessons on how to be a big, booming success, or on how to charm your worries away with pink thoughts. Our gospel did not come into the world with a fixed, silly grin on its face, and some light "Be good and you'll be happy" chatter. Jesus is being wounded worst of all by those of his own disciples who are distorting a message of redemption into a vapid "Cheerio."

But with these misconceptions cleared, look at the record of life. People who have acted on Jesus' word have found it as he told them. The experience of living by faith in Christ has brought its own verification of his teaching, a fundamental and enduring evidence of the truth of his revelation.

One of the greatest liabilities of life is that of prejudgment before any trial has begun, with a mind as closed as if it were set in concrete. That is true in any realm. We see it, in a strange bypath in the history of science, in the rejection of Galileo's discovery of the satellites of Jupiter. A so-called astronomer of Florence, Sizzi, disposed of the claim of Galileo in a brief which deserves immortality. He argued that because there were seven openings in the heads of men—two eyes, two nostrils, two ears, and a mouth—and seven metals and seven days of the week, there must be only seven planets, or else, as he pointed out, crushingly, "the whole beautiful system falls to the ground." Instead of looking at the evidence, he was playing a nice little game of Seven Up. It is a poor game of prejudgment, whether in the sixteenth century or the twentieth, whether in science or religion.

One of the earliest invitations to discipleship was, "Come and see." It is still a good one. Look at a few things which Jesus told men.

Inner Security

He said, "In me you may have peace." And men have found it as he told them. Not the placid surface of a stagnant pond, not the serene career of a contented cauliflower, but the deep inner security of a life amid turmoil, unafraid with any amazement. Here is the testimony of one of the first persons who found it that way, "I am sure that neither death, nor life . . . nor things present, nor things to come . . . nor anything else in all creation, will be able to separate us from the love of God." He had touched dependable rock. But we do not have to go back to the first century for evidence like that. A short time ago, in the stacks of a library, looking for something else, I picked up a book at random and read this dedication: "To my mother and sister, whose bodies were defeated in the battle against painful disease, but who, from that defeat wrested a spiritual victory which challenged all who knew them, and made glad the heart of God." That may seem an extreme case. But the word of Jesus can pass the test of extremes.

This peace of God is not like a rare flower, to be found only in a conservatory. It is more like a hollyhock; it will grow anywhere. Most of us, thank God, have seen it growing. There is something great here, which we may easily miss: a great inheritance. We are "heirs of God and fellow heirs with Christ." But we may be missing heirs, who have never really claimed or received the legacy of peace which is rightfully ours. We are heirs by relationship to God, and "if children, then heirs." Ours may be the inner security of God's sons and daughters in a home.

Again, Jesus said, "He who finds his life will lose it." And who that looks at life carefully can doubt that the surest way to lose life in its largest possibilities is painfully to try to preserve it? The best-preserved thing in all history is an Egyptian mummy. The surest way to make a mummy out of yourself is to give all your attention to preserving life. That truth comes with great pertinence to a generation which seems to have lifted up its soul to preserving. We try to preserve our looks. The beauty parlor business has become one of our major industries. We have made a religion out of preserving our money. Jesus' word shows that we can preserve life in the lowest sense by escape; we can escape burdens and sacrifices. But by doing so we escape life itself, in the largest meaning of the word.

How Poor We Are!

Many years ago Rudyard Kipling was giving a commencement address at McGill University. In the midst of the familiar warnings against preoccupation with wealth and fame, he said, "Some day you will meet a man who cares for none of these things, and then you will know how poor you are." As he said those words, they were prophecy. But they are also history. Centuries ago, there lived a Man who cared for none of these things. And, as multitudes have met him, they have known how poor they were.

That is the great hazard of living, that by saving our lives we shall miss life in its largest potential. Some time ago I was laid up with grippe in bed, and could not reach anything to read except one of my wife's magazines, *Better Homes and Back Yards*, or something like that. I learned about all the latest kitchen gadgets and the do-it-yourself delusions. In one article there was some psychological advice about not worrying, taking one day at a time, etc. I remember one sentence, "Whittle life down to your size." I said to myself, "That is not something out of the horse's mouth, but right out of the devil's mouth." That is what the man known as the Rich Young Ruler in the Gospels did. He "whittled life down to his size"—the size of a few acres and some livestock. Pigmy size! We are great whittlers! Life can be whittled down till it is like one of those little ships inside a bottle. I have read of one woman who read a novel, *East Lynne,* when she was a young girl. She liked it so much that she never read another novel all her life. So there are persons who read only one book, *The Life of John Jones,* that is, himself, or *The Life of Petunia Jones,* that is, herself. They become immersed in that Lilliputian epic and never really look at anything else. They do not ask to be carried to the skies on flowery beds of ease. All they ask is to be pushed in a perambulator, with a child's portion of responsibility and effort. Do not whittle life down to your size. Let God lift you up to the size for which he made you.

Power From Above

Jesus said, "You shall receive power." And men have found it as he told them. The words which were cried out in the first Christian generation, "I can do all things in him who strengthens me," have been repeated through all the years. There have been enhanced lives, empowered people, through the strange lifting force of a new object of devotion, a new faith and a new set of ideas.

I once saw in the Panama Canal a sight which seemed to me a true symbol of this fact of history. A ship was in the Gatun Locks. It would have to be lifted up to a great height if it were to go on with the voyage. The concrete walls of the lock rose above the ship like a skyscraper. How could it ever get up there? One thing did *not* happen. The engineer on the ship did not signal, "Full steam ahead! Everybody lift!" That would have done no good. The man in the control room on the lock quietly pushed a button and let in the water from Chagres Lake, high up in the mountains. The flow of power from above lifted the ship and sent it out on a new level. That is only a faint picture of what has happened in millions of lives, and what can happen in any life. The gift of the grace of God, the gift of power for living, can lift life and send it out on a new level.

Jesus said that he would be a disturber of loyalties. He said, "I am come to set a man at variance with his father and a daughter with her mother." Of course, Jesus has been the inspirer of great loyalties. But he has been a saving disturber of loyalties, detaching the emotions from one object and attaching them to larger ones. That is one of the world's deepest needs, disturbed loyalties. Our world is blighted with loyalty to muddled thinking, to petrified tradition, to sanctified stupidity; loyalty to the provincialism of clan and race. The world's hope is that men may be lifted out of partial loyalties into one high allegiance, the Kingdom of God.

The Only Way

Jesus said, "He who has seen me has seen the Father." There are no statistics on that. But there is the multiplied experience of the way that the Christlike God fits into the needs of the human mind and heart. That has given to hosts of people the conviction that "God stooping, showed us enough of himself for us to live by." Faith is still a venture. The mind and heart of man respond to the revelation of the God and Father of our Lord Jesus Christ.

Here is Katherine Mansfield writing in a casual letter, "God is now gone for all of us. Yet we *must* believe. And not only that, we *must* carry our weakness, our sin and our devilishness to somebody." Notice the musts. That is the voice of one woman. But it is the human race speaking. A man looking down from the top of the Empire State Building in New York, seeing the people like little midges on the sidewalk one hundred stories below, not as large as ants, said, "I guess that's the way the world looks to God." That is not the way God sees men. Jesus gives us another view. Here is the way the world looks to God:

> There were ninety and nine that safely lay
> In the shelter of the fold,
> But one was out on the hills away . . .

The searching God, for one person!

We are not digits in a column. That faith has lifted men to their feet.

That is something to sing about. So we sing about it, "O Love that will not let me go."

We are finding things in the social and international world as Jesus told us. A long time ago, in a far, far simpler world than ours, Jesus said, "I am the way." Today in a world in which man has outrun by far the sound of his own voice, in which he has achieved the power to destroy himself and his world, we can see more clearly than ever that he is the only way. There is no other name given whereby men may find survival than that which is given in Christ Jesus.

—THE PULPIT

2

The Impulse of the Resurrection

"She runneth therefore." (John 20:2.)

SMALL WONDER! THE FACT OF THE RESURRECTION STRUCK THE MIND OF Mary with a force that carried her along as though she were a projectile hurled by a gun.

Every few months the newspapers tell us that the most powerful explosive known to man has been invented, an explosive of such terrific force that it will hurl many tons miles through the air (the tonnage and the mileage increasing with each announcement). But that is all just a newspaper exaggeration. The most explosive force known to man is the impact of the idea of the resurrection of Jesus as it strikes the mind and heart of humanity. It has thrown men by its force 25,000 miles around the globe and has shaken the earth for nineteen centuries.

It is no accident or mere coincidence that in every one of the four Gospels the story of the resurrection is the story of a footrace. When we bring all the Gospel accounts together we have a swift succession of footraces. The thrill of the glad news, even before the heart was sure it was true, was so overwhelming that it started everyone who heard it running.

The finest picture of the first Easter which the imagination has ever conceived is not a picture of the empty tomb or even of the risen Christ. It is a picture of two faces, the faces of Peter and John as they raced to the tomb. Into their strained eyes filled with wonder there seems compressed the trembling hope of the whole world.

Those Easter footraces of the disciples well portray the most significant fact about the resurrection—that it brings a new impulse and movement to human life. When the meaning of the victory of Christ breaks over the mind life is no longer a walk. It leaps and bounds.

Great good news simply cannot walk. The word "marathon" suggests to us not so much the battle in Greece as the runner who sped forty miles with the news, well content to drop dead at the end, if he could but gasp out the word, "Victory!"

Our hearts rush out to grasp the assurance of endless life which the resurrection of Christ brings. When Mary made her way to the sepulcher, still engulfed in the gloom of Calvary, the startling wonder of the empty tomb quickened her step. "She runneth therefore," the Gospel of John tells us. How could she help it? So the heart leaps to meet the news of Christ's victory over death.

One of the traditions of the Cathedral of Winchester in England is the story of how the news of the battle of Waterloo was first received. It came by a sailing ship to the south coast of England, and by signal flags was wig-wagged to London. When the message reached Winchester the signals on top of the Cathedral began to spell the message, "W-e-l-l-i-n-g-t-o-n d-e-f-e-a-t-e-d," and then fog descended and hid the signals from view. The sad news of the incomplete message went on to London. When the message was read, "Wellington defeated," the whole country was in despair. After a while the fog lifted and the signals on the Winchester cathedral were still at work spelling out the complete sentence, "W-e-l-l-i-n-g-t-o-n d-e-f-e-a-t-e-d t-h-e e-n-e-m-y." The thrilling news raced across the land and lifted all hearts out of gloom into joy. "Wellington defeated the enemy!"

So the heavy gloom of Calvary fled before the victory of the resurrection. Out of the dark shadows of the tomb our hearts leap up at the news of victory. The resurrection puts the seal of reality on the great central truth of Jesus—that we are children of God, with a personal infinite, eternal value for him which shall never be lost.

The impulse of Easter puts a new momentum in life here on earth, for it puts a new value in it. The largest message of Jesus is not to tell us how long life lasts but what it is. Jesus did not come back to tell us that life goes on; he came to do far more than that. He came to tell us what real life is, here, there, or anywhere. Eternal life is not quantity of life but quality of life. It is here and now that we may live in the power of an endless life. Here and now we may find fellowship with God and a share in his great onward-moving purposes.

Sarah N. Cleghorn sets this truth in a memorable sonnet:

> We call this time, and gauge it by the clock
> Deep in such insect cares as suit that view,

As whether dresses fit, what modes are new,
And where to buy and when to barter stock—
We think we hold, based on some Scripture rock,
Claims on immortal life to press when due,
Imagining some door between the two,
Our deaths shall each, with presto change, unlock.

But this is also everlasting life:
On Monday in the kitchen, street or store
We are immortal, we, the man and wife,
Immortal now, or shall be never more,
Immortals in immortal values spend
These lives that shall no more begin than end.

Eternal life is self-forgetfulness in the great purposes of God. This new understanding of life strikes from our limbs the ball and chain of slavery to self. It raises the bedridden will to new power and bids us walk in the name of Christ.

Into our life today—if we will bare our heart and mind to it—this amazing explosive of the resurrection will bring a resilient bound and leap. Bliss Perry says, "Easter begins, like all deep things, in mystery and it ends, like all high things, in a great courage." It transforms human relations from the acquaintanceship of a short railway journey soon to be ended to a fellowship of eternal value. "The tomb is not a blind alley; it is a thoroughfare."

A recent critic has playfully recorded the effect which reading H. G. Wells has upon him:

No matter how discouraging things seem when I pick up a Wells' book, or how averse I may be to launching out on a crusade of any sort, I always end by walking with a firm step to the door (feeling, somehow, that I have grown quite a bit taller and much handsomer) and saying, quietly: "Meadows, my suit of armor, please; the one with a chainmail shirt and a purple plume." This, of course, is silly, as any of Mr. Wells' critics will tell you. It is the effect that he has on irresponsible, visionary minds. But if all the irresponsible, visionary minds in the world became sufficiently belligerent through a continued reading of Mr. Wells, or even of the New Testament, who knows but what they may become just practical enough to take a hand at running things? They couldn't do much worse than the responsible, practical minds have done, could they?

In a very high and reverent sense the gospel of Jesus and the resurrection send men into warfare with a quickened heart. At his "All hail!" we call for our suit of armor and leap into the fight. We know that our labor is not vain in the Lord. He has overcome the world, and his kingdom is an everlasting kingdom. It is tremendously worthwhile to fight against any odds, for life is stronger than death, love is stronger than hate, truth is stronger than lies.

"Where does your great river go?" David Livingstone would frequently ask the natives of the interior of Africa, pointing to the Congo. "It is lost in the sands," they always answered him. They had never seen the sea to which the river surely and irresistibly made its way. "Where does all your labor and effort go?" we frequently ask ourselves. And in moods of discouragement and fatigue the answer comes, "It is lost in the sands!" The victory of Jesus brings to our ears the roar of the distant sea, the assurance that our labor is not lost or void, but is joined to the divine power of righteousness destined to conquer the world.

A new thrill of movement comes into life as we return to it with the experience of the risen Christ in our hearts. The news is so great and glad that we must run to communicate it. The same irresistible impulse that set the disciples' feet flying along the road puts every life which discovers the meaning of the resurrection into swift and exuberant motion.

The disciples, running back from the empty tomb to carry the news, were the first of an endless succession of runners all with the same trembling joy in their hearts and the same free leap in their feet. Paul meets his risen Lord and runs with the news the rest of his life. The prison chains on his feet were never strong enough to bind his spirit. We find him writing from his little cell about "whensoever I go to Spain"—building castles in Spain of adventure for Christ in what was then the farthest limit of the world. Following the three Marys who first discovered the empty tomb and ran with the joyous news, there came along centuries later three other Marys, worthy to follow in their train, Mary Moffat, Mary Livingstone, and Mary Slessor, who had met their risen Lord and ran joyfully along the long, dark trail that led into the center of Africa to tell the overwhelming news. Or, to mention only one more among millions, James Chalmers received such an impetus from his vision of the risen Christ that he leaped to the end of a long road that led to the savage island of the South Seas, New Guinea, well content that, like the runner from Marathon, he could give his life to carry the word, "Victory!"

What does the Christian faith of immortality mean to us today? Surely, it must mean such a fresh amazement at the victory of Christ over sin and death that a sober, dignified, leisurely walk will not be possible. We must break into an apostolic stride, with Peter and Mary and John, and with eager heart and flying feet carry to the last and farthest of God's children the news of the eternal victory of Christ.

—THE HAUNTED HOUSE

3

Love Laughs at Locksmiths

"Bring my soul out of prison." (Ps. 142:7.)

OUR TEXT TOUCHES THE MOST FASCINATING THEME THAT HAS EVER gripped the imagination of man—the romance of escape. All through the long history of literature, all the way from the time when blind Homer held his audience enthralled as he sang the hairbreadth escapes of Ulysses, down to the days when we follow the exploits of Sherlock Holmes with bated breath, the story of an escape either from jail or peril has held the eager interest of all men.

There is a very deep reason for the unfailing interest in this romance of escape, for in a real sense it is the story of the human race in its struggle against jail doors. The long history of man is the story of an escape from jail, overcoming the prison walls of physical forces, the emancipation of the mind and spirit from the powers of ignorance and fear that enclosed them. Only in modern times have we realized what a long, heroic battle there was between powers of nature and the dawning mind of men. The deep, unconscious prayer that underlay every endeavor of primitive men was this: "Bring my soul out of prison." History is the divine answer of the Spirit of God to the spirit of man.

This deep prayer of the psalmist, uttered in a time of distress and despair, when the walls of adverse circumstances were steadily closing on him, pictures the largest service which religion can do for men. It brings jail delivery to the soul. By the grace of God, the enterprise of life may be just that—a gripping human and divine romance of overcoming prison gates and walls, the liberation of the soul from forces that chain it.

I

This prayer is a cry from the dungeon of our animal inheritance. It is a call for freedom from the dominion of physical appetite and sin. It is the first great step toward escape when we realize that the dominion of appetite is a prison. It is frequently accounted a palace, a stately pleasure house as opulently furnished as that of Kubla Khan, spread with silks and studded with jewels. But disguise the prison as we may, it is still a prison. In our sunlit moments we realize it.

Not all convicts are profligates by any means. Many are simply in prison in the sense that they are creatures of the senses. They depend absolutely on what they can eat and drink and see and hear for the whole of life. Their spiritual faculties are atrophied.

H. G. Wells has summed up this large class of people with a very expressive name when he calls them the "God-sakers," meaning the people who are always exclaiming, "For God's sake, let's do something!" When they are not going somewhere, or coming back from somewhere, or doing something, life is an empty and aching blank. Without resources in themselves they are dependent on the gratification of some one of the senses. It never occurs to them that life may have any deeper resources of enjoyment.

Paul answers his own question, "Who will deliver me from this body of death?" His triumphant answer is, "I thank God, through Jesus Christ our Lord." Peter's escape from jail affords us a very true picture of the means of escape of the human spirit from the dominion of the flesh. An angel came and let him out. That is always God's method. The first thing that was necessary was the angel to awaken him. The first step in our escape from appetite is the awakening of conscience, an inspiration at the awakening touch of the Spirit of God. After the awakening came the co-operation of the angel and the man, and soon he was on the street. It is by the co-operation of our will with the energizing, empowering Spirit of God that we vault over the wall, conquering the guard set to watch us, and leap on our way to freedom.

In these days when we are so much occupied, as we should be, with social vision, with the preaching of the kingdom of God as a social ideal, there is danger that we may slur over a fundamental message of the gospel:

He breaks the power of canceled sin,
He sets the prisoner free.

Those lines of the old hymn are a romance of escape, but they are no fiction.

To everyone fighting temptation this is, thank God, in the stark, literal meaning of the much-abused phrase, "gospel truth." There follow in the train of Christ, as the exalted language of the Te Deum portrays it, the glorious company of apostles, prophets, saints, and martyrs lifting their chorus of praise. But we ought not to forget that there also follow in his train a great and glorious company of escaped convicts.

Every soul must break out of a prison of things. We are dungeoned by possessions, smothered by a clutter of merchandise, the life flattened out by the accumulative instinct of selfishness. The prison house of selfishness is the common jail of mankind, caging men in the little cell of personal advantage.

There recently died in the village of New Hartford, Connecticut, an elderly man of wealth who was born and lived all his life in the same room in which he died. The newspaper account of his death stated that he had never slept in any other room and always had a great dislike of making any changes and grew angry when a new wallpaper or a new carpet was suggested. However broad may have been his interests, his actual physical life was spent in a one-celled universe. That life in a single room is a fair picture of the walled-up life of millions within the cage of selfish absorption; their contented, chained souls pace up and down as restlessly and uselessly as a grizzly bear doing his endless march behind the bars of his cage in the zoo. Frequently selfish lives are not a parade up and down one cell only, but before a tier of adjoining cells. Their interest bulges out to take in other members of their family, their relatives, and even the neighbors as far as three blocks in all directions.

What a wastage of life there is when the shades of the prison house of selfishness descend and the vision splendid is shut from view! The magnificence of the jail does not affect the tragedy of confinement. Last summer the attention of the country was fixed for thirty days on a gold mine in Jackson, California, in which forty-seven miners were entombed. Every effort possible was made to dig them out before death overtook them, but when finally the rescuers tunneled a way to them they were all dead. There they were shut up in one of the richest rooms in the world, with the walls and floor and ceiling literally lined with gold! Their prison house was worth millions; yet, in it they gasped their lives away!

That tragedy has a close parallel in the spiritual world, where the life of the soul has been snuffed out in a gold mine. Nor does it take the fabulous wealth of a gold mine to hold the soul a prisoner. A man's soul may be just as irretrievably lost among the cracker barrels of a corner grocery store.

The great emphasis of Jesus as he sought to lead men out of jail into freedom was that life was more than meat. That great truth can be heard through his discourses like the constant roll of the sea. We hear it in the parable of the rich fool, in the story of the rich young ruler, in the parable of the talents, and the good seed choked by thorns. That familiar teaching should echo and re-echo today above the noise of the marketplace.

We frequently hear church workers speak of the ministry of the church to "shut-ins." We have been speaking here of a very pathetic class of "shut-ins" who need a vigorous ministry. They are not dear old ladies or patient invalids who never get out of the house. They are the prison inmates who have built their own dungeons by their selfish absorption. The business of the church is not to give them glasses of jelly, smooth words, comforting prayers, or any other kind of flattering attention. The church has done far too much of that sort of thing. Far less often than we should have we declared in plain words to the selfish and respectable people around us: "You are locked up in jail. Your spirit is in prison. In Christ's name, come out!" Such spirits in prison need the strong words of the Lord to break in the doors of their selfish exclusion and let them out into a share of the vision and the service of Jesus Christ.

In the epistle of Peter there is a statement of haunting suggestiveness that Jesus "preached to the spirits in prison." Just what that means we do not know. The words lend themselves to a multitude of fancies. But this we do know, that Jesus preaches to "the spirits in prison" today and brings this great word of hope from a heart full of love: "If the Son therefore shall make you free, ye shall be free indeed."

> Self is the only prison that can ever bind the soul;
> Love is the only angel who can bid the gates unroll;
> And when he comes to call thee, arise and follow fast;
> His way may lie through darkness, but it leads to light at last.
>
> —HENRY VAN DYKE

Jesus came to preach deliverance to the captives. Have you had life's great adventure—its romance of escape? Outside the barred gates—waiting—"the Master is come and calleth for thee."

—THE HAUNTED HOUSE

4

The Dead Line

"Thou hast a name that thou liveth, and art dead." (Rev. 3:1.)

MARK TWAIN ONCE DESCRIBED A MAN AS SO IRREVERENT THAT HE HAD even been known to speak disrespectfully of the equator. There is another line, however, never exactly charted but not imaginary, about which no one will speak with disrespect. It is the Dead Line. It is a true International Date Line. For it is the line between yesterday and tomorrow. On this side of it is tomorrow. We face toward the future. When we cross it we face toward yesterday. Like the imaginary lines of the ocean we cross it unconsciously. It does not advertise itself; it has no outward sign whereby we may know it. But it marks a real division in the voyage of life. Out beyond the immediate horizon it waits for us all, a fearsome, mysterious thing. To chart our voyage so that we avoid the Dead Line is a major achievement of seamanship.

Our text suggests the Dead Line that crosses all life, not merely the lives of a particular class of workers. It glimpses the great problem of keeping life fresh, moving, growing, alive! That problem is a real one which calls for unceasing wakefulness. There is a point in many lives which corresponds to the first frost of the autumn. That coating of hoarfrost which appears some October or November morning is the dead line for plants. There is a nipping frost in human life which lays waste its powers and checks its advances in the same manner. It is not the result of an outside force, such as is the frost which chills the dahlia and chrysanthemum to death. It is an inner cause, the result of the mental and spiritual climate which we make for ourselves. We cannot blame the weather.

Broadly speaking, we cross the Dead Line when we cease to grow. "Go on or go under" is a law of nature which has never been repealed. The mind and spirit is just as amenable to it as plant life. That idea of the Dead Line, of course, is common and obvious. Let us try to explore it a bit in detail, in order that we may see more clearly the forces which expand and enlarge life and keep it fresh, and also the petrifying forces, noiseless, insidious, and constant, which tend to push us across the Dead Line.

1. The true epitaph to be written over many a promising mind and spirit would be: "Killed by routine." Routine seems to secrete a shell which forms about the mind and spirit of the one who gets completely in its power. In a letter written while he was Secretary of the Department of the Interior, Franklin K. Lane said that in the departments at Washington it took just about seven years for the nerve of initiative and imagination to atrophy. They will atrophy like any other nerve, when bound in the plaster cast of an inflexible routine. There are many things besides poverty which freeze the genial current of the soul, says Oliver Wendell Holmes. Routine is one of the surest of them. The only escape for the spirit is exactly that of the body confronting a zero temperature. Life depends on violent exercise. Only by swinging our arms and stamping our feet is the blood kept coursing through the veins and life preserved. So the imagination and initiative are saved only by vigorous use. The damage done by routine to the spirit does not come merely through regular and repeated activity. No fruitful contribution to life is ever made without concentration and the acquirement of skill. The real calamity is an avoidable one—the numbing of the faculty of surprise and wonder. It is in the loss of expectancy, the childlike heart to which the world is still full of a number of things which make it leap up. What a vivid flashlight of a heart which has crossed the Dead Line Robert Louis Stevenson has given us in his familiar verses:

> If beams from happy human eyes
> Have moved me not; if morning skies,
> Books and my food, and summer rain,
> Knock on my sullen heart in vain.

The vain knock of everyday wonders at a dulled and sullen heart is the announcement of Doom's Day. When curiosity dies, when eagerness has gone, when the whole pageant of nature and history in the making becomes a twice-told tale vexing the dull ear of a drowsy man, then we have crossed the fateful line into the Never-Never Land, "Never glad confident morning again."

"We need to train ourselves," says Father Bull, "in that aspect of faith, to have that buoyant expectancy of the improbable which refuses the dull estimates of common sense and joyfully expects in the future what is not suggested by the experience of the past." When that is preserved, life is preserved. And life, extended beyond any measure of three score and ten, may still be a wild, eager ride with high heart beating and lighted eyes searching the horizon.

> So with the wan waste grasses on my spear,
> I ride forever seeking after God.
> My hair grows whiter than my thistle plume
> And all my limbs are loose; but in my eyes
> The star of an unconquerable praise;
> For in my soul one hope forever sings,
> That at the next white corner of the road
> My eyes may look on Him.
>
> —G. K. CHESTERTON

2. We cross a definite Dead Line when *dissatisfaction gives way to a dormant content.* There is a preserving stir of life when we are at odds with the world and are restlessly seeking, no matter how quixotically, to remold it to our heart's desire. When we have our eyes on a goal, and ideal, far perhaps, but shining, and have not been overtaken by the dark nightfall of "What's the use?" we live. Painfully perhaps, wearied no doubt, yet there is no call to use the stethoscope—we are alive. It is when we stop sailing the seas scouting for pirates and privateers, and drop anchor into some sailor's snug harbor and haul down the belligerent flag that our real history ceases. The rest of existence can be covered by one sentence in the obituary: "Mr. X retired twenty years ago."

In this sense W. L. George's saying is true: "Life is like a pudding; the more you stir it the better it is." Truly orthodox Christianity is always adventure. That is one reason why it is the spirit of perpetual youth. It goes on making new discoveries, waging new wars for the liberation of the whole family of God—the life which is life indeed. There is a very suggestive phrase used in connection with the Methodist ministry—"taking a supernumerary relation." It describes one who is "above the number" listed in the active ranks, an extra, out of the combat, for one reason or another. We take a supernumerary relation to the whole forward enterprise of life when indignation dies and we conclude a separate peace with the powers and principalities of evil and sink back to a limp and beaten content. Louise Imogen Guiney, poet, essayist, and recluse, well expressed the creed of a supernumerary in her words, "The main business of the scholar is to live gracefully, without mental passion, and to get off alone into a corner for an affectionate view of creation." Take that Lilliputian view of life and stretch it alongside of Jesus' definition of life—"He that loseth his life shall find it"! It is like measuring a doll's house beside the universe.

3. *Materialism is a swelling "trade wind" which pushes us across the Dead Line* unless there is a strong hand at the helm. When the foolish dreams of youth are overtaken by a middle-aged "sanity," with a clear, keen eye for the main chance, when idealism gives way to the "practical," then we have reached the stopping place of life, in the high New Testament sense, and the conductor calls out, "This is as far as we go."

The heathen in his blindness
Bows down to wood and stone

in New York as well as in Benares, in Chicago as well as in Foochow. The blind passion for things wears down the soul as tuberculosis eats away the tissues of the body. A keen observer has pictured the things which make up the table of contents of life for a large number of Americans: "Automobiles and radios, buildings and bathrooms, furs and furniture, liners, hotels, and bridges, vacuum cleaners, cameras, bus lines, electric toasters, moving pictures, railways cars, package foods, telephones, pianos, novels, comic supplements."

Whatever pertains to the soul must be crowded into an appendix at the end as an afterthought, if there is any room in the already crowded volume. The result is that life is more like a Sears-Roebuck catalogue than a Golden Treasury. N. P. Barbellion wrote toward the end of that singularly brave and pathetic journal called *Last Diary*, "If I were to sum up my life in one word I should say *suffocation.*" In a very different sense from the one in which he used it "suffocation" would be the fitting entry at the end of the record of many souls. Not at the actual end of life but at the point where practical materialism overtook them and suffocated the life of the spirit, as completely as though the Woolworth Tower had fallen down on them. That figure of speech is not so far out of the way. For what has happened to a great many people whose spiritual faculties have deadened is that a great five-and-ten-cent store full of cheap and "practical" gimcracks has caved in on them and buried them in the debris.

> He who has lost soul's liberty
> Concerns himself for ever with his property,
> As, when the folk have lost both dance and song,
> Women clean useless pots the whole day long.
>
> —ANNA WICKHAM

In the fairy stories the climax which always made shivers run down our backs was when the ogre transformed a person into an inanimate object. I still believe in fairies, at least in ogres. For I have seen the black wand of materialism waved in the air and a growing soul transformed into the inglorious stage setting of modern life—a piece of overstuffed furniture.

4. *Self-satisfaction is an obvious Dead Line.* It is as clearly marked as the timberline on the mountains. "No growth beyond the point" is clearly marked at the spot where complacency sets in. When we stop to admire ourselves we congeal. Jesus waged continual war against self-satisfaction as the archenemy of growth. His picture of the Pharisee at prayer is a perfect demonstration. The Pharisee could no more hear anything that God had to say or say anything that God could hear than could a mummy in a glass case. That is always the penalty of self-satisfied egotism; it creates a spiritual vacuum in which all development ceases. In one of the letters of Grover Cleveland, given in his biography by McElroy, there is a shrewd observation on his intimate friend, Joseph Jefferson. He wonders whether the satisfaction with his role of Rip Van Winkle and the weakness whereby he liked to be the only person of consequence in his plays, did not prevent Jefferson from undertaking the really great dramas and thus developing into a greater artist. Self-satisfaction always prevents us from essaying the really great dramas of life which call for humility, toil, and pain. The little accomplishments in which we have become (to our own view) letter perfect are so much easier. The sweet salvos of applause which they win become a necessary drug—and, in a word, we have reached our terminal.

In the life of the spirit when the hunger and thirst after righteousness, inspired by aspiration to a lofty ideal of character, give way to a consciousness of petty superiorities to others, the soul is no longer a garden of God where the fruits of the spirit grow. It has become a cemetery.

5. *When intellectual life petrifies, we have the name of being alive but are dead.* "Wisdom," says Emerson, "consists in keeping the mind liquid or in resisting the tendency to too rapid petrification." What a labor of Hercules—to keep the mind liquid! A United States senator once remarked that God Almighty could not make him change his mind on our Latin-American policy. That was probably true. "Is God limited?" is a question frequently asked. In a case like that he must be sadly limited! The senator's mind was not in a liquid state. It was as finished, on that particular question, as concrete which has been poured into a mold and set.

To keep on this side of the Dead Line we must keep the mind accessible to fresh facts and forces which insure growth. The contents of the mind must be fluid enough to be penetrated with new ingredients, as the mass of dough is quickened with yeast. Mark Rutherford in the *Autobiography* paints an unforgettable picture of the opposite of this condition in his description of Wollaston, "His ideas, acquired long ago, had never fructified in him, but were like hard stones which rattled in his pocket." That rattle of hard, inflexible, finished ideas may very truthfully be called the "death rattle."

6. *Not to labor the point at all, not even the hastiest glimpse in the direction of the Dead Line could be taken without reporting that with the blunting of the sympathies we cross from life into death.* There are in the calendar of the Anglican Church days designated by a name which has haunting suggestiveness—"Ember Days." They are the lengthening days of autumn when the fires of the heart have sunk to embers, when the kindling glow of warm, tender sympathies dies down and a chill steals through the empty rooms of the house. The guests, dismissed with the poor courtesy of calloused indifference, creep away one by one. The lights blink out. The feast of life is over. A lonesome, selfish vigil by a dying fire is its poor substitute. Ember Days! God grant you may never see them!

"For God's sake do not forbid the years to teach you tenderness," wrote Barrett Wendell, during his last days, in a letter to a friend. What deeper, truer wisdom did anyone ever gather from the pilgrimage of life?

There is but one sure escape from the Dead Line. It is expressed in the words of an old gospel hymn—"Throw out the life line." Christ is the life preserver of the spirit, not in any narrow sense, but in the limitless sense of the redeemer of life from every force that withers and deadens its powers. To share with Christ his fellowship with the Father will keep the years lit up with a fresh wonder. To share with Christ his fellowship with men, his sensitive sympathy to every human need and appeal, will keep the heart warm and pulsing with the life blood of the soul—love. As we look out on life through his eyes we shall learn the things that are most worth while, the inner treasures which do not rust or mold, but which are the very fountain of perpetual youth, a well of water springing up into everlasting life.

—THE EAST WINDOW

5

Over the Wall

"By my God I can leap over a wall." (Ps. 18: 29.)

In these words David at the zenith of his career as king at Jerusalem recalls the athletic buoyancy of his boyhood days on the Bethlehem hills. His heart returns in the fullness of his years to the free life of the shepherd boy with its

> leaping from rock up to rock,
> The strong rending of boughs from the fir tree, the cool silver shock
> Of a plunge in the pool's living water.
>
> —Robert Browning

As his mind lovingly returns to that life of the hills, it occurs to him that the old acrobatic leap of his boyhood is a figure large enough to express the divine romance of his providential career. His has been a strange history, successively surmounting walls that rose up before him and overshadowed his spirit, and he gratefully recognizes that it has been by his God that he has leaped over them. If we will glance at three swiftly moving pictures in the life of this king, we will find that the words are not only large enough to give us the secret of David's life, but may afford a true transcript of any spiritual history.

The first is the dark picture of the man hedged in by the walls of a great sin. The man after God's own heart is overshadowed by the black murder done at the dictates of passion. We rarely see the real nature of sin so clearly as in David, a man so responsive to spiritual impressions, so full of the riches of heart's affection, so strong, so much of a genius, so steadily ascending in power and character! What a dismal anticlimax his sin was!

It would only have been in line with innumerable life tragedies if, in his remorse, he had thought of himself as fallen like Lucifer, never to rise again. That is so often the history, an aspiring upward path and then a drop into a deep well. And they accept the fall. How many spiritual histories could be told in the couplet of George Macdonald:

> There came a mist and a blinding rain,
> And life was never the same again.

But David did not stay in the pit. By his God he leaped over the wall. Read that interview with Nathan and its searching conviction, "Thou art the man," and then that marvelous prayer of penitence, "Against thee, thee only, have I sinned." Quick as a flash—the word is poor, for no flash ever went off so quickly as the movement of God's heart to true repentance—God answers, "I have forgiven thee."

The great thing about the sin of David was that it was a parenthesis. It was not a full stop, and after the break in the story the thread of grace is taken up again. David did not leap over the wall of sin by merely saying, "That was a bad mistake; I must do better in the future." We know how little that avails. We cannot lift ourselves out of the pit by our own bootstraps. We conquer sin, not by taking thought but by taking God, and are lifted from the mire by the strong cords of a forgiving, redeeming love.

The second picture is a brighter one. It is in the cave where his enemy, Saul, is sleeping in David's power. Between them the towering walls of antipathy, dislike, and fear have risen up as barriers, and the swift thought of the sword as an easy way to end it all rushes into David's mind. But he escapes by bringing into their relation the thought of God. This man Saul, this man that he does not like, and with good reason, is still the Lord's anointed, still has claims on his consideration.

What a high and strong leap this overcoming of the walls of resentment and prejudice is, we all know. Racial, social, and personal barriers to our sympathy rise up on every hand. Samuel Johnson said a very typical thing when he declared that "he could like everybody except an American." We all have our own bills of exceptions. It was Scotchmen with Charles Lamb, whom he said he had been trying to like all his life without any success. We say we can work with anyone *except* this particular person or that. "He gets on our nerves." We do not often overcome our imperfect sympathies by a reasoned process. We leap over the wall of dislike and exclusion only as David did, by getting a God's-eye view of the other man. It was only when the early church learned with Paul to see in the condemned Gentile and the barbarian without the law the brothers for whom Christ died that it was welded into that conquering union which knew neither bond nor free, Scythian nor barbarian. No matter what may be the extent of our estate or what mansions we may erect, we shall never succeed in building anything but a little prison house for our spirits unless we get the divine view of human relationships.

The last picture is a sublime one. The little child of David has died. But he refuses to accept as final the dark walls of death. He makes the magnificent leap of faith in immortality. "He shall not come to me, but I shall go to him." It is not the perfect faith as we know it in the New Testament. David did not have the ladder of Christ by which to make the surer climb. But it is probably the fairest foregleam of immortality to be found in the Old Testament.

In the shadow of that same wall of death we have all sat before; there we shall all sit again. No matter how far we have advanced in spiritual knowledge over the days of Israel's kings, it is still a leap of faith by which we get into the sunlight of hope and comfort. It even seems a longer leap to some today because of the many newly disclosed ties, showing our physical relationship to the other creatures. In the Museum of Natural History in New York City there is a striking series of the skeletons of the primates, arranged in the order of their ascent. At the head of the list there is a skeleton of a man, bearing a certain number, by its inclusion in that collection seeming to tell us, "Here *you* are. A little better than the other apes, a little more intelligent, more long-lived and adaptable. That is all."

All? No! Faith says, "I accept the horizontal lines that show my physical affinities to the other creatures of earth; but I see and hold to the vertical line that runs upward, binding me as a child to an infinite Father, in whose heart I have an eternal worth." Faith says with Paul, "O death, where is thy sting?" It says with Ruskin, "Why should we wear black for the guests of God?"

—FARES, PLEASE!

6

The Sunny Side of Ten

"To such belongs the kingdom of heaven."
(Matt. 19:14.)

MOST OF US REMEMBER SOME LINES BACK IN OUR OLD COPYBOOKS, WHICH ran like this:

> Give to the world the best that you have,
> And the best will come back to you.

In no place is the old truth so true as in the entrance requirement of the kingdom of God, "Except ye become as little children, ye shall not enter the kingdom of God." The Master demands the very best we have—the childlike qualities of teachableness and faith. It is an inexorable condition that we bring these. But the return which he makes, good measure, pressed down and running over, is that he enables us to keep unwithered by age and unspoiled by custom those very qualities of childhood. To be a member of the Kingdom is to keep oneself forever on the sunny side of ten.

James Russell Lowell, when passing once, in the outskirts of Boston, a building which bore the inscription, "Home for Incurable Children," said playfully to a friend, "They'll get me in there some day." That is just what he was—an incurable child, carrying over into his last years an irrepressible youthfulness of heart. That is what a real member of the Kingdom is—an incurable child.

On the sunny side of ten there is an atmosphere of trust. Have you ever thought of how much of the glory of childhood comes from the unruffled calm of its trust? It is only gradually that we come to realize that the years that set as lightly on our shoulders as a June breeze were years of intense strain and responsibility to our fathers and mothers. The child's world is a garden of delight because its boundless trust makes everything in it bloom as a spring day touches a valley and calls forth its beauty. Unsophisticated credulity is a childish thing, to be put away when one becomes a man. But a childlike trust is part of our permanent inheritance as joint heirs of Jesus Christ. "He careth for you." "He knoweth our frame." "He knoweth the way that I take." "He knoweth you have need of these things." A doctor told a student who complained of headaches and whose window looked off into empty space that he needed something in his view to "lean his eyes up against." It is a good thing to lean our eyes up against the background of the God and Father of our Lord Jesus Christ.

The child lives in the present. To a child on a picnic there has been no yesterday; there will be no tomorrow. "One crowded hour of glorious life" is his. He is unvexed by past regrets or future fears, while we, his elders, live so largely in the day before yesterday or the middle of next week. Dr. William Osler tells us the problem of happiness is a very simple one. It consists merely in pressing two buttons, one of which shuts off the past and the other shuts off the future. Two buttons, that is all. So beautifully simple! It is too bad that he neglects to tell us just how to do it! He who has the keys of life and death is the only one who can push the buttons. "As a thick cloud have I blotted out thy transgressions"; that is the only assurance which can shut out the peace-destroying past. "I will not leave thee nor forsake thee"; that is what lifts the cloud of future fears. The Christian who is persuaded that he is able to keep that which he has committed unto him may live as fully in the present as the most carefree child. The Jewish religion in the time of Christ knew only two days—yesterday and tomorrow. It is highly significant that the first recorded word of Jesus' public ministry was the word "today." Today is the day of salvation, of opportunity, of joy.

On the sunny side of ten we live in an ideal world.

When I was a beggarly boy
And lived in a cellar damp,
I had not a friend nor a toy,
But I had Aladdin's lamp.
When I could not sleep for the cold,
I had fire enough in my brain,

And builded with roofs of gold
  My beautiful castles in Spain.
—JAMES RUSSELL LOWELL

The world is full, then, of ideal personages and ideal forces. Prince Charming may appear from around the corner at any time. The pot of gold is at the end of the rainbow if we only hurry fast enough. The youthful Coleridge walking down the street, swinging his arms wildly, accidentally hits an old gentleman on the head and pauses politely to explain that he is cutting off the heads of Turkish infidels with his scimitar. From this realm of the ideal we emerge into what is called the real world, and a glory has departed. But the man of Christian faith, to whom God and the increasing purpose which runs through the ages are realities, lives in an ideal world. Creation to him is not a dreary mechanism of interlocked wheels, for the earnest expectation of the creature waiteth for the manifestation of the sons of God. His kingdom is an everlasting kingdom, and its members have the dew of their youth.

Ponce de Leon set out in the wrong direction to discover the fountain of youth. It is not in the everglades of Florida. It is the eternal spring, a "well by the gate" in Bethlehem of Judea.

—FARES, PLEASE!

7

Seven Years' Bad Luck

"He is like unto a man beholding his natural face in a glass: For he . . . goeth his way, and straightway forgetteth what manner of man he was." (Jas. 1:23-24.)

Enshrined in the superstition that it brings seven years' bad luck to break a mirror is a much deeper truth, having to do with a malady more deadly than awkwardness—for awkwardness is not always fatal. Even grotesquely awkward humans may sometimes survive and be fairly happy. I know, for up to the present date I have survived myself. The deeper truth of the common superstition is that it is a terrible thing to break a mirror in which you can see yourself as you actually are. It is an unmixed calamity with seven years' bad luck and multiples thereof in its train, to lose the priceless faculty of detaching yourself from yourself, and looking on the spectacle from the grandstand.

It is enormously hard to form a just estimate of ourselves. For that reason we need every aid to the process which nature has provided. The apostle James well pictures the difficulty when he says that "a man beholdeth himself in a mirror and goeth away and straightway forgetteth what manner of man he was." Dr. Rufus M. Jones says that these words of the apostle James are a great piece of psychological insight, as fresh and modern as though it were written by his own unapostolic namesake Professor William James. It is a notorious fact that none of us can visualize our own faces from memory. We see ourselves often enough, but the image fades out at once and leaves only a vague blur. One of the mercies of heaven, no doubt!

There are two priceless mirrors for the soul which should never be broken. They are *humility* and the *sense of humor.* These two are twins, or at least they are closely related, children of the same parents. They are truth-telling, polished mirrors in which we can take a darting glance and be enabled by their report to keep within the facts in our estimate of ourselves. If we keep them whole they will save us more than seven years of bumped heads and barked shins.

A sense of humor is a means of grace. "Now abideth these three," said an Irishman quoting Saint Paul, "faith, hope, and love. And the greatest of these is a sense of humor." His exegesis was all right. Is your hat four sizes too large for you? Your sense of humor will tell you all about it, and prevent you from allowing your exaggerated self-importance to make you ridiculous. If you look at this mirror long enough it will whisper to you in confidence that your ears look suspiciously like those of a donkey, that you had better wear your hair long to cover them up. Without that hint from your sense of humor your unrestrained actions would soon add to the gaiety of nations. You would label yourself as a near relative of that comic figure who announces, "I am Sir Oracle, and when I ope' my lips, let no dog bark."

A genuine sense of humility is the beginning of all wisdom and the secret of all growth. It is also a preserver from painful and ridiculous escapades into which we are so easily lured by conceit. A sergeant-instructor said these words to a cadet, and they are well worth reading at least once a week as part of our morning devotions: "No, ye'll no mak' an officer. But it's just possible if the warr keep on a while ye micht—micht, mind ye—begin to an' ye prractice harrd—verra harrd—hae a glimmer that ye'll never ken the r-rudiments o' the wurrk."

These mirrors can never be replaced, no substitute can ever be found for them. Handle with care!

Great souls are a wonderful gallery of mirrors. Not that they give us realistic views of ourselves, for they do not. But they help us see life in its true proportions. They walk before us, and our petty superiorities over our neighbor, which seemed of such momentous magnitude before, dwindle to the vanishing point. They change the Pharisee with his peacock strut and pious cant into the publican to whose lips only one prayer rises —"God be merciful to me, a sinner!" It is tragically bad luck to break that mirror, to put ourselves out of range of influence of great characters in history and in the present day, for their clear reflection of life's true greatness helps us to rise out of lives of tawdry insignificance.

Emerson presents us an ideal mirror to stand in front of when he says,

"Measure your present habit of thought and action by the remembrance of your dead, by the remembrance of three or four great men who are yet alive, by the image of your distant friend, by the lives and precepts of the heroes and philosophers. These all are only shadows of the primary sentiments at home in your soul." In such mirrors we can see ourselves in prophetic vision of what we ought to be and may be.

Christ is the mirror of all men, the measure of the stature of men by which we may estimate ourselves. There is a very poignant story of an artist in a Middle-Western town in the United States who achieved a great local vogue. His vivid and startling color effects were highly praised. He had but little training, but what he lacked in technique he made up in assurance. He conceived the idea of going to France in order to fulfill his destiny as the great painter of his day. He went to the Louvre and looked at the pictures. At first the somber and quiet hues of some of the great masters aroused in him a complacent disdain. As he stayed on week after week, however, the real soul of the artist which was in him responded to the masterpieces. It was a terrible agony of soul that the man went through when he realized that if those paintings represent art, his own best work was nothing but crude daubing, and that was the conclusion he came to when face to face with the best.

It is exactly that which Jesus Christ does for the race. As we look upon his achievement in the art of life, we see ourselves as the crudest of crude daubers. It is an immeasurable tragedy that for many men and women Christ is only a broken mirror. They swell up their Lilliputian chests, never realizing what malformed and undersized specimens of humanity they are. Sometimes the mirror of Christ has been dashed to the ground in anger because of the truth it tells about us. Sometimes it has been let slip out of clumsy hands. Sometimes the reflection of the Master has been allowed to become dim, covered with a film of dust through neglect and carelessness. It is an irreparable loss when the majestic figure of Jesus no longer walks before us. It means "bad luck" for all the years when we can no longer see life's true proportions in the form of him who saw life steadily and saw it whole.

—SKYLINES

8

The Old-Time Religion

"By faith Abraham went forth, although he did not know where he was to go." (Heb. 11:8.)
"Let my people go!" (Exod. 5:1.)

THE PRINCIPAL TROUBLE WITH "THE OLD-TIME RELIGION," AS THAT PHRASE is frequently understood, is that it is not old enough! We are all familiar with the song, usually pealed out in lusty tones:

Give to me the old-time religion,
It's good enough for me!
It was good enough for Moses,
It was good enough for father,
It was good enough for mother,
And it's good enough for me!

What a man who sings that song is clamoring for, when it is anything more than an emotional outlet, is not nearly so old as he thinks it is. He is usually thinking of the exact form of religious expression and practice familiar to him as a boy. And that is a very modern invention, comparatively speaking.

This whole sermon can be put into one sentence: If you want the "old-time religion"—and nothing is so desperately needed by the world today—be sure you get it *old enough.* Do not run back into the sixteenth century and stop there. Insist on the real thing. Go clear back to the beginning.

Notice swiftly three things about the frequent longing for "the old-time religion," with its inevitable implied disparagement of the Christian faith of the present day.

First, the sighing for the religion of yesterday is a *delusion.* Of course religion ought to be old. It can't be worth much if it is not. The sun which lights the earth was not made yesterday. The hills which give birth to the streams which water the earth are not a twentieth-century product. When we wish to make a thing as being really old we can say nothing so strong as that it is as "old as the hills." A religion to be worth anything must be so old as to be timeless. This truth is expressed in one of the most picturesque and suggestive titles of God in the Old Testament, "the Ancient of Days." It is only when we can say, "Lord, thou hast been our dwelling place in all generations," that we feel the lifting power of faith.

But while all that is eternally true usually the cry for the old-time religion is not a thirsting for the universal, timeless elements of religion—those large aspects of Christian truth which are the same yesterday, today, and forever. It is, rather, for those local and temporary forms which have become stereotypes of the mind. The paradoxical thing about it is that those particular interpretations which are revered as being old are comparative novelties. The rampant fundamentalist, for instance, seeking whom he may devour, who regards any interpretation of Christ more liberal than his own as one of Satan's masterpieces, is not merely so much concerned over the triumph of the Spirit of Christ, as over his success in ramming his own dogma down people's throats. He labels as "the old-time religion" a belief in the verbal inspiration of the Scriptures. That particular belief is really quite a new-fangled idea, as any student of the history of Scripture knows.

Many, if not most, of those who declare the old-time religion—which was good enough for Moses, for father, for mother, and for Shadrach, Meshach, and Abednego, and is consequently good enough for them—identify it with the theological interpretations and even with the science (there lies the rub!) held in certain localities two generations ago. Their attitude of mind is exactly like that of the old lady who bitterly opposed the stained-glass windows in the new church, saying that she preferred the glass "just as God made it." Both glass and theology are made out of elements supplied by God. But neither comes directly from the hand of the Almighty.

This vociferous cry for the old-time religion is an *evasion*. The chorus, "Give me the old-time religion," is one in which many join.

To the man looking out on a perplexing world with its new scientific understanding and social emphasis, the simple, individualistic, emotional religion of two generations ago was ever so much easier to get adjusted to. Earth is so much more bothersome than heaven! So the man who does not like to mix thought with his religion looks back longingly to the days when it was considered sufficient merely to sing about it.

The unintelligent sigh for yesterday's religion is *a repression of today's new insight.* It says lazily, "The old is better." Back to grandfather's world and to grandmother's Bible. Such a blind appeal to the near past and the local past strangles every new birth of conscience. Nothing could be more destructive of a genuine and creative faith than to model manners and morals and convictions by the standards of yesterday.

The emphasis so far has been negative. But I would like to make one as emphatically positive as I may and plead for the old-time religion as earnestly as any camp-meeting exhorter might. My only concern is that it be the genuine article!

Leap the centuries and you will find two things.

I

The old-time religion is the religion of Abraham—a religion of intellectual and spiritual daring. The "old-time religion" of his day was not good enough for Abraham. Not by a thousand miles! He traveled that far to Canaan to find one good enough. The religion which really is old is not a mechanical perpetuation of the dead forms of other days. It is pioneering for God into new fields and new days. Abraham went forth although he did not know where he was to go. Had he followed the practice of many today, he would have answered God's call to venture forth by a timorous "No thank you. Ur suits me all right. The old-time religion is good enough for me!"

He walked west with God, even when that daring exploit took him directly in the face of every time-honored and revered orthodoxy of his neighbors.

The Order of the Sons of Abraham created history. They have made the history of religion, beginning with Abraham and going on up through the prophets, on and up until there comes that utterly reckless innovator, Jesus of Nazareth, who announces in a perfectly scandalous way, "Ye have heard it said of old . . . but I say unto you." Any future history of Christianity worth recording will come from the same source—from men daring enough to push out into the world of thought and life, to adapt Christianity to the needs and temper of their time, men who dare to strip the husk from the kernel of truth and separate the accidental from the essential.

General Smuts, in that noble figure of speech derived from Abraham himself, said, "Humanity has struck its tents and is on the march." It is a tragedy if the church is left behind in a walled city. O for a baptism of that old-time religion of Abraham! Will Christianity go before this moving column of men as a pillar of fire, or will it be left behind like a collection of pyramids in ancient Egypt, dedicated to the past, peopled by mummies? Will the church have intellectual daring enough to make itself and its message at home in the new intellectual world we live in? Will it have the spiritual daring of Abraham to respond to the call of God which comes through the needs of the world today, "Get thee out"? Get thee out of the familiar and comfortable ruts of custom, out of the smug little dogmatisms which make void the Word of God through the accumulated tradition of unessential trifles! Get thee out of the world of petty ecclesiastical red tape and into the promised land of great fundamental human needs!

II

The old-time religion was the religion of Moses—a religion of social revolution. Perhaps "revolution" is a strong word. So be it. The religion of Moses was a strong thing. It was a blazing conviction which thundered at the established order in Egypt in behalf of the depressed, defrauded, exploited people, the command, "Let my people go!" The familiar hymn of praise to the old-time religion has one line which declares, "It was good enough for Moses." That is an unmitigated slander. After his vision of God in the desert Moses was not content with any worn conventionalities. He had learned that the will of God meant the release of the toilers, the bondsmen. The social gospel is not any new thing. It is one of the oldest things in the Bible. It was one of the first results of the vision of God which came to Moses. And any religion which does not have that social vision and throbbing sympathy for men at its very center cannot have any claim to being an old-time religion. It is a pale, bloodless modern substitute.

"Give me the old-time religion!" Let the world hear from millions of Christian voices the echoes of the command of God, "Let my people go." Let it reverberate through the United States, now left without adequate protection for its children against the exploitation of those who profit by child labor. Let it sound like the crack of doom thundering in the ears of Pharaoh in those states where children under fourteen years of age are forced to labor for ten to twelve hours a day under the shameful permission of the state. I believe that adequate protection requires a federal amendment prohibiting child labor. We are told by lawyers that we ought not to "clutter up the Constitution" with amendments. But let us repeat in high seriousness a remark first made in jest, "What's the Constitution between friends?" What is the Constitution between God and his friends, the children? I would much rather see the Constitution cluttered up with a dozen more amendments than to see the nation cluttered up with a million undersized, malformed children deprived of their birthright!

So we have arrived at the end—where every sermon should find its journey's end—at the feet of Jesus. The old-time religion is the religion of Jesus—a religion of active, sacrificing love.

—THE HAUNTED HOUSE

9

Meanwhile

"Waiting for and hastening the coming of the day of God." (II Pet. 3:12.)

OUR THOUGHT STARTS WITH TWO WORDS WHICH COME TOGETHER AND LEAP the years into our own day. The first is from II Pet. 3: "What sort of persons ought you to be in lives of holiness and godliness, waiting for and hastening the coming of the day of God." The key word in that is "wait." This was written in a dark day of persecution, when it looked like defeat for the Christian cause. The future was veiled; disaster was predicted. They were waiting. In the midst of all the uncertainties the light shifted to themselves. *Meanwhile,* in view of all this, what manner of men ought we to be? To this word, bring another, from a drama set in substantially the same era and in the Christian company. It is a word in Bernard Shaw's play *Androcles and the Lion* spoken by the gladiator Ferrovius. He was a giant, a man of force and violence, yet a Christian, drawn to the gospel of love, torn between two pulls. He says, finally, "The Christian God is not yet. *Meanwhile* I must serve the gods that are. I take service with Caesar."

Both these words come close to us. For we are in what may fairly be called an era of *meanwhile.* We find it hard to see ahead for one year, to say nothing of two. In so many ways—waiting. It doth not yet appear what we shall be, whether cinders on a global ash pile, or members of a surviving race which has mastered its new powers of suicide. That sense of waiting, of meanwhile, was vividly caught in a report of the bomb test last spring in Nevada by David Lawrence, the science reporter. He thus describes the tense waiting:

The silence was broken at last by a voice from the control point, counting off the seconds. "H hour minus ten seconds to zero." After five more seconds in which the passage of time grew ever slower, the voice began ticking off the seconds one by one.

"Five, four, three, two, one, zero." Out of the north came a light that penetrated the darkness of our goggles. It was a light out of this world, that had the intensity of a hundred suns.

So far, Mr. Lawrence.

It is no exaggeration to say that we do have a sense of a clock ticking—three, two, one, zero.

From a different viewpoint, our generation is certainly a meanwhile era, in its contrast to the stability of a time some of us can remember, the early 1900's. Then people counted on secure continuity, tomorrow the same as today.

> The world which was e'er I was born
> The world which lasts when I am dead.

But today, in so many ways we are just *waiting*. Take the striking contrast between the postwar mood after World War I and that after World War II. After the first world war there was expectancy. We had fought a war to end war. There was eagerness to build a new world. Youth building a new world. The blueprints were in process; the ground was clear. We get the echo of the mood in those strange-sounding words in which Woodrow Wilson announced the Armistice on November 11, 1918—"Armed imperialism is at an end. Who will ever seek to revive it?" But after World War II there was little or no expectancy. In that war there was no Rupert Brooke, writing eloquently, "Now God be praised who matched us with this hour. Honor has come back to earth again." There were no intoxicating slogans, no parades.

In this *meanwhile* there are large numbers of people who have made the choice of the gladiator, Ferrovius, saying, "I must serve the gods that are." And they do!

1. Many do it in *the economic and business world*. They say, "This is a corrupt age. Who can doubt it? The Christian God is not yet. The ideal conditions for a life of high integrity are not here. It would be fine, of course, to live and work in a world where honor rules. But obviously that is not now." So they say there is no use in being a fanatic, or butting your head against a stone wall. So they cut corners, take rebates, exploit where

they can and serve the gods of greed and gain. We can be sympathetic with the difficulty. We know it is hard to make a right-angled turn in the midst of moral traffic. It is like street traffic. I remember painfully a few moments driving a few years ago on Tremont Street in Boston, trying to make a left turn. Half the cars in the United States were coming behind me—the other half coming the other way. I just put out my hand and pretended to wave to someone on the curb and drove on. It was so much easier that way.

2. Also, the choice of the gods that are is easy and persuasive in *standards of personal living*. Many say, or feel without saying, "Just strike a mediocre level, with no nonsense about it, no painful ethical striving; it will save a lot of trouble." This has raised in many minds the dreary conclusion that this will not be widely advertised—the century of the common man—but the century of the *commonplace* man. Arnold Toynbee has insisted that every civilization which has perished has been overcome by barbarians within before it was overthrown by barbarians without. More than a generation ago the Spaniard Ortegay Gasset warned that Western civilization was threatened by barbarians within. He described the barbarian in our midst as the *mass man*, a term which is familiar and terrifying today—the man who holds no high standards for himself, who takes pride in his mediocrity. If he admires anything outside of himself, it is success. He admires the smart operator, the man who gets by, the fixer. Louis MacNeice has drawn his portrait:

Popcorn, peanuts, clams and gum,
 We whose kingdom has not come,
Have mouths like men, but still are dumb.
 We only deal in here and now,
As circumstances will allow
 The sponsored program tells us how.

They are so easy, the ruling codes and fashions, the gods that are.

3. Again, one of the tragic areas where the gladiator's choice prevails is that of *race relations*. Over the land a chorus rises, "The Christian God is not yet. So we will string along with the codes that are. After all, we did not make them, and we can't change them." So many people who can formally accept the doctrine of the fatherhood of God (as long as it is kept in a vacuum) and can say without batting an eyelid, "God hath made of one blood all men to dwell together," can accommodate themselves to a "Jim Crow" society and serve the gods of discrimination.

The real question is this, What is the *alternative* to serving the gods that are? What manner of men *ought we to be*, can we be, *meanwhile?*

There seem to be four things, at least, that can be said.

I

The first is obvious, and yet big. *We can refuse to call wrong right.* That has been the great service of a Christian minority in all ages. It can be done in the personal world, and in the larger world in the presence of powerful wrong. Last summer a man, depressed by world conditions and by the common feeling of individual helplessness, asked me, "What can you do when you can't do anything?" It is a tough question. I had no answer at the time. But later my mind drifted off to a little company who were confronted by just that question. It was the group of disciples of Jesus, watching the crucifixion. There is *pathos* in the simple record, "They stood there watching." There was the best they had known, the hope of the future gone down in crushing defeat. One thing they *did not do.* They did not look at the cross and say, "Well, I guess that settles it. Pilate was right. Caiaphas was right. Judas was right. Jesus was wrong." They said, "No. Wrong is wrong, no matter how popular and powerful." And history has put its seal on that answer, "Yet that scaffold sways the future!" It did sway it. That denial, apparently so powerless, was the beginning of new hope. Logan Pearsall Smith has recorded a conversation which tells much about a current mood and its remedy. He said that in a conversation with a group of young people he said that a certain act was wrong. "But," he continued, "that time-honored word seemed unfamiliar to them. They looked at each other and began whispering to each other, then one of them asked me in a hushed voice, 'It's what, did you say?' I repeated the word *wrong*, loudly. Again they whispered and again the spokesman came forward. 'Do you mind telling us how you spell it?' I shouted, 'I spell it with a W-r-o-n-g, *wrong!*' " The easiest thing to say is, "I move we make it unanimous." It is all that some men ever say. The world has gone forward on the feet of people who could say, "No!" We spell wrong with "W."

II

The power to make that denial rests on something deeper, *faith in a stronger power than wrong.* It was so with that group at the crucifixion. They had faith that the last word had not been spoken by the iron nails.

Faith is a stronger power than Rome. In a *meantime* era, we can have faith in a spiritual order of life, beyond the gods that are—*God.* Faith in

An older place than Eden
And a taller town than Rome.

—G. K. CHESTERTON

Some months ago I talked with an insurance man turned poet. Sometimes we think that all insurance men are poets of the romantic school. This man had come back from a summer in Europe and was telling of the most exciting thing he saw. In Rome he went from the ruins of the Coliseum where 100,000 people watched the gladiator's game, to the catacombs where thirty people made a crowd. Then a poet's gleam came into his eye and he said, "The catacomb was a larger place than the Coliseum." It was. In one of the catacombs was the inscription traced on the walls in the dark: "His kingdom is an everlasting kingdom." Larger future was there; God was there. To hold to such a faith is one thing we can do. As one scientist, Sir Arthur Eddington, once put it: "I would say that when from the human heart the cry goes up, 'What is it all about?' it is not a true answer to look only at a universe of fiery globes, moving on to impending gloom, and say it is about non-computed algebra. But rather it is about a spirit in which truth has its shrine, with potentialities of self-fulfillment in its response to right, and to God."

If life has no foundation of such a faith, if the only gods that are are man-made, if we trust in the wheels of a machine, we can lift only a shaky and pitiful prayer. With only that trust, here is what the General Confession becomes:

Almighty and most merciful machine,
We have erred and strayed from thy
Paths like lost screws.
We have put in those bolts which we ought
Not to have put in,
And have left out those bolts which we ought
To have put in.

That sounds like blasphemy. *It is.* But we ought to remember that that is ultimately the only prayer that can be made without God.

Go back to those words quoted from David Lawrence, about the atom tests—"a light out of this world." Our deepest need is other Light from out of this world. "God is Light." The Light of the glory of God in the face of Jesus Christ.

III

A third thing in a time of meanwhile is to hold the conviction that *quality of life outweighs quantity,* on the only scales that finally count. Nothing outward can ever make up for fatty degeneration of character. The verb "to have" is always a smaller one than the verb "to be." That is easily forgotten in a civilization so largely *quantitative.* Oscar Wilde once cried out, "Give me the luxuries of life and I can get along without the necessities." As he meant it, that was as idiotic rabble as words can be. But in a deep sense it is profoundly true. The finest luxury of life is integrity of mind and spirit. The easiest thing, of course, is to accept the judgment which Scott Fitzgerald said was that of many in the 1920's that "Life is a game in which everyone was offside, the referee had been chased from the field and there were no rules." There are rules and a Referee. To keep an ethic undebatable in the midst of all the debates that swirl around us and in us is the top prize of life. *Meanwhile,* in the midst of all uncertainties we can keep that. When we take the line of least resistance, which always runs downhill, and say, "It doesn't make any difference what I do," a paralysis of character and personality sets in.

This has been accepted as *undebatable* by many minds over many centuries. It has never been put into clearer, briefer form than in the classic words of Frederick William Robertson, words that will be heard for centuries to come:

> In the darkest hour through which a human soul can pass, whatever else is doubtful, this at least is certain. If there is no God and no future state, yet, even then, it is better to be generous than selfish, better to be chaste than licentious, better to be true than false, better to be brave than to be a coward. Blessed beyond all earthly blessedness is the man who in the tempestuous darkness of the soul, has dared to hold fast to these venerable landmarks.

That takes on the quality of a proposition in Euclid about the angles of a triangle.

Dorothy Parker has put memorably the degeneration which comes when an easy *moral relativism* displaces an *ethical absolute,* in verses which she ironically entitles "The Veteran":

> When I was young, and bold, and strong,
> Oh, right was right, and wrong was wrong!

My plume on high, my flag unfurled,
I rode away to right the world.
"Come out, you dogs, and fight!" said I,
And wept there was but once to die.

Now I am old; and good and bad
Are woven in a crazy plaid.
I sit and say, "The world is so;
And he is wise who lets it go.
A battle lost, a battle won—
The difference is small, my son."

Inertia rides and riddles me;
The which is called Philosophy.

When we say that "the difference is small," *rigor mortis* has set in. In art we are familiar with what is called a "one-man show." Now a one-man show, in many realms, can be a tiresome piece of exhibitionism, sounding like a tenor practicing the scales, "me, me, me, me." Or it may be, as it has been times without number, the most exciting drama ever put on. In moral choices we are all called to hold a one-man show.

A long time ago there was a one-man show—that of Joshua, who said, at a crisis, "You go where you wish, but as for me and my house. . . ." Just one. In the same great storybook, Joseph in Egypt put on a one-man show at a moment of choice, "Thou, God, seest me." That was enough. William Lloyd Garrison had only a one-man show, during the early part of his life, and a violent melodrama it was.

Browning asks the question: "Like you this Christianity or not? Has it your vote to be true if it can?" It is not a matter of majority but *choice.* Would it get your vote if it had no other votes?

IV

Finally there is one more thing we can do. We can keep a grasp on the truth that *one life counts.* That is hard to do in a time when so many great impersonal forces are at work. But the real truth is found in a line about the Webbs, Beatrice and Sidney, "They signed many minority reports which became majority actions." There is a lot of history in that sentence. A desperately Christian group, a pitifully small minority, has signed minority reports, for instance, against the murder of babies in the Roman world, against slavery, against the cruel exploitation of people in the early days of the industrial revolution. Napoleon said something like that. Speaking of the American Revolution he said, "The greatest issues of the universe were decided by the skirmishes of picket guards." They were. The Congress in Philadelphia bravely declared, "We hold these truths to be self-evident." But they were not self-evident to many except a few philosophers and poets. The average size of the American army was about five thousand men. Picket guards! That is a great role, and one to which we are called.

There is an alternative to "serving the gods that are." It is this: "We take service with him whose service is perfect freedom."

—An unpublished Sermon

10

Grace for City Living

"I have been in danger of cities." (II Cor. 11:26.)
"My grace is sufficient for you." (II Cor. 12:9.)

THIS SERMON COMES OUT OF THE STRANGE JOINING OF TWO TEXTS FAR apart, yet belonging together. The first is the Lord's word to Paul, "My grace is sufficient for you" (II Cor. 12.9). The other is Paul's own report, "I have been in danger of cities" (II Cor. 11:26). The promise of these texts is that there is a needed grace for living in a large city where so many must live and move and have what being they can manage. John Newton, the clergyman and hymn writer of Olney, England, has a good phrase for this need. When he moved to London from his village in the north of England, he made a fervent prayer for "London grace." He explained that by "London grace" he meant grace in a very high degree, "grace to enable one to live as a Christian even in London." Now John Newton knew a great deal about grace. If anyone were to put his life into fiction the publisher would say, "Do try to get it a bit nearer to probability so someone may swallow it." Not many people would "swallow" John Newton's life. He ran away to sea at the age of fourteen and was later sold into slavery. Managing somehow to gain his freedom he later became the captain of a slave ship, sinking to the lowest point of degradation to which a man could fall. Later in a hymn he wrote he put that experience into poetry and with it the confession that God's grace came even to the master of a slave ship.

In evil long I took delight
Unawed by shame or fear
Till a new object struck my sight

And stopped my wild career.
I saw one hanging on a tree in agonies and blood
Who fixed his languid eyes on me
As near His Cross I stood.

Thus, while his death my sin displays
In all its blackest hue
Such is the mystery of grace
It sees my pardon too.

John Newton made an about-face becoming finally a clergyman of the Church of England. His immortality will probably rest on two hymns which he wrote, "How sweet the name of Jesus sounds" and "Glorious things of thee are spoken, Zion city of our God." This man felt the need of a London grace. That would be grace in a very high degree, "grace abounding"—to use John Bunyan's phrase.

Paul's list of dangers, familiar to us as perils in the King James Version, make a suggestive and formidable list of the hazards of life. They were very real dangers to Paul. To read the list with an active imagination makes the blood run cold. No wonder Paul could exclaim, after going through some of them, "Here we are alive!" They were real perils, from the Jews who fought the Christian evangel, from Paul's implacable enemies, riots, beatings, dangers from both bandits and pirates. Not only was Paul one of the finest minds ever loosed on earth, but he was also one of the toughest men who ever went through an almost incredible endurance race. The drama of his life would make some of the popular "westerns" look and sound like an afternoon tea of the women's garden club.

He speaks of "danger in the city." This we can understand, for the danger of the city comes close to our time and situation. Our city life presents very real dangers to the life of the spirit. This does not mean, of course, that cities have been entirely antagonistic to the growth of Christianity. Some of the greatest seed plots of Christianity have been, and are today, in great cities. We have only to think of Rome, Geneva, London, Edinburgh, Boston. Nor is the old adage at all true,

God made the country
And the man made the town.

Both God and the devil are found in rural lanes as well as in city streets. Yet there is need for strong fortification of spirit, and what the Scots have called "bonny fighting," to carry on a vigorous and triumphant Christian life in cities.

I

One risk of life in a city is that of losing the sense of personal value and significance. Feeling rises in a city of two million, or in a city such as New York or London with eight million, "What does one person count?" The effect of a great crowd is that the individual seems lost. Is it not a symptom of the impersonality of our lives that on some toll road when one has put his coin in the basket a recorded "Thank you" comes out of the loudspeaker as the car drives away?

The story is told of a slave woman in Georgia watching General Sherman's army on its march from Atlanta to the sea. She had never been away from her plantation, and never seen so many people in her life. At the end of the long procession she said, "I reckon they haven't all got names." It was a really profound observation, for that is the effect of a great crowd, the individual is lost. It is as though he has no individual name. The Christian Gospel stands up to that saying they *have* got names. "I know my sheep by name." Against the pressure of the city's crowd, we need the inner assurance of the Gospel that every man is of infinite worth in the eyes of God. We need it especially living in cities.

In the 1950 census a woman was somehow overlooked. She called the newspaper editor and asked why she had not been counted in the census. The editor was a man of great imagination and told her that a census-taker would come to visit her, whereupon he sent one of his reporters over to take count of the woman's family. Upon returning to the office he asked the editor what to do with the information, and the editor said, "Put it in the wastebasket." The reporter said, "It doesn't mean anything to anyone, does it?" and the editor replied, "It meant a great deal to her." The Christian conviction is that it means a great deal also to God.

According to an ancient tradition there is a city in Palestine where Jesus once was lost. Such is a word of truth about any city, for any city may be the one where Jesus is lost. He is lost when we lose the sense of personal value and significance. William Blake's poem has a word to speak to us:

> He came to the desert of London town,
> Gray miles long;
> He wandered up and he wandered down,
> Singing a quiet song.

He came to the desert of London town,
  Murk miles broad;
He wandered up and he wandered down,
  Ever alone with God.

William Blake did it in London. You can do it in New York, or Chicago, or San Francisco.

II

Among the dangers in the city in our day is the intensified pressure to conformity. Many people in our cities look and act as though they had been stamped by a giant biscuit cutter, making them all the same shape and size. There is need for a thundering echo of the old plea, fitted to the city, "Come out from them, and be separate" (II Cor. 6:17). Not for the sake of being different, but for the sake of keeping a Christian quality in our life. A recent book has told the sad story of Everyman Gary Gray, who forgot how to say "I." It is the familiar story of group pressures in job, housing, car ownership, and the uses of leisure, if any. A great many people are in that mournful state. It is interesting, and also disturbing, to note that a hearing clinic at Northwestern University has discovered by experiment that one of the very hard words to be heard is the word "No." That is a sort of sinister symbol of the sad truth that very often the word "No" is not heard at all from some people in the city. Many people seem to spend their lives "window shopping," and their great response is "I want that." The lust of the eye is a hard pressure upon every individual to be like everybody else. Paul's word, "Be not conformed to this world," leaps across the centuries and the seas and comes to us with a terrible timeliness in our time. In cities individuality is pounded by agencies such as the newspaper, advertising, radio, television. They wield a mighty hammer: Be like everybody else—or else! From the jungles of Africa, Dr. Schweitzer describes it:

> The man of today is exposed to influences which are bent on robbing him of all confidence in his own thinking. He is called to surrender his spiritual independence by so much that he reads and hears. Parties and associations claim him for their own. Over and over convictions are forced upon him in the same way, by means of large electrical signs which flare in the streets of the city, and persuade him to buy shoe polish or soup.

The danger is not in compelling people to dress or eat exactly alike, but in the pressure to make people over. Organizations make people into their own image. To behave like the organization, to think like the organization.

J. B. Priestley makes this observation on "mass living": "People in the mass are not only losing their independence, but are losing any desire to be independent, and active-minded, sharply differentiated individuals. They prefer a mass existence, mass standards, with which they feel more comfortable in their circles."

One commentator on the social scene of our time has observed that life today is producing a population of what he calls "interchangeable men." If this seems exaggerated, more sobering is the word of the warden of the Federal Penitentiary at Lewisburg, Pennsylvania. "A symptom of today's youth is the abandonment of solitude which was once a trademark of adolescence and frequently that solitude was creative." He is right, for from the solitude often came the dream, the hopes and the aims that charged life with meaning. Longfellow was not just guessing when he wrote, "The thoughts of youth are long, long thoughts." You can see that youth in such frightening numbers has abandoned solitude in favor of pack-running, of associations like wolf packs which bury when they do not destroy individuality. They want to be initiated into the gang, and the price that they pay is the abandonment of self.

A mother of three children proudly remarked to a church visitor, "We are doing the very best for our children. On Mondays we send them to their school club; on Tuesdays they take music lessons; on Wednesdays they take dancing lessons; Thursdays they study elocution; Fridays they just play; Saturdays they go to the movies; and on Sundays we go for a picnic in the country." "Yes," replied the visitor, "but what are you doing for their souls?" The mother exclaimed wide-eyed, "Their souls? That's a bit old-fashioned, isn't it?" These two pictures deal with youth, but they reveal a hazard for all of us that goes with living in the midst of a crowd. The intensified pressure to conform, to be like everybody else. This is a twice-told tale, and there is no need to go over it at length. The big thing which the gospel brings is the assurance of the grace of God for city living—a New York grace, a Chicago grace, a San Francisco grace. "Be transformed by the renewing of your mind." There is suggestion as to how this can be done in the conviction of the Pilgrims at Plymouth, that they, though living in the new world, were still a colony of England. We, though living in the midst of all the pressures and dangers of city life, are yet a colony of heaven, and we will not go native.

III

Another danger of living in the mass of cities is that of losing the sense of personal relationship with people. There is a deadly sense of the anonymous in cities. In the city we are protected from having our feelings lacerated with sympathy and concern because we do not know the people concerned. We do not have such vulnerable hearts. When a person dies on the next floor of the apartment, only a few feet away, as a rule we do not know the family. The sorrow is anonymous. If the milkman falls down and breaks his hip, we do not know him, at least not well, and the most we can summon is an exclamation, "Tough break!" But in the country or small town we would know him, for he lives down the road. Our nerves are exposed painfully.

A task for everyone is to keep alive the sense of life in personal terms. There is a "London grace" for city living, even as for Paul there was an "Ephesian grace"; an "Athenian grace"; a "Roman grace." Paul was not conformed to the world, he was transformed by the renewing of his mind from the mind of Christ. "My grace is sufficient for you." God's grace was sufficient for Paul.

Jesus went up to the big city; it was big, even by our standards. Jerusalem was a city of hundreds of thousands of people; Jesus was a small-town man. A small-town man with his companions from the country going to the great city. His companions were tremendously impressed. They said, "Look, Master, how big everything is!" Like someone from the rural districts gazing up at the Empire State Building. But Jesus was more impressed with people. He said to them, "Look," and pointed to a woman putting all her living in the treasury. He said to them, "Look," and pointed to a widow put out from her house onto the street. Jesus was impressed, not with buildings, not with crowds, but with persons. His was a grace for city living.

The great phrase from the New Testament "The grace of our Lord Jesus Christ" is the grace of one who met life in terms of people. Jesus never talked about life generally or about philosophy in general; he saw and he talked about people in particular, the lame, the halt, and the blind; the least, the last, and the lost. That grace will be the grace for each one of us to live in the city. That grace is sufficient for us.

—An unpublished Sermon

11

Ashamed of Your Best

"I do not know the man." (Matt. 26:74. R.S.V.)

THESE ARE THE WORDS OF A MAN WHO, AT THE MOMENT HE SPOKE THEM, was ashamed of the best thing that had ever come into his life.

The story of the denial of Jesus by Simon Peter is inexhaustible in its dramatic interest and continuing meaning. Probably as long as time lasts attention will be given to the record of these few minutes in the life of Peter. The Gospel of Mark takes only one hundred and seventy words to tell the story. But it is like a jewel; we turn it around and see new lights gleaming from each facet.

With the most important aspects of that story we are not primarily concerned here. Surely it is one of the best-loved stories in the New Testament. The narrative of the recovery and forgiveness of a man who made a tragic blunder brings hope to all who have failed, to all who have made a mess of things; in other words, to all of us. One of the finest tributes ever paid to Christianity was in the words of the man who said that it "is the religion of all poor devils." That is where we come in.

Another aspect of the story speaks to us across the years, in its picture of a man ashamed of his best. Peter says of Jesus, "I do not know the man." Of course, in a deep sense, that was true. Peter did not know the man fully. He did not know his spirit and mind. To him, as to Philip, the reproachful question might have been asked, "Have I been so long among you, and you did not know me?" But the words were not true as Peter meant them. He did know the man. More than that, knowing him was the best thing that ever happened in Peter's life. One day a young man about his own age stood before Peter, looked him level in the eye, and offered to take him in on the ground floor of the greatest enterprise of human history. Jesus said, "Follow me." And Peter followed him. It was not only the best thing in his life; it was the only thing that ever gave him any distinction. Yet here, in a muddled moment, he went back on his best, ashamed of it.

There have been many striking instances of the same thing in other connections. It seems to be a continuous blunder. Take Sir Arthur Conan Doyle as an example. Among the many things brought out in the recent biography *The Life of Sir Arthur Conan Doyle* by John Dickson Carr is the evidence that the creator of Sherlock Holmes got awfully tired of him. The public had an insatiable appetite for Holmes. That is understandable by anyone who has had the chills run up and down his spine while reading "The Speckled Band" or any one of forty other stories. Doyle felt that if he did not kill Sherlock Holmes, Holmes would certainly kill him! So he killed Holmes off once, pushing him over the highest cliff in recent literature. But the public would not allow it, and Doyle had to pass a miracle and bring Sherlock back to life.

But more than that—he grew ashamed of him. Doyle said of Sherlock Holmes, "He takes my mind off better things." He thought that *The White Company*, a second-rate, run-of-the-mill historical novel, was far better than any of the Holmes stories. No one else agreed with him, but he was still ashamed of Sherlock—of the best thing he had ever done.

The same strange confusion of values occurred in the life of a lesser-known English writer, Beatrix Potter. As a young girl she wrote "The Tale of Peter Rabbit," a little story for children, which became a classic. I hope you met him at the right time, along with Flopsy, Mopsy, and Cottontail, and in lively imagination heard Mr. McGregor shouting at Peter Rabbit when Peter broke the glass in Mr. McGregor's forcing bed in the garden. Beatrix Potter grew up; that is, she grew older. After middle life she married a land owner in the north of England, a typical squire of the landed gentry. She went in heavily for "respectability." She grew into a fat, stuffy old lady and grew violently ashamed of Peter Rabbit. She never allowed his name to be mentioned in her presence. A strange note is added in the fact that she became an expert in the art of shooting rabbits! Again, as with Doyle, she was ashamed not only of her best, but of the only thing that ever brought her any distinction at all. Akin to that is the strange feeling, almost of disdain, which Tolstoi in his frantic later years came to have for *War and Peace*. Imagine that!

It can happen; it has happened to multitudes; it might happen to us—this monumental muddle of becoming ashamed of our best.

I

One obvious realm where we can see this distorted shame operate is in our American heritage of democracy. "Endowed by their Creator with certain Unalienable Rights"—that is our best! The principle of the right of the individual, rooted in a religious conception of man, came to the world in the eighteenth century as a dawn of hope. Today all too many seem strangely ashamed of it. They seem to regard it as something dangerous and subversive. In hysteria and fear we see the constant violation of civil rights, of many provisions of the Bill of Rights, including the right to vote and to receive education. Many of our officials, and politicians and citizens without office, are saying of the towering figures of our heritage of freedom and democracy, Thomas Jefferson and Abraham Lincoln, "I never knew the man."

Some senators, conducting a filibuster against civil rights for a large section of the citizens of the republic—and, incidentally, defending to their last breath the sacred right to drool—are saying plainly, "We do not believe in democracy. We have no use for it. You cannot have democratic government in the United States. We won't allow you. It is un-American." No lie circulated by the efficient lying machine of Russian Communism could be as harmful to the United States in the eyes of Asia as that. To many in Asia, to hosts of the two thirds of the world's population who have colored skins, the two best-known cities in the United States are not New York or Washington, but Scottsboro, Alabama, and Cicero, Illinois.

It is also very disturbing to realize that in recent years many people have become ashamed of another "best" in our high tradition, the role of America as a place of refuge and opportunity for the oppressed and persecuted of Europe. That sounds through our history like a great major chord of music. Yet that chord has been muted and silenced as we have watched one of the great tragedies of history, the suffering of millions of displaced persons in Europe. A large number have been admitted. The generosity of large numbers of Americans who have made possible the coming of many displaced persons, has written a bright page in our story. Yet it has been only a small part of what might have been done. The immigration laws have been bound up with restrictions and discriminations. Yet America's door open to the oppressed has been a noble "best." Those who have grown ashamed of it have forgotten that they have come from "D.P." ancestors. The sons and daughters of the "Mayflower" and other early ships came from displaced persons. The early boats had a great cargo.

> Laws, freedom, truth and faith in God
> Came with those exiles o'er the waves.

Very much later, other ships brought over in the steerage great assets to the democratic way of life in America. Part of our best is seen in the lines by Emma Lazarus inscribed in bronze on the base of the Statue of Liberty:

> Give me your tired, your poor,
> Your huddled masses yearning to breathe free,
> The wretched refuse of your teeming shores,
> Send these, the homeless, tempest-tost to me,
> I lift my lamp beside the golden door.

God help us if we ever grow ashamed of that.

II

The dreams and aspirations of their youth are what many people grow ashamed of. Like Peter, they are ashamed of the best things that ever happened in their whole lives. It is common to see people smile at the remembrance of these hopes and determinations, dismissing them with an apologetic sneer, "Oh, I was young them." What they really mean is, "I was alive then. I am dead now." Proof of their death is found in their regarding these dreams of their youth, their high idealisms, their hours of dedication, as naïve, youthful excesses.

People who have become ashamed of their best ought to ponder the familiar story of Jonathan Swift, once in the years when his mind was failing, looking at one of his early books and saying, "What genius I had when I wrote that." They should say of their dreams and high desires and endeavors of youth, "What greatness I had when I thought that, or did that, or tried that." Swift at least knew what his best was. That is a lot better than being ashamed of it. Louis Hector Berlioz gave a wise word of counsel to young people. He said, "Lay up in your youth a large stock of enthusiasms, for you will lose a good many of them on the way." That may sound like cynicism. It is just realism. The attrition of life does rob us of many youthful enthusiasms, so it is well to start with a generous supply.

Some of the enthusiasm will prove to be unjustified. But there is no need for total bankruptcy. There is no need for going back on our best. Much better than a petition in moral and spiritual bankruptcy is an old affirmation of solvency, "I have kept the faith."

Closely akin to that renunciation of the idealisms of early days is the strange sort of shame which many people often show over what is called the "narrowness" of their early life, of the home of childhood and youth. Now, of course, there have been and are many homes bound by legalism which cramps life. Often these homes are intensely biblical in their traditions but the parents seem never to have read in their Bibles these words, "The letter killeth, but the spirit giveth life," or the words of Jesus, "The Son of Man is Lord also of the sabbath." They do not realize that every institution and every tradition is to be judged by the manner in which it serves the abundant life of a child of God.

What is often called lightly, "narrowness," is only another name for what is truly a source of life and power, that is, moral and spiritual discipline. It is just the same with a life as with a river. Consider two views of the Mississippi River. One was at St. Louis years ago, at a disastrous floodtime. At the junction of the Missouri and the Mississippi there were no stoutly containing walls or levees. The result was a lake twenty miles across, which, in its complete "freedom" to go anywhere it was carried, was a menace to a whole countryside. Farther north at Keokuk, Iowa, there was a different scene. There the river has controls and limits. It is confined by narrow walls. It thus becomes a source of power to a whole region, furnishing light, heat, and power to many states. Discipline and control mean just the same production of power in a life as in a river.

A sharp picture of a person coming to the realization of what discipline, and a faith from which it came, mean, and the result which comes when it is gone, is found in the conversation overheard by a spectator at a performance of Thornton Wilder's play, *Our Town.* The play was a simple and impressive picture of a small town in New Hampshire two generations ago, an order of life shaped by the church and definitely expressing Christian standards and values. A prosperous New Yorker and his wife, who had evidently grown up in a small town like Grover's Corners, were talking while coming down the aisle after the show was over. The man was overheard saying to his wife, complacently, "Well, that's where we came from, baby." She gave him an unexpected answer, "Yes, and I'm wondering where we've got to." The play compelled a fresh appraisal of life. The woman saw that something precious had gone out of it, the best things their life had ever known.

III

It is in connection with religion, an articulate faith, that we find the crowning example of a person's being ashamed of his best. Through the centuries the upreach of faith has been man's best. We find it in old words, "The Lord is my shepherd"; "Underneath are the everlasting arms"; "My meat and drink is to do the will of God." A vital faith brings a qualitative difference into life that makes it impossible for anything else to be compared with it—"A day in thy courts is better than a thousand." In individual life, the awakening to a spiritual world beyond the things of sense, the response of the mind and spirit to God, is the finest thing in life. Yet some grow ashamed of it.

Some months ago I stood on the dock while the Queen Elizabeth was loading for the trip to Europe. There was a large pile of trunks, all of which bore the printed label, "Not wanted on the voyage." They were to be stowed away in the hold, as they were packed with things that were not needed during the short trip. But many have used the same label on the start of their voyage of life. They have written on religion, "Not wanted on the voyage." Put it away in the hold. This is a pleasure trip. I can't be encumbered.

So what might lift life above the animal level is discarded. And faith is needed, desperately needed, for the voyage of life. It has given and can give both momentum and direction. It can bring high meaning into a world which has become so largely and oppressively impersonal. Ralph Borsodi has given a memorable picture of a world increasingly denuded of personality. He writes that today the modern mother is often merely maternity case No. 8434, and her child, after being fingerprinted and footprinted, becomes No. 8003. At the other end of life a modern funeral in one of our great cities becomes an event in Parlor B on a certain day, with preacher No. 14, singer No. 87, rendering music No. 174, flowers and decorations Class B. That is, we are all cards in some vast index. That is where the Christian gospel comes in. It affirms that we are not cards, but children of God. God is the champion of personality. We are all familiar with the great words of the Book of Job: "I know that my Redeemer liveth." Those words are not to be taken with any narrowly theological interpretation of the word "Redeemer." It means in that context something different. It means that God is a champion of personality.

Still, I know One to champion me at last,
to stand up for me upon the earth.
This body may break up, but even then
my life shall have a sight of God;
my heart is pining as I yearn
To see him on my side,
see him estranged no longer.
(Job 19:25-27, Moffatt.)

That high faith is man's best. It is needed on the voyage of life. That faith is needed in our common life together as inhabitants of the earth. This is no hour to be ashamed of faith in the relevance of God to our world. There is an old gospel song not used much any more:

Jesus, and can it ever be
A mortal man ashamed of Thee?

It would be well to sing that song today. Ashamed of Jesus in a world going over the cliff of disaster because of disregard of him and his words? Ashamed of Jesus in a world in which fifty years of history have given an appalling vindication of his teaching? Ashamed of Jesus in a day when it appears more blindingly clear than ever before that there is no other foundation for human survival than that which is laid in Christ Jesus? It is no day to be ashamed of the old word of salvation in a world increasingly lost.

Ashamed of Jesus, sooner far
Let evening blush to own a star!

—MARCHING OFF THE MAP

12

Thanksgiving, Religion, and Patriotism

"If I forget thee, O Jerusalem, let my right hand forget her cunning, and let my tongue cleave to the roof of my mouth." (*Ps. 137:5-6.*)

THESE WORDS REPRESENT THE MOST PERFECT BLENDING IN ALL LITERATURE of religion and patriotism. Even over the centuries one feels a new heart-break in the words, a catch in the voice. This is the cry of an exile, desperately homesick. If one has never endured involuntary exile he may not be able to imagine what it was like. But anyone who has been an exile from his home does not need to be told what the words mean: "By the waters of Babylon, we sat down and wept." An exile from a loved worship, from all the dear and familiar ordinances of religion, an exile from home, the love of country rose in his heart like a flood. We can well imagine that the hills had something to do with it. Jerusalem was built on the top of a mountain—"as the mountains are round about Jerusalem." So the Lord was round about those who knew him, loved him, feared him. But when there were no hills!

This blending of the appeal of religion and patriotism is the mood of traditional thanksgiving. At its highest use it is more than a complacent bow of gratitude for personal good fortune or for the joy of family reunion. Thanksgiving, at its best, is a consideration of and gratitude for religion in the life of the nation. "This nation, under God" was Lincoln's phrase. Thanksgiving is the time to consider that we are a nation and that we are under God.

Religion and patriotism are two streams that run parallel, but they are not the same. It is blunder with terrible consequences to substitute patriotism for religion, to give to the state the worship and devotion which belong to God. The cult of nationalism has become one of Christianity's greatest rivals. On the other hand it has happened often that religion which is ethical and prophetic has been, and had to be, in conflict with national moods and trends. One result has been that the attitude toward country has been that of criticism rather than affection, of conflict rather than appreciation, like the candid friend whose candor is far more evident than his friendship. This has led many people to underestimate the genuine ethical and spiritual values that are in an enlightened love of country. A vast change has taken place in the last decade, with reappraisal of many of the tested values in American life, just because these values were threatened and attacked.

You may look at your own house with critical eyes—look at that silly roof! Did you ever see anything like it? It sticks out in little gables; the architect must have been drunk. But come inside. Behold the Holland Tunnel leading down to the kitchen and dining room. So you could go through every room. But suppose the house catches on fire and you stand there watching it burn. You see more than a silly roof or a long dark hall. You see your home. Values in spite of all the faults loom in a new magnitude. That kind of new look has been given to our nation before, during and after war. The house and the home have been on fire, forcing us to a reappraisal of the worth and values in the American tradition. It brings with it not a call to forget the valid criticisms that have been made, and can still be made, of our national life—such criticisms as John Dos Passos makes in his epic *U.S.A.*—but along with that we are called to a new consideration of the ground we stand on, a ground established by the founding fathers, Adams, Jefferson, Marshall, and the things of priceless service to humanity which have grown on that ground.

I

Thanksgiving brings us a fresh sense of the need for religion in our common life. We stand in need of a great power to preserve and sustain the best things in our life as a people. John Buchan described an atheist as a man with no invisible means of support. Our whirling globe needs invisible means of support. A life or a bundle of lives in a nation needs invisible means of support. The sum of wisdom is not in that ancient Babbit in Hamlet, Polonius, with his adage, "To thine own self be true." Is there any self to which one can be true which is not in turn true to something beyond itself? Tell the pilot of a ship, "To thine own self be true." It's a wonderful mouthful. But if a ship is to make any port the compass must be true to something beyond itself—the North Star. Say to an architect, "To thine own self be true." It's a good idea. But if the building he is erecting is to stand he had better have a plumb line handy. If a single life, or a nation of lives, is to stand firm under all the forces that play upon it it needs a plumb line of moral and spiritual realities.

There is today an impressive recognition of this need, an openness of mind to the need for other power than what is to be found in the ingenuities of a dazzling civilization. Here is report on the mood of the 1920's given by Professor W. P. Montague in his book *Belief Unbound.* He gives not his own judgment but reflects the feeling of great multitudes during that boom time.

> To the modern temper religion is coming to seem unnecessary because fear and sorrow are no longer major themes of our serious culture. There is a new worldliness that is the outcome, not of thoughtlessness and triviality, but of thoughtfulness and a new confidence in man's power to make life happy and secure by purely secular means.

Just roll that around in your mind for a moment! "Fear and sorrow are no longer major themes for our culture." Say that now when fear stalks down every city street and country lane in the world, when in the last ten years sorrow has entered the doors of hundreds of millions of homes. Fear and sorrow, so far from being outmoded by our inventions, are the major themes of our culture. It is not pious poetry but the hardest, most realistic truth, that a national structure needs a religious foundation. The search for material remedies to soothe or cure our spiritual distresses can have only one end—failure. Only when we accept the truth that man does not live by bread alone will there be laid a foundation stone of a civilization worthy of the name.

Can democracy survive the decay of its roots in an ethical, prophetic religion? This is one of the top questions of the day, for it is a historical fact that democracy has *never* grown without religious roots. It did not begin in Greece or early Rome, in Britain or Massachusetts. It began in Palestine. The dawn of Hebrew history commenced when Moses said to Pharaoh: "In the name of the Eternal, Let my people go!" He spoke for the right of man who was a creature and child of God. The Mayflower Compact was drawn up in the name of God. The Declaration of Independence begins with an affirmation about man and his endowment by his Creator. There is not a single problem in our own time, whether race, housing, medicine, that is not at its roots a religious problem. The largest service that one can render a tree or any growing thing is to preserve and sustain its roots, to give them life. The largest service we can render our country is to preserve and sustain the roots of her life, the religious roots from which has grown a free and just nation.

II

Thanksgiving should move us to love our country deeply enough to preserve her best. It is easy to overlook the patriotism of Jesus. No one ever loved a land more than he loved his. "O Jerusalem, Jerusalem, how oft would I have gathered you. . . ." He wept over his nation because he loved it. He loved the deepest and greatest things in it—its high heritage, its possible role in the world, all that it might be. He hated its worst—its corruption, its shameful compromise with Rome in the surrender of its devotion to God, its injustice and oppression of life. He dropped God's plumb line against it. That is the high office of patriotism. Not an easy "God Bless America," but God save America!

One night in the city of Philadelphia my imagination got away from me as I looked up at the statue of William Penn above the life on those streets. In a kind of waking dream I persuaded William Penn to come down and have a talk with me. There was much I wanted to know, much he wanted to know. Penn asked me the first question: "Are there any Quakers left?" I could say, "Thank God, yes!" I told him of the Friends' Service Committee. His face lit up.

"How do you people get along with the Indians?" he asked. I replied in shame, "There are no Indians." How would you like to tell William Penn what happened to the Indians over 175 years? "We killed most of them and pushed those who remained on a sorrowful march to the West."

"How about the teachings of Jesus that I believed in?" he asked. "We have lots of churches," I answered. "That's not what I asked you," he persisted. "What of the brotherly love of Jesus? I had a vision of a colony shaped by the mind of Jesus." What could I answer Penn? Is our common life shaped by the mind of Jesus in any way that he would recognize? He was a man far, far ahead of his time in his devotion to peace, a great pioneer breaking down the walls of partition between. Have we continued his demolitions? What of the colors that concern us—white, black, brown? This is not fantastic nonsense to judge ourselves before the questioning eyes of William Penn. This is our great heritage—the divine pattern for the life of a people together.

It is right that we be vigilant against subversive activity directed toward the undermining of our strength and security. But in the zeal of our search for any who are subversively active we overlook the fact that our nation suffers far more from subversive *inactivity.* A few deluded fools and dupes, a few determined traitors cannot hurt the nation in any way comparable to the hurt done by multitudes whose inactivity for the nation's good is deeply subversive of the nation's best.

At the approach of this Thanksgiving season it would be well if we brought one of the parables of Jesus out of the past into the present and opened ourselves to its searching of our own hearts. Two men went up in America to pray. And one stood and prayed by himself in a loud voice:

I thank thee, O God, that I am not as other men, that I am a hundred percent American. I thank thee that we are not as other nations, with a devalued currency, and our cities in ruins. I thank thee, O God, that we are the richest nation in the world; that we have ten times as many automobiles as any other nation, and a hundred times as many television sets. That shows what a great moral nation we are. I thank thee, O God, that all our superiorities to other nations have come to us not from good luck, or any other reason than our own worth. Hear us as we pray together:

O beautiful for dividends
  Of twenty five percent.
On steel and oil and real estate,
  On money wisely lent.
    O blessed land of bumper crops,
  May riches be our fate.
Increase our wealth and save our health,
  America the Great!

But the other American stood far away and would not lift even his eyes to heaven, but beat his breast and prayed:

God be merciful to me, a sinner. Forgive me for having allowed the things of the senses to smother the life of the spirit. Forgive me if I have ascribed our blessings to our own might or virtue, and have forgotten to be thankful to thee, O God, from whom cometh every good and perfect gift. Save me, and save America, O God, from the vulgarity of estimating the value of things by their size and not by their spiritual quality. Forgive us for the callousness with which we have looked at the evils which mark our common life. Help us to fulfill our high calling of being a servant of God among the nations of the earth. Hear us as we pray:

O beautiful for patriot dream
That sees beyond the years.
Thine alabaster cities gleam,
Undimmed by human tears!
America! America!
God shed His grace on thee,
And crown thy good, with brotherhood
From sea to shining sea.

—KATHARINE LEE BATES

III

We have wandered from Babylon to Jerusalem to the top of the Philadelphia City Hall. At the last we come back here to ourselves, to the homes where we live, to the church where we gather to thank God. And coming home we come sharply up against the need for the renewal of our own inner life and faith that we may have genuine spiritual wealth to give to the commonwealth. The religion of many people is like the spray of lavender pressed between the pages of a book that is never opened. It is a tender and touching moment to come upon a pressed flower, long since dead and dried, between the pages of a book, a flower that was put there long ago in the excitement or thrill of a memorable moment or a great love. The tender feelings may be dimly roused once again, but the thrill and power of the moment are gone. A man's religion need not be that way. A biographer, writing of H. R. L. "Dick" Shepperd of London, put it this way. "The stream of unceasing refreshment, of life-giving strength, depended for its powers on deep hidden springs, on its renewal from the melted snows of distant heights of the spirit." Even in Babylon the faithful children of Israel renewed their souls in memory of the distant heights of Jerusalem. Even in the common life that each one must live here and now he can find renewal and power at the distant heights where the soul finds its meeting with God.

—An unpublished Sermon

13

Vertical Living

"I will lift up my eyes to the hills." (Ps. 121:1.)

Beside those familiar words of scripture I would like to set another sentence from our own day which has turned my thoughts to that ancient affirmation. The sentence forms the title of a book of travels, the journeyings into as strange and mysterious territory as any explorer ever penetrated. Duff Gilfond calls her book *I Go Horizontal.* She refers to ten years spent in the flat, level world of sickness. Not ten hours in those ten years of sleeping sickness did she spend in a vertical position.

That phrase pictures both vividly and accurately what has happened in a large degree to our world. It pictures also a risk that every person must face in his own life. *I Go Horizontal* describes a world knocked flat, in many places approaching the ultimate horizontal position of death. In a deeper sense it describes also a life that largely takes its motives, goals, reliances, and compulsions from the flat material level, never looking up to the hills with the ancient psalmist for strength. Yet every passing hour demonstrates that something terrible happens when divine absolutes drop out of a man's landscape, when there is no vertical architecture in men's thinking. This old word of the psalmist, set against the backdrop of the world we live in proclaims the need for vertical living in a horizontal world.

I

Granted that in the word "vertical" we are using a symbol of an obsolete idea of space, there yet remains real meaning in that symbol. Horizontal living is to make of the common life a kind of random opportunism on a flat material level. Vertical living is to find a compulsion to right living in demands that are cosmic. It is a natural thing to hear a preacher affirm the need for vertical living. But today a great variety of unlikely people are proclaiming the same need with deadly earnestness. These unexpected, unordained evangelists for vertical living all point to the human disaster which overtakes life when the vertical dimension drops out of man's thinking. It brings the loss of any positive basis for a fundamental ethical code for Western civilization.

Here is Waldo Frank (who wears neither halo nor ecclesiastical gown):

> Europe has been in rough waters ever since it broke with the great tradition, the Hebrew-Christian tradition. The Christian tradition which had enormously enhanced the individual with pride of immortality and a God come down to earth, and the Hebrew tradition of justice and brotherhood. The great tradition is that the individual has purpose and direction and dignity and value because God is in him.

Here is Lewis Mumford who sees on the earth not only a horizontal conflict of arms but a vertical conflict of faith: "The main problem of the present hour is this: is there enough religion left in the mass of humanity to counteract the negative and diabolical religion that has swept to victory as fascism?"

Here is Herbert Agar putting it almost in the identical words of Duff Gilfond:

> We have learned in brief what happens to a world which has strayed too far from its moral purpose. All men desire life and we have seen that a social order without moral purpose fails to sustain life. The ancient Egyptians conceived of insanity as a flight from God in which the ego, fleeing its destiny, journeyed into the void and built a world of its own.

We wonder if a more accurate picture could be drawn of the last fifty years. It is not the preachers alone who are saying that the social insanity of our age is a flight from God into a void.

The idea of God may be accepted and still left as an emotionalized gesture hanging up in the air like a Maxfield Parrish castle in the clouds, connected nowhere with the earth. It is very easy and pleasant for religious faith to be magnificently and generously emotional in a social and intellectual vacuum, without facing and accepting the social compulsions arising out of that faith. One of the real dangers in a time of bewilderment and upset is that a backward-looking nostalgia may be substituted for an ethical religion. A sentimental longing to go back to a familiar day that has either gone or never really existed is substituted for the demanding task of taking the basic principles of Christian faith into the contemporary world.

From a preacher comes this nostalgic longing for the by-gone days of the 1870's. "Think of the years before the experts came. A small town on Sunday with everything closed down, everybody in church, hymns resounding down Main Street. The Sunday dinners. People in those days believed in paying their bills, and no one ever thought of getting something for nothing." Beautiful! If there were a Pulitzer Prize for the imaginative distortion of history that would certainly get it. The 1870's was the greatest era of corruption in American history. It was the age of the dinosaurs, the ruthless exploitation of a continent. And to find it trotted out as a golden age to which we should return! Just get enough hymns floating down a Main Street closed tight as a drum on Sunday and all will be well. That is a kind of Currier and Ives religion whose true symbol is the old oaken bucket. No cross rising vertically from a flat earth and bringing eternal demands upon life and conduct.

But when life does have a vertical God-ward dimension in the form of a cross there comes new power to move in new directions. Once some people came to Jesus on behalf of a sick girl for whom all hope had been abandoned. "Lay thy hand upon her and she will live," they appealed in faith. Their faith has had a continuing validation in experience. Of all the strangely mixed potentialities of life we may say, "Let the Master lay his hand upon them and they shall live."

This is true of the family. Family life is by no means inevitably a heaven. When there is forced propinquity without any inner cohesion it may be an outpost of hell—and not so very far out at that. But if Christ lays his hand upon it, if it becomes a dwelling place of love that seeketh not its own, it shall live.

So with a man's education. A college education may be merely the sharpening of claws for the competitive struggle so that one can get a bigger pile of loot. But if Christ lays his hand upon it, if in the secret places of the heart have been heard the words, "Freely you have received, freely give," it shall live as the servant of the common good.

It is true of an economic system. That can be, and has been, motivated by greed, becoming an ingenious means of collective suicide. But if Christ lays his hand upon it, if instead of the clenched fist of acquisition it should be truly symbolized by strong hands laid upon the tools for serving human need, it shall live. The true end of production is to bring a standard of living for all people that accords with the wealth-producing capacity of our time.

The urgency to work for Christian values in our common life is strong upon us. When Jesus was told on the day he entered Jerusalem to rebuke his disciples because of their acclaim he replied in words that seem fantastic: "If they did not shout the very stones would cry out." As we hear those words today they have the ring of tragic truth. Let us loose the checkrein of imagination as we think of the piles of stones on our earth that are crying out in unmistakable language. Think of the pile of stones in Coventry, England, where the aspiring vertical lines of the Gothic cathedral have been flattened out into a pile of rubble. Think of the waste heap of stones in Warsaw, in Rotterdam, in Barcelona. Stones cry out for order in the midst of chaos, for sanity in the midst of madness, for love in the midst of hate. The stones cry out because men did not cry out for order, for co-operation when they could. The stones heard the cries of another sort. One raucus yell was heard on the floor of the United States Senate: "Let Europe stew in its own juice!" It did stew and boiled over the world in a frightful brew. Not the stones but *we* must make an unyielding cry that comes down the vertical dimension from God. He who lifts up his eyes to God's hills will also lift up his voice in the cry for God's justice.

A picture of the alternatives before us appeared in a review of the week some time ago. It was a gleam of poetry in a mass of facts and statistics, as unexpected as to find a tulip blooming in an asphalt pavement. The writer was describing the coast road of Tunis along which the British Eighth Army and the American troops were moving. A historic road, he said it was; that road had felt many footsteps upon it: the beat of the troops of Hannibal's war elephants; the soft shuffling of the sandals of St. Augustine. At the barbarian overthrow of Rome Augustine lifted his eyes from the horizontal level of disaster unto the hills and saw a kingdom of God and of man, not made on earth but coming down from heaven.

II

Individual life also faces the risk that it may go horizontal, descend to the level of material life, become so preoccupied with the plains of living that the eternal hills drop out of the picture. In two words from Britain we find the contrast of horizontal with vertical living. J. B. Priestley, writing of his neighbors in a London suburb, says:

> No lasting vision of a nobler England haunts them. The reason for this is that such is their present style of life that no vision of any kind haunts them. They are living too near the surface of things. They are living too trivial and material in existence. They give themselves up to what I call a car and radio life. There is nothing wrong with either cars or radios, and I would not be without either if I could help it. But a life that hardly moves away from a schoolboy fussing with such things obviously lacks fullness and depth. Three quarters of the rich channels of communication in the mind are closed up. A large proportion of the young people of these classes marry and settle into a little bungalow, join the local tennis club, acquire a radio and car, and then might be simply a pair of cave dwellers for all the relation they have to the largest life of the community, or to the noble and enduring life of religion. The trouble with them is not that they live in bungalows but that they live bungalow lives.

Contrast that with the picture of vertical life on the bleak moors of Yorkshire. Emily Brontë's life was not easy in the rectory with a half-demented father, two sisters dying of tuberculosis, a brother reeling home drunk from the village tavern. These are among the brighter spots of the life of Emily Brontë. Yet she could write:

> No coward soul is mine,
> No trembler in world's storm troubled sphere;
> I see Heaven's glories shine,
> And faith shines equal, arming me from fear.

That is vertical living. For Emily Brontë a vertical Jacob's ladder was pitched between heaven and the Yorkshire moor. That ladder will reach down to any spot on earth. The sense of relationship to the eternal gives elevation and meaning to life. That sense of relationship comes not at the end of an argument but in the process of an experience. The beginning is simple, exposing the mind to realities that carry their own conviction. Watch a flower bulb; hold one in your hand. It is nothing promising; it looks like a retired onion. But exposed to the intangible but irresistible pull of the sun, something in the flower says, "This is what I was made for." It rises in a perpendicular when it is exposed to a compulsion that fits its nature.

I saw a mind yield to a coercion some time ago. A young woman from Grand Island, Nebraska, was on her way by train to the Pacific Coast. She had lived for twenty years on the flat plains of her native state; she had never seen a mountain. She told me she wouldn't like them; they would obstruct the view. Two mornings later I watched her as she looked up at the Sierra Nevada Range. She paid it the tribute of silence. The strong compulsion of a great shoulder of earth lifting into the sky was laid upon her.

So the compulsion of Christ has been laid upon men and women. As one has said, "There is a stinging persuasiveness" about Jesus. To those who will give an unhindered view as he walks before the imagination the validation comes, "Did not our hearts burn within us?" I will lift up my eyes to the hills. As it was in the beginning it is now, and ever shall be, he who was lifted up will draw all men unto himself.

—An unpublished Sermon

14

From Spectator to Participant

"And as they led him away, they seized one Simon of Cyrene, who was coming in from the country, and laid on him the cross, to carry it behind Jesus." (Luke 23:26.)

THIS IS A SHARP PICTURE OF A MAN TAKING ONE OF THE GREATEST STEPS that it is possible for anyone to take in life. He got down from the sidewalk into the street. He came from the side of the road where he was merely watching the parade and became part of the parade. He got down from the grandstand into the arena. He stopped being a spectator and became a participant.

That step is our theme here. It was a strange and sudden experience for Simon. It has been conjectured that he was a pilgrim from Africa, come to Jerusalem for the Passover. He was new in the city, just looking around. Standing on the roadside he saw a sorrowful parade coming—a common sight in that cruel Roman world—soldiers, sightseers, and in their midst a man carrying a cross too heavy for him. He fell under the weight of the cross, whereupon a Roman soldier reached out, grabbed Simon, "Here, you! Get under that cross." "Who, me? I have nothing to do with it. I'm just a bystander. I'm a stranger here." Nonetheless, they dragged him down from the side of the road and compelled him to take part.

It was compulsion, of course; nothing voluntary about this. It leads us to think for a moment of the great hosts through the centuries who have been compelled to carry crosses. One considers the tragic history of slavery—"The long drip of human tears." One thinks of the conscripts for armies in all the centuries. One considers today burdens laid on the backs of the colored peoples of the world. Moreover, the picture speaks sharply to our day: Lift the burdens from the backs of those compelled by man's cruelty to bear them!

But our theme today is not concerned with those compelled to be cross bearers, but those who do it voluntarily, those who have gone from just watching to taking part. That step is best described by a series of vivid pictures drawn from history in every age. There was Telemachus, the monk in the Roman Empire, who stood up at one of the gladiatorial contests and shouted, "In the name of God, stop!" It was a prophetic command, for the gladiatorial slaughter of human beings *did* stop. Come down to the last century: A young Boston Brahman—from the elite of New England, a sort of royalty—Wendell Phillips was standing on a Boston sidewalk watching a fugitive slave bound in chains being dragged down to a ship to be taken back to slavery. Phillips was so overcome by the monstrous injustice of it all that he left the sidewalk and walked with the chained slave. He kept on walking from that day forward, beginning a life devoted to the abolition of slavery. From the first century to the twentieth men have taken this momentous step, a step symbolized by Simon of Cyrene. May we look at this man Simon, going from a spectator to a participant, and by the grace of God see it as a mirror in which we may see ourselves in the twentieth century.

I

Take it first in the realm of religion. We can be spectators, looking at religious experiences from the outside, or we can be among those taking part on the inside. A British chaplain in the last world war has told of a sergeant briefing a company of soldiers for their first church parade. He wanted everything to be just right. He said, "When the Padre comes to the Creed and says, 'I believe,' that has no significance for you. You just stand at ease." We smile at that, but it is a picture of the way a great many people regard the Christian religion. The great affirmations of faith have no significance for them; they stand at ease, spectators, not taking any part themselves. The attitude of some church members to religion is like that of a person at a great banquet; he couldn't afford to be left out, but he has been forbidden by his doctor to eat anything. He takes no real part.

Some time since I overheard a conversation between two women. That is the way I learn most of the little I know—just overhearing conversations. One woman was talking about the Church of Sainte Chapelle in Paris; she was really raving about it. The other one apparently thought little of Sainte Chapelle. The first one said in amazement, "Didn't you think that that thirteenth century stained glass was marvelous?" "Oh," the other one said, "we didn't go inside; we saw it from a sight-seeing bus." You can't see the Church of Sainte Chapelle from a sight-seeing bus. You cannot see the Christian faith from a sight-seeing bus. You must see it from inside. What might look drab from the outside is radiant with light inside, just as the stained glass of Sainte Chapelle looks drab when seen from the outside, but when seen with the light shining through it is glorious beyond description. This is what happens when we go from being an onlooker and become a participant.

A common question we often hear—usually during a quarrel of some kind—is thrown out with a snarl, "Who do you think you are?" A good question to take quite seriously! What life means to us and what we can do with it depends largely on who we think we are. The Christian gospel has an answer to that question, if we become participants. We are not a chemical accident, not an educated ape. "Beloved, now we are the sons of God." You can ask Paul, going through the Roman world from one mob to another, from one riot to another, from one jail to another, "Who do you think you are?" Here is his answer: "It is no longer I that live but Christ who lives in me."

You can ask Martin Luther, standing before Charles V, the Holy Roman Emperor, "Who do you think you are?" They tell him that the German Princes would not rally to his defense, asking him, "Where will you be then?" Luther quietly answered, "Right where I am now, in the hands of Almighty God."

You can find the answer often in a businessman of today, standing up against some common practices. Ask him, "Who do you think you are?" I know of one such businessman; he is a purchasing agent. If you have any friends who are purchasing agents, you pray for them, for they stand in slippery places. Some men came to his office selling something, and a common proposal was made, namely that they put the price so that he could get a "kick back." He rose from his desk and said, "Get out of the office." One of the men was so surprised that he said, "Well, for God's sake." The purchasing agent replied, "That is the reason, for God's sake." There was a man who carried into the whole of life "For God's sake." He thought of himself as a child of God.

When we become part of that faith, it brings foundations against our insecurity, ultimates against our relativism, community against our separateness, liberty against enslavement, hope against despair. The words ascribed to Christ in the book of Revelation tell what happens in life when we become partakers of the faith, "Behold I stand at the door and knock. If any man hears my voice and opens the door, I will come in and eat with him and he with me." When we open the door of our mind and heart to God as guest life becomes illuminated. What was a dreary drudge becomes a way of great companionship and of lasting joy.

If we really become a participant in the Christian faith, we can go that way. The person in the midst of some of life's hardest experiences along a lonely way can say, "There are two of us, not merely one." The person facing hard choices and strong temptations can say, "There are two of us. I can do all things through Christ, who strengthens me." So, the person in the midst of hard tasks which seem beyond his enduring power can say, "It seemed there were two of us." We do not say with Tennyson, "my strength is the strength of ten because my heart is pure." We know too much about ourselves to say that. But we can say, "There are two of us going along this way together." From spectator to participant—see what it does!

II

Again over the centuries the figure of Simon getting under Christ's cross has one clear call for me and for you. "As the parade goes by in all its need, stop being just a spectator and take part in it." In the Gospel of Matthew there is a wonderful picture of Jesus by the roadside watching the human family. We read, "When he saw the crowd, he had compassion for them because they were harassed and helpless like sheep without a shepherd." His heart goes out and his life goes out to this family. How many times Jesus stopped before people, got down to their need. There was blind Bartimeus; when all the disciples could think of was to tell him to keep still, Jesus turned and spoke, taking his burden as his own. Another kind of need he recognized in Zaccheus; putting his own life into a detour, Jesus met that need of Zaccheus to be released from himself. Some people never really see the parade of humanity; they live behind a wall. Others, like Simon of Cyrene, step down from some safe, protected position and help carry the cross. Here is a bit of history from the last century of a girl who stepped down from the sidewalk into the street. It all began when Dorothea Dix served as a substitute teacher one Sunday morning at a church school in East Cambridge, Massachusetts. Such an activity would for many people rate a zero in entertainment value. But the session turned out to be an exciting affair; her pupils that day were four little mentally deficient children from the East Cambridge jail. When she learned that the pitiable little children were kept in jail like wild animals she exploded—and started off on a crusade that spread throughout the United States and a large part of Europe, a crusade which resulted in the rewriting of laws regarding treatment of the mentally ill. For a multitude of people in the days since, the letters "A.D." have meant not so much "the year of our Lord," but have meant "After Dix."

Contrast the words spoken by two men to see what becoming a participant means. First, the words of Henry Ford: "I do not believe a man can ever leave his business. He ought to think of it day by day and dream of it by night. . . . Thinking men know that work is the salvation of the race morally, physically, socially. Work does more than get us a living; it gets us life." The others are words of Jacob Marley, the ghost in Dickens' *Christmas Carol:* "Business!" cried the ghost, wringing his hands. "Mankind was my business. The common welfare was my business: charity, mercy, forbearance and benevolence were all my business. The dealings of my trade are but a drop of water in the comprehensive ocean of my business." Jacob Marley speaks for men who have seen the need to get down from the sidewalk into the street with compassion for the passing procession of humanity.

Taking up a burden is a nuisance to some people. One woman who had been asked to take up a needed job replied, "I don't like to be tied down to things." A common attitude but perhaps we ought to remember that we are followers of a Master who was willing to be nailed down to things—specifically to a cross—for the sake of his love for men.

An old Irish tale throws a clear light on a central truth of the Christian religion. It tells of a fairy, representing the pagan era in Ireland, dancing around the room in a farmer's home. Suddenly the fairy sees a crucifix on the wall. It stops suddenly and cries out, "Take away that ugly black thing!" That is only a tale, but the fairy's words do represent the idea of many people about the cross and the demand for sacrificial service. They think of it as a black thing; a burden on their backs. But to those who step into it, it is not a black thing but a radiant thing, a source of joy. It was with Jesus, who, for the joy that was set before him, endured the cross, despising the shame. The cross was not an ugly black thing to a man who seemed lost in China in missionary work—a former president of a university—James W. Bashford. Someone asked him, "Why do you bury yourself away out in China?" He replied, "Because I believe in a Resurrection." The cross has not been an ugly black thing to men and women who have gone down into difficult spots to take up burdens not their own. It has not been an ugly black thing to people who have taken responsibilities they did not have to assume.

Across the valley of the years we hear in Simon of Cyrene a call to participate, a fellow worker with God, a carrier of the cross.

—An unpublished Sermon

15

The Power of a Great Emotion

"Most of the crowd spread their clothes on the road." (Matt. 21:8.)

THESE WORDS GIVE A VIVID PICTURE OF PEOPLE CARRIED CLEAR OUT OF themselves by a great emotion. They forgot themselves. There was such surging of a great hope with the coming of Jesus that they threw their clothes on the ground for a donkey to walk on. That really was forgetting! Men and women normally were expected to own one cloak for about seven years. Their impulsive act was comparable to throwing a new suit in the dust or mud. They didn't all do it; the text says "most." Some no doubt prudently said, "Don't get excited. Keep ahold of yourself. Remember, these are your best clothes. You don't have to spoil them. It will be enough just to wave a palm branch." But the record reads, "Most of the crowd spread their clothes on the road." There was something that made them forget. On this Palm Sunday morning, with this picture in mind, we may think of the coming of Christ into our lives as a power that can carry us clear out of ourselves.

Notice this about the whole episode: A self-forgetting emotion and commitment was the thing that Jesus welcomed above everything else. He welcomed it here as he had welcomed it throughout his ministry. He had no use for easy sentimentalism. He rebuked that on one occasion. A woman got all worked up and cried out, "Blessed is your mother." She began to gush like a geyser, holding a Mother's Day celebration on the spot. Jesus cut it short: "Blessed rather are those who hear the word of God and keep it." He wanted to get her out of the world of sentimental twaddle into the world of religious and ethical reality.

Twice Jesus went into almost a lyric ecstasy over a self-forgetting emotion and dedication. Once was when a woman anointed him with a box of very precious perfume. Some of the disciples were indignant over the waste. "It might have been sold and the money given to the poor," they protested. We can hear them saying, in effect, "Go easy, sister. That stuff costs money." Dr. Goodspeed estimates that a jar of that perfume may have cost five hundred dollars. This emotion which made the woman completely forget herself—and five hundred dollars—moved Jesus deeply, as though he felt, "This is what I have been waiting for. This is the real thing." He said, "Wherever the gospel is preached in the whole world what she has done will be told in memory of her."

We see it again with the widow of Jerusalem who so far forgot herself as to put all her money in the alms box. Jesus almost leaped with joy, feeling, "This is the greatest thing in Jerusalem." He said, "Truly I say to you, this widow has put in more than all these who are contributing to the treasury." This is the real thing—then and now. On this Palm Sunday what can our faith in Christ's coming do for us?

I

The first effect of our faith in the coming of Christ ought to be that of lifting life out of itself in joyful forgetfulness. There is truth in these lines:

Take all away from me
But leave me ecstasy,
And I am richer then
Than all my fellow men.

True! That is life's great motive power. We must keep it, for it slips out of life so stealthily and takes so much with it. I think of religion in relation to some definitions of poetry. Emily Dickinson said, "If it blows the top of your head off, it's poetry." Said A. E. Housman, "If it makes you cut yourself while shaving, it's poetry." So we can say, "If it lifts you out of yourself in self-forgetfulness it is great faith." Yet it can drop out of life without your knowing or intending it. Religion is portrayed unforgettably in Vachel Lindsay's poem on Niagara.

Within the town of Buffalo
Are prosy men with leaden eyes.
Like ants they worry to and fro,

(Important men, in Buffalo).
But only twenty miles away
A deathless glory is at play,
Niagara, Niagara.

The women buy their lace and cry,
"Oh, such a delicate design!"
And over ostrich feathers sigh
At counters there in Buffalo.
The children haunt the trinket shops,
They buy false faces, bells and tops.
Forgetting great Niagara.

The main point in our religion is this: There is a deathless glory at play in the coming of Christ into our world, and into one life. It is not as one woman said of a sunset, "It's a wonderful sunset for such a little place." A wonderful sunset can happen any place. There is a deathless glory in any life that opens its doors to the coming of Christ. That is the breath-taking thing about our gospel, is it not? It catches the breath with wonder and hopefulness, the idea that God himself has stepped into the need and poverty and anguish of a world which has in it evil and incurable disease and battlefields and scaffolds and for each of us old age and dying powers. Unless in the Christian religion we find a lift into self-forgetting, outgoing emotion we can miss its true power.

Here is a marriage proposal made by an eminently respectable New Englander in Amherst, Massachusetts, over a century ago. This man kept a firm hold on himself. He told the lady that he had been measuring her in his mind and that with some changes she might fill the place as his wife. He wrote: "I hope I have no foolishness called romance; I am too well balanced for that sort of nonsense. But we might look forward to leading respectable and useful lives and enjoy the respect of the neighbors." I wonder how many women in this congregation would have been swept off their feet by such an overwhelming proposal, "to lead a respectable and useful life." That is a fair picture of what our religion can dwindle down to if we are not carried out of ourselves, if there is no feeling,

Were the whole realm of nature mine,
That were an offering far too small;
Love so amazing, so divine,
Demands my life, my soul, my all.

The true way to measure life is not by the number of breaths taken, but by the number *not* taken, when we are breathless in wonder and amazement.

I was once a member of a Board of Foreign Missions. Two candidates were turned down because the young men had "breathlessness and irregular heart beats." But that is what we all ought to have: the irregular heart beat of a self-forgetting emotion when Christ comes along our road.

That is what we do have on this day: not a historical remembrance accompanied by familiar music of an event long ago, but the power of a great emotional drive to joyful self-forgetfulness by the coming of Christ to us.

For thirty years I have carried a picture in my mind of something that happened in the corridor of the New Haven Hospital. I will carry it forever. A man I had never seen in my life came rushing up to me with a chart he had taken from the foot of a hospital bed. He grabbed hold of my arm, showed me the chart, and said, "Look! Her temperature's going down!" I do not know who he meant by "Her"—someone he loved. I never saw him before and have never seen him since. But to my dying day I shall never forget the spectacle of a man so overwhelmed by good news that he had to grab the first stranger he met and tell him all about it. That was the lift of a great emotion. We have good news which shall be to all people. May we keep its power, never letting it drift or drain away.

The danger of losing this power is real. We lose the real power of faith if we miss a great enthusiasm. We fail to get what life might give. A piano teacher said to a pupil, "You seem to play the piano with a feather duster. You never strike down deep to the music that is in the instrument." We can play our religion with a feather duster and never strike down deep. These are words of a man who struck down deep to great music: "It is no longer I who live but Christ who lives in me." Paul could say that in the glorious conviction that God had come in Christ, a conviction that produced an enthusiasm carrying him clear out of himself. This spreading of garments in the way is a thrilling thing to watch as it has gone on down through the centuries. People, projected by the power of a great emotion, have given fully of their best. And life has been made new. A man went into the five and ten cent store and asked the clerk if they had compasses. She replied brightly, "We have compasses for drawing circles, but not for going places." The gospel is a compass for going places. And how many places people have gone with it, carried by its power around the block and around the world in service. That scene along the road coming into Jerusalem is a parable of life, the great paradox of life, profoundly true, that only as we forget ourselves do we really find ourselves. Jesus put it unforgettably, "He that loses his life for my sake shall find it." He comes again this day that we may forget ourselves for his sake.

II

The other effect of the coming of Christ is to give our religious emotion a carry through. It is often said that the same throats that on Palm Sunday cried, "Hosanna! Blessed is he who comes in the name of the Lord," on Friday shouted, "Crucify him! Crucify him!" That is not quite true. They were not the same people. The high priest had hired a mob to demonstrate at a rigged-up trial that was a travesty on justice. But Jesus' friends were not there. Not even one voice was raised. Their emotion had no adequate carry through. The Hosanna ought to go through a week. It ought to go through a life. It can go through a life. The carry through of emotion is like a bullet going to its target on the power of initial impact. The great emotion that sees life through in service and response to human need comes from the initial impact of Christ who takes our head and heart, hands and feet, and sets them moving toward his targets at the impulses of God's love.

In one of those English detective stories where everybody is under suspicion from the butler to the Archbishop of Canterbury, who was spending the weekend at the scene of the crime, a disgusted detective says, "This was the perfect crime. He never left a fingerprint anywhere." Isn't that the perfect crime against life? Not to leave a fingerprint anywhere? Not to touch any life or institution or cause with a personal touch that leaves a mark upon it? Some people can go through life with gloves on, never really touching anything. Others, thank God, leave the mark of a great love on the people and the enterprises they touch. You can find that magic touch in unexpected places. A woman teacher taught for forty-five years in a two-room school in Ohio. One might say, "What a ghastly life! Forty-five years in two little rooms." Not the way God sees it. On her shelf is a book given to that teacher by one of her former pupils in which he wrote: "To the one who opened the gates of life and literature to me." It was signed by one of the notable preachers of his generation, Frank Gunsaulus of Chicago. The teacher had left a fingerprint on a growing boy.

Think of those who have left fingerprints on this congregation, parents, teachers, doctors, pastors, friends. We sing:

Take my hands and let them move,
At the impulse of thy love.

Those who have moved their hands in love for our sake have given life a glory beyond all telling. Their hands have moved at the impulse of him who came in the name of the Lord.

Epstein's statue of Jesus on trial is crude and strong. The Master's hands are tied. A poor woman looking at it cried with revealing simplicity, "If we could only untie the hands!" This is our task—to untie the hands of Christ. We may do it by grasping our world with his hands of love. And his is a love that does not let us go but comes again and again "in the name of the Lord." In his coming is power to see the task of God's purpose through.

—An unpublished Sermon

16

The Richest Hill on Earth

". . . for whom Christ died." (*I Cor. 8:11.*)

MANY YEARS AGO I WAS DRIVEN ALONG THE MOUNTAIN ROADS FROM HELENA to Butte, Montana. Winding among the hills and valleys the road suddenly rounded a sharp curve; ahead was a long, bleak scarred mountain. The man driving the car turned and said, "That is the richest hill on earth." It was the Silver Bow Mountain. More wealth in the form of copper had been taken out of that hill than any other hill on earth. Since 1876 the mines in the Silver Bow Mountain have yielded over thirteen billion pounds of copper—$2,500,000,000 worth! Before the discovery of copper millions in gold and silver were taken out of the hill. Tragedy has marked the story, for every crime known to man has been committed in connection with that wealth—robbery, corruption, gambling, murder, arson, lust. All these have been part of the richest hill on earth.

That phrase lay dormant in my mind for over ten years. It came back while I was with a company winding its way through the narrow streets of Jerusalem. On the Via Dolorosa along which Jesus is supposed to have traveled on his way to the crucifixion, our guide stopped and said, "Nobody knows just where Calvary was. The city has been buried three times during the centuries. It was probably not far from that hill." The phrase came suddenly to my mind again, "The richest hill on earth." For in a higher and deeper sense, not from Silver Bow but from Calvary has come the greatest wealth the world has ever known. Out of it have come the world's hope and the spiritual momentum that makes it possible to look for redemption.

All the light of sacred story
Gathers round its head sublime.

Will you move your imagination up to that hill now and look at it to really see what happened there and what it means? The cross may be a window through which we may see the realities of God beyond.

I

First of all, the cross of Calvary is a reality through which we see the nature of God. Those who have looked longest and deepest at Calvary have seen more than a tragedy, or a martyrdom, or what is called, loosely, "inspiration." They have been persuaded that they have looked through a window and seen the ultimate truth of the universe, a God of love. There is a shocking medieval painting of Christ on the Cross. Behind him is a painted figure of God. Such art is foreign to our taste. We do not paint pictures of God. It was not foreign to the New Testament; God was in Christ reconciling the world to himself. That is what makes Calvary the richest hill on earth. That God himself has stepped into our human life, with all its pains, weariness, grief, and sin, making our struggle his own—this makes our gospel a breathtaking thing.

Sara Teasdale makes this lyric confession:

Places I love come back to me like music,
Hush me and heal me when I am very tired.

We all have them. They come into the mind like a breeze with healing. But one place above all that men love comes back to them like music, Calvary.

There is a green hill far away,
Without a city wall,
Where our dear Lord was crucified,
Who died to save us all.

—CECIL F. ALEXANDER

Think of what it brings into a life to realize that Calvary is a window into the heart of God. Emily Dickinson has written some vivid words about the Book:

He ate and drank the precious words
His spirit grew robust;
He knew no more that he was poor,
Nor that his frame was dust.

He danced along the dingy days,
And this bequest of wings
Was but a book. What liberty
A loosened spirit brings!

Note those words—"He danced along the dingy days." There are times we all think we live in dingy days. But if we eat and drink these precious words—God so loved the world—take them into our hearts and lives, they can change any dingy day into a hopeful confident walk with God.

Calvary is not man reaching up; it is God reaching down. Calvary is the richest hill on earth because it is the gift of God's power. Power comes by opening your life to God, as the Gatun Lock in the Panama Canal is opened to the waters of the lake above it and the ship is lifted. Life is lifted when you let in the life of God.

Arnold Bennett has put into words a memorable picture of the cross in its pull on the deep places of the heart. In his novel *Clayhanger* he tells how Edwin Clayhanger, who said, "There is no virtue in believing," and his girl, Hilda Lessways, stared cynically at a Sunday-school pageant in the streets of a midland town. They watched it with a good deal of derision, for it was not a very glamorous spectacle, until the children began to sing:

When I survey the wondrous cross
On which the Prince of Glory died.

Then Hilda, hitherto unaffected by religion, was deeply moved, and when she turned her face away to hide her emotion, Edwin asked, sharply, "What is the matter?" Whereupon the girl flashed out, "It would be worth anything in the world to say those words and mean them." We can say, not "It *would be* worth anything to mean those words," but "It *is* worth anything."

II

Second, we never really see Calvary in its full meaning until we see ourselves in it. There is a fierce light that beats about the cross. In that light we see ourselves; we see the play of motives that are active in our own lives. The motives that pushed Jesus to the cross are in our lives—greed, the desire for security, the grasp of advantage, the fear of the crowd, indifference to the suffering of others. Calvary was an event in history;

but it is also an event in our lives if, with clear eyes and a heart that is not afraid to look at ourselves, we see our likeness to those who drove Jesus to the cross.

Look for a moment at one of the attitudes that allowed the crucifixion to go on—indifference. It is hard to realize that there were hosts of people who watched the painful march to Calvary and never batted an eyelid. They did not take part in the crucifixion; they just didn't care. They were indifferent; they were accessories to the crime. The same indifference often makes us bystanders. We see evil about us and say, "Oh, yes, but I'm busy; I can't be bothered." Another crucifixion is on its way. In the matter of racial injustice we are sure something is wrong, but, "Why should I stick my neck out?" Another crucifixion is on its way. There are people who go through life protecting their necks. Their necks are more important than their souls. In the face of continual danger of war, with some trigger-happy maniacs wanting to explode bombs over China instead of Nevada, but, "Sorry, I have troubles enough of my own." If we have indifference like that another crucifixion is on its way.

As we think of ourselves in this light from the cross the question comes: What place does Jesus have in our lives? Revelation of how we rank Jesus was given some time ago by the publishers Grosset and Dunlap. To publicize a new history book a panel of twenty-eight historians, educators, and journalists were asked to rate the 100 most significant events in history. First place: Columbus' discovery of America; second, Gutenberg's development of movable type. Eleven events tied for third place. Tied for fourth place: U. S. Constitution takes effect, ether makes surgery painless, X ray discovered, Wright Brothers' plane flies, Jesus Christ crucified.

So Jesus ties for fourth place! That was the best he could do on this rating of importance. Where is he in my life? Fourth place? Or eleventh, or nineteenth?

Before the Cross of Jesus
Our lives are judged today.

At the exit from the National Gallery in London is a large receptacle. The doorman explains its use, "That's where the art students drop their conceit as they go out." To look at Calvary and really see ourselves in the picture is to drop our conceit and cry, "God, be merciful to me, a sinner."

III

Third, we do not really see the cross until we see it as a way of life for ourselves. It is the way the Master went, shall not the servant travel it still? The cross is not only something to receive, it is something to do. It is not merely something to sing about, "In the cross of Christ I glory," though we should thank God for that. It is a quality to put into action; "the love of Christ constraineth us" (II Cor. 5:14, K.J.V.). That has been the most powerful source of social action the world has ever known.

T. R. Glover once observed, "Four words destroyed slavery, 'For whom Christ died.' " Our hope is that the same four words will someday destroy war, someday destroy racial discrimination and segregation, someday destroy exploitation. Someday! This day of the cross should lead us to face what I think is the greatest danger the Church faces, the danger of partisanship that goes deeper than our Christianity. It is a terrible thing to say, but it is found North, South, East, and West, that the deepest thing may not be our religion but our prejudices, our habits, our partisanship. We keep these in a secret room before which reads the warning, "Keep Out!" If we see the cross as a way of life for ourselves we will offer our minds to Christ, to bring our thinking—cost what it may—into line with the mind, the life, the sacrifice of Christ.

A recent book entitled *Redesign Your Home for Easier Living* is recommended as a housewife's dream—forty-five housekeeping tricks, thirteen clues to easy dishwashing, et cetera. It all feeds the delusion that easiest living is the happiest living. Jesus said, on the contrary, I will redesign your life for harder living!

There is a striking poem by Genevieve Taggard on the old superstition that was strong in Europe and in particular in Ireland, that it was not safe to die until one had taken a stick in his last hours and marked on the earth the sign of the cross. These are her words:

> Mark the earth with a Cross before you die.
> Take a small stick and bend down
> And make two marks—two
> Only, on the ground. Ask no one why.
> Mark, before you die, the earth for a sign. You
> Are not a soul, you cannot die
> Rightly until you scratch a small mark on the ground.

Lean and write and be done and gone,
And the wind be with you.

Lift that up to its larger meaning—not superstition, but reality. Leave somewhere on earth the sign of a cross written on your life. Some sign of unselfishness, sacrifice, love, that reminds men of him who marked the earth with a cross.

—An unpublished Sermon

17

News from a Graveyard

"Except a corn of wheat fall into the ground and die, it abideth alone." (*John 12:24.*)

IT IS NO ACCIDENT THAT EVERY STORY OF THE RESURRECTION IN THE GOSPELS ends up as the story of a footrace. Good news cannot walk. It runs. The good news of the resurrection of Jesus struck the minds and imaginations of those who first heard it with such force that they started running. As Easter breaks over the world this morning it is news—tremendous, stop-the-press news, that is related to every life and every issue in our world.

In Ernest Poole's novel *The Harbor*, published about forty years ago, one of the characters is an impatient and headlong reformer, who has a strong disdain for history as being unimportant. "History," he says, "is just news from a graveyard."

That is a notable phrase—"news from a graveyard." Of course, that is a rather common idea of history, held by people who suffer from the blight of contemporaneousness and believe that the world began last Saturday night.

The phrase is a memorable description of Easter. More than that, the best news in the world is always "news from a graveyard." Take that jonquil blooming alongside the house, in a beautiful yellow and green. That's the best news in the world of nature, the sign of spring after a long winter. It is news from a graveyard. Except the bulb, by losing its life, finds it. Out of the grave comes the good news of the flower.

The best news about America is not in the morning paper. It is news from a graveyard. News from a graveyard in Springfield, Illinois, the grave of Abraham Lincoln—for that is news of what America might be at its best.

The best news in the international world is not the latest report from Korea or China. It is news from a graveyard—in a Washington Cathedral, the grave of Woodrow Wilson, the legacy of a vision of a family of nations, a linked and steadfast guard set on peace on earth.

The best news for all the world and all the years is news from a graveyard in Jerusalem, a grave near

> . . . a green hill far away
> Without a city wall,
> Where our dear Lord was crucified,
> Who died to save us all.

Continually we lift up our hearts to the good news of Easter as it comes into a world full of bad news.

I

Easter is good news about the universe, about God. It proclaims that the world is not an orphan asylum, not a machine shop, not just a whirling ball, hurled through endless space. It is a home. At its heart is not just something but Someone. It is the breathtaking news that love is the ultimate power in the universe. In Walter de la Mare's poem "The Listeners" there is the ultimate question men ask:

> "Is there anybody there," said the Traveler,
> Knocking on the moonlit door;
> And his horse in the silence champed the grasses
> Of the forest's ferny floor.

We are all travelers, knocking on the door of the universe and asking, "Is anybody there?" And the Easter faith answers, "There is Somebody there!"

Eternal life is credible because we believe in God the Father. We believe that the God who has created personality can and will preserve that personality, the supreme creation in the universe.

Any real sense of eternal life comes, if it comes at all, from conviction as to the kind of a world we live in, a world in which spirit is a reality. That is, a world view which results when we take the highest and best we know as a clue to ultimate reality. It has been pertinently said, "We do not believe in immortality because we find reasons that compel us; we rather look for reasons because we believe in God." Easter is not removed from daily life if we can say with Robert Browning:

> The World's no blot for me,
> No blank—it means intensely
> And it means good.

Professor William E. Hocking has stressed, in his *Thoughts on Death and Life,* that the meaning of the various parts of life depends on the meaning of the whole. If we believe in God faith in the conservation of life's highest values becomes an inevitable part of our whole view of life.

It is in that truth of God's abiding Fatherhood that we find the abiding reason for faith in immortality. If you are actually God's child what other can ever conceivably take your place? It is perfectly reasonable that God might create another world or another universe, to replace this one. But what could replace a child? Susanna Wesley had nineteen children. That is a good many even for so notoriously competent a mother. It is highly probable that she got their clothes mixed on occasion. But do you imagine she ever got them mixed? Did Samuel sort of fade into John, and was Charles a misty blending of both? Would she have cared little if one slipped out of her life, finding ready comfort in the fact that she had eighteen left? If you have any doubt about it read her letters to her children. Each one had his own individual place that none of the others, not all eighteen together, could fill. A child is unique and irreplaceable. How much more must the Fatherhood of God imply an eternal place in the Father's heart for each child?

II

Easter is also good news about man, about ourselves. I got to thinking about a central truth of Christianity not long ago in an unusual place. I was marooned in a little town for two hours on a Sunday afternoon waiting for a train. So I went in to the only building that was open, the post office. There I occupied my time looking at the art gallery that decorates the walls of every post office, pictures of men wanted for robbing the United States mails. Several of them looked like some of my best friends! Rewards were offered for their capture, five hundred for some, a thousand dollars for others, and for one—evidently a grand duke of the profession—five thousand dollars. Each man had a price on his head.

Then it struck me suddenly that those pictures were a crude but real suggestion of the heart of the Easter message, that every man has a price on his head, a divine price tag, an infinite worth in the sight of God. That was the message with which Christianity went out to a hard Roman world, where men were cheap—the message of Jesus and the resurrection. It went down into ghettos and slave quarters, where men were bound with every conceivable fetter and chain, and put into their minds a new valuation of themselves, "Beloved, now are we the sons of God and it doth not yet appear what we shall be." That faith lifted men to their feet and sent them out into life with a new consciousness of worth. So that news comes into our lives today—fortifying us for any amazement by the new price put upon us, the infinite eternal worth of the soul. Easter affirms that in a universe that is so careful about the indestructibility of matter, the highest, most precious creation of all will not be lost. That is something to sing about. So we sing on Easter—"He is risen, Hallelujah!" That great faith has perhaps never been more persuasively expressed than in the quiet but tremendous words of Professor George Herbert Palmer on the death of his wife, Alice Freeman Palmer. These are his words: "Though no regrets are proper for her death, who can contemplate the fact of it and not call the world irrational if, out of deference to a few particles of disordered matter, it exclude so fair a spirit?"

Have we really received this great news from the graveyard where a tomb stood open? There is great wisdom in what may seem the record of a trivial conversation between a young woman and a professor of history at a dinner party about fifteen years ago. The girl, not knowing what to talk about, suddenly said, "Have you read *Gone With the Wind?*" The professor said, "No." Then she said, "You'd better hurry up, it's been out six months." He asked her, "Have you read Dante's *Divine Comedy?*" "No," she said. "Well," he replied, "you had better hurry up, it has been out six hundred years."

So we ask, Have you really read the story of the resurrection, read it so that it really gets into the secret places of the heart, where the springs of life are coiled? It's been out nineteen hundred years. It has changed the world for millions. It can do the same for you.

III

Easter, again, is good news about humanity and the future of the world. Easter is the affirmation of a tremendous social force in the struggle against evil and injustice—the force of a living Christ in the world. That has been put vividly in what I think is one of the noblest lines of modern poetry. It is in John Masefield's poetic drama, *The Trial of Jesus*. Procula, the wife of Pilate, is deeply concerned over the crucifixion of Jesus. A Roman soldier, Longinus, comes to report that he has found the tomb of Jesus empty. Pilate's wife asks, in great excitement, "Do you believe his claim?"

LONGINUS: If a man believes anything up to the point of dying on a cross for it, he will find others to believe it.

PROCULA: Do you believe it?

LONGINUS: He was a fine young fellow, my lady, not past middle age. And he was alone and defied all the Jews and the Romans, and when we had done with him he was a poor broken down thing, dead on the cross.

PROCULA: Do you think he is dead?

LONGINUS: No, lady, I don't.

PROCULA: Then where is he?

LONGINUS: Loose in the world, lady, where neither Jew nor Roman can stop his truth.

"Loose in the world, lady"—that is the social hope of the world today, tomorrow. Our labor for a better world is not vain in the Lord. The divine force revealed in Jesus is a continuing reality in the world. Jesus is loose in the world—a divine force wherever love struggles against hate, wherever justice fights against exploitation, wherever truth battles against lies.

Sometimes we see a proclamation about an escaped criminal, a dangerous man at large. That is what Easter says, in a far different sense—to every evil power that preys on human life, that would use persons as things—"Dangerous man at large." Jesus Christ has broken jail! "He could not be holden." He is loose in the hearts and minds of men, and he will win the battle.

The tremendous social implications for Easter are found in this truth that what we are willing to do for men depends ultimately on our conception of what they actually are. If we put on them the rating of immortal souls, that act of faith brings a new and powerful momentum into action on their behalf. When we carry that estimate of men into our action Jesus really does get loose in the world, as an overturning and saving force. A missionary friend of mine once told me of being called into a textile mill in China, to identify a child worker, just eleven years of age, who had fallen asleep at a machine and been mangled to death. He said that as he looked at the pitiful body he realized that the whole affair was a profoundly theological question: What is she? Just one of 400,000,000 things in China, things which were very useful in producing a 200 per cent profit? Or is she a child of God, endowed with eternal worth? It makes a difference. But we do not have to go to China for examples. We must ask the same question wherever things are set above persons in value.

Finally, will you think for a moment of the great Easter parade of earth. I do not mean the Easter Parade that is familiar, the one along the Avenue, the fashion parade, the glittering show of hats and clothes. That is a bright pageant of color, but a shabby anticlimax if it means that Easter is chiefly concerned with the milliner, the florist, and the tailor. Look at the real Easter parade as it starts at the open tomb of Christ and marches down through the centuries, the shining company of those who have lived in the power of an endless life and have joined Christ's warfare against oppression and wrong.

We need that Easter parade today, for humanity walks in the valley of the shadow of death, the shadow of atomic war. And our souls from out that shadow shall be lifted only as Christ gains the victory over greed, over the lust for power, over aggressive nationalism, over race conflict.

Watch that Easter parade as it has turned into devastated areas of the world, where man's eternal worth to God has been denied, against the strongholds of slavery and exploitation. All the world is waiting for that Easter parade today—groaning and travailing in pain waiting for the revelation of the sons of God, waiting where the worth of men is obscenely denied, where men are being used as missiles in war.

This truth emerges. One sure way of deepening and strengthening men's faith in eternal life is by the practice of treating men as sons of God. No doctrine can live in the intellect which does not renew itself in experience. If the social implications of immortality are made the guide for individual and social practice, that very experience will give a reality to the faith itself which centuries of argument, ritual, and preaching could not give.

—MARCHING OFF THE MAP

18

"Wie Befinden Sie Sich?"

"He came to himself." (Luke 15:17.)

A familiar salutation made by German people, "Wie befinden sie sich?" means "How do you find yourself?" It is a form of greeting like "How do you do?" or "How are you?" It is well to remember that this greeting, even though followed by a question mark, is not really a question. It is a salutation and not a medical inquiry! It is dangerous to ask some people, "How are you?" They will tell you.

But here we do take the salutation as a question, one of the most serious questions that could be asked of any person. "How *do* you find yourself?" One literalist replied to this German salutation, "I never lose myself!" But people do lose themselves, their potential remains undiscovered. Lord Byron wrote some words that truly fit himself:

> This should have been a noble creature
> With all the energy which should have made
> A goodly frame of glorious elements
> Had they been wisely mingled; as it is,
> It is an awful chaos . . . light and darkness,
> And mind and dust and passions and pure thoughts
> Mixed, and contending without end or order
> All dormant or destructive.

In other words, he got lost and never found himself. Byron was no exception, for life is a problem in finding the potential self of each one of us. There is a profound statement—one among many—in the story of the Prodigal Son. We read: "He came to himself." He came to his highest potential as a son of his Father. It is a great hour, a great day, a great year when a person truly "comes to himself" and realizes the potentials that are wrapped up in him.

It is well to remember at the start that a man finds his best self only when he digs for it. It is hardly accidental. Your potential is buried among many things. Sometimes it is as though a department store had caved in on a person, burying him in the rubble. Balzac once said about writing, "You have to dig frantically like a miner under a landslide." For your best in living as well as writing you have to dig for it. A woman was talking to the sculptor Gutzon Borglum about his statue of Mr. Lincoln. "Mr. Borglum, how did you know Lincoln was in the marble?" Whether the sculptor knew it or not, he had to dig for Abraham Lincoln. We all have to dig for our minds, our skills, our souls.

I

"Wie befinden sie sich?" *You find yourself in the challenge and demands of a hard task.* Michelangelo really came to himself—that is, he displayed his greatest powers—when he painted the ceiling of the Sistine Chapel in the Vatican in Rome. Abraham Lincoln came to himself in the stupendous demands of saving the nation.

Old residents of St. Louis used to like to tell of two men, just out of jobs. They were two former soldiers, both graduates of West Point. One day they met on a street corner. One was peddling wood raised on his wife's farm. He had just resigned from the army. The other had been head of a military school and had been let out of that post. He had written: "I am out of money, out of a job, and out of hope." The first man was Ulysses S. Grant. The other was William Tecumseh Sherman. They *found* themselves in the great demands which leadership of the Union armies in the Civil War thrust upon them. That is not a tribute to war; it is a tribute to the self-discovery possible when one throws oneself into a hard task.

This is true whether the tasks are large in a physical sense or of smaller size. The Galilean fisherman, Peter, found himself in the task placed upon him as an apostle of Jesus Christ; the task of allowing his faith to be part of the Rock on which the Master would build his Church. You find yourself in a great task.

II

"Wie befinden sie sich?" *You find yourself in the gifts of life that have come to you.* Have you ever seen a child stand on the shoulders of a man to watch a parade? Look closely and you will see there a picture of every man, yourself included. We all stand on the shoulders of someone—frequently on many shoulders. Once in a while we hear some half-wit chattering about being a self-made man. It is just a confession that he is a fool. We stand on what has been given us. A man once asked a surgeon, "How do you do it? With life and death in your hands, there you are all alone." The surgeon replied, "I do not go into the operating room alone. Louis Pasteur goes in with me. Joseph Lister goes in with me." So it is with every man, who he is and what he is is the gift of many, near and far, distinguished and unknown. You find yourself in the best things given to you, in the life you have lived, exciting adventures of the mind opened to you by fine minds who awakened your mind, the riches of friendship given by those who have walked with you, the sense of responsibility which has grown out of great tasks someone gave you to do, the lift of ideals given you by someone who held them high before you. You find yourself in life's gifts.

III

"Wie befinden sie sich?" *You find yourself in other people.* You find yourself when you see other people with the sensitive eye and the sympathetic imagination. One of the never ceasing miracles of life occurs when a person who has been all bound up in himself, usually resembling "a clod of ailments," is suddenly released to find a self he never knew he had in response to the needs of another, in the occasion to bring joy to another. Now the best self emerges as the figure emerges from the marble under the sculptor's touch.

A shoemaker, a man of very little formal education, William Carey, found himself as a man of increased power when he went out as the first foreign missionary to India. But so also has many a woman found herself in expanding the walls of her home and extending her love to a larger company than can be gathered within her four walls. Recorded in the book of Acts is the story of such a woman. Her name was Dorcas, and she made garments for the poor.

In the outthrust of life we find ourselves. We find ourselves by putting ourselves out to service. Jesus put it memorably, "He that loses his life shall find it." We find ourselves in outgoing effort. You never find yourself in a rocking chair, unless it be that you rise from the chair to go forth in the service of life. You find yourself in other people.

IV

"Wie befinden sie sich?" *You find yourself in God.* It was said of Heywood Broun that he always wanted to be known as a man about town. Before his life ended he came to realize that the most important town about which a man can be known is the City of God. That is true of anyone. We find ourselves only in relation to a spiritual world. A great statement of this truth comes not from a preacher but from a philosopher, William James, who wrote: "The visible world is part of a more spiritual universe, from which it draws its chief significance; that union or more harmonious relation to that spiritual universe is our true end. We and God have business with each other and in that business our highest destiny is fulfilled." We and God have business with each other. In that great business we find ourselves. In the purposes of God, making for a transformed and better world, people have found themselves. Paul put it in a sentence, "You are complete in him." In the purposes of God you find yourself.

—An unpublished Sermon

III

Teacher of Preachers

In the Minister's Workshop and Communicating the Gospel are Halford Luccock's only books on homiletics. In these two volumes he summed up the most important things he had to say about preaching. *In the Minister's Workshop,* particularly, contains the core of his teaching. During the twenty-five years he was at Yale he held virtually every lectureship on preaching in the United States. These dealt with a variety of themes but the essence of what he had to say on preaching is summed up in the Lyman Beecher lectures of 1953, *Communicating the Gospel.* For the present volume excerpts are taken from these two books, *Christianity and the Individual,* and the symposium *Protestantism.*

III

Teacher of Preachers

In the Minister's Workshop and *Communicating the Gospel* are Halford Luccock's only books on homiletics. In these two volumes he summed up the most important things he had to say about preaching. *In the Minister's Workshop*, particularly, contains the core of his teaching. During the twenty-five years he was at Yale he held virtually every lectureship on preaching in the United States. These dealt with a variety of themes but the essence of what he had to say on preaching is summed up in the Lyman Beecher lectures of 1953, *Communicating the Gospel*. For the present volume excerpts are taken from these two books, *Christianity and the Individual*, and the symposium *Protestantism*.

1

The Sermon, Preaching, and the Preacher

The Nature and Purpose of the Sermon

In the first two centuries the spoken word was the chief agency, not only of evangelization, but also of edification, building converts up in the faith and the practice of it. It was not the only agency. There was the fellowship. There were the beginnings of forms of worship, the practice of sacrificial sharing, the instruction of converts. But preaching was the chief reliance.

The very character of the first church buildings is an evidence of this emphasis. They were designed for preaching. Hence, they did not follow the model of the Jewish Temple, which was split into separate courts, or of pagan temples, such as the Pantheon, into whose construction the need for preaching did not enter, but followed the model of the basilica, or court of justice, emphatically a place designed for speech. For this reason early Christian churches were called basilicas. The building was oblong in shape, with a raised platform at one end. These buildings were used for preaching, passing in time from the simple exhortations of the post-apostolic years to the more polished and artistic sermons preached to thousands of hearers in the large basilicas such as those of Ambrose at Milan and Saint Sophia at Constantinople. The outstanding names are those of great preachers: Origen, Basil, and Chrysostom in the East; Jerome, Ambrose, and Augustine in the West. This early era of preaching stands in glaring contrast with the darkness that descended over the Church in later centuries, when preaching lost its place.

To quote John Ker . . . a major lesson of the Christian history is that "the church that cannot and will not preach, and preach well, will go down."

—Protestantism

Remember this: Do not overestimate or underestimate the place and power of the sermon in the life and work of the Church. That power has been grossly overestimated. Much of Protestantism, historically, has laid on the sermon, as a chief or exclusive instrument of its work, a burden that it cannot possibly carry. Protestantism has made an unfortunate excursion into Greek mythology and come back with Atlas as the symbol of the preacher carrying the whole world of its work on the shoulders of his sermon. The load is too great. One of the blessed recoveries of our century has been to recognize the pulpit as one, and only one, instrument among many. "The eye cannot say to the hand, I have no need of thee." The sermon cannot say to the fellowship of the church, to worship, to nurture and education, "I have no need of thee." Maurice Egan has said that if the Protestant church ever dies, the dagger found in its heart will be the sermon. We can dismiss that as the judgment of a Roman Catholic, of sacramentarianism. But we ought not to shrug it off too lightly. For it does point to our grievous overestimate of the power of the sermon alone.

—COMMUNICATING THE GOSPEL

When the sermon becomes an end in itself, it makes void the word of God by a tradition.

This undue elevation of the sermon as an end in itself has frequently prevented it from becoming a means of bringing Christ to the people. The words of Jesus: "Whosoever will be great among you, let him be your minister" apply to the sermon as well as to the preacher. It is truly great only as it stoops down, puts aside the rhetorical sins that do so easily beset it, and serves men at a particular point of need.

—PROTESTANTISM

A sermon is like a brick: It fulfills its function only as it is placed in relationship, in a structure. On this point Gaius Glenn Atkins speaks with his usual wisdom: "Preaching is having a hard time just now because too heavy a burden has been put upon it in our evangelized Protestantism; preaching was never meant to carry out the program of an institutional church; it was never meant to do the whole work of making religion real." That remembrance must be the backdrop of all thinking about sermons; otherwise there is a fatal distortion. Preaching, separated from its roots and accompaniment in the life of a parish and community, becomes an aerial plant with a faint color and deficient life. The sermon has true meaning when it is seen as one of many agencies of the spiritual life. When it alone is used to build, the building sags.

Preaching should be a sector of truth and not an arc. An arc is a portion of the circumference of a circle; a sector is a V-shaped wedge in a circle, which includes a portion of the circumference but goes by radii to the center. "Arc preaching" deals with a segment of the circumference of life; "sector preaching" includes circumference but goes to the center. A true, as well as clever, description of preaching that stays on the circumference is found in the oft-quoted remark of Arnold Lunn: "There is no market for sermons on the text: God so loved the world that he inspired a certain Jew to inform his contemporaries that there was a great deal to be said for loving one's neighbors." Paul did "sector" preaching; he dealt with the varied circumferences of life in the Judean and Greco-Roman world—family life, the care of children, eating and drinking, the treatment of slaves—but from that circumference he drove a wedge of thought deep to the center, to the unveiling of God in Christ.

No mere arc on the circumference of life today, no matter how surely drawn, is adequate in a world waiting for the relating of life to central reality, to God.

—IN THE MINISTER'S WORKSHOP

The Aim of Preaching

It is a significant addition which Dr. Henry Sloane Coffin has made to Phillips Brooks's classic definition of preaching as "truth through personality." Dr. Coffin says that preaching is "truth through personality *to a person*." It must be aimed at a definite receiving end.

—CHRISTIANITY AND THE INDIVIDUAL

The gospel was not merely an idea, a message, but an idea in process of communication. We see it portrayed all through the New Testament in terms of motion. When it loses that motion of communication, it ceases to be itself. The disclosures of form criticism of the gospels have enabled us to see the gospel, the message, formulated and shaped by the purpose of communication. Incidentally, form criticism does much for the morale of the preacher. It reveals that the preacher is not an excrescence, an appendage to the fellowship. He was not a Johnny-come-lately to the church. He was a prime mover. In the beginning was the word—the word of the teacher and preacher. Our gospels did not originate as histories or biographies, but as short theological sermons. So let the preacher drop his inferiority complex and lift up his head. He was there at the beginning of the drama, Act I, Scene I.

—COMMUNICATING THE GOSPEL

A sermon is like a wrestling match, or rather two wrestling matches, first with an idea and then with an audience, with the absorbed tenseness of those first moments which will determine whether one can get an effective hold on idea or on people.

—IN THE MINISTER'S WORKSHOP

The preacher is a bridge builder. That is a notable title in religious history, *Pontifex Maximus*. The *Pontifex Maximus*, the great bridge builder, is the messenger who throws a bridge of clear communication across the chasm between the speaker and the hearer. The gospel cannot go over a shaky bridge.

—COMMUNICATING THE GOSPEL

A symbol of the preacher's task is the vivid illustration of William James in which he used the relation between two mill wheels to picture the problem of bringing ideals into moving relationship with the machinery of everyday living. The upper mill wheel above a lower one may be turning, but unless there is some sort of peg joining the lower one to the upper, the motion of the upper wheel will not turn the lower one. The upper wheel may represent ideals, faiths, professions; the lower one, the practices of everyday life. Often there is little or no connection between the two. There is need to drop down a peg from the upper to the lower wheel so that faiths and ideals may be brought into effective relation to the machinery of everyday experience. Preaching has much to do with "pegs."

—CHRISTIANITY AND THE INDIVIDUAL

The aim of preaching is not the elucidation of a subject, but the transformation of a person. When we have said that we must hurry on to add that all through the Christian centuries a most effective instrument in the transformation of a person has been the elucidation of a subject. The first Christian sermon at Pentecost was emphatically the elucidation of the subjects of Hebrew history and prophecy. It resulted in the transformation of people.

Yet the purpose of the preacher is not to explain something but to persuade people to think, and to act, in a certain way. One of the hardest tasks in any theological seminary is to take students who are spending three years in a world where, inevitably and rightly, the emphasis is on explaining something, and persuade them that in a church and congregation they are in a different world which demands a different goal and approach. The most wonderful demonstration of that difference is in Jesus' conversation with the woman at the well in Samaria, a sermon to one person. There we see him, with love and skill, turning what might have been an academic discussion of history and worship into a personal appeal and the conviction of sin. Our task is to give to doctrine a moving presentation which goes beyond exposition into persuasion. The sermon must be judged operationally by its effect on the hearers.

—COMMUNICATING THE GOSPEL

[Dick] Sheppard always talked to persons; he never merely sprayed the solar system with words. In that lay his genius and his far-spreading influence. He had simplicity and directness; he was as clear as sunlight, his themes were basic ones of Christian doctrine and experience, even though his range in doctrine was far less than the full octave of the New Testament. It is not surprising that his preaching seemed deceptively simple. Many have even felt, "That kind of preaching is easy." The answer to that is in two words—"Try it." It is just as easy as great simplicity in painting. So one might conceivably say of the "Angelus," "Why, it's just a simple thing, a man and a woman standing in a field. That's easy!" Or of the "Madonna of the Chair," "Just a woman holding a baby. How trite!" It is a high art to be able to take elemental things and make them *live*. Sheppard did that.

—THE BEST OF DICK SHEPPARD

One crux of the matter is a conscientious moving of the truth in a narrative or word of other centuries and other places into the midst of present experience. It is the absence of the engaged "clutch" of the present-day parallel which meshes in with the machinery of the mind and heart that has made so much alleged expository preaching irrelevant and obsolete. A strange incident in recent American history throws a great deal of light on this art. That was the broadcast made by Orson Welles out of H. G. Wells's scientific romance *The War of the Worlds*, a story of an imagined invasion from Mars. Orson Welles broadcast it as though it were actually happening at the moment over in New Jersey and up in Westchester, just a few miles from the studio. Neither he nor the officials of the Columbia Broadcasting Company ever dreamed that anyone would accept it as present fact. But the realism and the near location of the imaginary invasion from Mars were too great for tender and jumpy minds. The actor described the attack of weird creatures from Mars armed with "heat rays" as they descended upon a section of the state of New Jersey. The spectacular radio broadcast was interspersed with hair-raising "news flashes" that threw into a panic a large number of men and women, who had not heard the preliminary radio introduction and explanations. They thought that the Martians were really attacking the world and that its end had come. They fled to the streets, tried to buy newspapers, called up studios and the police, and otherwise behaved as delirious grasshoppers.

At the time many thought, "What a tribute to H. G. Wells!" But later H. G. Wells gave a disgruntled interview denouncing the effrontery of Orson Welles. He said that all the trouble came from Orson Welles's taking liberties with the story by moving its location. If he had left it in Brighton and London, no one would have been excited. But "by moving it to a close location, he got a nervous reaction."

Those are words for a preacher to ponder well. When we leave the Bible stories in Palestine all is well; the congregation can sleep safely and murmur, "Never touched me." It is when we move the good Samaritan from the Jericho Road to Main Street, just around the corner; or move the rich fool from Judea to our own neighborhood in Nebraska or Texas; or move Judas into our own congregation, that the trouble begins; and that is when real preaching begins.

The Preacher Himself

"He seemed to be the channel of a communication, and not the source of it." These words, written by Walter Bagehot after hearing a sermon preached by Frederick Denison Maurice, are more than a perfect tribute to a great preacher. They describe all true preaching. In real preaching the preacher is a channel, not a source. That truth is pictured in the word commonly used for the sermon—"message"—something sent through a channel. It is the prophet's charter. "The word of the Lord *came*." As the Old Testament prophets reached back into the dim, shadowy realm of inspiration, they were conscious, not of their own wisdom or wit, but of something spoken and heard. "Thus saith the Lord God of hosts, Go . . . and say." "Thus shalt thou say unto him, The Lord saith thus." The primary fact about preaching is that which is behind the preacher—the reality of a God who speaks. Any discussion of preaching which does not begin there might as well not begin at all.

—IN THE MINISTER'S WORKSHOP

One very great obstacle to communicating the gospel today is a curious perverse desire of many preachers to be known as profound. They use strange translation of the injunction of II Tim. 2:15: "Study to show thyself obscure." So many, in a frantic effort to be profound, succeed only in being muddy. This strange yearning to be difficult, and thus receive the accolade of incomprehensibility, has never perhaps been more frankly expressed than in the envious sigh of Hugh Walpole, the novelist, who wrote, "I'd rather be like Virginia Woolf than anything else on earth. How nice if people said, 'This new novel of Hugh Walpole's may be very beautiful, but we can't be sure because we can't understand a word of it.' . . . I'd truly love that."

There are preachers as well as novelists who would truly love that! Yet no man can serve two masters. Let no pride of mind or of reputation seduce the preacher away from the task of being a messenger. Let the preacher be proud. Let him drop all benumbing sense of inferiority, but let his pride parallel that pictured in old words. "Let not the wise man glory in his density or mystification, but in clarity to the wayfaring man." Let him lift his head in solemn pride, knowing that if anyone understands him, he is in a great succession—in fact, the Apostolic Succession.

[It is a] sense of urgency [that] will preserve the zest of preaching. Without it the sermon so easily becomes just a weekly chore to be dragged through. Then the preacher has touched bottom, emotionally and spiritually. His Saturday-night dirge becomes "Tomorrow and tomorrow and tomorrow creeps on this petty pace" from Sunday to Sunday. But if he is seized with the conviction that something momentous is at stake preaching can be an exciting wrestling match. It is a wrestling match, first, with an idea, if you can discover one, and second, with an audience which can get away with all the agility of a greased pig. The thrilling question comes out, "Can I get a half nelson on this slippery audience?"

The glorious uncertainty of it keeps the mind on tiptoe. We can say with Ulysses:

> It may be that the gulfs will wash us down:
> It may be we shall touch the Happy Isles.
>
> —ALFRED TENNYSON

The passion of an evangelist will save the sermon from the last indignity, that of having the deadly drip of a tired commercial.

This involves a tremendous thing, nothing less than actually believing that he that loseth his life shall find it. It is easy to say. It sounds rather well. But it is hard to believe to the extent that we build our work on it. It involves subordinating every other ambition to what often seems the less glamorous one of making plain the way to God.

A commonly used phrase may lead us, I think, . . . It is the phrase "He rang the bell." Used, as it often is, of a preacher, it usually has a vulgar meaning, indicating that he did something sensational, had a personal triumph of some sort, flung himself from a pinnacle and dazzled the audience. But there is another, and a high, meaning of the phrase. It comes from the Roman Catholic celebration of the Mass. It is a high moment for the believer, who accepts the Roman doctrine of the Mass, when at the elevation of the host a little bell rings, signifying the presence of God. That is our calling, brethren, to ring the bell in that high meaning, to communicate the sense that "this is none other but the house of God, and this is the gate of heaven." (K.J.V.)

We cannot communicate the gospel if we fail to express the astounding wonder which is at the heart of the revelation. That, all too often, is the lost dimension of preaching. It represents an unchanging need of the human mind and heart.

We are stewards of the mysteries of God. The faithful steward will say with Paul, "Behold I show you a mystery," and not denature it into platitudes for retarded or tired minds. If anyone says to you that you are preaching over his head, there is a good answer in three words. Use it. It is, "Raise your head."

Over the desks of many of the broadcasters in London in World War II, sending messages beamed to enemy countries, was printed the question,

"Is what you are saying worth a man's risking his life to hear?" That is enough to rock any man back on his heels. It is enough to rock the preacher back. Is what you are saying truly a word of salvation; is it important enough for a person to risk changing his life when he listens? When we apply that stern test, how many of the effects that we love so much, the silken words that we love to stroke, are irrelevant? For a traveler along the road, it is a far better thing to find a road sign, even in stark simplicity, than a painting by Picasso.

—COMMUNICATING THE GOSPEL

Think of that first Christian theological seminary which was conducted by Jesus on the hills of Galilee. The first lessons were a long, long way from what many of us would have put first. In that curriculum there was an orientation course for new students; but it was not exactly of the kind which are designed in theological schools today, when the curriculum is revised every second year. I must confess that had I been Dean of that seminary I would have put in a course in "The Social and Political Problems of the Mediterranean Basin." Was that not the world which the disciples would have to face? I would have put in a course on "The Strategy of Propaganda Amid the Greco-Roman Culture." Jesus put first, in the curriculum of companionship, quite another lesson—Our Father. He saw clearly the issues involved in bringing the good news of the Kingdom into that world. He knew the clashes that would come. He told his disciples, "Ye shall stand before governors and kings." But he knew that if they did not face God it was not much use to face anything. That is elementary, but it is not irrelevant to our whole church life. Our first task is not to get people to *do* something, but rather to *receive* something, ourselves to share something. Jesus' first word to his disciples was not "go," but "come." We frequently reverse the order. We start with alarms and excursions, and the expeditions are often futile and shortlived because we have not first freely received; we have not shared Jesus' calm faith in God and fellowship with God.

—CHRISTIANITY AND THE INDIVIDUAL

2

Life-Centered Preaching

The Need for Life-Centered Preaching

In the narrative in the book of Acts which recounts Philip's evangelization of the Ethiopian Treasurer we have a suggestive model. "Philip began at the same scripture, and preached unto him." (Acts 8:37.) Philip began at the very point at which the other man had arrived in his experience and interpreted it in the light of Jesus. It was one of the first instances in Christian history of what has been called "life-situation preaching." Beginning *there*—that is the chief point in preaching to personal needs. It is not so much beginning with scripture, but bringing it to a place of particular experience and need.

It is in the failure to meet this need of the immediate situation that the traditional type of expository sermon is most lacking. An athletic coach once said to a student practicing the long jump, "You go so far back for your run that you are all tired out when you come to the place to jump." The preacher of the traditional expository sermon who goes back for a sight-seeing tour of Palestine as a prelude to the sermon runs back so far that the audience is all tired out when it comes to the place to jump. Often there is no time for the preacher to jump; frequently the audience is so far gone that it does not notice whether he jumps or not.

—Christianity and the Individual

The preacher's craving must be that of Thackeray when one of his novels achieved a moderate success among the intellectually elite. It had what is called a success d'estime, a thin prize, too much like a moral victory in football. Thackeray was completely dissatisfied. He cried out, "My tunes must be heard in the street!" That must be the preacher's ambition. We must cry, "My tunes must be heard in the street!" Or rather, we must hear our Master cry, "My tunes must be heard in the street!" That is where they were heard in the first place. They were heard in the streets of little towns in Galilee, and along the roads. We read, "And the whole city was gathered about the door," and "There was no longer room for them, not even about the door." His tunes must be heard in our streets.

—COMMUNICATING THE GOSPEL

A speaker in an evangelistic service was launched on a hortatory flight in which he quoted with great fervor Kipling's poem "If." All the "ifs" were recited, concluding that if you can do all these things "You'll be a man, my son." When he had finished a man in the audience asked this profound question: "What if you can't?" That is the hardest question which ethical exhortation has had to face all through history, "What if you can't?" Christianity has faced and answered that question. Its answer has been the demonstration of lives brought into energizing contact with power greater than their own, the power of God.

—CHRISTIANITY AND THE INDIVIDUAL

[This kind of preaching] sharpens the evangelistic point and edge of preaching. It relies on the sharp particular persuasion rather than the easily dulled general appeal. It gives to the great words of evangelism, "Repent and believe," the force of specific content, the persuasion to turn from some particular destructive and unchristian way of acting and thinking, and the persuasion to accept the Christian faith at a localized point where the need for its resources is evident. Evangelistic preaching, as that high term is frequently used, has often been debased into what someone has described as a "bunch of borrowed illustrations tied up in baby ribbon." Carlyle once commented on a sentimental and inadequate book about Margaret Fuller that if you seek a fact in it, "you are answered (so to speak) not in words, but by a symbolic tune on the bag-pipe, symbolic burst of wind-music from the brass-band." Wind music from the brass hand is not a means of effective evangelism.

—IN THE MINISTER'S WORKSHOP

Lasting help to bewildered people in real need does not lie in smart phrases. To people who look for light on the handling of life, far more is needed. Emerson has given in his Journal a picture of an audience in a village church, which deserves to be framed in every pastor's study:

At church to-day I felt how unequal is the match of words against things. Cease, O thou unauthorized talker, to prate of consolation, resignation, and spiritual joys in neat and balanced sentences. For I know these men who sit below. Hush quickly, for care and calamity are *things* to them. There is the shopmaker, whose daughter is gone mad, and he is looking up through his spectacles to see what you have for him. Here is my friend whose scholars are leaving him and he knows not where to turn his hand next. Here is the stage driver, who has jaundice and cannot get well. Here is B, who failed last year and is looking up anxiously. Speak things, or hold thy peace.

When we actually see people with eyes like that, nothing less will be adequate than a miracle of incarnation by which a word becomes a *thing* real enough to hold to, stout enough to lift.

—CHRISTIANITY AND THE INDIVIDUAL

That calls for theological preaching with a dimension of depth. For modern society is what Professor Tillich calls it, an eccentric world, a society which has lost its spiritual center. And when man loses God as his center he loses himself. From another viewpoint the terror of our time has been that primitive man has returned. He must be met with primitive Christianity. This calls for more than the preaching of doctrine. That could be done by indoctrination, a not too difficult task. Of course we need the preaching of doctrine. But merely to announce the doctrine in solemn tones is not to convey it. That is a trouble with some preaching by theological students and young graduates. They are entranced by points of doctrine, and they mistake the announcement of these points with confronting the congregation with the good news. What is merely stated is never presented. We must convey the reality to which the doctrine points—God. And who is sufficient for that? In that task we cannot be reminded too often that it is the duty of a shepherd to feed the sheep and not to entertain the goats.

—COMMUNICATING THE GOSPEL

Help in How to Do It

The newspapers not long ago printed a story of a doorman of a New York theater who had guarded the stage door for seventeen years and in all that time had never once seen a performance on the stage inside the building! It is possible for a preacher and members of a congregation to become that sort of doorkeeper in the house of the Lord. The attention can be centered on the circumference, the incidental, the mechanical, and lost to the central living drama of salvation in individual lives and collective life which alone gives any meaning to the organization.

In preaching this gospel of salvation the most promising starting point is in people's own experience of dissatisfaction. The preacher need not worry about not finding any sense of dissatisfaction with life, as a place to begin. He will find it, for it is there. He need not give a great deal of effort to the task of making people dissatisfied with their own experience of life. His chief task will be in the interpretation of people's feeling, often unconscious, about life, the feeling of unrest and frustration and inadequacy. One of the finest tributes ever paid to spiritual counsel was that which the woman at the well of Samaria paid to Jesus, "Come, see a man, who told me all things that ever I did." There was more in her exclamation than the wonder over a stranger's knowledge of some things in her past history. It was the recognition of the insight of one who had plumbed down into her life and intepreted the meaning of her condition. We do not start with a "plan of salvation"; we do not first announce dogmatically a remedy. We begin with the person at the point which he has reached in experience, and interpret that experience of inarticulated dissatisfaction and unrest, of ill-defined yearning, in the light of Jesus' interpretation of life.

In strong contrast to this, is the form of sermon preparation described by Dr. Albert B. Coe, thinking himself into the lives and needs of people, a practice shared by an increasing company of ministers. Dr. Coe says:

> It is my custom to spend much time here in the church alone. I walk up and down the aisles. I sit in my pulpit, drinking in God's light through the rose window. I imagine the different individuals in the pews, seeking an intimate comprehension of each one's needs and praying for the power to meet the need in a sane, intelligent, inspired way. From my pulpit I go to the street that passes the church, see the people passing—bright faces, sad faces, the man out of work, the Negro feeling the tightly drawn cord of racial discrimination. There is a woman with all the lines of distress written on her face. There is a man seeking the divorce court with his heart wracked indescribably. There they go—unhappy faces, on which are written doubt and scorn and yearning and a thousand evidences of a lack of integration with life and the universe. All the faces reveal a hunger for reality. I reach out to all of them.

In such an imaginative sharing of the experience of people, the sin that doth so easily beset a preacher—the ambition to preach an impressive sermon—drops out, and speaking becomes more like taking a towel and girding oneself and stooping down to perform human service.

—CHRISTIANITY AND THE INDIVIDUAL

This approach makes of the sermon a means but never an end. Is there not an arresting meaning for the preacher in the words of Jesus, spoken in an entirely different connection: "The kings of the Gentiles exercise lordship over them; and they that exercise authority upon them are called benefactors. But ye shall not be so: but he that is greatest among you, let him be as the younger; and he that is chief, as he that doth serve"? How many times have we seen or read about the "great ones" high and lifted up in the pulpit (recall that terrible phrase from another day, "princes of the pulpit"), lording it over their subjects in the pew with an onrush of overpowering oratory or by turning on the charm of personality. In either case the interest centered on a display of ability more than on the lowly serving of those sitting at meat in the pews. Jesus said, "It shall not be so among you." One way of guarding that it shall not be so is to keep the present need of any sort of people, rather than the exhibition in the pulpit, in the focus of attention. The only way to true greatness in the pulpit, as in all other realms, is the paradoxical way of making oneself the servant of a particular task. The history of literature is full of demonstrations of this truth. Whenever a writer conceives of himself as writing for posterity he becomes a wooden thing, in spite of talent. When he has written for a particular contemporary audience, trying to meet it with a specific service, he finds life and length of days. Posterity is a perverse mistress to work for. She rarely pays any attention to what was written especially for her, but she is often curious about what was written in supreme unconcern for her. Paul wrote great literature, not because he said, "Go to, now; I will write an ode to love which will go ringing down the centuries; watch me carefully," but because he had his whole mind, with all of its endowments, intent on the task of making Christ formed in the lives of those to whom he wrote and spoke.

This kind of preaching, where the particular object is the main thing, cuts across the traditional classifications of sermons into doctrinal, biblical, ethical, or topical, as Dr. Fosdick has so clearly shown. It may be three of them at once. It may fall into any classification because it employs doctrine or Bible as a means of making life more abundant, not for the primary purpose of inculcating doctrine for its own sake or of teaching the Bible—just as a physician's purpose is not to empty his medicine chest, but to cure a sickness. In the treatment of doctrine, for instance, life-situation preaching follows the wisdom of one who advised, "Always get ahold of a doctrine at its preaching end." There is a preaching end of every great Christian doctrine—many ends. If someone raises the objection, "Suppose you can't find a preaching end to a doctrine?" the answer is, "Then it isn't an essential doctrine."

This focus on the situations in which people are found, and the desire and ability to bring spiritual resources for meeting them, can be greatly helped by the preacher's reading. A cloud of witnesses surrounds us—people in real-life experiences, in fiction, drama, biography, and history. The personal contacts of anyone with actual experience are necessarily circumscribed. No one but Baron Munchausen ever saw everything personally. But the vicarious adventuring in other people's lives may bring back a rich cargo of insight and wisdom; that is, if it is done in the domain of real literature and not in the romance which is merely the mental equivalent of a sleeping powder. The questions can be asked: What was really the matter with this person or that? Why didn't life add up to more with him? What was the flaw? What was the real trouble with Becky Sharpe or Paul Dombey, Sr., or a hundred others in the dramatis personae of literature and history and biography?

—IN THE MINISTER'S WORKSHOP

In the attempt to bring the resources of religion to lives under various tensions it is so easy to fail to make them available at the point of practical need. There is much worth the remembrance of a preacher in the century-long discussions of the battle of Waterloo. Waterloo has been fought and refought by military experts ever since 1815. The question is, "Why did Napoleon lose, when he had superior numbers and other advantages?" There has come to be some general agreement that a disengaged French army is a big part of the solution. There were really two battles going on at the same time, one at Ligny and one at Waterloo. One army under d'Erlon spent the time wandering around between the two battles without getting into either of them. A great many sermons have done just exactly that. There are two real battles in Christian warfare. One is in the social world, the struggle to build love and justice into the structure of society. The other is to bring spiritual energies into life so that they may turn the machinery of everyday living. A great amount of preaching and teaching is like a wandering, disengaged army, never really getting into either end of the battle. For instance, the sermon which is a traditional, conventional tribute to Jesus is like the lost army of d'Erlon at Waterloo. It does not count in the struggle for a more Christian society, nor does it make available untapped resources for personal life.

—CHRISTIANITY AND THE INDIVIDUAL

Part of the disastrous wall around learning has been built of a specialized jargon. There is no need to whip that villain around the block again. He has already received his more than ninety lashes. But he is still alive, adding to the confusion of tongues, preventing the transmission of meaning. Here, we must be careful not to confuse necessary technical language in many fields with meaningless "Jabberwocky."

> Beware the Jabberwock, my son,
> . . . .
> The Jabberwock, with eyes of flame,
> Came whiffling through the tulgey wood,
> And burbled as it came.

—LEWIS CARROLL

It does burble. So many writers and speakers, in their desire to become profound, succeed only in becoming polysyllabic. The words are not synonyms. There is so much that is buried in a tomb of official jargon—once called gobbledegook. But by any other name it reads as badly.

—COMMUNICATING THE GOSPEL

The weakness of vague preaching, usually in theological generalities, is pictured in the story to be found in Lloyd Lewis' life of General Sherman, entitled *Sherman, Fighting Prophet*. He records an incident in the battle of Shiloh, when the Union troops were pushed back by the Confederate army under Albert Sidney Johnston, almost into the river. One teamster was struggling to drag a gun carriage up through the mire of the river bank. He had his shoulder to the wheel, when an evangelist of the Christian and Sanitary Commission seized upon that strategic moment to do some evangelistic work. He said to the teamster in a sepulchral voice, "Do you know who died on a cross?" Without looking up the man answered, "Don't ask me any riddles. I'm stuck in the mud." The mere repetition of theological phrases seems like a remote riddle to a man who is stuck in the mud! A great many people are stuck in the mud these days, bogged down in circumstances where headway seems impossible, straining at loads beyond their immediate powers. They need sources of energy to be made available at the point of need.

—CHRISTIANITY AND THE INDIVIDUAL

We would not be guilty of the wrong frequently done to Jesus, sometimes strangely enough, in perverted tribute, which reduces his thought and words to the naïve simplicities of a third-rate mind. No surer way has been found to distort Jesus than to fail to recognize his intellectual power and penetration. He dealt with traditional questions of religion and ethics with a profundity that was shocking to many of his contemporaries.

Nevertheless, Jesus spoke directly to the "great unwashed." That is what they were, literally. They did not do ceremonial washing. Jesus did not belong to the Judean Institute of Arts and Letters. He wore no old school tie. We can detect in the gospels some of the intellectual swank and snobbishness which his preaching met. "The Jews marveled at it, saying, 'How is it that this man has learning, when he has never studied?' " Jesus' first disciples met the same sneers from the elite. The judgment of the elders and scribes on Peter and John was that they were "uneducated men."

New Testament research has thrown much new light on the *Koine*, the common speech in which the New Testament was written. Its truth carries best in common speech. There is an illuminating passage in Acts 22. Paul was in danger of his life from mob violence in Jerusalem. He starts his defense, and then we read, "And when they heard that he addressed them in the Hebrew language, they were the more quiet." When the message came in their own language and not in an unfamiliar tongue, they heard. It is always so. When language has no roots in human experience, when it offers no first aid to the senses, there is small response.

—COMMUNICATING THE GOSPEL

The Dangers of It

There is need for one short but earnest word about one deep pitfall in this matter of bringing the resources of the Christian religion to the point of practical need. It is the delusion that personal needs can be completely met or best met by what is often called "practical preaching." The result of that fallacy is the impotence of pedestrian didactic advice which rarely rises six feet above the ground. Many preachers have learned from humiliating experience that "common sense" cannot do the energizing creative work of religion.

It is very easy for preaching to be too "practical" to have any practical results. It can be too psychological to effect any psychological transformation. It can be too much on the level of daily life to perform the miracle of a lift to a new level of power.

That note of demand for the highest can never be absent from preaching which reaches down into the deepest needs of life. A very real danger of a psychological emphasis in preaching is that it may so center on the individual's comfort and happiness and success in adjustment to his environment that it ceases to be definitely Christian, lacking the note of redemption, in finding onself by losing oneself. Rose Macauley has given a prescription for choosing a book in which to read oneself to sleep, which might serve as a description of preaching from which the note of Christian challenge is lost. "Take a novel," she says, "lightly titillating, but not furrowing the surface of the brain. Let the story amuse, thrill, interest, delight, it matters not which; but let it not animate, stimulate, or disurb; for sleep, that shy night bird, must not be startled back." There is no failure of responsibility in a preacher to his people more subtle or deadly than that of allowing his preaching to become a thing which "interests" and "delights," but does not "animate" or "disturb."

—CHRISTIANITY AND THE INDIVIDUAL

The words "preoccupation with self," suggest another danger in concentration on life-situation preaching. It may serve to focus people's attention on themselves and their own problems and ailments. Thus may be fostered an enervating self-concern which shuts one out from the salvation which comes from finding life through losing it. A preacher may, with mistaken motherly solicitude, hover over a congregation, take its pulse and temperature, and whisper anxiously, "How are you feeling now, dear?" —when all the time the principal ailment of the people may be fatty degeneration of the will. Thus the last state of that congregation becomes worse than the first. Its mind is never lifted up for any great length of time from a preoccupation with ailments by the sounding of the truly redeeming challenge, "If any man will come after me, let him deny himself, and take up his cross, and follow me." The Good Physician used shock treatment and radical remedies. He practiced moral surgery: "Go thy way, sell whatsoever thou hast, and give to the poor"; "Let the dead bury their dead"; "Pluck out thine eye." These are not little pills or a gentle massage. They are words of life, stern, demanding, yet leading to salvation.

—IN THE MINISTER'S WORKSHOP

The worst thing that religion can do for a person—and it has often been done—is to remove all tensions prematurely and superficially. A life in which that has been done has really entered the vegetable kingdom. Such a person is more like a contented cauliflower than a man struggling toward the achievement of a soul.

They climbed the steep ascent of heaven,
Through peril, toil, and pain,

is just as true of the Pilgrim's progress toward Christian personality as it is of outward achievement. Storm and stress is an inseparable part of Christian maturity. Mrs. Barbara Spafford Morgan says that winning self-consciousness is like being exiled from the Garden of Eden; the old blissful state of wholeness is gone. But that is the price of growth. Right here is the immorality of some preaching and evangelism. It has aimed to give comfort and peace, and in doing so it has chloroformed the strivings and discontents of the soul. The Christian dealing with tension lies not in abolishing conflict but by bringing unity of personality on a higher level.

—CHRISTIANITY AND THE INDIVIDUAL

3

Social Preaching

The Need for Social Preaching

TERTULLIAN WROTE OF "MEN ALREADY CIVILIZED AND UNDER THE ILLUSIONS of their very culture." True of Rome in the third century, true of America in the twentieth! What a theme for the preacher, the illusions of our culture! And what an enemy to fight and strip of its deadly weapons. The illusion of one of its prophets, that "the business of America is business"; the illusion of the rich fool, as we often practice it, who gave all his attention to problems of production and not any to distribution—he was called a fool, you remember—the term still applies; the illusion that meat is more than life, and raiment more than body; the illusion that spiritual diseases can be cured by material remedies. In recent years we have had many striking portrayals of the truth that man cannot live on illusions. That truth became flesh and walked on the stage in Tennessee Williams' *A Streetcar Named Desire*, in Eugene O'Neill's *The Iceman Cometh*, in Arthur Miller's *Death of a Salesman*. The Big Lie must be overcome by the truth that makes men free.

An additional urgency comes from the situation, deeply disturbing, the great gap which exists between ministers and hosts of laymen, a great majority, certainly, in their thinking on social and economic issues. Periodically the chasm widens. It has stretched to an ominous width at the present hour. One distinguished layman, Dr. Douglass S. Freeman, of Richmond, Virginia, has viewed this division. He writes of

> the grim fact that many laymen have refused to accept or at least to apply, the economic implications of Christianity in business and government. Some

have countenanced one code for the church and another for the counting house; one code for the pew and another for the pulpit. They have preached personal unselfishness and upheld national selfishness; they have given more heed to their brother's church envelope than to his pay envelope. For fear that they may put the church into politics, some have failed to have Christianity defend social justice.

The situation is not too far removed from what happened to a parade on Fifth Avenue in New York, many years ago, when the Twenty-seventh Division, returning from World War I, marched up the avenue. The parade took five hours to pass. There had to be some interruptions, so that the crosstown cars could get through. At Twenty-third Street at one time the parade was suddenly halted, just after the drum major of the band had passed by, separating the band from the leader. The drum major went on marching up to Twenty-ninth Street, swinging his stick gaily up in the air, while the band was held up six blocks behind.

That lonesome drum major has resemblances to many a pastor. He is leading on, giving his message in devoted seriousness, but his band of laymen, who he hoped and prayed would be following him, are blocked by many obstacles a mile behind and hardly seem to be moving at all! If the church is to move in any way like a mighty army, the gap between the minister and laymen must be shortened.

—COMMUNICATING THE GOSPEL

One of Sir James M. Barrie's plays bears the title *What Every Woman Knows*. What a volume covering the years since 1929 could be compiled under the title *What Every Pastor Knows!* What wealth of detail could be gathered to amplify and support the statement that every moral and spiritual problem known to pastor and priest has been aggravated and intensified during the "years of the locust," 1930-1936, intensified by the lack of economic security. The task of maintaining self-respect, the task of maintaining high standards of chastity, when so many young people see no prospect of being able to marry, the task of maintaining the spiritual values of home, about which the pulpit so loves to exhort—all these are made immensely more difficult. Yet we have people within the churches, spiritually deaf, dumb, and blind, who keep droning on, like a parrot that can say only one sentence, about the need for saving individual souls, and not bothering about economic forces which make for the break-down of Christian personality. Right here is the pitfall of a terrible hypocrisy to be avoided at all costs. We all depend on security. We need the realism of Jesus who said that man shall not live by bread alone, but also said, "Your heavenly father knoweth ye have need of these things."

—CHRISTIANITY AND THE INDIVIDUAL

Help in How to Do It

One constant aim will be to strive to develop in people a sensitiveness to evil, some share in the sensitiveness of mind which Jesus manifested. He had a nervous alertness to the presence of faith and goodness; equally quick to detect the contamination of the air which came from dark purposes and designs. "See their thoughts." "He knew what was in man."

This quality of spirit, so greatly needed, found expression in the strong words of Peter Cartwright, the frontier evangelist. Coming into a little settlement which was a sinkhole of iniquity he loudly announced, "I smell hell." He had not yet seen the evil, nor heard it. He smelled it. He had the nose of a foxhound for wrong. It is a great gift. A sharp nose is an instrument for ethical evaluation. If we do not have it, we become like the idols denounced in the Ps. 115: "Noses have they, but they smell not." In the heyday of laissez-faire economics, when the doctrine of no government interference put its blessing on the slaughter of child workers, there were a few Christians who made violent protests. They did not have any equipment of scholarly economic theory. They had something better—noses. They smelled the hell covered with fair words. There are processes and customs today in industry, race relations and politics which literally "smell to heaven." We need the training and consecration of the nose.

One other help is to remember that we are advocates for unseen clients. The people whose cause we plead are rarely ever in the pews in front of us. It is difficult to speak for those who are not present to those who are present. The conventional preacher can easily forget those out of the range of vision. To remember them calls for a costly offering—a dedicated imagination. The preacher must do his work surrounded by a great cloud of witnesses of two sorts, those who have gone before and a cloud of clients. The clients are pictured in the vivid words of George Adam Smith who said that the Prophet Amos could always see "the pinched faces of starved peasants looking through the picket fences." No fence must shut them out. They are the people in need, far away, across the tracks, across the sea. But, much farther away, across the lines of likeness, of color, of class, of religion. If their cause is to plead at all in the hearing of many in the congregation, it will be pleaded by us.

A help is found in the continuous stress on one great principle which covers much ground, to measure the world as Jesus measured it. He measured it in terms of people. That principle is like the magic tent in the Oriental fairy story, made of material so delicate that it could be folded up and held in the palm of a man's hand; yet when it was unrolled and set up it could shelter an army of thousands of men. So the principle of the worth of a person in the sight of God, as revealed in Christ, guides in person-to-person relationship and spreads out to include a world. This truth is compressed in an antithesis of Barth's, "We believe in a civilization of things; Christ believed in a civilization of persons."

Think of the contrast between the eyes of Jesus and those of his disciples. When they came up to Jerusalem, they saw buildings. They cried, "Look, Teacher, what wonderful stones and what wonderful buildings!" Jesus also said "Look!" But he saw people. He said, "Look at that woman over there, putting in two copper coins into the treasury. Out of her poverty she has put in everything she had." He saw the people who were deprived of the privilege of using the Temple as a house of prayer. He saw defrauded widows. If we can help people to look at the world as Jesus did, we give them a new slide rule by which to measure. Then they can see that many of the world's boasted advances become its diseases, measured by the effect on people. They can see that while our society has done wonders with the mechanical arts of multiplication, it has done far less with the ethical art of division. They will be more able and ready to go on to the dangerous edge of things for the sake of people, for whom Christ dies.

One help is obvious, but often disregarded. That is to find the source of our message in our gospel. Then the sermon does not come as a strange and questionable addition to the word of God. One elementary handicap that often hinders preaching on social issues is that it is separated from the preaching of the gospel. Frequently a congregation does not respond to presentation of social implications of the faith, not because the people are born reactionaries, which they are not, but because the man is not preaching. They look up bewildered and say, "Jesus, I know, and Paul, I know, but who are you?"

The preacher's concern must always be not change for the sake of any social change but to help people find what might be the will of God as a guidance for action. That is one reason for the effectiveness of biblical preaching, for in that we are dealing with things which are so largely accepted by the congregation.

If we are to impart the message, we need the courage of the specific. The individualistic commitment to abstract virtues is not enough to make any evils tremble or to assault any stronghold of wrong. The courage of the specific does not mean the indulgence of an insufferable dogmatism about actions. It does not mean the identification of Christianity with any order or institution or proposal. We cannot say that Christian teaching demands that any needed reform, such as the elimination of racial discrimination, demands federal rather than state action. But we can get the subject raised in specific terms so that our preaching shall not be a pea-soup fog. Speaking in specific words will get us into trouble. But there is no other way to avoid the vicious sentimentalism of the advocacy of ends without the provision of means. Or the sentimentalism of refusing to carry an idea to its logical conclusion. I do not know any better picture of the futility of ends without means than a bit of history of Oxford University. After years of debate the dons of one college finally voted to allow the buildings to be lighted with gas. But when asked to grant permission for gas pipes to be installed, they stoutly refused. They were in favor of gas in general but not gas in pipes.

Jesus did general teaching such as the Beatitudes, and the persuasion to trust God. He also had the courage of the specific, as in his rejection of the whole ceremonial code. Jesus was not crucified for saying, "Consider the lilies, how they grow." What brought him to the cross, as far as men were concerned, was saying, "Consider the thieves in the temple, how they steal."

It is the specific action which puts our faith squarely against the ruling anti-Christian and sub-Christian codes of our time. Recall the shout which greeted the Christian martyrs in the Colosseum, "To the lions with the atheists!" Strange-sounding words, to call the Christians "atheists." But the crowd was right. They were atheists. They did not believe in the gods of Rome, in Venus, in Bacchus, in a philandering Jupiter, or in the emperor. We need the cultivation of a stubborn atheism, of Christians making clear that they do not believe in the gods of our marketplaces. Saying, "We do not believe in Bacchus, or in Venus, the goddess of lust, or in Mercury, the fleet-footed god of clever thievery, or in Mars, or Vulcan." Vulcan is the chief god of many Americans at the present hour, the god of the forge, the armorer. His altars are everywhere; our whole economy depends on him. His sign in which we trust is a pillar of smoke from giant chimneys by day and a pillar of fire by night.

If we are to worship the God and Father of our Lord Jesus Christ we must be more aggressive atheists about all others.

—COMMUNICATING THE GOSPEL

The Genteel Tradition in Preaching

Bishop John V. Vincent of The Methodist Church used to have a lecture entitled "The Power of the Parlor." As I look back and recall that title, there is much more in it than meets the eye; much more than the bishop meant. Much preaching has been held captive by the power of the parlor; that is, attention has been directed to those areas of life which were visible from a trimly curtained parlor window. The result has frequently been a paralyzing remoteness from what was pressing painfully on people and from those forces which were blocking the evangelistic and nurturing work of the church.

Gentility comes not from the presence of God in preaching but from his absence. There was not too much preaching of God, but too little, in any vital way that meshed into life. God is not genteel. Our God is a consuming fire. Perhaps that truth has grown too rough for a refined generation of good taste. A minister recently wished to use in a service the Russian hymn "God, the all terrible," and failed to find it in the index of the *Pilgrim Hymnal.* Later he discovered that the first verse beginning "God, the all terrible," had been omitted, the hymn now beginning with the second verse, "God, the all merciful." Have we grown so softhearted and softheaded that we cannot stand the mention of an all-terrible God? If so, we have traded a great birthright for a pitiable mess of pottage, for without an all-terrible God we have little with which to confront the all-terrible evil of our world.

The only power big enough to face the ghost of Caesar stalking through the world today is God. Such a meeting calls for a very ungenteel preaching of the majesty of God. The issue of God against Caesar is not a future, but a present one, in nearly every community in America.

—THE CHRISTIAN CENTURY

4

The Craft of the Preacher

The Role, Purpose, and Psychology of Structure

In the craftsmanship of the preacher first place must be given to one of the basic principles of much modern architecture, "form follows function." That applies all the way from a chair to a skyscraper. If it is a chair why not make something to sit on, instead of a disguised feather-bed? If a gymnasium is being built, why make a Gothic cathedral? The previous question is always, "What is the function of this talking?" A student years ago reported his consternation on finding in the pulpit where he was a supply preacher a little card on which was printed the question, "What are you trying to do with these people?" That upset him, for he was not really trying to do anything. He was just preaching. There is a parallel in the art of stage managing. The stage manager's work begins long before the first rehearsal. The first need is to get clearly in mind what the author is saying, and then to bring everything, voice, costume, scenery, properties, to that one focal point. We are all familiar with the division of spoken and written words into three forms, the solid, liquid, and gaseous. Dean Inge said that the solid is the form taken by books written by professors for or at each other. The gaseous, alas, needs no definition! We all know it. The liquid form gives more promise. When learning is held in solution, it may convey the invitation to people, "Ho everyone that thirsteth, come and drink!"

In preaching, as in all creative writing, the thing of first importance is not plots but people. A novelist gave good advice to a young writer when he wrote, "Do not rack your brain contriving plots. Get out among people. See them, hear them, study them." It is good advice to the preacher.

—Communicating the Gospel

Much that has been said and written on "structure" in the sermon might be put into one sentence: The power of a sermon lies in its structure, not in its decoration. This is equally true of beauty, in spite of a common tendency to find beauty in ornament rather than in form.

In this respect the relationships between architecture and sermons are many and significant. In buildings, all the way from a Greek temple with plain Doric columns or a Gothic cathedral in its sublimity of mass and shape to the simple beauty of proportion in a rectangular Georgian Colonial house, beauty comes from structure and form. Doric columns may give way to elaborate Corinthian capitals, the cathedral may be enriched with exquisite sculpture, the Georgian house acquire a notable doorway with fluted sides and rounded top. The great beauty and power of the building lies still in its form.

Aristotle expressed this truth, applying equally to building with words, in his dictum that "beauty depends on order and a certain magnitude." That is basic foundation for all forms of expository, argumentative, and persuasive writing and speaking—including, emphatically, preaching. To get it well in mind will help to keep in remembrance the truth so important to a maker of sermons, that ornament often blurs what should be the clear, hard beauty of structure. Where an essential rightness of order and outline is not present, even a frieze rivaling those of the Parthenon will not make up the deficiency.

—IN THE MINISTER'S WORKSHOP

Often ideas do not come through clearly because there is no subordination. They do not serve one master. The result is a tangle, with a result something like that of the woman who heard a series of lectures on Nazism, Freudianism, and Confucianism, and came to the conclusion that Hitler's theory of the libido was due to the influence of Confucius. Or, nearer home, like the preacher who united Marx, Freud, and Jesus in one all-comprehending muddle. Such milling around of ideas never brings people to the unifying experience of the Mount of Transfiguration, when they see no man, save Jesus only. They do not see, in shining light, the deed of God in Christ.

—COMMUNICATING THE GOSPEL

For one thing, [structure] gives to the hearers continuous clues to what it is all about. That is an eminently reasonable service. A sermon is not a species of detective story, inducing a maze of baffled speculation about whether it is this or that. It is more like a highroad well posted with legible signs indicating, "This is where we are now; the next place will be so and so." A panorama without pattern is a distraction to the mind, no matter how bright the occasional vistas. Evident structure and a consecrated devotion to clarity, which sets the preacher free from a self-regarding fear of letting the outline appear point by point, give the hearer a necessary map of the journey. Stages of movement, definitely announced, clarify the mental trip as helpfully as do the announcements of the railroad conductor when he calls out, "This station is Utica; the next stop is Syracuse." That may be stooping to a lowly service, but it does serve the traveler in a way that no eloquence alone could match.

A word frequently heard on the radio is well worth a preacher's remembrance: "There will be a brief pause for station identification." A good idea! Then the hearer knows exactly where he is on the radio map. When the preacher makes clear the point at which his sermon has arrived, he too gives a needed pause for station identification. He says in effect: "This is where we are. Let's keep that in mind, pull ourselves together, and go on to the next step."

Movement is another indispensable advantage of sharp, clear outline. Any discourse designed to win and hold human attention must have movement. The eye and the mind are so designed that they follow movement involuntarily, and the public speaker had better remember it. People's attention will follow a thing as long as it is moving; when it stops they relax, as though the plot had sagged. A young preacher in a country church, one summer Sunday when the windows and doors were open, was greatly disturbed by the rivalry of a bird flying around the sanctuary. He felt rather bitterly the trivial-mindedness of the congregation in watching the bird instead of listening to him. There was no "trivial-mindedness." The people were merely exhibiting a law of attention. The bird was moving, and perhaps the preacher's sermon was not. The sermon should move along straight lines rather than revolve in circles around the same spot. Even when one is purposely speaking on one point, there must be certain aspects of it progressively brought under the focus of the mind if one is to respect the powers and limits of attention. This is true in optics. The eye cannot remain focused on one black dot; its very nervous mobility compels it to travel to other dots in the same area. It is oriented to movement, and so is the attention of the mind.

An effective sermon is marked by progress, and progress is impossible without structure. Progress includes movement, but it is more and other than movement. It is strategic and cumulative movement toward an assigned goal. The grand old Duke of York, when he went up the hill and down again, had movement but little progress. A sermon should gather strength as it goes along, reaching a climax or a series of climaxes. That can be achieved only under a planned strategy of operation, with the successive objective to be taken well mapped. Otherwise, even when the idea is good, there will be a tendency for the sermon to run down hill after the central idea has been unfolded. Unless there is an outline that compels progress the sermon will trickle like a thin stream running down from a spring. That is the reason why one of the commonest questions in the theatrical world is, "How's your second act?" Does it gather strength and go on, or does it trickle out? A critic has made an acute comment on the later novels of H. G. Wells, that after they get a good start, they sit down like a baked apple. Sermons "sit down" too. Sometimes they sit down lumpily for as much as five or ten minutes at a time, giving the whole thing a static quality.

One critical point in any kind of outline is that at which the central idea or proposition is "broken up" into significant and relevant aspects, divisions, and relationships. Unless this is done, the sermon is liable to stop in its tracks and go into circular repetition. Or else the value of the initial idea is lost by not being carried through to practical implications. The analogy to the task of the diamond cutter is close and instructive. The skill required in splitting up a diamond by striking it at the right spot so that it will fall apart in regular fragments and not lose its value by being ground to mere chips and dust, is a very great one. Expert diamond cutters have looked at a large diamond for weeks, studying to find the place to strike the careful blow which will break it up into unmarred fragments. Needless to say, the moment of striking the blow is a tense one. So much depends on finding the natural grain of the diamond and aiming the stroke of the hammer so that it will fall into natural divisions.

The preacher, too, must split his diamond carefully. The critical point of the sermon is the breaking point, where, after clearly revealing the central idea, it is "cracked open" so that it may fall into significant divisions.

But structure and outline in sermons are not all a matter of logical sequence and order and progress in relation to a subject. There is also what might be called a psychological outline that must be kept in mind, one that takes account of the emotional rhythm of an audience. A sermon is not a chapter in a textbook, where ideas can be unfolded in a near vacuum. It is a co-operative achievement with an audience, and the audience must be kept in mind at all costs. Thus, material which is immensely valuable in getting into contact with an audience and holding that human contact may often seem a wasteful detour from the point of view of strict logic. But it justifies its place in the structure by the indispensable service it renders. Frequently very unfair and unskilled criticisms of preaching have been made by amateurs, often theological students, who have never grappled much with the difficult and mysterious task of holding an audience. Such critics often complain that the preacher was not doing very much with his subject; they do not notice that he may have been doing remarkable things with his audience, and often by the use of material at which they looked with pedantic disdain. That is one of the most evident differences between an amateur and professional speaker, in the best sense of professional. For the competent professional knows that there is not much use in holding to your subject if you lose your audience. There must be an emotional outline, so to speak, a chart of keeping in touch with the audience, as well as the orderly outline in developing the subject.

—IN THE MINISTER'S WORKSHOP

A homely story which Ralph Waldo Emerson records has permanent wisdom. With the help of his son he was trying to get a calf to go into the barn. His son was pulling from the front and the great philosopher was pushing from the rear. Nothing happened, except that the calf was singing, "I shall not be moved." An Irish servant girl, only a few weeks away from the old sod, came to the back porch and stood there laughing a moment. Then she went up to the calf, put her finger into its mouth, and gently drew it into the barn. She knew how her audience took in ideas. That calls not only for knowledge of people, but also for humility, of sacrificing the joy of issuing papal bulls in our most infallible manner, and asking humbly, How may this truth reach these particular people? Paul was doing essentially that when he sought to be all things to all men.

—COMMUNICATING THE GOSPEL

Using the Imagination

One of the most helpful of all the rules of thumb which can be given is this: Turn the ear into an eye. No rule can be universal in its application to a profession, and that one certainly is not. There are many occasions when the habit of writing and speaking in pictures is a cheap and easy escape from the discipline and duty of hard, straight thinking. A beautiful illustration is a vain thing for safety when there is need for an argument to be carried home in clear, direct words. This must be granted. Yet the rule of thumb has real wisdom for many occasions; for when the truth is put in pictures and images which make one see as well as hear, not only is the immediate impression greater, but the memory lasts longer. This is particularly true in what can be called an eye-minded generation. People in our mechanized world take in so much of all they get through the eye. The heyday of the picture magazine makes one wonder whether the next generation may not find that reading anything longer than a picture caption brings on prostration and a splitting headache. Indeed, until the advent of the radio the ear was rapidly disappearing as one of the organs of sense. Recently, also, the craze for jazz and swing has been an aid to the ear in its rivalry with the eye, aided by the amazing spread of interest in the best in music. And of course the advent of the sound-track moving picture played a timely part in saving the ear. In the days of the silent movies, multitudes became so accustomed to seeing that they became very poor listeners. Complaints that they could not hear from a pulpit or platform were common, and very often they were merely an excuse to cover a sense of hearing that was growing atrophied from disuse.

The harvest which the preacher places at the service of God and man is the fruit of a "double eye"; that is, the ability to see a thing not only clearly in itself but also in its possible relationship to something else which does not register on the physical retina. This double eye sees the object and the symbol, the object and the parallel in some other realm. In a reverent sense we can say, for example, that Jesus saw with a double eye. He considered the lilies with the physical eye, seeing them, no doubt, with an optical alertness beyond that of his disciples. But with the other eye he saw the lilies as symbols of the care of a Heavenly Father: "Be not therefore anxious." The preacher can add to the statement of Jesus, "If . . . thine eye be single, thy whole body shall be full of light," this additional word for his own guidance: If thine eye be double, thy whole message shall be full of light.

This mental and visual double life can be cultivated, without degenerating into that distressing preacher's myopic vision which sees things continuously in terms of sermons. For, verily, the preacher's mind shall not live by sermonic bread alone, but by everything that proceedeth out of the creative mind of God. Yet the alertness which can see a true analogy, a fruitful use of observation, is a beautiful instrument of service and one which can be developed.

—In the Minister's Workshop

"He left the synagogue, and entered the house."
(Mark 1:29-31.)

We do no violence to the meaning of this passage, and to many others in the gospels, when we remember Bushnell's saying that "preaching is a gift to the imagination." It is always dishonest to read into any words of the Bible what is definitely not there, as though ideas foreign to it were actually present in it. But when, dealing honestly with what is in the passage, we allow it to stimulate the imagination and conscience, as a picture and symbol of the truth extended into experience, we help it to fulfill its high function as a lamp unto our feet and a light unto our path.

—The Interpreter's Bible

The chief trouble with sermonic illustrations, which are indispensable to preaching that etches into the mind, is that they are too often falsely considered as a sort of thing apart by themselves rather than a quality of writing and thinking. They are hung on the body of the sermon as bright ornaments are hung on a Christmas tree. They did not grow there. The wire which ties them on is all too often visible. They are decorative rather than in any sense structural like an arch or a keystone. Then all too often the illustrations are treated as Pharaoh treated the Egyptian slaves—they are expected to make bricks without straw, to make sermons without coherent, consecutive thought.

—In the Minister's Workshop

Work Habits of the Preacher

Work at long range. The most helpful sermons come, as a rule, not when one is looking for "something for next Sunday" (that very strain and urgency freezes the genial currents of the mind), but when one is just reading the Bible, on the alert and mental tiptoe but giving himself up to it without regard to any particular occasion, as part of a continuing habit of life. It is one of the perversities of the human mind that you can usually do a thing better when you don't have to do it at all. Emerson recognized this perversity and made it an ally. In his journal for October 14, 1834, he wrote: "I will say at public lectures and the like, those things which I have meditated for their own sake, and not for the first time with a view to that occasion." It is not from that which is meditated for a particular occasion that the richest harvest comes. The core of the Christmas sermon that meets the occasion may come from the brooding over the Scripture that was done in May. Many ministers have found it productive to keep the study of two books of the Bible going together for a period, one in the Old Testament and one in the New—I Samuel, for instance, and the Gospel of Luke, and then when these are finished, say, Jeremiah and Romans. A good commentary is an invaluable companion for the journey, but the study should not become a critical or technical one. That can come in another part of a preacher's study. The process in mind here is rather a "double eye" reading, with one eye on the story and the ideas, whether in Egypt or Samaria or Jerusalem or Corinth, and the other on Chicago or Jersey City or Fargo—wherever one lives. One eye on 1000 B.C. or A.D. 30 and the other on the twentieth century. It is as though we were reading in double columns—as indeed we will be.

This kind of Bible reading is not a passive affair. It means plowing work. A youth once wrote in a "confessional" magazine, "My father was a farmer, but he loved nature so much he wouldn't ruin her with a plow, so we were always poor." If the preacher loves the Bible so much he won't ruin it with a plow, he, too, will always be poor, in the study, pulpit, and parish. Phyllis Bentley, the novelist, writing of fiction, describes the intensely active process of looking at a scene, which is much like the way of a preacher with a scene in scripture: "For scenic background I visit a setting perhaps a half a dozen times and simply sit and look at it, letting my mind range over its possibilities. Under the process the setting changes; it becomes something of my own." This kind of meditating, whether for novel or sermon, is as active a process as that represented in Rodin's statue "The Thinker," where the tense muscles proclaim that an activity of the whole man is going on.

Another positive value is in helping to avoid the danger of trying to arrive at an outline too soon. This is one of the commonest causes of mediocre and commonplace sermons. An outline, or general conception of a sermon, arrived at prematurely, before one has walked around the subject and seen it from various points of the compass, is nearly always a wooden outline. There are exceptions, of course; there are bound to be in a realm as unpredictable and mysterious as the mind. Men do occasionally get into that shadowland called inspiration. Sometimes there comes, with the suddenness of a revelation from outside, like a flash of lightning, a way of developing or impressing a truth that seems to have the inevitable quality of something ordained from the foundation of the world. But such occasions, even for the genius, are rare. For the large majority of preachers, counsel in the words of Habakkuk applies: "Though it [the vision] tarry, wait for it; because it will surely come"—the vision in this case being the plan or line of march of the sermon. And—make no mistake about it—it will usually tarry. So wait, not somnolently, but actively, engaged meanwhile on the rewarding process of trial and error.

The old Greek myth of the birth of Athena, springing fully armed out of the forehead of Zeus, has been an evil influence on many preachers. They expect sermons to be born that way, to leap in full panoply, with introduction, points, and conclusion, out of the mind. They forget that the miraculous birth of Athena was just mythology. Sermons are not born that way in the course of nature. They come from a long succession of slow unfoldings, of following promising leads which turn out to be mare's-nests, of grim hanging on to an elusive idea, of mental labor pangs.

Often what is found to be the most productive lead for a sermon is not the thing which is put down first, second, or third but the thing which is put down as the seventeenth possibility. The preacher looks at this idea, come lately, sitting at a lowly place at the bottom of the table and says, "Friend, go up higher." For often the last shall be first.

From time to time, as this is going on, the sermon maker will watch to see if an outline is ready to emerge. This, ordinarily, will not all come at once; it will grow. Some one proposition will demand a place irresistibly, to be followed by others. One caution, already made, is not to try to force a final form on the material until it is "ready." When the outline does appear, then it can be imposed on the material. Certain parts of it will fall into the appropriate places; other parts will be discarded. Of course, certain illustrations and considerations will already have been attached to the affirmations they support or enforce at the time when they were put down just as raw material, of possible usefulness. The process of the material's falling into shape under the influence of an outline is much like an experiment frequently made in physics classes. Metal filings are scattered on a thin metal plate. Then a violin is played near the plate, and the filings form themselves into regular and changing patterns. The outline, sometimes at least, is like the melody played on the violin. It causes the material—the facts, ideas, narratives, questions—to move, almost of themselves, under the various aspects or divisions of the theme.

The first suggestion is to wait, to delay the building by taking off time enough to engage in the process which balks at hurry, that of imaginative creation. The first task is not to manipulate anything, texts, ideas, or illustrations. It is to stop and look and if possible see, to see both the truth as it is set in life and the people whom it is designed to help. Just to sit and look and ask, What is it all about? and to feel one's way with the truth and theme into the lives of people—that is the best kind of acceleration in getting on. Then the kindling pictured in the Psalms takes place, "While I was musing the fire burned."

Unless one does that, tactics, to use a military figure of speech, displaces strategy; the means of working out an idea or theme gets a false priority over the purpose and goal of the undertaking. This pause for the effort of imaginative creation, before any details cloud up the picture, is a stage all too frequently skipped or slurred; it cannot be omitted without loss to the warm human quality of the preaching or its closeness to experience. Storm Jameson, writing of the novelist's problem, turns to the Greek myth of Proteus and says that it is the novelist's first job to "hold the beast in his hands till it turns into proper shape." That, too, is the preacher's job. It takes time, and humility, but it is the delay which makes ultimate speed possible.

A second method of proceeding which has been useful to many men is to make sure there is enough material in front of the eye and mind, so that they can act on it selectively. In practice this often reduces itself to a very simple process, and one which may seem to be distracting and even trivial. But it need not be either. This method, is, after the theme has been chosen, with some idea of its general development in mind, to put down on paper, without any worry about logical order or continuity, anything that comes to mind that has any real connection with the subject. Much of what one puts down will not be used at all. Do not fret about that. If this seems to involve a lot of lost motion, remember that the purpose is to get the mind out of neutral into an active engagement with the subject. That in itself is an accomplishment of major importance. So just let the mind run along, with what the psychologists call "free association." Put down things which you know, even as you put them down, you won't use. Even that helps to get the machinery oiled and running. The thing which is not used in the sermon as it takes shape may be a sort of mental billiard shot which sends the mind bumping into another idea which seems to belong unmistakably in the sermon. Thus the stone which the builders reject does become, by a roundabout bouncing, the head of the corner. At least, you wouldn't have found the head of the corner without the intervening step of the rejected stone.

A third suggestion in beginning work is to ask oneself certain questions, to be applied as keys to see whether they will not open doors into the meanings of the truth or theme. The provocative value of this cross examination of the theme, and of the preacher, is very great in the way in which it starts the mind on new trails. Here are a few sample questions to ask oneself in getting started:

1. What is the particular truth or statement that comes out of this Bible passage? How can it be shaped as an affirmation?

2. To what possible situation or realms of experience does it apply?

3. How can it be made vivid and easy to remember, either in (a) describing the need or situation or (b) describing the solution or cure?

4. What are some causes of the condition or situation discussed?

5. What might be some effects of the solution proposed if it were really adopted?

6. Has this solution or remedy ever really been tried or demonstrated by anyone? If so, give examples.

7. Does the sermon tie a knot in the memory?

8. What are some objections to the solution proposed, or the affirmations made; or what may be some real difficulties? This is done to be fair with an audience, or to anticipate the unvoiced queries or skepticism in an audience. In church, hearers do not heckle the speaker; hence he must do it himself on occasion if he wishes his persuasion to have the utmost carrying power. St. Paul does exactly this in the great fifteenth chapter of I Corinthians. He heckles himself, thus making a dialogue instead of a monologue: "But some man will say, How are the dead raised up? and with what body do they come?"

It would be hopelessly mechanical to think of asking all these questions, or a list of similar ones, of any theme. But the use of some of them may act as a self-starter for the mind.

The working of this ally [the "unconscious mind"] can be described in a few sentences which would have no place in a textbook of psychology but which do fit the experience of a multitude of literary workers. There are two stages. The first is to get a theme, a question, an idea to be developed, rammed down so deeply into the mind that the "unconscious" can go to work on it while the attention is otherwise engaged, probably even during sleep. From this basement workshop of the mind, with its machinery running so silently that it never intrudes, the results of the work will be "shoved up," as it were, for the conscious attention to examine, weigh, and pass upon. That may sound like a fairy tale, but it is true. The heart and lungs are not the only organs continuously active. Part of the brain works on a twenty-four-hour shift.

The second stage is to give to the unconscious mind time to take up the question and produce its results. It does not start with the trigger and is as balky as a mule if one tries to hurry it. The problem must be posed early enough to allow time for the work.

A homely and a far too simplified analogy is to be found in placing an order for a meal in a lunchroom where the kitchen is on the floor below. The order is called down the dumb-waiter shaft, and unseen hands put the order on the stove. After an interval it is sent up to the floor above. Mental creation is never that simple! But it frequently follows that pattern. A question on which a person is brooding is given sufficiently hard thinking and exploration to amount to an "order" and sent down to the unconscious for some material on it. After an interval, during which the mind's attention is given to other things (the interval may be a night, a day, a week, or much longer), something is "sent up" to the light of attention in response to the order so vigorously and effectively placed by hard preliminary thinking.

—IN THE MINISTER'S WORKSHOP

IV

Interpreter of Literature

Acknowledgement that creative literature has much to say to religion about life is widespread in the 1960's. Such recognition was not common thirty years ago. Halford Luccock's courses in literature and religion at Yale Divinity School and his books *Contemporary American Literature and Religion* and *American Mirror* brought a generation of students to understand in a new way the social function of creative literature and gave them a new appreciation of the religious use of such writing. The excerpts here are from the two books which he wrote in this field. The sections on Millay and Hemingway demonstrate the perspective and pathways by which he approached an author and the truths which he found speaking to the problems of faith. He never subordinated literature to preaching, or thought of reading as utilitarian to homiletics. His lifelong interest in literature vastly enriched his mind, opened windows for his understanding, and so served as an abiding resource for preaching.

1

The Social Function of Creative Literature

"SIR," SAID SAMUEL JOHNSON, IN ONE OF HIS BOOMING PRONOUNCEMENTS from Sinai, "a book should either help us to enjoy life or endure it." If this magisterial verdict had been widely accepted it would have shut out a large library of authentic literature. Dr. Johnson left out two of the great services of literature, that of helping us to understand life and to feel it. [Much of the writing of the thirties] records the impact of the depression . . . on millions of people. Such writing does not help anyone in the enjoyment of life; it is not designed particularly to add to the resources for enduring it. But it does help to understand and to feel. For that reason it should have a permanent historical importance.

Examining literature on a basis not purely literary, but frankly social, is not entirely unrelated to the judgment which time ultimately makes. The centuries are strewn with literary figures imposing in their day, forgotten now, forgotten because it was ultimately revealed that they did not have anything fundamental to say. Longfellow greatly outshone Herman Melville during their lifetime. A later century has completely reversed that judgment. Melville had much more to say, both to his own time and to all time.

Incidentally it may be noted that this strong concern for public speech on great questions has posed anew an old dilemma of the poet—and for the novelist and dramatist also—a dilemma which is continually evident in the writing of these years. It is the dilemma that talents which are dedicated to the specific ills of any year often do not survive the immediate situation; while on the other hand, writing in a social vacuum, which does not have any relationship to the major questions and experiences of a time, lacks depth and pertinence.

The creative literature of any period is never an accurate mirror of its life. It is bound to be full of distortions. Many important features of life are not reflected back at all. It is easy to see, for instance, that the most widely acclaimed literature of England during the generation when the industrial revolution was gathering momentum made a very inaccurate and clouded mirror of the life of the people. Much nearer, we can now see that characteristic American literature of the 1920's gave very inaccurate reflection of the gathering forces which burst into full power in the 1930's.

For one thing, the present time is too soon to make an appraisal of permanent worth, either of the experience of the decade or its literature. "Art," says Santayana, "is a delayed echo." It is too early to listen for the fullest and clearest echo of experience in art. More delay must intervene before that. Again, the most accurate and vivid movements of the seismograph recording the economic earthquake are not to be found in what is called creative literature, not in fiction, drama, or poetry. They are to be found in the reporting of the period; the factual records; the history of the milling years; the mountainous records of the debates, political, economic, and social; the prodigious federal exploits in the field of social welfare; the history of scores of movements which made up the whirlpool after the Niagara of 1929.

Yet the creative literature of the 1930's preserves many authentic portrayals of experience. And if, at the very beginning, we forswear any ambition to assess either the permanent worth of the literature or the ultimate meaning of the history, we will have much data for an understanding of the years as they seized and shaped human life in America, and the experience they brought, economic, intellectual, moral, and religious. It will be a genuine, if limited, mirror, reflecting life as no other glass can do. There is a real portrayal of the genuine service which literature can render to an understanding of a time in a device frequently used in the motion picture production of a novel. On the screen is shown a closed book. Then the cover opens and characters, endowed with life, come trooping out in procession. That is the authentic miracle of great fiction. We can truly say that in some of the literature of the depression decade the years became flesh and dwelt among us, full of truth, if not always of grace. Out from the economist's charts;

from the banker's trial balance, those grim records of trial and error; out from industrial indexes; from the tortuous jargon of legislative bills; from geologists' reports on the land itself; from the portals of the Supreme Court, and the doorways of thousands of homes, there step lives to dwell among us in our imagination and understanding. The ever-renewed wonder of fiction and drama is well expressed in a verse of the Psalms, "one shall put ten thousand to flight." That is, the story of one person, one family, one group, if the artist is able to re-enact the old miracle of Eden and breathe into their nostrils the breath of life so that they become living souls, will have a power that far exceeds the records of ten thousand cases buried in a mausoleum of statistics. We see this clearly in regard to war. No ten-volume history can compare in the power of emotional effect with the story of one man—Sergeant Grischa—or one group, as in *All Quiet on the Western Front.* So in our present period when we have spent half an hour with Clifford Odets' *Waiting for Lefty,* when we have driven from the dust bowl of Oklahoma to California with John Steinbeck and the Joad family, when we have lived on the inside of the Ford Factory with Wessel Smitter's "Russ," in *F.O.B. Detroit,* then we get the very feel of life and crawl under the skins of people.

—AMERICAN MIRROR

2

The Religious Use of Creative Literature

ORGANIZED RELIGION CAN NEGLECT THE LITERATURE OF ITS TIME ONLY AT its peril. To say that seems an utter commonplace, yet it is a tragedy which has often happened. The creative writing of any time is one of the most authentic sources of knowledge of the tempers and distempers of that time, in which religion must live and move and do whatever work of redemption it is to achieve. To neglect it is like a physician neglecting to take a patient's pulse or temperature, for literature is both.

Often we hear ministers and others cry out at the low tone of literature, seemingly oblivious that their criticism is not so much of literature, which is a symptom, as of the life of a generation, which is a cause. We repeatedly hear the question, for instance, Where have the heroes of literature gone? A pertinent question, which we shall try to face. But many forget, in asking it, that the real answer is not that authors are degenerate and perverse, but that they are voices of their time; and ours has not been a moral climate in which heroes are nourished as naturally and luxuriantly as daisies in June. Whatever we have done for democracy, we have not made a world safe for heroes. As T. S. Eliot said, in the early 1920's, "The age objects to the heroic." Whatsoever a generation soweth that shall it also reap; and a generation that soweth to the flesh shall of the flesh also reap the neurotic alcoholics who stagger through the novels of Ernest Hemingway and Theodore Dreiser.

[Any] judgment on the absence of religion from literature stands . . . only as long as we confine our definition of religion within the rigid and traditional limits of articulate belief and theology. When we refuse to accept the strict demarcation of religion into an isolated province on the map of life and think of it as an attitude and spirit which pervades the whole, a total response to life, we find much of the literature of today occupied with the examination and interpretation of those experiences which are and have been of vital concern, historically, to religion. It is merely a commonplace to observe that one of the continuing and most significant marks of fifty years in religious thought and life has been the overflowing of the artificial canal banks with which religion has been enclosed. The history has been a parallel to the Niagara river, flowing through a deeply cut gorge, against the banks of which it bounds and surges in restraint, finally making its way out into the broad expanse of Lake Ontario. Perhaps the figure of speech will hold a bit further. For waters enclosed in the Niagara gorge were not always thus narrowly confined; back of the temporarily compressed river lay the spaciousness of Lakes Erie, Huron, and Superior. Men have caught a fresh glimpse of the range of religion in the last half century, as they have reread with unbandaged eyes the charter of Christianity as proclaimed by Jesus.

A study of the literature of today ought to show three real relationships to religion. For one thing, it will disclose much of what might be called "implicit religion." The voice of the day in poetry, drama and novel includes much that expresses attitudes and spirit which mark the Christian conception of life. It will not often be labeled formal religion. Some of it may even be listed, because of one feature or another, as an irreligious or immoral influence. One looking only at the surface, or interested only in pasting labels, may easily overlook or wrongly identify it. But those who are looking for the thing itself, for the understanding of life, for the sensitiveness of injustice, for the pity and sympathy born of love and of respect for the capacities of the soul, a devotion to truth which makes men free from the blight of lies, will find this attitude and spirit an inseparable part of religion in human life. They will find much of it, often strangely stirring and beautiful, in unlikely places. It will be found in Dreiser as well as Upton Sinclair, in Eugene O'Neill as well as Carl Sandburg.

Literature is of first concern for religion also in that it shows the symptoms of a time, its need, its voids, its sore spots, its hopes, its despairs. The competent novelist of any period is an indispensable diagnostician for anyone who would seek to heal the hurt of humanity. We can learn far more of the soul of nineteenth-century England from Charles Dickens than from John Henry Newman. We can learn more, to take an extreme example, of the sickness of soul of New York City from Michael Gold's *Jews Without Money* than from all the reports of the Federation of Churches published in the last thirty years. If more religious leaders had had the wisdom to see life through the eyes of dramatists and novelists, and had not exhausted so much of their spiritual energies in denunciation, they would have felt more deeply and known more accurately the sickness they desired to heal.

In addition to these services, contemporary literature renders an indispensable ministry to religion in the challenge which it presents. It holds out to organized religion the sacrament of disturbance. It saves religion from the soporific of its own anthems. Literature acts as an open window into the sanctuary, through which the screams of life, its wails, its fighting cries, its hollow revelry, come in to mix with the "Peace, perfect peace," of the hymnbook. Its often unconscious pictures of the futility of life empty of faith come as a challenge to faith; its dramas of the bankruptcy of hope may confront and stir those who believe in divine resources in life; its aching portrayals of the oppressed may bring rebirth to those who pray to the God of Amos and of Jesus; its deep etchings of the loneliness of man without God may act as a divine recommissioning to those not wholly dead.

—CONTEMPORARY AMERICAN LITERATURE AND RELIGION

Where are the ethical and religious elements in all this varied expression? Why search for the ethical in a time when most writers carefully avoided the very appearance of ethical purpose or preoccupation? Why concern with any religious implications in a body of literature in which explicit religion as a subject or indeed as a part of the life portrayed in fiction was faint and blurred, when it is found at all?

The answer, of course, is that the ethical qualities of experience and the transcript of it are inherent in the thing itself. They do not depend on labeling. They do not depend on any consciousness of ethical purpose. There is no such thing as literature divorced from moral or religious implications. R. Ellis Roberts argues this in an extreme form, but with recognizable cogency, when he says that the nonsense of Edmund Lear and Lewis Carroll, and the simple lyrics of many nature poets, presuppose both in author and reader the profoundly ethical thesis that mere joyfulness and gaiety are right for men. If that be true there is in such portraits of the life of the Negro in the United States as are found in *Uncle Tom's Children* and the drama *Stevedore* the profoundly ethical thesis that such life is profoundly wrong for men. If we pause, in a deserved attention, reverence even, for the thing that is, pause to see what is portrayed and to listen to what honest voices of our time are saying, we will find that they are full of ethical interest, insight, and judgment, and valid religious implications. Often the very absence of religion in the life recorded and in the recorders themselves is negative testimony of the first importance to service of religion to life.

By the "real thing" in this connection we mean attitudes and cherished values which find a place in religion. The term legitimately includes evaluations of the worth of man which have an overtone of a universe of spiritual values; the spirit which cares desperately for "the least of these," and the sense of sin, though it is rarely called by that theological term, the sense of missing the mark of man's high calling; in a word, the deep dissatisfaction of the prodigal in the pigpen, even though there is no explicit declaration, "I will arise and go to my Father."

There is also to be considered as belonging in the field of religion the negative aspects, expressions of the strong sense of the tragic nature of human existence, the rejection of traditional beliefs which are felt to be inadequate, the substitution of other faiths, or hopes, or the rejection of all faith and hope.

What has not been recognized as it should be is that this body of literature of sympathy, protest, and struggle has been an unorthodox but genuine expression of [the great prophetic tradition, coming down from the eighth-century Hebrew prophets, through Jesus, including the prophetic witness of Judaism, Catholicism, and Protestantism]. One large hindrance to that recognition has been the habit of many religious people of being so shocked at vulgar language that they have failed to be shocked at the far more important things. No doubt, thousands of readers, for instance, were so shocked at the offensive expressions in the early part of *The Grapes of Wrath* that they failed completely to respond to the tremendous meaning of the book. One urgent need of Christian education is that of getting people to be shocked at the right things, the big things which are truly shocking, the violations of human dignity. The emotional reactions of Jesus have much contemporary relevance in this connection. He was shocked by different things from those which appalled the churchmen of his day. He was never bothered a bit by ceremonial impurities or any form of words; he was profoundly upset by wrongs to man, such as devouring widows' houses, over which others never blinked.

The great common religious experiences of the human race have found continued and varied portrayal. In the midst of all the changes in the world, the ancient themes of the centuries have held the attention of men and found expression in the recording of the experience of men. There is evidence of the pondering of ultimate questions concerning man's nature and destiny, his sense of insecurity, his bewilderments and doubts, the disturbing experience of conscience and the dark problem of evil.

In Eugene O'Neill, for instance, in spite of the absence of familiar theological presuppositions and vocabulary, there is a strong grappling with what are ultimately religious as well as psychological questions, the consciousness of guilt, the sure wages of sin, the visitation of the sins of the fathers on the children. O'Neill's play dealing most explicitly with orthodox Catholic Christianity as a refuge and salvation over modern man may be disappointing dramatically and inadequate in its representation of Christian experience, yet it testifies to an intensely serious interest in religion and contains many acute insights into man's spiritual struggle and quest for redemption. The common idea that the sense of sin is a belated hangover from an earlier unenlightened day finds no support in O'Neill.

—AMERICAN MIRROR

3

The Resistance of Religion to Creative Literature

Among the reasons for the church's failure to profit as it might from an appreciation of the services of realistic literature, there are six which stand out prominently. The first is the fact that the church has feared any kind of criticism. It has given grudging welcome to any observation and insight which challenged its traditional outlook on life or its official orthodox interpretation of life. There have, of course, been exceptions to this generalization in the unbroken line of prophets who, from the days of the great prophets of the eighth century B.C. down to the present, have refused to mouth the soothsaying of an official optimism complacently blind to fact. This fear of criticism is, of course, not peculiar to the church; it is one of the liabilities of institutionalism. Its operation in the ranks of organized religion has resulted in an opposition to realism in every form of literary art. It has been like the device of the mind in repressing what is unpleasant or what does not fit into its ruling and fixed ideas. There has been the additional influence which comes from the fact that the mind of traditionally religious people has been oriented to sentimentalism by the nature of much of the preaching to which they have listened. For much preaching has been sentimental in the primary sense that it has been more concerned with creating the greatest emotional effect on the audience than with discovering the real truth about the material dealt with.

A second reason is the historic devotion of both Protestantism and Catholicism, with different emphasis and degree, to Puritanism in individual moral life. This is particularly true in the whole realm of sex. A great deal of realistic fiction has forsworn allegiance to the taboo on sex; it has often presented scenes dealing with sex and comment on sex and marriage relations quite in conflict with the traditional teaching and mores of the church. The result has been that work containing what has been termed "immoral tendencies" has been either disparaged or put under as much of a ban as was possible. This, in spite of the fact that often the very novels and poems condemned were filled with passionate indictment of monstrous immoralities of another sort, both individual and social.

A third reason for the church's failure to profit from realistic literature is the wide prevalence of a standardized and false view of "spirituality." One of the greatest weaknesses of Christianity as an agency for spiritual and ethical transformation lies in the commonly accepted idea of spirituality. The farther religion has been removed from the concrete situations, choices, and issues of life, the more "spiritual" it becomes. It would be both unfair and ridiculous to imagine that this charge is of universal application. Perhaps it does not apply to the majority. But such a vague, abstract, emotional idea of the "spiritual life" does find wide enough acceptance to have made it blur seriously the ethical understanding and spiritual insight of the churches. "Spirituality" has been so predominantly associated with emotional states and personal habits, so tied up with pious devotional practices, so measured by participation in services of worship, that problems and issues of tremendous spiritual significance to millions of people have been shut out from inclusion as spiritual concerns. Membership in the Altar Guild has been often accepted as a mark of spirituality. Work against child labor and tuberculosis, or for a minimum wage, is "secular." That perversion of prophetic religion has played a large part in closing the eyes of people within the ranks of the churches to the fresh resources for understanding the world which much present-day literature has supplied.

Another reason, already suggested, is that traditional religion has been tied up with an unreal outlook on the world, turning a blind eye and a deaf ear to what is considered not uplifting. It has had a viciously unwholesome preoccupation with the wholesome. It has made the tragic mistake of reading too exclusively the contents of its own Sunday-school libraries. There is a remark by one of the characters in Norman Douglas' *South Wind*, commonly cited as the apex of cynicism: "There is so much that is wholesome in real life. Let's keep it out of our books." That is cynical. But religious leaders and church people in general would have made ethical and spiritual gain if they had kept more of the "wholesome" out of their reading. If there had been a greater capacity for clear seeing and less addiction to soothing syrup the churches would have been saved from that falsely optimistic and romantic view of life which has done so much to make religion seem and be unreal. They would have seen more of what Micah saw, what Jesus saw, of life. The church has immured herself too much in a Victorian pattern of life, or a rural pattern, and the grim facts of our present industrialism do not fit into either one. It has been said of Henry Adams that his principal difficulty with life was that he had an eighteenth-century education but had to live in the nineteenth century. Change the figures for the centuries and apply it to the church: It has had a nineteenth-century education but has had to live and work in the twentieth century. Dorothy Parker has, quite unintentionally, given an accurate picture of this inadequate grasp of the factors shaping the lives of millions of people in her poem entitled "Interior":

> Her mind lives in a quiet room,
> A narrow room, and tall,
> With pretty lamps to quench the gloom
> And mottoes on the wall.
>
> There all the things are waxen neat
> And set in decorous lines;
> And there are posies, round and sweet,
> And little, straightened vines.
>
> Her mind lives tidily, apart
> From cold and noise and pain,
> And bolts the door against her heart,
> Out wailing in the rain.

The heart of religion, in its great prophetic hours, has been "out wailing in the rain." Its divine business is not with wall mottoes but with "cold and noise and pain."

There are two other reasons for this lack of appreciation of and learning from realistic literature. One is that it demands the pain of thinking, while the literature of naïve romanticism or rosy optimism can be met with feeling and singing—or, best of all, with sleep. Sir Joshua Reynolds said truthfully: "There is scarcely any expedient to which man will not resort in order to evade and shuffle off real labor—the real labor of thinking." That is not cynicism; it is merely truth. Another reason is that organized religion has had too great a reverence for the businessman, in the roles of both autocrat and wizard. It has been too deeply involved in the established order, has given too many hostages to the status quo, to suffer gladly facts or a point of view which threaten to upset it.

—CONTEMPORARY AMERICAN LITERATURE AND RELIGION

4

A Case Study of a Poet—Edna St. Vincent Millay

EDNA ST. VINCENT MILLAY DURING THE DECADE [OF THE 1930's] HAS BEEN a dialogue between Miss Jekyll and Miss Hyde. To demand of the writers of such a time that they see life steadily and see it whole, when from lack of such an accepted body of conviction they saw life in flickers and in disjointed pieces, would be to expect the impossible. Periods of great literature make it clear that it springs more readily in a time dominated by a common outlook than in a time, such as in the 1930's, when it was lacking. The fact has a close bearing on the relations of religion to literature. Martin Turnell has well expressed it in relations to poetry: "While the medieval poet was living in a ready made world and was provided by the theologian and the philosopher with his subject matter, the modern poet having no such advantage, has tended to create a world of his own." This accounts in part for the distressingly "private language" like a telegram in code, that has made much very modern poetry so baffling to the reader.

In his poetry since 1935, MacLeish has expressed strongly a new spirit, which turns its glance outward to the present world and feels the necessity for a poet's dealing with a social system out of joint, if not actually doomed; also for the necessity of coming out of every sort of ivory tower to partake in mass action movement to right injustice and save a threatened world.

A less marked but similar movement can be seen in Edna St. Vincent Millay, in her progress from "a privateness of feeling to a world of thought"; from the egoistic preoccupations of her early work, when her candle-burning-at-both-ends seemed a cosmic conflagration to a concern for the outward world, shown in the bitterly savage "Epitaph for the Race of Man" in her *Wine from These Grapes* and the varied social observation and denunciation scattered through *Conversation at Midnight.*

Edna St. Vincent Millay's . . . work does not present the clear direction marked in the poetry of MacLeish and to a less extent in Benét. In her book published in 1939, *Huntsman, What Quarry,* she reverts in a majority of the poems to earlier moods and themes of personal emotion. Indeed, the critical reception of that book indicates the difficult position of a poet. If he follows the content and mood and form of his earlier work, some critics will sigh, "Alas, alas, mere repetition; just the mixture as before." If he turns to new fields, he gets, from some, the counsel to be himself and not make futile efforts to change. In *Wine from These Grapes,* Miss Millay has sharp and powerful expressions of the mood of rebellion and protest which so marked the years, and the quickened and enlarged interest in society and its fate. A new planet has swung into her ken, most memorably shown in the bitter "Epitaph for the Race of Man," a passionate protest against the obscene idiocy of war. The poet's concern with a disintegrating world is shown again in the group of poems, "Say that We Saw Spain Die," in *Huntsman, What Quarry,* in which the figure of a dying bull in the ring is made to serve as a symbol of the Spanish Republic, betrayed by the democracies and slaughtered by its fascist enemies. Written before the outbreak of World War II, the poem shows a grasp of the worldwide importance of the Spanish tragedy, which the years following underlined in deep red.

In *Conversation at Midnight,* Miss Millay uses new forms as well as content. Instead of the skillfully carved sonnet sequence, there is the attempted reproduction of familiar talk, employing the devices of slang, unfinished sentences, even doggerel. Typical figures representing different economic, social, and religious points of view engage in a "bull session." A stockbroker, a Franciscan priest, an agnostic painter, a Communistic poet, an advertising man, and a short-story writer are made to express characteristic clashes of opinion and denunciations. The opinions of the author do not emerge clearly; possibly there is some sympathy with many of the divergent convictions. At any rate, there are pungent diatribes against most of the ills of the time, such as the lack of leisure; the living in a bath of barbaric noise which threatens to atrophy the sense of hearing; the bane of meretricious advertisement, "daily slop," in the words of the advertising man; the hypocritical emptiness of religion and also the defense of the church by Anselmo, the priest; the futility of war; indictment of both conservatism and Communism.

Her *Conversation at Midnight* has many passages reflecting her feeling of the habit of conformity and the pressures of a mechanized, mass-production world tending to depersonalization.

[Edna St. Vincent Millay is an author] who has continually revealed an intense preoccupation with finding a substitute for a discarded religious creed. In an early poem, "The Blue Flag in the Bog," there is an aspiration, at least, toward the faith into which she had been born. The woman in the poem prays to "Father, Son and Holy Ghost" to "reach a hand and rescue me." Her cry is heard and she receives "the whole of His white robe, for a cloak against the night." There is nothing to parallel that in the later poems. Instead, the dominant themes are a despair about humanity, a preoccupation with death, and also a devotion to beauty and human love as the only substitutes she can find for a religion. She finds no guiding hand in the universe. She resents death, sees in it "unpatterned blackness without horizons," but there is neither evidence of nor desire for immortality. Beauty is the high value—"cleave henceforth to beauty." She seeks "beauty where beauty never stood." It is usually the beauty of nature which she feels and for which she has a sensitive appreciation. "O world I cannot hold thee close enough." Yet occasionally there is a recognition of abstract ideal beauty as in the much quoted sonnet, "Euclid alone hath looked on beauty bare." The other pole star is human love. Yet both fail as sources of lasting hope, faith or joy, or as a fortification against futility or despair. The years return, "like one hack following another in meaningless procession" ("The Harp Weaver"). When love is gone, "there's little use in anything as far as I can see" ("Ashes of Life").

The most bitter despair over the human race, touched with a savage contempt for its imbecility in failing to find a substitute for war, is in the savage lines of Edna St. Vincent Millay in her "Apostrophe to Man." It recalls the bitterness of Swift:

Detestable race, continue to expunge yourself, die out,
Breed faster, crowd, encroach, sing hymns, build bombing airplanes;
Make speeches, unveil statues, issue bonds, parade;

Convert again into explosives the bewildered ammonia and the distracted
cellulose;
Convert again into putrescent matter drawing flies
The hopeful bodies of the young; exhort,
Pray, pull long faces, be earnest, be all but overcome, be photographed;
Confer, perfect your formulae, commercialize
Bacteria harmful to human tissue,
Put death on the market;
Breed, crowd, encroach, expand, expunge yourself, die out,
HOMO called SAPIENS.

—AMERICAN MIRROR

A vehement protest, more direct and sharp, marks many of the poems of Edna St. Vincent Millay. Her poem written after the final decision in the Sacco-Vanzetti case is a powerful expression of restrained emotion and challenge. After a moving description of a New England homestead she concludes:

What from the splendid dead
We have inherited—
Furrows sweet to the grain, and the weed subdued—
See now the slug and the mildew plunder.
Evil does overwhelm
The larkspur and the corn;
We have seen them go under.

Let us sit here, sit still,
Here in the sitting-room until we die;
At the step of Death on the walk, rise and go;
Leaving to our children's children this beautiful doorway,
And a blighted earth to till
With a broken hoe.

Edna St. Vincent Millay has combined in an unusual manner a sensitive appreciation of beauty with both social sympathy and rebellious protest. A typical note in her verses is this:

The anguish of the world is on my tongue.
My bowl is filled to the brim with it; there
is more than I can eat.

A frequent theme in the poetry of protest is the appeal to Jesus in pointing the contrast which he makes to attitudes taken, complacence revealed, evils tolerated by individuals and organizations which bear his name. Illustrative of this is Edna St. Vincent Millay's sonnet "To Jesus on His Birthday":

For this your mother sweated in the cold,
For this you bled upon the bitter tree:
A yard of tinsel ribbon bought and sold;
A paper wreath; a day at home for me.
The merry bells ring out, the people kneel;
Up goes the man of God before the crowd;
With voice of honey and with eyes of steel
He drones your humble gospel to the proud.
Nobody listens. Less than the wind that blows
Are all your words, to us you died to save.
O Prince of Peace! O Sharon's dewy Rose!
How mute you lie within your vaulted grave!
The stone the angel rolled away with tears
Is back upon your mouth these thousand years.

—Contemporary American Literature and Religion

5

A Case Study of a Novelist—Ernest Hemingway

NATURALISM MAY ROUGHLY BE CALLED A THEORY OF FICTION WHICH AIMS to include "nothing but nature." It was inevitable that the scientific movement of the latter part of the nineteenth century, especially that reverential awe of science which elevates it to a philosophy, should reach over into the field of fiction. The term was first used by Zola in France, and its accepted meaning was largely defined by Zola's practice in fiction. Man was both the creature and victim of "nature," taking that term as the sum of physical influences affecting man. Naturalism dethrones man from his traditional seat "a little lower than the angels," and gives him a place with his relatives in the zoo. "We naturalists, we men of science," wrote Zola, "we must admit nothing occult; men are but phenomena and the conditions of phenomena."

The naturalistic canons of fiction were employed in America by Stephen Crane and Frank Norris in the 1890's. The most thoroughgoing and consistent practitioner of the twentieth century in America is Dreiser, with Sherwood Anderson, Jack London, Hemingway, Masters, Faulkner and others showing its influence.

Naturalism claims to approach life in a scientific spirit, to deal with nothing but facts, to observe from the outside. This intention has very often been violated, as frequently in Dreiser. In the analysis and description of personalities and their action there is often pressed into service a philosophy imported from cloudland, one which has no more foundation in demonstrated fact than the medieval castles suspended in pink clouds in Maxfield Parrish's pictures. Naturalism has brought the liberty of an enlarged and unexpurgated dictionary. It has made an almost religious principle of "frankness." Vital areas which had been regarded as a forbidden zone by "genteel" literature were dealt with in the endeavor to study and portray the whole personality. It was natural that, inasmuch as sex had been the most interdicted topic, it should receive a major portion of attention. This fitted in very well with the new Freudian emphasis on sex relations by many novelists, following the lead of Zola and Flaubert, preceded any wide influence of Freud.

Naturalism brought a new doctrine of determinism. John Calvin came back to earth in a new incarnation. The determinism of the twentieth century was not theological but physical. It was also, in many writers, social and economic. Man was a marionette in whom free will was a mocking delusion. This view did not ordinarily involve belief in fatalism in the sense in which it appeared, either by design or by malignant chance, in Hardy. It is rather the blind action of physical forces. A new type of determinism came also from looking at the spectacle of man helpless against the social forces of his environment or the vast impersonal processes of modern industry.

Of far-reaching moral influence has been the effect of Freud on the idea of sin. Freud says that the most bitter blow to human vanity is "the discovery by the psychoanalysts that the ego is not master in his own house." Similar expressions of determinism have led to the substitution, by many, of environmental conditions and influences for moral choices as the source of evil. The result has been the weakening of the sense of moral responsibility and the feeling of guilt. This has filtered down into the thinking of many who have never been directly influenced by the new psychology.

Literature has shown many traces of the effect of the new psychology. In the United States, Eugene O'Neill, Sherwood Anderson, William Faulkner, Ernest Hemingway, Dorothy Canfield, Ellen Glasgow, James Branch Cabell, Robinson Jeffers, and many others in varying degree show its influence.

—Contemporary American Literature and Religion

The delight of big muscles and violent action as a heritage of the war is seen most clearly in Hemingway. Here is the clinical report given by Max Eastman:

We took this young man with his sensitive genius for experience, for living all the qualities of life and finding a balance among them—and with that too obvious fear in him of proving inadequate—and we shoved him into our pit of slaughter, and told him to be courageous about killing. And we thought he would come out weeping and jittering. Well, he came out roaring for blood, shouting to the skies the joy of killing, the "religious ecstasy" of killing—and most pathetic, most pitiable, killing as a protest against death.

Where in any author before was such a parade of violence, hangings, shootings, suicides, caesarian operations with jack knives, abortions, gangrene, bullfights, prizefights, all preserved in alcohol? The style in which these epics of assault and battery were written has been the most widely imitated style of our time, giving rise to what has been called "the Joe Muscle School" of writing.

—AMERICAN MIRROR

To Ernest Hemingway has been assigned the role of the chief interpreter of the "lost generation." Few American writers of the present time have attained a greater prestige; few have been so widely imitated, at least in manner and style. It is an ideal style for a generation to some extent under the influence of a behavioristic psychology and philosophy. It deals with outward actions rather than inward states. It holds emotion under effective restraints. It is a style stripped of verbiage, almost bullet-like in its short declarative sentences. It proved popular; it was easy to imitate; hence the market was flooded with minor Hemingways. As the style is stripped of surplus words, so the characters are stripped of soul; we are told the exterior facts about them; any inner strivings of spirit are beyond the restricted gaze of the author. It is indeed a spiritual "waste land" which is pictured. The land is peopled by the tribe of the hard-boiled bullfighters, prizefighters, gunmen, prostitutes, professional soldiers, dope fiends—"the simple annals of the callous," as Lee Wilson Dodd described his volume of short stories, *Men Without Women*. His first great success, *The Sun Also Rises*, depicts a group of human derelicts in Paris, on whom the sun has set, enveloped with a cloud of postwar pessimism and aimlessness, in which alcohol inebriates but does not cheer. The success which that book attained is due partly, at least, to the manner in which is expressed the popular aversion to romanticism and sentimentality. It portrayed a paralyzing disillusion so strongly that in the words of Clifton Fadiman, "he takes a spiritual malaise and translates it into something vivid, vital, even splendid, giving to bitterness an exuberance that joy itself cannot match." It is hard to find much exuberance in Hemingway, outside of his spirited zest in extolling brute force and cruelty and aside from the love story in *A Farewell to Arms*, which owes its strength not so much to callous realism as to deeply sentimental romance. Mr. Fadiman's comment, however, does probably indicate a real source of attractiveness in Hemingway, that he has most powerfully expressed the disappointed idealism, cruelly shattered by the war and its aftermath. His strongest novel, *A Farewell to Arms*, brings to bear on the war a clarity of objective observation which makes its incidental criticism of war all the stronger.

No more penetrating comment on the moral world of Hemingway's characters has been made than that of Joseph Wood Krutch in his discussion of Hemingway and Aldous Huxley. He writes of the characters described by Huxley and Hemingway:

> In a generally devaluated world they are eagerly endeavoring to get what they can in the pursuit of satisfactions which are sufficiently instinctive to retain inevitably a modicum of animal pleasure, but they cannot transmute that single animal pleasure into anything else. They themselves frequently share the contempt with which their creator regards them, and nothing could be less seductive because nothing could be less glamorous, than the description of the debaucheries born of nothing except a sense of the emptiness of life.

Hemingway's *The Sun Also Rises* is the classic picture of "the lost generation," set in a barroom that stretches across France from the English Channel to the Pyrenees. The utter absence of any religion or idealism is accurately matched by the absolute absence of happiness or a remote reflection of it. The following satirical comment on it, written by Marion Sanders, has deep truth under its style of banter:

> It is the great moral tract of the age. It will drive all the amateur reprobates in the English speaking world to cold showers and bran muffins. Mr. Hemingway has painted the most unalluring picture of vice yet achieved, to my knowledge, by mortal pen. It is the same old orgy from start to finish. A pathetic round of drinking, cussing and immorality. Good enough for the week-ends, but a man has to have a vacation some time. No one can stand a continuous grind of monotonous gaiety forever. It's just an endless cycle of dreary dissipation. After hearing Mr. Hemingway's characters classify each other for the ninth time as good or bad drunks (practically the sole diversion of these poor drudges), you feel that they really have a nice hectic game of croquet coming to them, just to put a little color in their drab lives. They may be bad eggs, but surely God never meant the least of his creatures to be so bored.

As Mr. Krutch remarks with sharp insight concerning Ernest Hemingway and Aldous Huxley:

> To them love is at times only a sort of obscene joke. . . . But the joke is one which turns quickly bitter on the tongue, for a great and gratifying illusion has passed away, leaving the need for it still there. . . . If you start with the belief that love is the pleasure of a moment, is it really surprising that it yields only a momentary pleasure?

Hemingway's *A Farewell to Arms* is not so directly critical of war as [is the work of some other authors]. Its wide success was probably due more to the author's style, to the grip of the narrative, to its love story, and to its generous supply of sex episodes. Yet by its very restraint, its entire absence of patriotic heroics, it brings strong criticism of the official version of war. The aversion of the common soldier to the language of glory dear to the heart of the orator and employed in military citation and monument inscriptions is well illustrated in the words of the hero, Lieutenant Henry, an American who enlisted with the Italian army on the Italian-Austrian frontier, when a friend tells him, grandiloquently, "What has been done this summer cannot have been done in vain."

> I was always embarrassed by the words sacred, glorious, and sacrifice, and the expression in vain. We had heard them, sometimes standing in the rain almost out of earshot, so that only the shouted words came through, and had read them on proclamations that were slapped up by bill-posters over other proclamations, now for a long time, and I had seen nothing sacred, and the things that were glorious had no glory and the sacrifices were like the stockyards at Chicago if nothing was done with the meat except to bury it. . . .
>
> Abstract words such as glory, honor, courage, or hallow were obscene beside the concrete names of villages, the number of roads, the names of rivers, the numbers of regiments and the dates.

"The things that were glorious had no glory and the sacrifices were like the stockyards at Chicago"—these clear words of Hemingway's convey the honest report of an open eye and interpret a whole library of war fiction and poetry. They are also an index of a significant social force and an asset to any thoroughgoing religious view of the world.

—CONTEMPORARY AMERICAN LITERATURE AND RELIGION

Social upheavals have always had a bad effect on established writers. Ernest Hemingway's endeavor to deal with economic problems in *To Have and Have Not* reminds us of the words written about Byron, "When he tries to think he is a child." The new struggle gave to many literary figures, as it gave to many business pundits and economic wizards, the appearance of dust-covered antiques.

[Hemingway's] collection of short stories, *Winner Take Nothing* (1933) [are likewise unsatisfactory]. Set in the low point of the depression, they have a curiously remote and irrelevant quality. Indeed, the urgent problems of the depression have made clearer the highly specialized world of Hemingway's hard, tough characters. They seem as much an "escape" from the major issues of the time as the most romantic historical novel or woman's magazine serial. They are noticed here for the inner emptiness of the characters, the absence of normal human values of the characters. They fit, as fiction, perfectly into behavioristic psychology; they have action, but no moral absolutes or even moral values that are at all transcendent to immediate conduct. Hemingway's much imitated style is an admirable medium for the content. It is a cliché to call it clipped and stripped of verbiage. It represents a world clipped and stripped also—stripped of standard human spiritual equipment. In this sense, they are "grotesques" to the same degree that many of Caldwell's misshapen characters are. That famous style has been described as a combination of "a grunt and a hiatus." There is a notable hiatus where the soul is frequently found. He is an amazingly skilled observer; one has the feeling that if he ever looked at anything really worth describing the result would be great literature. But the game of continually observing and reporting the behavior and speech of a static world of characters much alike, hard, stupid, cruel, greedy, and lustful, is not worth the candle of the skill. The title *Winner Take Nothing* strikes the note of futility felt through the stories. The central characters do take nothing from life. They are for the most part his favorite primitives, or "simples," hardly distinguishable from morons, some of them inarticulate prizefighters. The opening story, "Fathers and Sons," revolves about a theme of not remarkable freshness, fornication; the hero of "The Mother of a Queen" is a prizefighter touched with megalomania. The humane qualities have been so depleted that a blood transfusion is necessary.

Yet one cannot overlook the fact that in a world in which the reversion to the primitive looms as the most disturbing feature, in which a dehumanized mentality with sadistic gifts runs amuck, the people whom Hemingway records are of real importance. For our present interest, however, the stories give evidence of a fact of first importance about literature and its relation to morals and religion. That relationship has been expressed forcibly, not by a professional moralist or a preacher, but by a practicing novelist and short-story writer, Margaret Culkin Banning.

> Books without any moral standards or any hope of them, especially the ones which pride themselves on such lacks, are beginning to approach the end of a blind street. They have nowhere to go. It is hard to keep on making interesting stories out of people who are only game and unafraid and headed for the rocks. The fiction readers have found this out. The writers are finding it out. Alcoholism is all right as a fictional setting for a while; but anyone, even a reader, gets tired of being with people who are tight all the time. He gets tired of being with people who keep on going to bed with each other. It stops being interesting and credible.
>
> If realistic fiction is to hold its readers today, it must have as much of a moral pattern as has sound contemporary biography. This implies an adherence to no single rule of conduct, nor to a definite set of morals. Fiction is not propaganda. But it does mean that in so far as there is effort in the world toward creation of a better society and the preservation of the spiritual quality in life, fiction must take cognizance of these things or lose its public.
>
> All this is a long way around Robin Hood's barn to say that fiction is no more devoid of moral standards than is life. And at the moment it needs heroes and heroines in the literal sense quite as much as the world does. Perhaps a few more are on the way.

—AMERICAN MIRROR

V

Expositor

Notwithstanding that all eight of Luccock's expository volumes were closely read, this section of the anthology has about it a truly random aspect. It is a sampling of what the author wrote and how he wrote it. Selections were made not according to some prefabricated scheme by which the whole gospel might be expressed, or the Bible systematically covered. The hope is that by what appears here one may understand further what the gospel meant to Halford Luccock and what disciplines he felt that it laid upon the faithful. It is further anticipated that one might see in these selections how a gifted and holy imagination opens the scriptures to shed new light and speak with greater clarity.

Eight of his twenty-seven books were of biblical exposition, including what will quite probably be his most enduring work, the exposition of the Gospel of Mark in *The Interpreter's Bible.* The editor has drawn heavily on this study of Mark seeing in it the author's finest penetration and revelation of the gospel. In this whole section of exposition, in view of the fact that excellence shows all the way from the early 1917 work on the *Parables of Jesus* to the posthumously published work on Paul written in the last months before his death in 1960, some conscious effort was made to include a greater number of pieces from early books, some of which are now out of print. Comparatively fewer pieces are gathered from the late volumes on Paul which none the less contain some of his most characteristic writing.

The amount of material included was governed altogether by consideration of balance in the book, not by considerations of excellence. The pieces here printed by no means exhaust the work of comparable quality that could have been added had space had wider limits. At this point we are most keenly aware of the nonsystematic character of Luccock's lifework. The fact that more excerpts may appear under one or another of the headings in this division is fortuitous. It does not necessarily reflect a greater concern in the author's total work. It must be said with emphasis that especially in the brief divisions concerning the church, the sacraments, prayer, and the resurrection, this is not a summary of the author's faith or theology. These are *some* of the things Luccock had to say on *some* of the occasions when he wrote of these matters.

The titles of the eleven divisions have all come from particular expositions and were not intended by the author to compartmentalize any other group of writings that have been placed with the title pieces.

1

Four Mighty Words—Expositions on the Divine Yes, the Promises of God

"For whom Christ died." *(Rom. 14:15.)*

One of the best commentaries ever made on these four mighty words was the sentence of T. R. Glover, "Four words destroyed slavery, 'For whom Christ died.'" Our hope is that the same four words will someday destroy war, someday destroy racial discrimination and segregation, someday destroy exploitation.

Paul brings here the crowning argument against allowing our selfish indulgences to injure people by the example we set. The people who might be injured are a special brand of people, the elite of the earth. *All* people are a special brand; *all* people are the elite of the earth. They are the men and women "for whom Christ died."

The truest description of the Christian doctrine of man was made in the early days of the Christian church by a deadly enemy, Celsus. His was the oldest literary attack on Christianity of which any details have survived, about A.D. 178. We know of it from Origen's reply, *Contra Celsum.* Celsus wrote, "The root of Christianity is its excessive valuation of the human soul, and the absurd idea that God takes an interest in man." Exactly! Paul never made a much better description himself! Celsus penetrated to its very heart.

It should never be forgotten that these four words are a profoundly theological affirmation. There is no power in the foggy idea that Jesus was a sympathetic person who sent his good wishes to everybody. Nor is there power to destroy evil in a general fog of sentimentality. The Christian faith roots in specific fact and specific revelation.

A few years ago an outdoor theater was opened in Cold Water Canyon in Beverly Hills, California. Over the entrance to the auditorium was to be inscribed, "Amongst our eternal hills we build a shrine, sans creed, sans dogma, inspiring all mankind."

There is a good answer to that in one word, really the only fitting word, "Fiddlesticks!" All mankind will never be inspired by an intellectual vacuum. Here is what has inspired man, "For whom Christ died."

—PREACHING VALUES IN THE EPISTLES OF PAUL

"All the promises of God find their Yes in him."
(II Cor. 1:20, R.S.V.)
"He is the divine 'Yes.'" (Phillips.)
"The divine 'yes' has at last sounded in him."
(Moffatt.)

A tremendous word—the divine yes—for a world of so many negations. It is a positive affirmation sounding like a roll of thunder amid and above the many denials of human speech, its fears, its frustrations, its betrayals. Our world is full of road blocks. It stretches out like the streets of Paris during its many turbulent revolutions. There are barricades erected across so many roads which say sternly "No!"

Yet the ancient thunder still sounds, the divine yes to all the hopes and aspirations of humanity. "All the promises of God," writes Paul, "find their Yes in him." The hopes and dreams of man find their yes in him. The lines of Phillips Brooks seem like a translation of these words of Paul:

The hopes and fears of all the years
Are met in [him] tonight.

H. M. Tomlinson has a postwar picture which culminates in what is a good name for Christ in our badly dented world. In his *Wreckage at Sunset* he muses on a passing gun wheel in a military parade, and writes: "Just for an instant we surmise that those wheels cannot be endlessly turning; a calm morning will come, with no ships blowing up, and no houses on fire. Only the silent ruins will be there, waiting for the recreative Word." The Word made flesh is for our broken world the recreative word.

Christ was born into a world sunk in negative pessimism. Like our world it had its longings as well as its depressions. Gilbert Murray wrote of it, "How earnestly the world was looking for peace at this time appears by inscriptions set up in Asia Minor and elsewhere in honor of Emperor Augustus. The nations had received the *Pax Romana*, but as a philosopher was to say before the century was out, that while Caesar may give peace on land and from piracy at sea, he cannot grant peace from sorrow and envy." A greater than Caesar was here! All the promises of God and all the deep hopes of men find their Yes in him. With Him it is always Yes.

—MORE PREACHING VALUES IN THE EPISTLES OF PAUL

"This is my beloved Son; listen to him." (Mark 9:7.)

Consider how many occasions there are when the words "This is my beloved Son; listen to him" have been and are the supreme wisdom. When a life looks out on the world in the early years, when it is choosing its goals and its way, its ambitions and aspirations, then listen to him who rejected the proffered kingdoms of this world for the larger kingdom of God. When life goes into eclipse, when darkness covers the face of the sun, in sorrow and failure and despair, then listen to him who was a man of sorrows and whose revelation of God brings the sustaining word of comfort and the enabling word of hope. When life waxes in might and gathers power or riches, when the siren voices of self-indulgence are sounding, then listen to him who can save life from going to pieces. So, too, at every turning point of human history, as the nations stand choosing between life and death, *This is my beloved Son; listen to him,* whose way of brotherhood is the only way of survival.

"Who do men say that I am?" (Mark 8:27.)

Who do you say that he is? A poetic idealist, a beautiful, sentimental figure, obsolete in our changed world? Some have said that. A picture to hang in a church, but to be kept within its walls? Some have said that.

An inspiring leader for social causes, but not the revealer of an ultimate God? That too has been said. A dear companion for the home, blessing its intimate love, but no master for business or politics? That too is said every day. Your life, your attitudes, your sense of values—who do they say that he is?

To say *Thou art the Christ* means that he is accepted for the mind, as the revelation of God and of the meaning of life. It means that he is accepted for the spirit, that his spirit of love marks our own. It means that he is accepted for the hands and feet, that we shall help him lift the burdens of men, and run the errands on which he sends us.

"Why does he eat . . . with tax collectors and sinners?" (Mark 2:16.)

The question of the Pharisees also gives a picture of the *uncontrollable Christ*. They asked the disciples, "Why can't you keep your teacher within decent limits?" He would not stay behind the sanctified fences of accepted usage and tradition. He was always leaping over them into forbidden territory. It was upsetting to their status quo, and hence unendurable.

How endlessly that scene has been repeated and how modern it all sounds! The uncontrollable Jesus has disturbed many of his professed followers in all centuries. Jesus got "out of hand" in the appeal of the early church to the Gentiles. Through the book of Acts we can hear the Judaizers snarl, "Why doesn't this Christ stay within the decent limits of Judaism?" The spirit and message of Jesus were uncontrollable in the evangelical revival in England in the eighteenth century. Many churchmen bitterly complained that he was not kept locked up in the churches, but was out in the open fields and street corners, consorting with nonrespectable sinners—miners, and the dregs of city slums. Jesus was uncontrollable in the missionary movement of the nineteenth century. Many churchmen echoed the violent words shouted at William Carey—"Sit down!" But passionate hearts and minds had taken seriously Jesus' words, "Let us go on to the next towns"—into Calcutta, Canton, Rangoon, and Tokyo. Jesus was uncontrollable when he burst the bonds of a traditionally individual, personal religion, and men saw him as a Savior of society as well as individuals. Jesus was and is and will be uncontrollable. A Savior could not be otherwise.

"The beginning of the good news about Jesus Christ." (Mark 1:1.)

We cannot grasp the meaning of that great title, "The good news about Jesus Christ," unless we loose the checkrein of our imagination a bit and see some of the pictures that unroll.

It was good news when it was first proclaimed. It moved up and down the country roads of Galilee and the city streets of Jerusalem, and men and women were made whole. Jesus said, "Follow me," and men gladly followed him, their life deepened with new faith and enlarged with new purpose.

It was good news as it went out to the hard Roman world in the first century. Down into the ghettos and slums of Greek and Roman cities, where life was bound with every conceivable chain, the good news came with a proclamation that lifted men to their feet. "Beloved, now are we the sons of God." (I John 3:2.)

It has been good news down through the centuries, out through all the nooks and corners of the globe, until it reaches the last outpost on earth. There is great meaning in the old childhood jingle:

Matthew, Mark, Luke, and John,
Bless the bed that I lie on.

The Gospel of Mark—and the others—has blessed the bed that humanity has lain on—beds of pain, of sorrow, of despair. It has come into every human situation and blessed it. It is good news when life unfolds and looks up with aspiration, good news when life meets sorrow, when life goes to smash, still the best of good news when life comes to an end. It is good news in the common life men live together, when groups clash. To a life torn apart by human greed and human passion, *it is the good news of him in whom "all things hold together."* (Col. 1:17.)

—Exposition of Mark in THE INTERPRETER'S BIBLE

"Bethesda . . . where a crowd of invalids used to lie, waiting for the water to bubble." (John 5:3, Moffatt.)

Here were a group of invalids depending for their cure on some external commotion. They put all their trust in "bubbles."

Society is very much like a boiling spring. It has its periodic fashions and crazes. A new word, a new interest, leaps into prominence; the surface of the pool of life is disturbed; it bubbles. And a church, in a mood of invalidism, sees the new upheaval, and says, "Lo, here! This is the thing which will put me on my feet. I can jump into the center of these bubbles and grow strong again!"

The man at the pool was saved not by the coming of an external disturbance but by the advent of a Person. It is the advent of Jesus Christ into the midst of our life which is the one hope of salvation. By faith are we saved—faith in the meaning of that fine definition of it given by Dr. DuBose—"the setting of our entire selves Godward."

The kingdom of heaven cometh not with observation of bubbles.
—PREACHING VALUES IN NEW TRANSLATIONS OF THE NEW TESTAMENT

"A wise man's words are like goads, and his collected sayings are like nails driven home; they put the mind of one man into many a life." (Eccl. 12:11, Moffatt.)

D. H. Lawrence, in a postscript to a letter to Katherine Mansfield, wrote, "Don't worry, Kate; Jesus is a back number." Leaving aside entirely the matter of what particular cheer that announcement might bring to a young woman dying of tuberculosis, we cannot help but wonder that Lawrence or anyone should call Jesus a back number in a day like this. Jesus a back number in a world that has gone down into the valley of the shadow of death through disbelief in his reading of life? Jesus a back number in a world in which hunger and bankruptcy are daily writing a dark underscoring to Jesus' teaching that men rise and fall together, that they are tied in a living tether? Rather the truth lies with him who observed that Jesus was the only man who came out of the war with an enhanced reputation. The one hope of salvation for the world is to put his mind into many a life.

—Preaching Values in the Old Testament in the Modern Translations

"You killed the pioneer of Life." (Acts 3:15, Moffatt.)

A pioneer is one who enlarges the possible area of life, one who pushes back horizons and blazes the trail into new habitations for humanity. The word catches many of the essential and unique meanings of Jesus for the world. He, above all others, was the great enlarger of life; the one who pushed back the horizons of men's minds, sympathies, and lives; the trail-breaker to new heights.

Jesus pioneered a new and living way into the heart of the Father. He threw open a new home to the race—in the very heart of God himself.

Jesus opened up a new quality of life; he led men into new regions of power.

Jesus crossed old frontiers. The ancient barriers of race and clan and color and class, with all their fearful taboos, with their high walls of exclusion, had no meaning for him.

This conception of Jesus as the pioneer of life saves Christianity from being merely a refuge. Christianity is an achievement, a venture, a discovery. Its motto cannot be "Safety first." It must pioneer.

—Preaching Values in New Translations of the New Testament

"Killed the Prince of Life." (Acts 3:15.)

How subtly and unconsciously it can be done—killing the Prince of life! "Guide of life," Weymouth translates the phrase, bringing into view a supreme service of Jesus to human life. It is so easy to put the guide of life to death, to give Jesus, as a shaping, directing influence in life, a premature but effective burial.

We can do it by burying him absentmindedly, under a clutter of interests, all of which are given the precedence accorded to "must" legislation by a legislative assembly with a crowded schedule.

We can frame him as a religious picture in the hallway of our lives, a beautiful, gracious decoration, but rarely noticed.

We can make him a constitutional monarch, smothering him with all the trappings of royalty, but denying him all real power, until he becomes as futile a figure as King Victor Immanuel of Italy at the present time.

We can bind him into a book of history. In the British Museum there is stored away a phonograph record of a speech broadcast to the British empire by King George V on Christmas day, 1933. The record has been specially prepared so that it will be usable five thousand years hence. Meanwhile it is interred in a museum. So have the speeches of Jesus been laid away by many in a vault of history.

The Prince of life—is he alive in our world?

—THE ACTS OF THE APOSTLES IN PRESENT-DAY PREACHING. VOL. I

"Your outlook is not God's, but man's." (Matt. 16:23, Moffatt.)

Any outlook has four dimensions, depth, height, length, and breadth. And those dimensions may be clues to the inexhaustible meaning of these words—God's outlook.

Jesus revealed a new *depth* to life. He plumbed beneath all outward observances to the heart; beneath all outward acts to the motive.

Jesus' revelation of God puts new *height* into man's outlook. Without God we have a worm's-eye view of the world.

The inclusive love of Jesus gives a new *breadth* to our vision and concern. We are so adept at building fences which shut out other races, nations, classes. On his release from a long prison term, a prisoner looked out across a valley and remarked, "I haven't looked more than two hundred yards in front of me in twenty years." Many men are prisoners in a self-made jail. They have erected walls of exclusion about their minds. Jesus had no use for fences.

Length to our thinking is a mark of God's outlook. "God does not pay every Saturday night." We chop time into convenient blocks, of sevens, thirties, and three sixty-fives. The middle of next week is the usual outpost of our thinking. With God's outlook the present moment partakes of eternity.

—PREACHING VALUES IN NEW TRANSLATIONS OF THE NEW TESTAMENT

"Friends should be kind to a despairing man, or he will give up faith in the Almighty." (Job 6:14, Moffatt.)

Here comes across the hills from yesterday a word whose timelessness and importance for today can scarcely be exaggerated. Indeed, it is to be questioned whether any message could have more urgent significance for the future of Christian faith. For here, flung out from the midst of intense experience, like a spark struck from flint, is the insight, perhaps stated clearly for the first time in history, that the supreme difficulties of believing in a good God are not intellectual but moral. The inevitable result, Job says, of unkind treatment at the hands of men, is decay of faith in a kind God. . . . Put into the language of our time, this truth of Job amounts to this: The most profoundly constructive theological work of our day will not be in the strictly theological field at all. It is social. It will not be in the reshaping of an argument but the reshaping of a world.

—PREACHING VALUES IN THE OLD TESTAMENT IN THE MODERN TRANSLATIONS

"Do you not know that the saints will judge the world?" (I Cor. 6:2.)

"Don't you know that Christians will one day judge the world?" (Phillips.)

Our first response to this question is, "How fantastic!" We are liable to go on from there and add, "How idiotic!" We look about the earth and back through history and do not see saints on any throne of power.

Paul says "the saints will judge the world." The saints have passed judgment on the world, they have sat on judges' benches. Judges' benches have turned into thrones of power. To say this is not to make an excursion into idealism, into what *ought* to be, but to examine history, to see what *has been.*

Keep the New Testament conception of a saint in mind.

The saints were not an elite corps. They were those who made up the Christian fellowship. They were "separated people" who had come from the world around them into a "special allegiance" to Christ. There is a real and permanent meaning in that the saint is separated from the dominant forces which rule so many, separated from the frenzy of accumulation, from the dominance of the senses, separated from the eat-drink-and-be-merry which rule so many.

The saints, in that primary sense, do judge the world. They have judged it. Their lives and minds have given a standard for the judgment of the world. The saints have preserved the moral and spiritual standards by which the world is judged. In time, in many things, the world has acknowledged the judgment. The saints judged the Roman world in the custom of exposing unwanted babies so that they died. It was a common custom. They were only nuisances, girl babies, no market value. The saints judged that world and rendered the verdict that such girl babies were not nuisances but daughters of Almighty God. So it was with the carnival of murder, the gladiatorial games in the Coliseum. To the outward eye, it was the Roman Empire judging the games. To the eye of history, and of God, it was the saints judging the barbaric games themselves.

The saints judged the world in the matter of human slavery. It is hard to realize how deadly the grip of the slave trade on England in the eighteenth century. It was as though the slave trade were a giant octopus which swam up the Mersey River to Liverpool and extended its slimy tentacles until it had in its grip the bank, the business houses, even some of the churches. Then the saints, among whom were Wilberforce and Clarkson, judged the world of the slave trade and obliterated it.

The saints brought into clear visibility the standards of God. The true picture of the judgment throne is the parable of the last judgment in Matt. 25: "When the Son of man comes in his glory, and all the angels with him, then he will sit on his glorious throne. Before him will be gathered all nations." Picture? Yes. But the great reality of history. For a central theme of history is the progressive working out of Christ's judgment of the world. The world has been judged by One who walked over only an infinitesimal small fraction of it.

—PREACHING VALUES IN THE EPISTLES OF PAUL

The Eternal is my . . . retreat. (Ps. 18:2, Moffatt.)

A religion which gives comfort without rebuke, satisfaction without repentance, is the most immoral thing in the world.

—PREACHING VALUES IN THE OLD TESTAMENT IN THE MODERN TRANSLATIONS

But the court of the last judgment is a bankruptcy court so far as earthly wealth is concerned. What value would a complete command of the French language be to us if the examination we had to stand were on mathematics? Just as much value as learning, wealth, power, with or without religious connections, will be when God will judge us on the basis of something entirely different, our attitude toward men and the reality of our neighborliness.

—STUDIES IN THE PARABLES OF JESUS

"And they crucified him." (Mark 15:24.)

The stark simplicity of these four words is impressive. It is an unadorned statement of what happened. And it has tremendous power.

But the Crucifixion is not only a fact. It has come to be seen as the central, pivotal fact of history. Those who have looked most deeply at it have found it a window into the truth behind it. We are familiar with events which have served as windows. According to the traditional story, Galileo took a long and deep look at a swinging chandelier in a cathedral and saw behind it the truth about the heavens, the movement of the earth. According to tradition, Newton took a long and deep look at an apple falling from a tree and saw behind it the truth of gravitation. So those who have taken a long and deep look at Calvary have seen behind it the truth about God and man.

The Crucifixion is a revelation of God. On Calvary there was more than the martyrdom of a good man, earth's best man. There was more than the inspiration of a great example. The Cross is a window through which we can see the truth behind it—"God was in Christ reconciling the world to himself." (II Cor. 5:19.)

The Cross is a judgment on sin. In the fierce light which beats on that hilltop we see what sin is and does.

The Cross is a way of life. "Take up the cross, and follow me." The love of Christ here supremely revealed, constrains us to a life of love, of sacrificial dedication to God's will.

"And with him they crucified two robbers." (Mark 15:27.)

The criminals to be executed were handled in lots. Jesus was crucified with those whose time had come. Beyond that routine procedure there is an unintended but true symbolism. He who was called "the friend of sinners" died with them, one on each side. He who came to seek and to save those who were lost is found among them at the very end. In the early days of his ministry the question was asked in bitter rebuke, "Why does he eat and drink with . . . sinners? (2:16.) Here, as he breathes his last, he is still in their company.

This silhouette of the three crosses on Calvary should constantly remind us that the Seeker and Savior of men belongs among those who need to be saved. From first to last Jesus was "at home" with those who needed the good news of the kingdom. He was "at home" nowhere else. One clear word comes to the church from a cross with "robbers" on each side: "In all your thinking and acting keep in the midst of those Christ came to save."

"And he saw that they were distressed in rowing." (Mark 6:48.)

There is true eloquence in those words *he came.* There is true history in them too. Into unnumbered lives, distressed with hard toil, beset with heavy winds, and engulfed with mounting waves, he has come. That is history. He has come with empowering assurance of God's care. Into the home of grief, of discouragement, of failure, of anguish, he has come. And, as here on the Sea of Galilee, he has come in the darkest peril. This verb "to come" has present and future tenses as well as past. Jesus "came" to the disciples in distress. He "came" to many others in desperate hours. But there is also a glorious present tense, "he comes." And a glorious future tense, "he will come."

—Exposition of Mark in THE INTERPRETER'S BIBLE

2

Living by Imperatives—Expositions on the Imperatives of Prophetic Faith and Mission

We must obey God rather than men. (Acts 5: 29.)

THE WORD "MUST" FREQUENTLY HAS THE CLANK OF A BALL AND CHAIN about it. We do not instinctively like it. We can all have a good deal of understanding of Queen Victoria's feelings when she snapped at Gladstone, who had told her she must put her signature to a document in front of her: "Do not use the word must to me."

Yet there is no rattle of fetters to the word as Peter and other disciples used it to the high priest. It did not have the drag of chains; it had the lift of wings. It is the word of men whose lives had an undebatable compulsion. They traveled a rough road, which wound through riots and jails. But along it they marched to the music of a great imperative. . . .

It is a great way of living—living by imperatives.

Where does human life find its authentic imperatives? Three suggestions may be worth exploring.

Let us put our imperatives in front of us rather than behind. It is a red-letter day for anyone when he stops being pushed from behind and starts to be pulled from in front, when the most powerful imperative is not the crowding necessities that tread on his heels, but something he wishes to overtake, something he aspires to.

Let us put our imperatives at the place where Jesus meets our nature.

Let us put our imperatives at the place where Jesus cuts across our world, where his way of life stands in stark opposition to dominant codes of action.

"You shall love your neighbor as yourself."
(Mark 12:9)

The parable of the good Samaritan, the man who overstepped all existing borders to do concrete, costly acts of love, makes clear that love of neighbor has no barriers. When we take the command as an absolute, there emerges into fuller view a necessity we have met before: We have to love our neighbor, as well as God, with the mind! We must bring the best thought we can summon and the fullest knowledge we can acquire to the task of determining what specific actions and policies promise best to be the embodiment of intelligent goodwill to men. So the words become like the little tent in the Oriental fairy tale, made of material so delicate that it could be folded up and contained in the palm of a man's hand; yet when it was unrolled, it would afford shelter for an army of thousands of men. This little "tent"—love your neighbor—small enough to apply to the family next door, when "unrolled" by a consecrated imagination, covers the earth. It involves the patient exploration of what the largest, lasting good would be to all "neighbors" with whom we are tied in the big bundle of life, to the laborers who maintain the fabric of the world, to all groups of race and nationality. It goes into questions of penology, of the social safeguarding of health, of international policies. And after that dedicated thinking comes the dedicated giving of the whole self.

—Exposition of Mark in THE INTERPRETER'S BIBLE

"Futility of futilities, all is futility. (Eccl. 1:1, American.)

"A vain, futile affair." (Moffatt.)

When we lay this futilitarianism in literature and life down beside the New Testament, we quickly discover some sources of this mood. The sense of futility always crowds in to fill a spiritual vacuum. Life becomes a futile thing when it lacks a faith in the high meaning of its *origin.* It becomes a futile thing when it lacks a faith in the high meaning of its *goal.*

"Beloved, now are we the sons of God"—such a sense of our origin and status redeems life from blankness, from a random quality. "Knowing . . . that he was come from God"—with these words the Gospel of John prefaces its description of the highest achievement of Jesus' life.

> *"At the door of the gateway, I saw twenty-five men, among whom I noticed Jaazaniah the son of Azzur and Pelatiah the son of Benaiah, the popular leaders! 'Son of man,' he said to me, 'these are the men who make wicked plans and offer evil counsel in this city; they argue, "Houses have been recently rebuilding; all is well! The city is a cauldron, and we are the flesh, safe inside it!" So prophesy against them, prophesy, O son of man.'" (Ezek. 11:1-5, Moffatt.)*

The modern sound of these words almost takes our breath away: "Houses have been recently rebuilding; all is well." They sound exactly like a front-page newspaper interview with some Pooh-Bah of the financial world just printed this morning. "I predict," says the sage, "a swift upturn. New houses and office buildings are going up. Everything is fundamentally sound."

Ezekiel had a quaint idea that the permanent prosperity of Jerusalem depended on its moral foundations. He rejected the popular real-estate religion. He predicted a collapse of all flimsy prosperity which rested on a basis of new houses, but which had no place for eternal laws of the Eternal. He looked at the waste of human life piled up in the streets and heard the voice of God saying, "Prophesy against them, prophesy, O son of man."

—PREACHING VALUES IN THE OLD TESTAMENT IN THE MODERN TRANSLATIONS

> *"Now this man obtained a field with the reward of his iniquity." (Acts 1:18.)*

These words present a sharp etching of at least a part of the tragedy of Judas. A villain in the plot was real estate. Judas paid for a solid piece of ground with thirty pieces of silver—and his soul. . . .

The exaltation of real estate results in a subtle distortion of values, whereby whatever is not real estate becomes "unreal" estate. That way of thinking takes hold of the spirit and brings death to it. . . .

"As real estate increases to dominate the mind and soul, the quest for spiritual and social values declines." Walter Weyel in his book *Tired Radicals* puts into contemporary terms the working of this law. He writes with irony of those among us who "marry pleasant wives, beget interesting children, and begin to build homes in the country," and retire disastrously from all real participation in the human struggle for a fairer future. . . .

Look also at the reverse of the process which went on in Judas as it is found in Acts 4:36: "And Barnabas . . . having a field, sold it, and brought the money and laid it at the apostles' feet."

Barnabas took the proceeds of real estate and invested them in unreal estate.

—THE ACTS OF THE APOSTLES IN PRESENT-DAY PREACHING. VOL. I

"They bound Jesus and led him away and delivered him to Pilate." (Mark 15:1.)

A sorry parade: The religious authorities turning over to the political power an issue which was primarily religious and was their own responsibility. Jesus has been sent to Pilate far too many time. Take, for instance, the big question of the training of the nation's children in religion and morals. Far too lightly Christian churches have turned the matter over to the state.

Questions in which Christianity has a great concern have been limply handed over to political and economic powers with an evasive apology: "This is a complex matter. You take it, Pilate." Whatever is God's affair, the welfare of men, women, and children, is the responsibility of the Christian church, and no church may sidestep it.

—Exposition of Mark in THE INTERPRETER'S BIBLE

"His habit at this time was to teach in the Temple by day, but to go out and spend the night on the Mount called the Oliveyard." (Luke 21:37, Weymouth.)

For the last week of his life Jesus was a commuter. In this physical aspect of his life he followed exactly the habits of that great, thronging modern tribe of suburbanites who flock into the city to work in the morning and at five or six in the evening go out again to the little village on the outskirts of the city.

If we look closely at the life of Jesus during these days and nights we find more than a physical resemblance to the motions of the modern suburbanite. His life has, in those last five days, a peculiar message to those who go back and forth.

The great danger of the commuter is that he may avoid responsibilities at both ends of his trip. The railway train may be used—unconsciously at times—as a way of escape from burdens and responsibilities, both in the city and at home. Jesus bore the burdens and responsibilities at both places.

The tasks of the Kingdom remain undone for the lack of energy that is lost somewhere on the road between the two points. Many a suburbanite is truly "a lost soul" as far as any genuine participation in the causes of human welfare are concerned, outside of his own business affairs.

The road between Jerusalem and the Mount of Olives was not a road of evasion for Jesus. He gave himself supremely in both places.

After the great earthquake of a few years ago in Tokyo no one was admitted into the city unless he came bearing rice and a candle; in other words, food and light. There was no room for merely another person to be carried. That same passport ought to be ours whether we come into the bustling city or the quiet countryside—food and light—strength and sympathy, skill, brought and shared.

"They put on Him a general's short crimson cloak." (Matt. 27:28, Weymouth, first edition.)

These words are symbolic of much that has happened in Christian history. In those tragic hours immediately preceding the crucifixion there were many cruel indignities heaped upon Jesus. But one of the crowning indignities was dressing him up in the cloak of a Roman general. What a piece of irony it was, to dress the Prince of Peace in the trappings of a war lord! But the same indignity has been often forced upon Jesus by his friends and adherents, and that wrong is still being done him.

—PREACHING VALUES IN NEW TRANSLATIONS OF THE NEW TESTAMENT

"They entered together into the synagogue of the Jews." (Acts 14:1.)

There is saving grace in a message that disturbs. Any new creation, in nature or in art, involves disturbance. No disturbance, no new life. Physical birth is a deep and dangerous disturbance. Jesus was the greatest disturber of history; he set a son against his father, a daughter against her mother.

A good test of our teaching and living is, Does it disturb anyone or anything? Not superficially but deeply. We are too intent on cheerful messages. When a man is dangerously sick, he needs not a cheering message but a saving one. And the saving message may be both mentally and physically disturbing—an operation. Dallas Lore Sharp gave utterance to a common fallacy in his advice to writers, "The world is sad enough. If you cannot say something to help or cheer it on its way, keep still." That advice makes an utterly false identification of help and cheer. The thing that may ultimately help may be, and often is, not immediately cheering at all.

The disturbance that saves a too quiescent and complacent world is sharply concrete. What is vague lacks upsetting force.

When someone asked Albert Einstein how he discovered the theory of relativity he answered, "I challenged an axiom." Thus it is that new revelations and discoveries, a new society, are brought about. Our calling is to challenge in the name of Christ the axioms of an unchristian society.

"*Let us go* somewhere else." *(Mark 1:38, Moffatt.)*

At the very outset of the ministry of Jesus, as recorded by Mark, he evades two deadly dangers which have beset his cause ever since: He refuses to become *localized;* he refuses to become *institutionalized.* The future of Christ's church depends to a large degree on the measure to which the paralysis of those same two calamities can be avoided.

It was natural that the townspeople of Capernaum should say, "Stay here!" Jesus' healing had been a blessing to the town. His presence would become a permanent asset. He was among friends. What would be better than just to stay? To Jesus there was one thing better—the road to the world. He came not to be a town doctor but a world's Redeemer.

Threatened, for the moment, by loving but mistaken hands which would have imprisoned him in a local provincialism, Jesus said, "Let's go somewhere else." In those words and in that spirit there was the universal destiny of Christianity, its unresting outthrust into all the world. It broke through the bounds of Judaism, broke out of the wider bonds of the Roman Empire, burst the bonds of Europe, across the Pacific. Christianity has lived because as each new frontier came into view, men with a spirit akin to their Master's have cried, "Let's go!" Always that preservation of Christianity as a world force has been won only by overcoming the seductive voices, which demanded, as on the first day at Capernaum, "Let's *stay*."

Jesus' departure from Capernaum, on the road that led eventually to Jerusalem, Calvary, and all the world, was a refusal to become *institutionalized*. The Prophet, the Teacher, the Redeemer, would have been transformed into a kind of impersonal clinic, a hospital and dispensary. Another institution, a blessed one of course, but still an institution, in the town's life. Whenever Christianity has been expressed in a statement of doctrine, in a form of organization, and men say in satisfaction, "That just fits. Let's keep it this way forever," the institution begins to set like a plaster cast, throttling the spirit within. It is inevitably so. The Christian gospel is *yeast*, not concrete. It should ferment, upheave, grow, not solidify. The hope of the Kingdom depends on the persistence of the Spirit of Jesus, "Let's go somewhere else."

—PREACHING VALUES IN NEW TRANSLATIONS OF THE NEW TESTAMENT

"But the Chief Priests stirred up the crowd
to have him release for them Barabbas instead."
(Mark 15:11.)

Barabbas is a figure terribly alive in our world today, in his personality, what he stood for, and the choices he compels. There was much in Barabbas to win the vote over Jesus in the courtyard of Pilate. There is much in those who resemble him now to win the voice of the crowd.

For one thing, Barabbas was a nationalist. He had a commonsense slogan, "Judea for the Judeans." It was a stirring emotional appeal that warmed the blood. He had been in an insurrection against the hated Romans. To many his intense patriotism had far greater drawing power than Jesus had, with all that talk about loving one's enemies.

Again, Barabbas was a man of violence. There was no "sentimental nonsense" about him. Life was clean cut and straightforward. "Get a club." You need not use your brains. Use muscle. Compare that to what Jesus had said: "Blessed are the peacemakers." Could there be any question who was the practical man of affairs, the realist?

Barabbas regarded evils as external. Such simplicity is always attractive. Drive out the Romans and all will be well. This Jesus, who went so much deeper and called for repentance, was altogether too complex and difficult.

Is it not clear that Barabbas, the nationalist, the man of violence, the one who sees evil as external, as something in the other fellow, is a powerful figure in our world? To those who do not think, the program of violence, the reliance on arms, the emotional hysteria of nationalism, is beautifully simple, when you stand it over against the repentance demanded by Jesus, the long, slow processes of peacemaking, the faith in love and brotherhood. Across the years Pilate's question still sounds in the ears of each of us—"Which do you choose—Barabbas or Jesus?"

—Exposition of Mark in THE INTERPRETER'S BIBLE

"If you salute only your near relatives, what praise is due to you?" (Matt. 5:47, Weymouth.)

That's our long suit—saluting our near or fancied relatives. To those within the sacred circle, gathered round the same totem pole of race or nation or class privilege and profit, we are adept at saluting. We "snap into" attention, the heels click smartly, and the hand goes briskly up and down.

Frequently our salutes are confined to one subdivision of our own little tribe, with some such deforming result as that pictured in the creed of the Pendyce family, given in Galsworthy's novel, *The Country House:*

I believe in my father and his father and his father's father, the makers and keepers of my estate, and I believe in myself and my son and my son's son. And I believe that we have made the country, and shall keep the country what it is. And I believe in the Public Schools, and especially the Public School that I was at. And I believe in my social equals and the country house, and in things as they are, for ever and ever. Amen.

Yet that pathetic credo would serve for millions of people.

Bigger and Better Salutes are Needed:

1. *The Salute Across Race Divisions.* The form of this salute is with the uplifted hand. It is the hand lifted up to one Father and stretched out in the grasp of brotherhood.

2. *The International Salute.* Nations are learning better salutes. The world cannot go on if nations are to form merely a mutual irritation society. But the salute of good will and trust across national boundary lines demands the overpowering of self-centered, egoistic, aggressive nationalism. The signs found on buses in large cities should be posted conspicuously in the world's parliaments, "Courtesy will prevent accident."

3. *The Religious Salute.* Across the lines of different religions must come the recognition of the common pilgrimage of all men in search of the one God.

4. *The Salute Across the Picket Fences of Caste and Class.*

—PREACHING VALUES IN NEW TRANSLATIONS OF THE NEW TESTAMENT

3

Hopes and Chains—
Expositions on the Marks of the Christian Life

"Because of the hope of Israel I am bound with this chain." (Acts 28:20.)

REAL HOPES ALWAYS HAVE CHAINS ATTACHED TO THEM. HOPES ARE WINGS, we are told. We have all seen great hopes act as wings to life, giving lift and buoyancy to hard days and long years. All true. Yet a cherished hope binds one as by a chain to obligations implicit in the hope itself.

It was in that deep sense that Paul had hope of Israel. Because that hope in the God of Israel, revealed in Jesus Christ, sang within him, he willingly wore chains. The iron chains on his body were only the symbols of a deeper and stronger chain. He was the slave of Jesus Christ. "The love of God constraineth me," he wrote. Because of his hope for men, for Israel, for the world, he bound his life under great obligations, as the servant of all.

Do we hope deeply enough to wear gladly the chains which inevitably accompany great hopes? We hope for peace. Do we wear the chains of that hope? For it has chains to be worn; chains that will bind us to a just way of life, so far as we can lead a just life in an unjust society; chains that will bind us in a fellowship of struggle with the exploited and defrauded; chains that may well bring us contempt, hatred, perhaps martyrdom.

We hope for the coming of the day when the knowledge of the Lord shall cover the earth like the waters of the sea. Are we bound in the chains of that hope? Do we put our lives under the obligations, the ardors and endurances, which that earnest expectation lays upon all who hold it?

—THE ACTS OF THE APOSTLES IN PRESENT-DAY PREACHING. VOL. II

"Then they will see the Son of Man coming in the clouds." (Mark 13:24-30.)

Contrast the faith that God will act redeemingly in human history with the characteristic "messianic" hope of the twentieth century—modern man's secular apocalypse. He looks for a world of wonders which science and industry will provide. He has exchanged his august faith in God's coming action for a faith in the kind of plastic heaven that comes out of a factory. We are kept in a state of nervous excitement with prophecies of the world of tomorrow, a paradise of chromium and ceramics, of helicopters and television, of egg-shaped automobiles and layer cake houses, of skyscrapers made of glass and clothing made of soy beans! What a trade! Heaven for earth, God for gadgets, the coming of Christ in the life of the world for the coming of a salesman's paradise! Such a degenerate "messianic" hope can serve only to emphasize what need we have to hold fast the essence of the N.T. epectancy, a confident faith that the God who has acted in the coming of Christ is acting still, and will act at and until the end of time!

"Take heart, it is I; have no fear." (Mark 6:50.)

In every great crisis of history, when everyone who hopes for a world preserved from destruction is *distressed in rowing* against head winds, the sense of God at the center of the universe is a deep necessity. The great issue is that of irrational hope against rational despair. Not fantastic hope, nor, in the common meaning of the word, romantic hope, but irrational hope, hope that comes from other sources than reason. Rational despair is a mood that besets and grips millions. But irrational hope is based on something that is not the creation of logical reason. It looks to God as the unpredictable and ultimate, though often forgotten, factor in human affairs. There is no more urgent task for the church than to open the hearts and minds of despairing men to a Voice which says, *Take heart, it is I.*

—Exposition of Mark in THE INTERPRETER'S BIBLE

"Look to him, and you shall beam with joy." *(Ps. 34:5, Moffatt.)*

"Look at me and so be jubilant." (American.)

One of the most noted of all the verbal mistakes attributed to Doctor Spooner of Oxford, and which came to be known as "Spoonerisms," was his use of the words "the tearful chidings of the gospel," when he meant to say "the cheerful tidings of the gospel."

The pulpit has often made that same miserable substitution. "Tearful chidings" are a poor substitute for cheerful tidings of great joy.

—PREACHING VALUES IN THE OLD TESTAMENT IN THE MODERN TRANSLATIONS

"Never mind." (I Cor. 7:21.)

"Don't let that worry you." (Phillips.)

Paul gives here a fine study of measurement, trying to save people from mistaken magnitudes.

It is a great phrase, "Never mind." Do not let the great goal of life be missed by making other things first. Carry this idea of relative magnitudes into other realms of life. Notice that there is a *right* way of using the words, and there is a *wrong* way of using them.

There is a bad sense of the words "Never mind." Some people use it of religion. To them it is not important; it is mainly a matter of words, and they are not important. So they say, "Never mind." They are just as wise as the woman on a ship which had had its rudder broken off in a high sea. She consoled the captain by saying, "Never mind. It was down where nobody could see it. It won't make any difference." To throw over religion makes just as much sense. In both cases, the rudder and religion, it is what steers the ship.

People diminish the great moral and spiritual realities, the mountains of personal life into inconsequential trifles. In the presence of life's highest concerns, they toss off a jaunty, "Never mind."

Among Christians there is often a poor use of the words, when people think of the matter of sustaining their religious life by daily devotions.

They feel, "Never mind," as though the religious life would sustain itself. It is just as wise as for a person to pay no attention when his bank balance has reached the vanishing point, and to say of that, "Never mind."

Now look at the good places to use the words.

In the first place, *one great gift of the Christian faith is to be able to say to the worries and anxieties* that mount so in these days, "Never mind." The wearing down of the spirit by the steady beat of anxiety can be overcome by trust. "Cast all your care upon him for he careth for you." Not to say it lightly or frivolously, but in seriousness and confidence to look up to the hills of God whence cometh our help, is to win victory over fear and nervous breakdown.

Secondly, when your friends and neighbors have more of this world's goods than you have, and things which you could very well use, learn to say, "Never mind." We can say it and have no covetousness in our heart and mind, if we take time to realize the real prize of life. You *have* the gift of God's grace. Jesus puts the right value on life's possessions. He asked, "What shall it profit a man, if he shall gain the whole world, and lose his own soul?" If we remember that life is more than meat, we can say, "Never mind," and say with Paul, "I have learned in whatever state I am, to be content."

Thirdly, if you feel, as most of us do feel at times, that our life has been a failure in that we have not arrived at a "top" place, and have no great fame or position, we can say emphatically to ourselves, "Never mind," or rather let us hear God saying it to us. For Jesus said that life in the high sense is not to be wasted in worrying over the question, "Who shall be greatest?"

—PREACHING VALUES IN THE EPISTLES OF PAUL

"And Jesus said to him, 'If you can! All things are possible to him who believes.'" (Mark 9:23.)

All things are possible to him who believes, must of course be taken in the light of Jesus' teaching and life. If they are taken in sodden, unspiritual literalism, they become immoral nonsense. They offer the believer no justification for acting as if he possessed a private magic, some legerdemain to be used for personal advantage. Jesus rejected all that for himself in his temptation, and he rejected it for his disciples. Edna

St. Vincent Millay in a noble sonnet says that "love will not fill the thickened lung with breath," nor set a broken leg. Neither will faith. Faith will not enable one to caress rattlesnakes safely, or to pluck money from the air, or to live without food. Yet in the wide realm of the kingdom of God and of God's continued action to bring in that kingdom, whether for one human life or for the world, there is no barrier that can be set against the divine invasion: none but our own cardinal weakness—that often we believe more firmly in the power of the demons of evil than in the power of the God of love. Certainly in the bright lexicon of faith there is no such word as this "if," take it what way you please.

"You will not always have me." (Mark 14:7.)

The opportunity to have Jesus, in the sense of the experience Paul had and millions of others after him, "Christ liveth in me" (Gal. 2:20), is not a constant. There is a tidal quality in life. There are opportunities which must be taken at the flood, for there comes an ebb when they cannot be so readily taken, if at all. There is the particular flood tide of youth, when one may have Jesus as the guide and master of a whole lifetime. We cannot have that always. There is the voice of God in conscience, but if it is not heeded it grows faint. We cannot have it always. There is the appeal of need, but if we do not answer it we soon grow deaf to it. One dare not miss the solemn note. *You will not always have me.* "Seek ye the Lord while he may be found." (Isa. 55:6.)

"He who endures to the end will be saved." (Mark 13:13.)

There is a fruitful suggestion in the comment, "*Endure* is more than survive." The difference is worth careful exploration. Of course, in an atomic age the question of survival is a real one. Yet to survive as human beings is very different from enduring as Christians. It is a lesser thing. Surviving is a matter of existence; enduring is a matter of faith. To survive is to keep on breathing and eating and sleeping; to endure is to keep on straining and wrestling and holding out—to the last notch.

"A woman, whose little daughter was possessed by an unclean spirit, heard of him and came." (Mark 7:25-30.)

The outstanding feature of the story is Jesus' evident admiration of this woman's energy and brains. Her quick reply, salted with wit; her keen and nimble mind; no doubt the very courage of her repartee—all of it met with his appreciation.

Energy and brains—how desperately they are needed in the work of God's kingdom! They are superb, indispensable materials. Jesus needs clear, quick brains for his cause. It is not enough to have "a heart of gold and a head full of feathers." Feathers are poor building stuff. We give silver—and sometimes even gold—to Christ's church. Have we ever really given our energy and brains?

One reason why our civilization has so little to say of profound significance is that so many of Christ's disciples have an impediment in their speech. His word does not sound out clearly to the world through them. They choose rather to be "God's mutes." To the ringing appeal of the psalmist, "Let the redeemed of the Lord say so" (Ps. 107:2), they reply, "Kindly excuse me, I do not want to go on record." We read in Prov. 15:23, "A word spoken in due season, how good is it!" But it is never the season to speak for one who has the *impediment* of selfish preoccupation. The silencing impediments of caution, prudence, and cowardice will prevent us from speaking boldly for God in the presence of wrong. What stirring eloquence in the simple words the evangelist uses to describe the restored voice, *His tongue was released, and he spoke plainly*. God needs our voice, speaking plainly, that his voice may be heard.

"And he appointed twelve." (Mark 3:14.)

What mortal alive at the time could have guessed that over against the momentous magnitude of this act, when Jesus went into the hills and called disciples, the glory that was Greece and the grandeur that was Rome, all the marching legions, were as dust in the balance? Who that was alive in the early years of the eighteenth century could have imagined that the most important event in Europe was not the victories of the Duke of Marlborough, but the fact that in an obscure rectory in Epworth,

England, a mother, Susanna Wesley, was teaching her children to pray? Yet that is the sober judgment of history. In Isaiah we find a mathematical formula for it all: "A little one shall become a thousand." Freely, though not fantastically, interpreting that, we can say that one trained and dedicated disciple becomes mightier far than a thousand casual hearers.

"To be with him, and . . . to preach and . . . to cast out demons." (Mark 3:14-15.)

Very concisely but impressively Mark here lists three things the disciples were to do. The three activities make up a timeless three-point program for a valid Christian ministry, both for ordained, full-time clergy and for laymen. Forms of those activities have changed and will change. But the essence has remained, and will remain, the same.

To be with him—our mood often is "Let's get going." The result is breathless hurry rather than staying power. The amount of good we bring depends on how much we have been with him. How much we can give depends on how freely we have received.

To preach—the world needs a new word, "A new commandment I give unto you, that ye love one another." We are sent out to preach that word, the Word made flesh.

To cast out demons—in the gospel of Christ there is authority to heal those disorders of the spirit from which so many nervous and mental disorders come. To bring individuals into a right adjustment to God, is often to bring healing to the center of life.

—Exposition of Mark in THE INTERPRETER'S BIBLE

"*Love . . . knows* how to be silent." *(I Cor. 13:7, Weymouth.)*

The words, "Love . . . knows how to be silent," suggest the great variety of occasions when the supreme gift which love can bring is the sympathy and understanding which expresses itself in silence. There is vast true meaning in the phrase, "a healing silence." It frequently comes with a positive blessing like the stopping of a riveting machine.

It is one of the rarest refinements of sympathy which is able to discern occasions which call not for speech, however tender or eloquent, but for that deeper ministry and communication of heart possible only through silence.

A love that knows how to speak but does not know how to be silent has not entered the deepest places of human intercourse.

There are so many calls in life—mute, unspoken calls—for the love that knows how to be silent. They are as various as the many mysterious silences of the natural world. These particular silences, each with a quality of its own, have been suggestively enumerated by Edgar Lee Masters in his poem, "Silence," in which he speaks of the "silence of the stars and sea, of the sick, of a great love, of a great hatred, of a spiritual crisis, of defeat" and of many other high hours of life.

This silence of love is not indifference; it is not merely poverty of something to say. It is a positive form of self-communication. Just as silence is needed to hear a watch ticking, so silence is the medium through which heart beats are heard.

There is the silence of love when someone makes a mistake, when a shallow soul would let loose a stream of comment and advice; the silence of grief, when any conventional stereotyped words are a noisy sacrilege; the silence of worship, of whose healing we have far too little in a vocal, chattering age; the silence of a parent when a child is making a decision and whose love restrains him from making the child's decision for him, and who allows the child the great but glorious risk of growth; the silence of loving trust, which asks no hesitant questions even when baffled.

These are but a few moments of love at its best.

"Love makes no parade." (I Cor. 13:5, Moffatt.)

It is hard to imagine any word which would so clearly and picturesquely express the very opposite of the true spirit of love. It expresses vividly the subtle egotism which is so often alloyed with love or even substituted entirely for it and yet passes for the real thing. Making a parade is a gratification of the insidious and deeply planted desire for self-display, the concern for getting personal credit in every action and relationship. When the parade instinct is let loose the parade itself becomes the chief thing, and the distinctively Christian virtue of spontaneous, self-forgetful love is lost amid the fuss and feathers and display.

The subtle danger is that when a parade of affection, whether in words, motions, or deeds, is staged, the parade exhausts the emotion. It satisfies with a premature substitute the real energy of love which should expend itself in deeds and not in formations and gestures.

> "*I have come that they may have* life . . . to the full." *(John 10:11, Moffatt.)*

The problem of life, then, is to get out of the realm of fractions, to cease to live on a mere fraction of our inheritance and powers, and to live *to the full.*

Our age has given great study to the task of adding years to our life and has succeeded marvelously. In the last fifty years the span of the average life has been increased by fifteen years. But the deepest problem is not to add years to our life but *life to our years.* That is the gift Jesus came to impart—"*life* to the full."

In contact with the Spirit of God the gates are opened by which a liberating divine energy and joy come into life. The New Testament experience of the Spirit of God brought and brings the power of living life to the full.

Love of God brings a unifying power to life.

Sacrificial love to man brings strange recreative power. As the author of *The Lady of the Decoration* says in words worthy of a place in the New Testament: "The most miserable, pitifully smashed up life could blossom again if it would only blossom for others."

> "*Mary has chosen the best dish, and she is not to be dragged away from it.*" *(Luke 10:41, Moffatt.)*

Life is not a *table d'hôte* affair. It is an *à la carte* menu. You can't have everything, though many are trying, with an impossible eclecticism, to take everything in the world in an indiscriminate gorge. Life's business is a terrible choice.

The best dish at life's banquet is fellowship with God—the nourishment of the teaching of Jesus.

It is a timely figure of speech for our day, when so many forces of social compulsion are reducing life to a severely standardized *table d'hôte,* where people take what is laid down for them and go through life without any real exercise of sovereign choice.

And choice there must be, if life is to have any coherent meaning. What shall it be—the upholstery of a house or the spirit of a home; fashion or the fine and mellow graciousness of spirit which can ennoble the routine of everyday living however simple; a shifting vaudeville or the concentrated purpose of the New Testament?

Henry James, in a letter to a friend, advises a choice of the best dish, in a word of counsel, that might very well have come from this tenth chapter of Luke—"Let your soul live; it is the only life that isn't, on the whole, a sell."
—PREACHING VALUES IN NEW TRANSLATIONS OF THE NEW TESTAMENT

"I will obey thee eagerly, as thou dost open up my life." (Ps. 119:32, Moffatt.)

New Testament religion begins in the passive voice and then, having freely received, freely gives. There is deep truth in the observation that Christianity is not first a demand. It is an offer. And unless the offer is accepted, the demand cannot be met.

We have missed the essential lesson of the New Testament if we think of it just as a summons to "try harder." There would be no great good news in that. The "new creatures" we meet in the book of Acts and the Epistles were not people who tried harder. They were men and women whose lives were opened. True, Paul never ceased to "press on." But that was not his secret. He gives it to us himself—"Who loved me." He began in the passive voice and was projected into the active. Before he was concerned with what was done by him, he was concerned with what was done to him, for him, and in him.

"Sore they pushed me." (Ps. 118:13, McFadyen.)

It is doubtful if humanity can be separated into two more significant classes than the two suggested by this verse from Ps. 118: Those who are pushed and those who are pulled.

Pilate was pushed—"desiring to please the crowd." Paul was pulled —"the love of Christ constraineth us."

And you—are you pushed or pulled?

—PREACHING VALUES IN THE OLD TESTAMENT IN THE MODERN TRANSLATIONS

"They rehearsed all the things that God had done with them, and that he had opened a door of faith unto the Gentiles." (Acts 14:27.)

The most important thing in life is not the kind of experiences we have but what we select from them for keeping. The disciples made a selection out of their total experiences on the trip which is described in the thirteenth and fourteenth chapters of Acts. This report might have been vastly different and still completely true. They might have chosen to remember their mishaps—a record hard to match. They might have dwelt lovingly on every hair-raising detail. "Oh, it was terrible! We were beaten. We were stoned. We were driven out of town. We had the most barbarous treatment." But they "rehearsed the things God had done with them." They made an anthology of their own, a "Golden Treasury" of great positive providences, beside which any misfortunes were incidental. They made an apostolic selection. Here was the big thing—through them God opened a door to the Gentiles.

"That if he found any that were of the way, whether men or women, he might bring them bound to Jerusalem." (Acts 9:2.)

Recall the times when you have heard the fervent exclamation, "That man is a Christian!" What did it mean? Orthodoxy? Never—that is, never outside a Sanhedrin of some sort, the ears of whose members were attuned to catch the correct click of proper syllables. Membership in a church? Alas, no! When that exclamation wells up with undebatable conviction, it is always in tribute to one who is "of the way," whose manner of living brings a reminder of Jesus.

To the pagan priests the Christian sect was "a way of heresy." It is still a "bad" word. The way of Christ is a dangerous heresy in many of the centers of power and authority in our time. Of course, some who follow the way are honored. Indeed our brightest laurels are reserved for a Father Damien or a David Livingstone. But it is no mere cynicism to say that honor seems to vary directly with the square of the distance from the areas of privilege. Father Damien held out no threat to any entrenched power. Neither did Livingstone. But where existing forms of political or economic dominance are threatened, Christ's way is a heresy.

"And behold an angel . . . awoke him saying,
'Rise up quickly.'" *(Acts 12:7.)*

The traditional tribute to beauty of speech is, "It was like an angel's." We assume—though we cannot verify the assumption—that an angel's words are always sweet and beautiful. It is worth while to gather together the slight data afforded by the Bible on the sort of speech angels used. What did they say in their appearances recorded in the Bible?

Once we begin on that exploration, we pull up suddenly at the startling results. We discover that the words addressed by the angel to Peter in prison, "Rise up quickly," are typical of biblical angels. Nearly always they say the same thing—"Get up. Rise quickly." And those are not always the pleasantest words to the human ear. Sometimes they are unwelcome as the jangle of an alarm clock. The angel of the Lord said to Gideon, "Go in this thy might" (Judg. 6:12-14). An angel said to Elijah, "Arise and eat" (I Kings 19:5). In the nativity story, "an angel of the Lord appeared to Joseph in a dream saying, 'Arise'" (Matt. 2:13). An angel of the Lord appeared to Philip saying, "Arise" (Acts 8:26). At the tomb of the risen Christ an angel says to the disciples, "Go quickly and tell his disciples."

Certainly "arise" is one of God's most frequent words to man. The words of Jesus to his three disciples in Gethsemane, "Rise, let us be going," are his eternal message to his church. They are words always in season, always needed to lift a disciple, or a church, out of lethargy, out of comfortable chairs and beds into a standing position ready for movement. There is much truth in the saying that we think differently when we are lying down and when we are standing up. When we arise and face a task our minds take on a new quality. That angelic speech is preliminary to all great action—"Get up. Face this. Get going."

—The Acts of the Apostles in Present-Day Preaching. Vol. II

"Then returned they unto Jerusalem from the mount called Olivet, which is nigh unto Jerusalem, a Sabbath day's journey." (*Acts 1:12.*)

This journey was a little over half a mile. . . . Thus . . . when the disciples returned from the ascension of Jesus to take up life again in Jerusalem, it was a short walk physically. But in its implications it was a long and momentous journey—a journey many people never take.

In Edinburgh, Scotland, there is a street rich in historic memories, running down from the Castle to Holyrood palace. It is called the "Royal Mile" from the many royal processions which have passed along it, going from the castle on the hill to the palace below. . . .

"The Royal Mile" is a name which with profound fitness may be applied to this road from Olivet to Jerusalem. Consider some of the real meanings of the journey from that starting point to that destination.

It was a journey from vision to deed. Out on the hilltop of Olivet there was the vision in the sky. Back in the city, less than a mile away, lay the place and the task of giving the vision meaning through action. It is always a royal mile when anyone travels from vision to deed.

It was a journey from the passive voice to the active voice. The standard New Testament grammar has well over a thousand pages closely printed in small type. But a chief point of New Testament grammar can be stated in one short, simple sentence: Spiritual life begins in the passive voice, but it is never completed until it gets into the active voice.

It was a journey from the abstract to the concrete. That journey, in whatever realm of life it is taken, is always a royal progress. . . . Yet how often that mile from easy and pleasant abstraction to rough concreteness is an untraveled road!

It was a journey from privilege to need. Olivet was a height of fellowship. Down in the crowded streets of Jerusalem, in their squalor and darkness, there was the same panorama of stark need, physical and spiritual, which every great city always presents, be it in A.D. 31 or in A.D. 1938. Many people have traveled a hundred thousand miles who never once have known the incomparable experience of going this pathway. The city of God is always to be found at the end of a royal mile.

"But when he was well-nigh forty years old, it came into his heart to visit his brethren the children of Israel." (Acts 7:23.)

Life began for Moses when he got on the rim of his world, when he began to grow in awareness of people and of what life meant to them. That is when life in the fullest sense begins for anyone. This is not a matter of duty, charity, kindness, so much as of intellectual adventurousness. It is the dedication of the imagination to social ends. It is the projection of mind into the lives of others, so that we get a real feel of the burdens which cut cruelly into other shoulders. Thus we escape from the little one-celled universe of our individual desires and emerge into life.

Life began for Moses when he got into a fight. That is when life begins for anyone. To say this is not to stress the virtues of pugnacity; it has none. Nor is it to extol the oversimplification of the complex issues of life and society into clear sharp black and white; that is a delusion which easily besets radicals and reformers. It is rather the feeling of moral alternatives, the response to the struggle of humanity which pulls on something deeper than reason. Life began for Moses when he stopped strolling as a neutral observer and became part of a struggle for justice and human right. It is the reddest of red-letter days in the life of anyone when he gets down from the grandstand into the arena of life.

—THE ACTS OF THE APOSTLES IN PRESENT-DAY PREACHING. VOL. I

The Pharisee and The Publican

"Two men went up into the temple to pray; the one a Pharisee, and the other a publican." They went up in Jesus' day. They went up to church last Sunday. They will be there again next Sunday. They live on our block. They walk our streets. They come into our houses. We see them everywhere we turn, even when we look in the mirror.

The Ten Virgins

Think of the lonely personal battles in the Bible, such as Joseph's resistance of temptation, Moses' choice of God's people, Job's struggle with despair, Jesus' temptation. Remember this; there will come times to you when you will desperately need courage to perform duty, patience under pain, comfort in sorrow. How is your present life preparing you to meet these crises successfully? The foolish virgins were not the victims of a relentless and unforgiving friend. The exclusion represents, rather, the solemn truth that opportunities pass and can never come again. Certain doors shut, never to open again.

—Studies in the Parables of Jesus

"But when Jesus saw it he was indignant."
(Mark 10:14, R.S.V.)

This matter of the indignations of Jesus throws a clear light on his spiritual greatness. He never showed indignation over personal affronts. All through the scourging and crucifixion "opened he not his mouth." The only reference he made to his executioners was, "Father, forgive them." It is a humbling experience to compare his indignations with our own. What most quickly rouses ours as a rule is some injury done us, real or fancied, some slight, some rejection. Then we blaze like a freshly lighted fire. While many of us continue to look out on evils that engulf vast numbers, or on injustices that cry to the skies, with undisturbed equanimity . . . a needed daily prayer is this: "God grant us the indignations of Jesus."

The phrase *receive the kingdom,* makes clear what the characteristics are which distinguish those who truly enter it. The marks of the child which are stressed are dependence and receptivity. The child is dependent. He looks to the parent for all that he receives. He has no sense of achieving things himself. It is all a gift. So, Jesus says, must be the mind and spirit of one who receives the kingdom of God.

Another mark of the child spirit which is a mark of the kingdom is that of spontaneity, of impulse, "the capacity to act at once" on what they understand. The impulse is not strangled by calculation and cautious skepticisms. Jesus always welcomed the spontaneous impulse, as in Peter's confession, and the woman's breaking of the alabaster box of precious ointment. That is indispensable to the enterprise of the kingdom. Talleyrand once said profoundly, even though cynically, "Distrust first impulses. They are nearly always right." True! It is the checking of childlike spontaneity which has frustrated so much Christian achievement. There is evangelical wisdom in the remark, "Don't look before you leap. If you do, you will decide to sit down." One finds throughout Christian history far too much calculated, skeptical looking and far too little leaping. Let this mind be in you which is also in a little child—"*For to such belongs the kingdom of God.*"

—Exposition of Mark in THE INTERPRETER'S BIBLE

4

Hearers and Doers— Expositions on the Theme of Personal Response

"For it is not the hearers of the law who are righteous before God, but the doers of the law who will be justified." (*Rom. 2:13.*)

TWO MEN MET ON A BUS. THEY EXCHANGED FAMILIAR QUESTIONS, ONES we hear every day.

One asked, "What do you know?" The other asked, "How are you doing?"

Two questions, both important. The first, "What do you know," has always been extremely important since the dawn of time. The whole history of science lies in the answer to that question. It will always be important.

But the second question, "How are you doing?" is a completion of the first question and is vastly more important.

In our world today we have overestimated the values of hearing. We are always beset by one of the persistent delusions of life, the comfortable feeling, which is a constant boost to our complacency, that by hearing about a situation or a need, we have actually done something about it.

For this reason, the word of Paul's that only the doers of the law, not the hearers, are justified, comes as a needed and arresting reminder to us all. It is tremendously needed in our religious life, for it cuts the importance of merely hearing down to size. A small size!

Kierkegaard wrote one of his vivid parables on the danger of becoming a specialized hearer of religion, an occupation so absorbing that it left no inclination to *do* anything about it. He imagined that near the cross of Christ had stood a man who beheld the terrible scene, and then became a professor of what he saw. He explained it all. Later he witnessed the persecution and imprisonment and cruel beating of the apostles, and became professor of what he had witnessed. He studied the drama of the cross, but he was never crucified with Christ in his own life. He studied apostolic history, but he did not live apostolically. He was a hearer, not a doer.

That is a sin that does so easily beset us. We see its infection in the words of a minister who said testily, when a bothersome call came over the telephone, "I am writing a great sermon on sympathy, and do not have time for individuals."

Give us to build above the deep intent,
The deed, the deed.

—JOHN DRINKWATER

—PREACHING VALUES IN THE EPISTLES OF PAUL

"And Pilate again said to them, 'Then what shall I do with the man whom you call the King of the Jews?'" (Mark 15:12.)

This is the inescapable question about the unavoidable Christ. Pilate could not get away from it. He had to do something about Jesus. We can no more get away from it than could he. Jesus stands in front of us. We have to do something with him. The crowd had a simpler answer to that question—"Crucify him." Pilate accepted it as a command and carried it out. It was the easiest thing to do, the line of least resistance. What shall we do with him?

We can crucify him. It may seem preposterous to say that. But there is a continuing crucifixion that goes on. Whenever we take the words of Jesus in anything but deep seriousness, whenever we try to kill in our world the things he lived for and died for, we take part in the Crucifixion. We can patronize him. Many do exactly that. We can insist that he was a very good man, an interesting man, who said some very good things, particularly the Golden Rule, which has wide popular approval. And we can speak of it all just as we would praise a drawing made by a six-year-old child. We approve it, and that is the end of the matter. It really has nothing to do with us. Or we can ignore him. But we must not imagine that ignoring him is the same thing as escaping him. We can no more escape Jesus by ignoring him than we can escape dying by ignoring death. We can, however, blot him out of our lives and go on as though he had never lived, and as though he had never died. In doing so we will blot out our highest and richest potentialities.

—Exposition of Mark in THE INTERPRETER'S BIBLE

The Rich Fool

No vice is as hard to detect as covetousness. There is a sharp warning in the statement of a priest that he had every conceivable sin on earth confessed to him except that of covetousness. It usually appears first under the guise of "thrift," "diligence," or "prudence," and is warmly welcomed. Then its coils tighten about the heart without our recognition and early ideals of unselfish service and sacrifice, our habits of generosity and capacity for enthusiasm are quietly strangled. It is hard to recognize the process. Anyone knows when he has been drunk, but who can tell when he is growing covetous?

Consider the place this man would occupy in your community. He would be proudly referred to as "one of our substantial citizens." He would be made a director of half a dozen enterprises and his commonplace remarks gravely recorded in the newspapers. There is a strong possibility that he would even be elected a trustee of the church. Think of the meaning of these two facts: Society honors a prosperous, progressive, and efficient man of this type; Jesus called him a fool.

—STUDIES IN THE PARABLES OF JESUS

"And throwing off his mantle he sprang up and came to Jesus." (Mark 10:50.)

This is a perfect picture of the headlong response. The very words seem to spring and jump. They are violently active. Bartimaeus did not fold his garment carefully and neatly and say to a bystander, "Please look after this a minute. I'll be back." He threw it away and leaped to his feet.

Such headlong response to the words "he is calling you" is something we greatly need. We are so careful about "springing," so cautious about going "all out." We like to look before we leap. And so frequently, after a look, we do not leap at all. This blind beggar did not care about his garment. He forgot it, caught up in a great hope and a great trust. Are we so careful of our garments, of our interests of one sort or another, that we fail to have the throb and the joy of headlong discipleship? Do you leap at the words "He is calling you"?

—Exposition of Mark in THE INTERPRETER'S BIBLE

The Prodigal Son

While he is yet a great way off the father's eager eyes discern the returning boy, and he runs out to meet him. He erects no barriers of reproach. He does not scrutinize his son's motives for coming back. His heart is filled only with a flood of joy that the long-lost boy has returned, and the welcome is unconditional and complete. God is quick to discern the faintest movement of the heart toward him. "He takes ten steps to our one."

"When he came to himself." (Luke 15:17.)

There are several levels in "coming to oneself." It is a lifelong process really to "come to oneself" and find the true reach of one's capacities and the utmost possibilities of one's service. For the prodigal in the barnyard it was leaving the far country of sin that was the result of coming to himself. But there were other and later steps to be taken after he got home in order to reach the full possibilities of his personality in service. Is there not some step for you right now—some higher ideal of personal life, some additional service undertaken, some habit relinquished, which shall be a coming to yourself in a larger way for you?

Suppose the prodigal had met his elder brother before he had met his father, what would have happened? He would have gone back to the far country undoubtedly. He would have been discouraged from his purpose to come back by the cold, suspicious, cynical attitude of his brother. What a terrible ending it would have made to the story!

Bring this possibility close home. What do you think does happen in thousands of similar cases? *Are not many wanderers kept away from their father's house because they meet the elder brother in the vestibule?* Are you the elder brother some returning sinner has met? *It is a very serious thing to consider that the only chance some people have of seeing the Father God is what they see of him in our character and action.*

—STUDIES IN THE PARABLES OF JESUS

"And he broke down and wept." (Mark 14:72.)

In Christian experience great living begins in tears. It is God's starting point. When Peter broke down and wept, all pride, of which he had much, and all self-sufficiency and self-trust dropped away from him. Only humility and shame were left. The deep mood of repentance, his sorrow for sin, made possible an utter dependence on God, which is the beginning of sonship. There is a true New Testament insight in Thomas Moore's poem *Paradise and the Peri.* One who is charged with bringing to heaven the world's greatest treasure finally comes with a tear of repentance, which proves to be the most precious thing that earth can produce. It is indeed. Sorrow for sin, followed by repentance, removes the pride and self-regard which block God's entrance into life. Man's extremity, the low spot of his self-revulsion, is God's first real opportunity.

"I came not to call the righteous, but sinners."
(Mark 2:17.)

What would you think of the crew of a lifesaving station who gave all their attention to the station itself, made the quarters attractive, planted gardens, designed uniforms, provided music, and thus pleasantly occupied, shut out the roar of pounding breakers, driving ships and men to destruction on the rocks? Incredible, we would say, and rightly. Yet is such a fancy far removed from a church, so intent on its own interior life, its housing, its decoration, its material well-being, that the plight of those outside, in need of salvation in Christ, is forgotten or becomes subordinate to other things? The church is not a company on a summer hotel porch; it is a lifesaving crew. How many churches, just at the time when the needs around them were growing greater, have packed up and followed "the righteous" out to a new location in a pleasant residential section, where peace, perfect peace, reigns! In some such fashion we can get away from the disturbing cries and burdens of sin and need. But there is a price to be paid for it. We also get far away from him who came to save sinners.

"He saw Levi." (Mark 2:13-15.)

Note also the change which occurred when Levi became a follower of Jesus. He had been a tax collector. His life had been devoted to gathering. Now he turned to distributing. It was a deep-seated change in motive and goal, from gathering taxes to distributing the message and gifts of God. His Roman employers had commanded, "Gather, collect, gather!" Jesus turned all this around, "Freely ye have received, freely give."

Many changes come when Jesus is followed as teacher and Master. This is one of the greatest. The clutched hand of gathering becomes the open hand of distributing, a vital change in orientation, in central drive. Levi no longer used people as a means. God's children became ends in themselves.

This great change should find expression in our common life together. Our whole economic world has been too largely and tragically centered on gathering, on production, on profit taking. It must face the problems of distribution, that the abundance of God's earth may be more equitably divided among God's children.

—Exposition of Mark in THE INTERPRETER'S BIBLE

"But Peter said, 'Not so, Lord, for I have never eaten anything that is common or unclean.'" (Acts 10:14.)

The words echo down the centuries and the present day catches their reverberations. It is startlingly clear that on the housetop the authority of custom and habit was higher with Peter than a fresh vision of God. To the man whose mind turns on an "I have never," fresh revelations of

God are always of minor authority. In that vision God was breaking the mold of tradition. But in Peter tradition was not easy to break, for it had the solidity of rock. His was a highly geological state of mind.

In our universities there is a department of economic geology. No department of geological economics is ever listed—not by that name. Yet economics is often completely geological, so solidified into an "I have never" tradition that a world convulsion which explodes the dogmas of classical economics all over the map does not disturb the devotion of the economists among the ruins.

This narrative in Acts not only gives a picture of the "I have never" disease, but is an inspiring case history of a cure. From his initial resistance to a new idea, Peter moved on to an enlargement of mind. The word of God was brought into contact with the concrete situation, in this case the man Cornelius. When Peter allowed the specific case to be lit up by the general truth, he put himself on the line of discovery.

—THE ACTS OF THE APOSTLES IN PRESENT-DAY PREACHING. VOL. II

"He . . . began to drive out those who sold and those who bought." (Mark 10:15.)

Notice that it was the concrete act which was the dangerous thing. Kirsopp Lake says it was this overt attack on the financial interests that was the real cause of the accusation subsequently brought against Jesus by the priests. It is possible that if Jesus had confined himself to words, the power of the hierarchy plus the power of Rome would not have felt compelled to kill him. It is the act which is dangerous. But it is also the act which has saving power. Our Christian witness grows impotent as the proportion of acts to words goes down.

—Exposition of Mark in THE INTERPRETER'S BIBLE

"And they laid hands on them and put them in ward unto the morrow; for it was now eventide." (Acts 4:3.)

Two things come immediately to mind in connection with this overnight imprisonment of Peter and John. They are both instances of what might be called universal tendencies. We are struck by the effort of the authorities to imprison ideas. It has always been a delusion of threatened power and privileges to imagine that a fermenting idea can be securely locked up. That delusion has contributed much to the world's progress, for jails have in all the centuries proved to be the most favorable places for intellectual and spiritual fermentation that have ever been devised.

This action is also an instance of the easiest way of dealing with any problem—put it off till tomorrow. Lock it up overnight. Get it out of sight. . . .

There has been no more effective weapon in all the devil's armory than this suave doctrine of "the unripe time"; no more effective way of blocking the kingdom of God than the evasion of "putting it off till tomorrow." So readily is the gospel locked up in a moratorium, "for it is now eventide" and the light of truth is dimmed by gathering clouds. We do it with war. We do it in times of industrial strife. Men say—not often bluntly, but under cover of high-sounding devotion to "law and order" —"This is no time to insist on civil liberties. Let's lock it up till tomorrow."

Against this frustration of God's good news by obstruction and postponement stands a very effective little word, frequently found in the New Testament: "Today."

—THE ACTS OF THE APOSTLES IN PRESENT-DAY PREACHING. VOL. I

> *"And certain men came down from Judea and taught the brethren, saying, 'Except ye be circumcised after the custom of Moses, ye cannot be saved.'" (Acts 15:1.)*

This conflict between the strict Jewish party at Jerusalem and in Judea and the more liberal adventurous church at Antioch illustrates the eternal tension between the crowd at headquarters and the people in the field. There is a certain type of mentality, fairly consistent in all fields of action and in all professions, which may be represented by the initials used in armies, "G.H.Q."—General Headquarters. . . .

The clash between administrators and practitioners occurs also in the field of education. Bliss Perry vividly pictures the state of affairs in that field: "The whole tendency of American institutions is to breed ten administrators to one real teacher. I used to pass University Hall [at

Harvard] with something of a small boy's dread of passing a cemetery; for teachers lay buried there under their roll-top desks." Education is always in danger of selling its birthright of teaching for a mess of overhead administration. This is increased by a vicious tendency, connected with the false standard of "success," to rate a man's progress in his profession by the distance he is removed from its actual practice. The fledgling Ph.D. in a central board of education, who has hardly ever, if at all, been guilty of the lowly business of classroom teaching, is rated, both by salary and prestige, higher than the most fruitful classroom teacher in the city. The secretary of a church board, the ecclesiastical administrator of any sort, frequently stands higher than the man who is still immersed in pastoral work. Indeed this judgment could be reduced to a mathematical formula: "Success" varies directly with the distance from the actual practice of an art or profession.

The gist of the matter seems to be that real growth, in an individual or an institution, occurs at the tip of the root rather than at the base. The grasp of the fresh, great meaning of the Christian gospel came at the frontier in Antioch, not at the headquarters in Jerusalem.

"Thou wentest in to men uncircumcised and didst eat with them." (Acts 11:3.)

This is a little gem of narrative. It explains with perfect clearness what is the unforgivable sin against established orders and vested privilege—action. Words, no matter how bold and swelling, can be winked at. Action is unforgivable.

Peter is "on the carpet" before the leaders of the Judaistic faction in the Jerusalem church, for the crime of extending the blessings of the gospel to Gentiles. Inclusion of Gentiles in the Christian groups meant a violent breaking down of the walls of Jewish exclusiveness. It was a disturbingly new idea, one that held a real threat to the authority of the inner group. Notice that these people did not object to Peter's preaching to the Gentiles. The unpardonable thing was his carrying into action the implication of the words he had proclaimed. "Thou didst *eat* with them." You not only talked but you did something to make the talk real.

This bit of history needs to be etched into our minds. It is the deed, not the word, which brings opposition to the Christian revolution in life. Of course, often the powers that be have no great love for Christian words.

They will repress such words if it can be conveniently done without too much uproar. But words are frequently harmless. Indeed they may serve as a safe outlet for discontent and protest. But deeds are a declaration of war, not to be ignored.

Among the humorous performances of Nazi Germany—though it is tragic too—is the passage of Goebbels' decree abolishing dramatic and literary criticism. That eminent cultural authority ordains that "criticism shall be replaced by contemplation and description." But Nazism is not the only system which thus seeks to shackle criticism. Often in a capitalistic democracy, economic power insists that the benevolent workings of the system be only raptly contemplated and piously described. No criticism by deeds of opposition. In a strike situation, for instance, the unforgivable sin, to employers and chambers of commerce, is action. Testimony before the Senate Civil Liberties Committee in July 1938 exposed the technique of the Republic Steel Company in dealing with those whose sympathy with strikes reached the stage of action—those who *did* something about it. "Thou didst *eat* with them."

Two truths emerge. First, it is *action* which counts in the carrying of the Christian evangel to our world. Action is what the world pays attention to. Words are so easy, so pleasant and satisfying that they are frequently subjected to a 99 per cent discount by the cynical pagan powers of our world. In religion, as in criminal law, it is the overt act which is the crime. A recent novel defines a liberal as "a person who holds the right views but lacks the courage and single-mindedness to do anything about them." Cynical? Yes. But how often has it proved true of liberal Christians! In an old comedy of Thomas Shadwell's there is a knight, Sir Nicholas Gimcrack, who practices his swimming in dry security, outstretched froglike on a table. "I hate the water," he confesses. "I content myself with the speculative part of swimming. I care not for the practick." We smile at Sir Nicholas' frankness, but how much swimming on land have we done? Resolutions, perorations, noble sentiments—but we "care not for the practick."

Yet Christianity must act if it is to find concrete leverage in the world. A woman recently went into a five-and-ten-cent store and asked for compasses. "We have compasses for drawing circles, madam," the clerk said, "but not for going places." Christian truth has often been a compass for drawing circles, endless discussions that go round and round. But it is emphatically a compass for going places, for movement, for action, for definite arrival at definite goals.

A second truth is that action on Christian lines will always rouse opposition. We will do well to fortify ourselves by remembrance of that fact, lest we be driven into a blue funk of fear every time the inevitable opposition arises.

—THE ACTS OF THE APOSTLES IN PRESENT-DAY PREACHING. VOL. II

The Two Foundations

One very popular substitute for following the teachings of Jesus is to admire them. It is popular because it is so much easier. It is always in good taste to admire Christianity, and it costs nothing. Admiration of this kind is worth just what it costs. Several years ago a plow was sent over to Africa and fell into the possession of a tribe of natives in the interior of the continent. Not knowing what else to do with it they set it up on a pedestal and worshipped it. The plow was designed to strike down deep into the soil and prepare it to produce fruit. To be set up for admiring worship was a perversion of its purpose. So the purpose of the gospel of Jesus is to plow down deep into men's lives and make them fruitful in the largest sense. It is a poor substitute for this to pay to the gospel a few cheap and easy and empty compliments. Dr. Crothers compares the difference which frequently exists between the principles people admire and those they use to two pokers for the fireplace. The fine brass poker in a polished stand is to be looked at. When we really have to do anything to the fire we get out a dingy little black poker which stands somewhere out of sight. So we keep in public view, he says, the beautiful principles we admire and supposedly believe. But when we really have to do anything, we follow some much less attractive principle of action which we keep out of sight.

—STUDIES IN THE PARABLES OF JESUS

"And the widows stood by him weeping and showing the coats and garments which Dorcas made while she was with them." (Acts 9:39.)

Dorcas was the founder of an International Ladies' Garment Workers' Union, one of the greatest labor unions of all time, with branches in all lands. The rate of pay has been small, the hours long, but the union has never gone on strike. Otherwise it has been a highly successful craft union in the needle trades. Indeed, so great a part has this union of women played here in America that Dorcas seems more like a character in New England than in Palestinian history. There is high drama and pathos in the words, "showing the coats and garments"—those eloquent memorials of a life of love. What a collection it would be if the coats and garments made by all the Dorcas societies of all these years could be assembled! What a record of all the changes of style and of the costumes of all climes! Those garments are recorded somewhere in a grand inventory.

The legacy of Dorcas is an inward history as well as an outward one of flying needles. Elizabeth Fry, the Quaker ambassadress of God to those who were in prison in early nineteenth century England, describes that inward history in recording her first prickings of conscience over her life of privilege in the midst of need. She wrote, "I feel like a contemptible fine lady, all outside, no inside." A great many "fine ladies" have ceased being "contemptible" by getting outside themselves and inside others' needs, thus discovering and developing a new "inside" for themselves. It sounds like a contortionist's trick, but it is a marvelous trick for making a more Christian life.

There is eternal need of this Ladies' Garment Workers' Union, a union of heart to feel and hand to do. Our day needs to carry the spirit of Dorcas beyond the immediate and obvious task of supplying garments into the wider issues of social housekeeping, that justice may displace the obvious charity of clothes dispensing. Our day must express Christian love, not by merely passing out garments and jellies, but by securing a fairer share of the world's wealth for the workers who so largely create it.

—THE ACTS OF THE APOSTLES IN PRESENT-DAY PREACHING. VOL. II

"When saw we thee ahungered?" (Matt. 25:37.)

It is well to remember that the love which wins the welcome, "Come, ye blessed of my Father, inherit the kingdom," is a love which goes out of its way to find the stranger, the sick, the unclothed, and the prisoner. It is rather easy to "brighten the corner where you are." The fundamental Christian message is to brighten the corner where someone else is and which you go out of your beaten path to find. It has been truly said that if people could actually see the misery within ten blocks of them, they could not eat their dinner in peace. The Christian conscience must annihilate those ten blocks and spoil the dinner! We eat too many dinners in peace anyhow. When Richard Watson Gilder was on the Tenement House Commission of New York he wanted to find out the cause of the many tenement-house fires. He had a fire department gong placed in his bedroom and every tenement-house fire was reported on the gong, so that he might go. He went out of his way to serve. His love was so great that he allowed himself to be riotously disturbed by the needs of others. That gong connecting his home with the lower East Side is a fit symbol of the Christian love which this parable demands.

The Good Samaritan

Many people are much more ready to discuss the immigration problem than to care for an immigrant on the next block. It is easy to love men when that means only a vague feeling of goodwill to humanity in general. Religion becomes easy and useless just in proportion as it grows vague.

The Good Samaritan's help was not only personal, it was self-sacrificing—getting down from his beast and lifting up the wounded man. His service was thorough. He did not leave his task of rescue half done, with the pious hope that the man would "get along all right," or the vague request to "write me if I can do anything for you." Much effort is lost because it is scattered too much. Dr. Cabot says that Paul's "this one thing I do" has become "these forty things I dabble in."

"When I can find a moment, I will send for you." (Acts 24:25, Moffatt.)

"I will find time later." (Goodspeed.)

There is this unique characteristic about time which we overlook: We can *lose* time, but we can never *find* it. We have to *make* it.

Felix found lots of moments for what he wanted to do—to satisfy his curiosity about Paul and open the way for a bribe. We read that he sent for him "pretty frequently" (Acts 24:26), but he found no moments to face the big issue squarely and render a judgment. Such moments are never found. They must be made.

A feature of our modern life which keeps us from deliberately making time for the highest uses and betrays us into the old fallacy of Felix is the note of *strident immediacy* so characteristic of the mood of today. So many things must be done right away to keep up with the "swim" that those long processes of growth which are life's finest fruit find no sufficient time to mature.

Are you a vagrant? A vagrant lives by finding things. Life has no high choices, no seizing of time for creative purposes. A vagrant, in his relation to time, ambles through life a helpless Micawber, hoping time will "turn up." Felix was a vagrant, even though he sat on a throne.

—PREACHING VALUES IN NEW TRANSLATIONS OF THE NEW TESTAMENT

"Never envy . . . but always reverence." (Prov. 23:17, Moffatt.)

This is an inevitable alternative.

If a man has no high sanctities, he will have low superiorities. The only guarantee against the gnawing of envy is a greater preoccupation with a reverence which lifts the whole life to a higher level.

We can take our choice.

—PREACHING VALUES IN THE OLD TESTAMENT IN THE MODERN TRANSLATIONS

"When he had driven the people out." (Matt. 9:25, Goodspeed.)

Jesus' concern was to dismiss the crowd; ours is to gather one.

Is it not probable that the reason we are able to do so little with the crowd is that we do so little apart from it? Does not a man's final and lasting influence with a crowd depend on what he does away from the crowd—alone?

That is a truth so easily forgotten in an age of publicity. The glare of the crowd has the same effect on a man and his message as the glare of the desert. The streams dry up. There is often deep irony in the phrase "a public man." For the man who revels in the crowd depends upon it. He becomes more and more the public figure and less and less the *man*. Many a preacher has allowed his message to become a thin trickle of soothing syrup, because he could not dismiss the crowd and replenish life from deep inner springs.

It is a strong verb used here. Jesus had to *drive* out the crowd. So do we, if we are not to be trampled down. Can you get along without the crowd, more eager for inner realities than marketplace notice, measuring life's significance by the eternal standards of God rather than by inches of newspaper space? What we can do in the crowd depends on what we become away from it. If we cannot dismiss a crowd, we will never be able to do much else with it.

—PREACHING VALUES IN NEW TRANSLATIONS OF THE NEW TESTAMENT

"Ye judge yourselves unworthy of eternal life."
(Acts 13:46.)

In that deep and beautiful story of Italy under the heel of Fascism, *Bread and Wine*, there is one episode where a woman innkeeper, a devout Catholic, thinking from his kindly actions that a certain guest might be Jesus returned to earth, is at a loss what to do in this situation. So she hurriedly consults the government's list of rules for keeping an inn. She is greatly disappointed to find no directions covering a possible arrival of Jesus. We may smile at that. But here is something not to be smiled at: Does our way of life leave any room for a possible arrival of Jesus in our world, the near world of our personal contacts or the farther world of our environment? Or do we desire that God's kingdom come only provided it doesn't upset anything to which we have become accustomed?

This question comes to the church as well as to the individual Christian. Is it worthy of the tomorrow—God's tomorrow—of its gospel and prayers?

—THE ACTS OF THE APOSTLES IN PRESENT-DAY PREACHING. VOL. II

5

Hell Is Paved With Stumbling Blocks—Expositions on the World, the Flesh, and the Devil

"Never . . . put a stumbling-block or hindrance in the way of a brother." (Rom. 14:13.)

It is fascinating to watch Paul at work here. He takes a controversial question—hot in the hour of conflict—and lifts it out of the furnace up to an entirely new level. He lifts it from the level of "me and my stomach" up to Christ's level, where concern for my stomach, whether to eat meat that had been offered to idols, gives way to concern for the souls of men.

Moral and spiritual stumbling blocks are deathtraps. We have heard that hell is paved with good intentions. *Hell is also paved with stumbling blocks.*

So many stumbling blocks and hindrances have prevented spiritual progress that might be made. A church largely wrapped up in itself has been a tragic stumbling block to serving the community filled with people with many kinds of acute need. The indifference of good people to a town's welfare has often been a hindrance to advancing that welfare.

This word is Paul's vivid picture of the responsibility of personal conduct. In families we see clearly the crime of putting stumbling blocks in the way of youth. Often children stumble over a *bottle.* A bottle of strong drink has caused a stumble; the turning point on which the life of a parent has centered has been "me and my gullet."

Sometimes the stumbling block is *example* in general. Parents, not on malicious purpose—but just as disastrously as though malicious—cannot control their desires with any consideration of what harm the children might take from example. Paul gives a crowning blow on example when he explains, "Surely we shouldn't wish to undo God's work for the sake of a plate of meat!" (Phillips). But that is exactly what a parent often does! Sometimes the stumbling block in the way of children is more intangible. It is the empty place where a father ought to be. He ought to be by the young person's side at times of choice. He is too busy. So the young man or woman stumbles for lack of guiding friendship. There was an old Civil War song, sure to bring tears: "There Shall Be an Empty Chair." Sometimes the empty chair is father's. Sometimes it is mother's. The empty space causes a stumble.

—PREACHING VALUES IN THE EPISTLES OF PAUL

"If your hand causes you to sin cut it off." (Mark 9:43-48.)

Jesus applied this to the whole life of the mind and soul. Whatever hinders entrance into the kingdom is a fatal liability. There is a touching scene in the life of young Arthur Wellesley, who became the Duke of Wellington. On leaving home to begin his army career he deliberately smashed his beloved violin to bits. That seems extreme and fanatical, but it showed the intensity with which he realized that no man can serve two masters. He had chosen one profession, not two. The choice of the kingdom must be that unanimous.

"They . . . divided his garments among them, casting lots for them." *(Mark 15:24.)*

There are two shocking things here. One is the gruesome contrast, a dice game at the foot of the Cross. Right in front of their eyes was the crowning event in history. The soldiers could not be blamed for not realizing that. But it was an evident tragedy. Even the dullest ought to have seen that this was something and someone out of the routine. Mark records that at the end one Roman soldier did see exactly that (see vs. 39). But to the majority of the military guard it was all in the day's work, scarcely more than a chance to gamble for very small stakes—some second-hand garments.

The imagination runs out in all directions to other times and places, where people, confronting in their day events that were shaping destiny, were engaged in sacrilege. Mark the dull and brutal unconcern of the multitude in the face of the world's appalling tragedies. Millions of people go down into the valley of the shadow of death. The whole future of the human race is at stake in what happens. And all the while the feverish playing of the commodity market goes on, the clamorous clutch for more profits, more goods, more advantages, and in a hurry. It is the latest chapter—will it be the last?—in a continued story that began on Golgotha, gambling at the foot of the Cross.

The other suggestion is equally shocking. All that these soldiers appear to have seen in Jesus was his clothing. That they divided among them. They took his garments—that was all. From the man himself they took nothing. What disturbing reminders there are in every detail! Countless numbers that have taken the name "Christian." They have taken the historic forms with which the gospel of Jesus has been clothed—the creeds, the organization, the ceremonial practice. But of the Man himself, the Master, the Savior, with power to change the inner spirit and the outward face of life, they have taken little more than these soldiers. *They . . . divided his garments among them.* "Lord, is it I?"

> *"The chief priests and the scribes were seeking how to arrest him by stealth. . . . lest there be a tumult." (Mark 14:1-2.)*

Beyond this historical situation, the words *arrest him by stealth* offer a suggestive picture of another kind of history, the history of the spiritual life of the Christian. When Jesus is removed as real master, the process usually goes on secretly, "with subtlety" (A.S.V.), "by craft" (K.J.V.). If the surrender of allegiance were a matter of open, forthright demand—such as martyrs, early and late, faced—if it were a dramatic choice, "Renounce your faith publicly, or die," most Christians would make the martyr's choice, death rather than outright, final denial. But life is not that simple. Its choices come by "stealth"; Jesus slips out when we are not noticing it. No trumpet announces the hour of decision. Little by little, compromises gnaw away fidelity and resolution; small neglects, here one, there another, "with subtlety" change the whole climate of a life;

the calls of God to service are refused, not with any resounding "No," but simply because they are lost amid other pressures.

"What have you to do with us, Jesus of Nazareth? Have you come to destroy us?" (Mark 1:24-25.)

This question, first recorded as the frightened shriek of the disunited forces of evil, is the cry of evil power in all centuries and in all languages. It is still being vociferously and angrily shouted today.

It is the cry of greed. "What have you to do with us, Jesus? Mind your business. Our business is our own. Get back to Palestine. Get back to the Bible. Get back to the church. Get back anywhere, so long as you do not interfere with our profits." The powers that exploit men and women and children insist that profits are sacred, and protest that the teachings of Jesus have no jurisdiction over them. To bolster their case they throw words at Jesus and at those who proclaim judgment on mammon—words such as sentimentalist, romanticist, dreamer, impractical. It was the language of the slave trade. It is the language of the profiteers of slave labor, commercialized vice, a debauching liquor traffic, race discrimination. It is the language of entrenched power everywhere, of oppressive government, of dominant militarism, of shifty diplomacy. It is the language of unrestrained individualism. "I have a right to live my own life" usually means, "What have you to do with me, Jesus of Nazareth?"

—Exposition of Mark in THE INTERPRETER'S BIBLE

"Then all the people of the neighborhood of Gerasa asked him to go away from them, for they were terribly frightened." (Luke 8:36, Goodspeed.)

It would be instructive to make a list of the people who said to Jesus, "Get out!" It would provide not merely a study in New Testament history but likewise a picture of many forces in present-day life. For the burden of the world's attitude to Jesus in many areas of life today is exactly the same as in many towns of Galilee and Judaea. It can be expressed in two words, "Get out!"

1. The people of Capernaum threw Jesus out of town (Luke 4:29). He had healed a man and challenged their traditions.

2. The people of Gerasa cried feverishly, "Get out!" They were afraid for their property and the placid order of their town. His coming had been the occasion of the loss of property. They preferred pigs to a miracle worker.

3. Herod told Jesus to get out. His ideas did not suit the purposes of the government, Herod being the government.

4. A Samaritan village kept him out. They had a violent, ineradicable prejudice against his race.

Here were four instances of people who threw Jesus out of their town, and as far as possible out of their life and affairs.

The same four antagonisms to Jesus operate powerfully today. Jesus is told to get out because his teachings run counter to sacred traditions and practices; because they would reduce business profits, if applied; because they challenge some purposes of governments; because they condemn cherished race and class and nationalistic prejudices.

—PREACHING VALUES IN NEW TRANSLATIONS OF THE NEW TESTAMENT

"He also changed his prison dress and dined at the royal table." (Jer. 52:32, McFadyen.)

Here was one who had once been a monarch himself accepting the patronage of his master, allowed to dress in a more elaborate manner than his fellow slaves, put on a pension, and graciously allowed to look on his captor every day. A dramatic descent—from king to a pensioner at another king's table.

What an accurate picture it is of religion when it allows itself to be patronized, when it takes orders from a worldly master and wears his livery and is flattered by his condescension in allowing it a place in his household!

We see Christianity in many institutions and in many realms of life, sitting, like this Hebrew king in exile, a prisoner,

Bound who should conquer,
Slave who should be king.

"Never learn to live like pagans,
dismayed at portents in the sky;
pagans are dismayed at them,
but their rites are inane."
(Jer. 10:2, Moffatt.)

Two marks of pagan mentality are stressed here—dismay and inanity. There is a close relation between the two. Pagans, Jeremiah says, are dismayed at outward events because their inner life is inane.

There is a deep insight in the selection and joining of these two characteristics. They describe essentially what pagan living is, an inner emptiness, resulting in an inadequacy to meet outward contingencies and situations. A life inane at the center will be dismayed at the circumference. Where there is fatty degeneration of character at the heart of life, there will inevitably be panic and rout on the field of action.

A woman in Indiana recently sued her husband for divorce. One of the items in her petition was the fact that when she had trouble with her eyesight he bought her a pair of glasses at a five-and-ten-cent store. There are a great many people whose only vision of life is through five-and-ten-cent-store lenses. There is no vision of eternity; consequently there is dismay at the portents of time.

"Better a joy at hand than wants that roam abroad." (Eccl. 6:9, Moffatt.)

In one sense this is true. But in a deeper sense, in which the author of Ecclesiastes wrote these words, this is the sorriest creed to which one could subscribe. It is the perfect expression of a prudence which smothers the spirit, sinks life to an animal level, and renounces all "high-erected thoughts which pierce the night like stars."

We have heard much of a Five-Foot Shelf of books. We have had a five-foot religion persuasively urged on us. Here is a five-foot creed. It votes for man's grasp; it leaves out his reach.

"Stick to practical affairs. Shun the wants that roam abroad, that demand infinity and eternity and humanity for their satisfaction."

"Elihu went on." (Job 35:1, Moffatt.)

He did. Endlessly. For twenty-five centuries he has been going on. That low drone and boom you hear comtinually on the fringe of consciousness, that's Elihu—still "going on." A new name has been invented for his type of omniscience in late days, and a good one—a "Sophomoron." Age cannot wither his infinite loquacity.

No wonder the book of Job has forty long chapters, since it contains a condensed summary of four speeches by Elihu!

Elihu, then and now, is marked by two unfailing qualities—an impregnable self-righteousness and ludicrously inadequate instruments with which to measure the earth and plumb the depths of life. His premature assurance is never jolted either by curiosity or a new fact; consequently, there is no cessation of the Niagara-like flow to his words.

"I will now justify my Creator from a wide survey of the truth." (Job 36:3, Moffatt.)

The unconscious humor lies in Elihu's use of this word "wide." At least two inches wide. . . . How often, in the hands of researchers and self-admitted experts has a partial exploration of a problem, coupled with a superstitious faith in the magic of measurements, been elevated to a petrified credo! Of that type of unhesitating research man with his "wide" survey of the truth, Elihu is an example who should raise searching questions in those who see and hear him.

What a familiar figure he is, light-heartedly throwing a net of affirmations to catch the universe! He can outlaw and outdate the whole of religion if you give him two minutes of your close attention in which to do it. That impressive roll of papers bulging out of his pocket is his wide survey of the truth.

—PREACHING VALUES IN THE OLD TESTAMENT IN THE MODERN TRANSLATIONS

"They began to be sorrowful, and to say . . . one after another, 'Is it I?' " (Mark 14:18-19.)

We betray him when we try to make him fit into our way of life and thought, instead of changing our thoughts and ways to fit into his. Judas may have done that. The familiar word of Whistler is in point. When he was told by one of his patrons that a certain picture would not fit into his room, Whistler replied: "Man, you can't make the picture fit the room. You must make the room fit the picture." Jesus is not to be fitted into our life. Our room must be arranged to fit him.

We betray him when we give way to the cautious feeling that he is "going too far."

Three words, "Is it I?"

Live with them.

"He will come . . . and give the vineyard to others." (Mark 12:9.)

Our attention ought to be given to this with deep self-searching. When the natural channels through which new revelations might be expected to come into the world are for any reason blocked, God moves into life through unexpected and hitherto unrecognized channels. He has never been blocked by the rejection of his truth on the part of those agencies and institutions which might most naturally be expected to be the means of its proclamation. There is a suggestion of this in the profound symbolism of the Christmas narrative. In the nativity stories Jesus was born in a barn. That was highly irregular. There were places in the organized life of Judea where babies should be born. A barn was not one of them. But all the others were closed. So God used an irregular place—a stable. New revelations of God might be most naturally expected in God's church. But if that is closed he can always use some unrecognized place. History shows that he has done so. When in the presence of evils that literally cried out to the skies, the church—or majorities within it—has been as dumb as a stone statue, God's truth, God's justice, God's love for the least and lost, have found expression outside the church. His revelation has been received and proclaimed by oppressed groups, in lay movements, in the missionary enterprise, in labor unions, in political action. The words *give the vineyard to others* should lay upon us the responsibility of recognizing the messengers of God when they arrive, and of making room within the church for the new revelations of him who came to set at liberty those who are oppressed.

"He went away sorrowful." (Mark 10:22.)

He went away sorrowful. What exactly did this man lose? When we examine it, we are ready to award him the prize for having made the world's biggest blunder. He missed a great friendship. What else in all human history could compare to that prize, an elbow-to-elbow companionship with Jesus, hearing him, seeing him, being loved by him? He missed a great development. Think of what the men who accepted Jesus' invitation became! Someone has said that one can lie awake on a hot summer night in Illinois and hear the corn grow. We can put our ear down close to the New Testament and "hear" Peter grow! He grew out of the narrow nationalist into the prophet of the universal love of God. This man might have grown out of provincial ownership into universal sainthood. He missed a great adventure. When he saw the little group of disciples disappear down the road, he did not know that they were walking directly into the center of the greatest romance in history. He might have been the author of a gospel. His influence might have endured to the end of time but for a few acres and a few bags of gold!

—Exposition of Mark in THE INTERPRETER'S BIBLE

"This was your sister Sodom's crime: She and her daughters lived in pride, in plenty, and in careless ease." (Ezek. 16:49, Moffatt.)

Here is a trinity, not of heaven, but of hell—"pride, plenty, and careless ease."

It is not in any chance sense that these three ideals are called a trinity of hell. Look anywhere in the modern world and see the hell they have made. Join pride and plenty and the result is always the third member of the trinity—indifferent ease. When they sway the minds of any considerable portion of a nation's population the result is as told in the words immediately following in this same verse, "She never lent a hand to the weak and wretched."

The combination of these three traits develops a crustacean callousness to the defrauded and exploited, to those outside the holy circle of plenty, to those on whom swollen pride looks down.

Two trinities. We can take our choice. Grace, Mercy, and Peace. Pride, plenty, and careless ease. One makes heaven. The other makes hell.

—PREACHING VALUES IN THE OLD TESTAMENT IN THE MODERN TRANSLATIONS

"Other seed fell among thorns." (Mark 4:7.)

The strangled life is one in which there is *no great priority*. Everything is of the same size and importance. There is sharp point in the alarm of a schoolboy who, in reading a list of the chief causes of death, discovered a new fatal disease unknown to him. When asked what it was he spelled out the word "miscellaneous." It is a terrible disease! Millions have died from "miscellaneous." The life of the spirit sickens when it is buried under a landslide of miscellaneous things. An eager young woman, deeply stirred by Arnold Bennett's book *How to Live on Twenty-four Hours a Day*, said, "I am going to concentrate." "On what?" asked Bennett. "Oh," she answered, "on lots of things." When we concentrate on lots of things we concentrate on nothing. Life needs a saving priority—"Seek ye first the kingdom of God."

"Thus making void the word of God through your tradition." (Mark 7:13.)

Goodspeed's translation of these words is very suggestive—and embarrassing: "You nullify what God has said by what you have handed down." It raises the question, What is your private nullification act? What part of the word of God do you rub out and make of no effect for you? Can any of us honestly say we have never done that? Some of us nullify

Jesus' words "forgive seventy times seven." There "the Galilean is too great for our small hearts." Unrelenting and vindictive, we find those words disconcerting. "Voided." Jesus said, "Take up the cross, and follow me." (Mark 8:34.) But it is far too much trouble to take up a cross. That spoils our eager, unhampered stride through life.

What do you nullify?

"Beware of the leaven of the Pharisees and the leaven of Herod." (Mark 8:15.)

The spirit of the Pharisees—it is the spirit of externalism, of the elevation of observances and regulations into the priority which belongs to the moral and spiritual. Whenever any interest, advantage, or form of cherished custom displaces the moral requirements of God we have *the leaven of the Pharisees.*

The spirit of the Herodians was worldliness. Today we would call it secularism. It developed to a high art the serving of God and mammon. It made a supreme virtue of expediency. There are churches in which a comfortable adjustment to power and popularity would almost seem to be one of the articles of the creed.

Jesus said, "*Take heed, beware.*"

—Exposition of Mark in THE INTERPRETER'S BIBLE

"I hate men who are half and half." (Ps. 119: 113, Moffatt.)

"I hate dissemblers." (American.)

The reports from political conventions in which half a vote is frequently recorded for some candidate are puzzling. All that suggests itself to a layman as an explanation is the possibility of some delegate giving his vote to two different candidates. That is not the explanation of the fraction one half in so many tallies. But it is often the explanation of the shameful one half when the roll is called on moral issues. Jesus gets exactly one half a vote from some of his followers. And the kingdom of God will be a long time in coming if it has to move

Half a vote,
Half a vote,
Half a vote,
Onward.

"This world of men, where all around us the ungodly strut, and where base creatures rise to power." (Ps. 12:8, Moffatt.)

One of the most profound pieces of advice to which anyone can give heed is that common direction which we see and hear on trains and street-cars, "Watch your step." We had better watch our steps, lest we swing into an ungodly strut.

It is noteworthy that Jesus' first invitation to his disciples was to walk with him. He taught men a new step. "The great among the nations lord it over them," he said, "but it shall not be so among you." The path to service goes over pathways where strutting would be impossible. It goes along the Via Dolorosa. No ungodly strut has ever gone along that dark lane. Watch your step!

—PREACHING VALUES IN THE OLD TESTAMENT IN THE MODERN TRANSLATIONS

6

The Authority of Hazarded Lives—Expositions on the Cost and Disciplines of the Christian Life

> *"It seemed good unto us . . . to choose out men and send them unto you with our beloved Barnabas and Paul, men who have hazarded their lives for the name of the Lord Jesus Christ." (Acts 15:25-26.)*

Here is the supreme spiritual authority and credential, the authority of hazarded lives. The Christian group at Antioch wished to give the highest commendation to the representatives whom they were sending to a conference with the heads of the church at Jerusalem. So they sent "men who have hazarded their lives for the name of the Lord."

The men of Antioch grasped the very genius of the Christian gospel. "Here," they wrote, "are men who have hazarded their lives." That, now as then, is the final authority of Christianity in its appeal to a skeptical world—the proof of the cross, of devoted and hazarded lives.

There is no other comparable authority. There never has been. There never will be. It was the original authority of Jesus. "I, if I be lifted up, will draw all men unto me"; "I am come to give my life a ransom for many."

—The Acts of the Apostles in Present-Day Preaching. Vol. II

> *"And they were on the road, going up to Jerusalem, and Jesus was walking ahead of them." (Mark 10:32.)*

The border between Galilee and Jerusalem is the most important borderline in any life. It tests the reality of our profession. When we cross it in our lives and actions we go from comfort into pain, from ease into jeopardy, as Jesus did. But if we do not cross it, we leave the road which leads to fullness of life, and to power.

"And Peter took him and began to rebuke him."
(Mark 8:32.)

A Christianity diluted into a very cheerful and sensible religion, in which God's act of redemption in Christ has dropped out of notice, is emphatically of Satan. A sensible and optimistic doctrine of "progress," from which all realization of the costly suffering and pain of overcoming evil is eliminated, is a perennial masterpiece of Satan. A conception of Christian discipleship reduced to common sense, in which there is no room for the "foolishness of the Cross," is a satanic triumph.

"He charged them to take nothing for their journey except a staff." (Mark 6:8.)

Jesus' forbidding his disciples to take elaborate equipment says clearly to everyone who goes out to witness, "The main thing is to get on with the work." Do not get bogged down with a burdensome sense of responsibility for paraphernalia. *No bread, no bag, no money,* the simplest clothes. Travel light, so that the work may get the whole of your undivided mind and soul. The emphasis has a pertinence for all time. More than once the urgency of the mission has been lost through a worried concern about incidentals. A fussy preoccupation with accessories, or a delay until the perfect equipment was ready, has blotted out the evangelistic purpose. The means can supplant the end. The word "impediment" once meant "baggage."

The same compulsion to put first the task of carrying the message rests on a company of disciples, a church. Reliance on equipment, on the ecclesiastical equivalent of bag, money, and clothes, has all too often pushed into the background the command to "go." There is always danger that by the time a great idea gets completely organized and housed, the original impulse will be forgotten. The detail of the collecting bag is endlessly suggestive. The business of collecting money can take the place of the business of evangelizing. Masonry, money in the purse, ecclesiastical furnishings, have become not only obstacles to the mission, but substitutes for it.

"And he said to them, 'Where you enter a house, stay there until you leave the place.'" (Mark 6:10.)

Never let your desire for comfort take your attention from the work. Nothing else really matters. The chief question is not, "How do I like it?" but "How is the work getting done?" An undue insistence on comfort, the desire to have everything just exactly right, lodging, food, people, pay, can ruin the work of anyone sent out on a mission for Jesus. It puts the self at the center of attention and God on the fringe. Do not let the search for comfort transform an apostle into a "fuss-box."

"He is beside himself." (Mark 3:21.)

"He is mad" has always been an ultimate tribute in Christian history to those who served, not two masters, but One. Paul won that distinguished service decoration. Festus cried, "Paul, you are mad!" Francis of Assisi was "mad." William Carey was "mad." In one of his early stories Sinclair Lewis writes of a man who had a project for organizing a "Society for the Promotion of Madness Among the Respectable Classes." Fantastic? Yes. But after all, not a bad name for the Christian church.

Yet it has been a firm article of the world's faith, a seemingly unshakable faith, that good results can come of evil methods. That is the faith which instead of moving mountains prevents mountains of evil from moving. Men have believed that they could cast out cruelty by more cruelty, violence by more violence, war by more war. The illusion that Satan can cast out Satan extends into all realms of life—that truth can be established by lies, that liberty can be advanced by repression, that temperance can be promoted by drinking, that democracy can be enhanced by arbitrary measures, that religion can be served by compulsion. Evil will always produce evil. Good ends cannot be achieved by evil means, for the means have a subtle but inevitable way of becoming the ends.

"They left their father Zebedee in the boat . . .
and followed him." (Mark 1:20.)

All the disciples left something behind. The first four left fishing boats, their livelihood, and their homes. Figuratively, but quite truly, they "burned their boats behind them," like invaders, rendering it impossible to do anything but go on. They left no way of retreat open. It was not the kind of venture of which they could say, "We will try this for a while, and see how it works out." They followed. There was a finality about it. The question inevitably comes, "*Have we left anything?*"

To many those words "*they left*" have had a painfully literal meaning, a meaning common enough in the missionary church of the first century. "Leaving" has always been the hallmark of missions and evangelization. Thousands have become "displaced persons," uprooted from familiar scenes, to be "placed" in God's work.

But for most of us the word "leave" does not necessarily involve departure. Home and occupation may be tools for God's building enterprise, and great ones. There are, however, if not places, then things to be "*left.*" At Christ's call we should leave behind our cherished prejudices, so familiar and easy to get along with; our recumbent inertia; our aversion to the pain of new ideas—Ellen Glasgow wrote of her heroine Virginia that "she was willing to die for an idea, but unable to conceive one"—our self-determination, reluctant to follow the Master. Leave these and follow.

—Exposition of Mark in THE INTERPRETER'S BIBLE

Israel clamours,
"A prophet is a crazy fool,
a man inspired is a man insane!"
(Hos. 9:7, Moffatt.)

Very familiar language. It has been the standard clamor which has greeted the prophet in every age; which has greeted the pioneer in any area of achievement. The dedication of the monument in November, 1932, at Kitty Hawk, North Carolina, to Wilbur and Orville Wright, called to mind the clamor which, before their successful air flight, so heartily labeled them "fools." Classic, almost, is the comment of one of their fellow townsmen in Dayton, Ohio, in 1903, after the flight had taken place: "I don't believe it. Nobody's ever going to fly; and if anybody did fly, it wouldn't be anybody from Dayton." The magnificent logic of the last half of the preceding sentence is characteristic of clamors against the prophet.

Whenever a man brings any thoroughgoing criticism of an established order from a spiritual and ethical point of view he may securely count on hearing in his ears the echo of the words hurled at Hosea: "A prophet is a crazy fool; a man inspired is a man insane."

Jesus heard it. He was counted mad. Paul heard it. "Paul, thou art beside thyself!" was the judgment of a typical man of the world.

There are three things which every prophet should do about this clamor.

He should expect it. It is the seal on his ordination. If he never hears it, if the word "fool" is not familiar music to his ears, he may well enter into deep heart searching, to learn how and where he has failed to catch the spirit and follow the leading of his Master. He may well remember that his Master pronounced the solemn warning "Woe unto you, when all men shall speak well of you." For that is the end. The soft purring of universal approval means that the man has made so complete an adjustment to his world that he no longer counts as a saving force in it.

He should understand it. What other immediate defense could a challenged order make than to discount the prophet by calling him a madman and a fool? Could William Lloyd Garrison have hoped to escape the enraged snarls of the proponents of slavery? Could any challenger of the sanctity of the profit motive reasonably look for sweet reasonableness on the part of all whose basic assumptions he assails? "Fool" and "lunatic" are among the mildest epithets he wins. An epithet is the readiest substitute for an argument which a hard-pressed man has ever found. The more devoid of argument he is, the warmer the epithets he hurls.

He should accept it. "Fool for Christ's sake" is the most honorable title a man has ever borne. A serious believer in Jesus, a genuine follower, is always "insane," if the world's common sense is made the standard of judgment. If he has not that touch of "madness" he has achieved the moral mediocrity of common sense. The worst disaster which has ever overtaken Christianity is not persecution; it is the engulfment by the world's common sense. Look at the age of enlightenment in the eighteenth century when organized Christianity almost sunk for the third time in the flood of spiritual obtuseness, which called itself the reign of reason. It is the foolishness of those who take Jesus as God's word and God's way for the world which is the saving salt of the earth.

—PREACHING VALUES IN THE OLD TESTAMENT IN THE MODERN TRANSLATIONS

"Paul, thou art mad." (Acts 26:24.)

This charge of Festus puts clearly what can never be dropped out of Christian faith if it is to be still a living thing—a certain irrationality, a venturesome thrust of mind and life, which goes far beyond the prudences, the cozy axioms, the arithmetic and logic of a world of Festuses. This charge of Festus is one of those high tributes paid to Christianity by men who imagined they were condemning it. The most incisive and penetrating tributes to Christianity have been paid by enemies or non-adherents. It is almost as though there were some infallible instinct at work in singling out as marks of shame those very traits which are Christianity's enduring glory.

It is a tribute devoutly to be coveted. When the Christian faith and purpose cease being something mad, something above the world's probabilities and proofs, above its shrewd prudences and readily obtainable ends, it ceases being Christian and becomes just another dull passage in the annals of pedestrian common sense.

To say this is not to be unmindful of our tremendous debt to those who have made clear the deep reasonableness of the Christian faith. Yet the Christian religion never strikes its most compelling notes, never gets into the treble clef, until it frankly admits the charge that it is tinged with irrationality. That is, it trusts in realities and insights which it believes to be true but which can never be completely proved by the world's logic. It sets out on roads that are never completely seen. Faith in love as the ultimate power in the universe must ever run beyond, must ever rise above any rational underpinning. It must have a touch of madness.

—THE ACTS OF THE APOSTLES IN PRESENT-DAY PREACHING. VOL. II

The Ten Virgins

Church activity or church membership without righteousness is another kind of "foolish-virgin goodness" which counts for nothing. Ecclesiastical machinery is simply the form without life, without vital goodness. Church membership is a good expression of righteousness. It is a poor substitute for it.

The Pearl of Great Price

This parable sounds a needed warning today. We live in a time of comfort and convenience and of toleration, and there is a strong tendency toward cheap and easy religion with few duties attached. People are searching for bargains everywhere else and look for them in religion. The preacher or the sect with a "marked-down" religion to offer at a low cost is popular. Someone has keenly said that there is something radically wrong with the Christian whose favorite song is "I'm glad salvation's free." It is a sign of a far more healthy religion when one sings:

Love so amazing, so divine,
Demands my soul, my life, my all.

—STUDIES IN THE PARABLES OF JESUS

7

Where You Come in— Expositions on Prayer

"Here you can join in and help by praying for us." (2 Cor. 1:11, Phillips.)

THESE WORDS, "HERE YOU CAN JOIN IN," ECHO A QUESTION THAT RUNS through many lives like a continued beat of a drum: "Where do I come in?" Often when any kind of project is proposed, the question springs out of hiding to the foreground, "What is there in it for me?"

It was heard in the very beginning of Jesus' teaching of his disciples. We read, "Then Peter said in reply, 'Lo, we have left everything and followed you. What then shall we have?" (Matt. 19:27.) The persistent question gets a start in the history of the gospel and the church, "Where do I come in?" So down to the present have we heard in one form or another, often unspoken, "What do we get out of it?" The request resembles that of desiring to be first-class passengers on a cruise. These people feel that special attention is due them.

Paul uses here almost the same words, but in a vastly different sense. He tells the Christians at Philippi, "This is where you come in." He does not mean the distribution of gifts and advantages. He lifts the question to a higher level, to the highest level, that of prayer and communion with God. He asks the converts that he may have their co-operation in prayer. The place where they come in is in a fellowship of intercession. There are many places and undertakings where they come in, but this is one of them, partnership in communion with God in prayer. Paul asks their prayers for him, that blessings to him may be carried to others.

This plea for a fellowship in prayer comes down through the centuries to our day and to us. We need urging to *practice* prayer. We are in an analytical age. We are busily engaged in destroying the flower to see what it is made of. Many of us are far more ready to explain prayer than to pray. Yet no one can reduce intercessory prayer to a diagram or a syllogism. We cannot have it and tie it up with a neat Q.E.D., either negative or positive. But we can practice prayer for others. We know that God touches the world through human lives. God makes a larger entrance into human lives through lives that are open to his coming and influence. So the world is "bound by gold chains about the feet of God."

That is our first service. Some years ago E. S. Waterhouse pointed out that when Jesus said the harvest was too big for the available help, he did not say, "Work harder," or "Get more helpers," but he said, "Pray to the Lord of the harvest." First things first.

We should never forget that prayer is an active affair. It has been said of Rodin's statue of "The Thinker" that the man thought with his whole body. The person who makes an effective prayer prays with his whole life.

—MORE PREACHING VALUES IN THE EPISTLES OF PAUL

"And he said to his disciples,
'Sit here, while I pray.'" (Mark 14:32.)

The story of Gethsemane pictures the only effective preparation for the loneliness of decision and crisis. That preparation is in what Jesus had—fellowship with God. He was not really alone when the disciples slept in the garden. The great Companion of all his years was there. He did not have to improvise a fellowship; it had run through his life on lonely hills and in crowds. He came to and came through the crisis in the strength of an established communion.

"He rose and went out to a lonely place and
there he prayed." (Mark 1:35.)

That, for Jesus, was the secret of sustained life and power, that opening of his soul to the unseen force of his environment—God. It is for man the secret of the sustained life of the spirit.

There can be no fulfillment without a lonely place. Lacking it, life lacks the dimension of height. And that is precisely the case in multitudes of lives. The very physical conditions of existence seem often enough to make solitude impossible. A woman put it picturesquely to her pastor: "You tell us that Jesus said to enter into your closet and close the door. In our apartment there are no closets and there are no doors." Life has become so public and gregarious. It is hard to shut our doors against the insistent intrusions of the outer world, of the radio, and of all the other constant invaders of the lonely place.

We must make a lonely place. Nothing that enriches and empowers life ever just "happens." It is made. Jesus never "happened" to find himself alone. He went out to put a stout fence around some corner of time and space. The crowded life which never does that has no means of renewal, of cleansing, of fortification. Private prayer is beautifully pictured in Keats's line: "I stood tip-toe upon a little hill." Jesus did it in Galilee. You can do it anywhere.

—Exposition of Mark in THE INTERPRETER'S BIBLE

"Enable thy servants to proclaim thy message with fearless courage." (Acts 4:29, Weymouth.)

This is one of the first recorded prayers of the Christian church. Suppose it had been a model of all Christian prayers—forgetful of safety and gain; intent only on the fearless courage of proclaiming Christ.

We need to make that the chief burden of prayer, for we are so open to the mounting hesitations of what Wordsworth calls "the uncourageous elder years." Whether we are so elderly or not, we soon meet the uncourageous years. Instead of the assault on the world's evil, so full of risk and toil, we begin to play what is known in sport as "a defensive game."

We need a fearless courage to proclaim a spiritual universe amid a growing fashion of materialism, to proclaim a gospel of moral austerity in a day of tolerated license, to proclaim a gospel of justice and brotherhood in the face of powerful forces of exploitation.

—PREACHING VALUES IN NEW TRANSLATIONS OF THE NEW TESTAMENT

"Asked to receive an alms . . . and leaping up . . . praising God." (Acts 3:2-8.)

Here is a notable journey in religious experience, from begging to praising. When we first glimpse this lame man at the gate of the temple he is using the house of worship selfishly. It was a good post for individual advantage, a good place from which to get something for himself.

But as he passes out of the brief spotlight of history he is not merely in a different physical posture, but in an utterly changed spiritual posture. He is no longer begging; he is praising. Between the two there is a great gulf fixed. The gulf must be crossed if religion is to be a reality or a growing experience.

We see the contrast between begging and praising in the conception and practice of prayer. Prayer in so many lives never gets beyond the business of begging. In other words, it never really becomes Christian prayer. When prayer is used merely as a sort of beggar's whine it is prostituted to low ends. It is futile in so far as the transformations which can be wrought by prayer in personal life are concerned. The really great miracle in Christian experience is well pictured in the story of this beggar. He began with asking for his personal advantage, but he rose to worship.

—THE ACTS OF THE APOSTLES IN PRESENT-DAY PREACHING. VOL. I

The Pharisee and the Publican

The word "Pharisee" means "Separatist" and this particular one more than lived up to the name. No "separatist" who, in his thinking, holds himself aloof from others can pray in the Christian sense. The grim and certain penalty of separating ourselves from our fellow men is that we separate ourselves from God. Can you imagine the Pharisee standing with the publican and saying, "Our Father, . . . forgive us our trespasses and give us this day our daily bread"? Yet no other kind of prayer is acceptable.

Have you ever thought of the serious implications in the fact that Jesus said of the Pharisees, "Let them alone"? He was the most undiscourageable optimist who ever walked the earth. He saw the good possibilities in the greatest sinners. Yet he regarded this self-satisfied, hard formalism of the Pharisees as the most hopeless thing in the world.

—STUDIES IN THE PARABLES OF JESUS

8

Inspired Amateurs—Expositions on the Church

"They therefore that were scattered abroad upon the tribulation that arose about Stephen, traveled as far as Phoenicia and Cyprus and Antioch, speaking the word." (Acts 11:9.)

THE STUDIES OF RECENT YEARS HAVE ADDED GREATLY TO OUR KNOWLEDGE of what has been accomplished by people from sheer love of a task. Kevin Quinagh has collected a surprising gallery of what he calls "inspired amateurs." Herschel was a musician who became one of the greatest of astronomers. Grote was a banker who became the historian of Greece. Priestley was a preacher who discovered oxygen. Schliemann was a merchant who excavated Troy. Spinoza was a grinder of lenses who took high place among the philosophers.

The most priceless gift that can come to a church is a singlehearted spirit in the men and women who make up her ranks, their willingness to give to the work of the Kingdom all the strength and devotion they can spare from their vocation. In spite of all the professional skills at its disposal, the church is close to bankrupty if there be lacking the sense of personal responsibility and devotion which was in those who were scattered abroad and traveled "speaking the word." Jane Addams powerfully experienced that essential sense of responsibility in connection with the cause of peace, a field in which she was an "amateur." "Looking back upon those efforts of hers, extending over almost forty years, one cannot but be reminded of that strange dream she had 'night after night,' when she was a little girl; that dream that she alone remained alive in a deserted world, and that upon her rested the sole responsibility of somehow making a wheel which should start again the world's affairs; the dream that she was standing in the same spot in the blacksmith's shop, 'darkly pondering as to how to begin,' and never knowing how. It was because in life as in her dreams she felt her responsibility as 'sole,' that she could never stop pondering or trying. She tried to make wheel after wheel to start the affairs of peace."

—THE ACTS OF THE APOSTLES IN PRESENT-DAY PREACHING. VOL. II

"To the saints and faithful brethren in Christ at Colossae." (Col. 1:2.)

Here is one of the earliest names of the Christian church—"Saints and faithful brethren." Difficult, but what a glorious name to live up to!

There are many varieties of churches through the years. Let two stand in extreme contrast. One is the church, met with here and there, which has been preoccupied with mechanics. One scurrying activity follows another and looms larger than the practice of love. It might be called "The Church of the Holy Fidgets." In its busiest busy season it looks something like the practices of Moslem pilgrims at Mecca. They reverently kiss the Black Stone, solemnly go around the Kaaba three times running and four times walking, run to a neighboring holy hill seven times, run to a second holy hill, and then stop to catch their breath while they listen to a sermon. Quite a field day! "The Church of the Holy Fidgets" has the same kind of ecclesiastical genius.

The other church might be known by the name of an actual church in Chicago—St. Stephen's Church. It is called "The Church at the End of the Road." That is a fitting location for a church of Christ. There are so many people who come to the end of their road. They have reached the end of their hope, of their strength, of their money. Go through the gospels and recall how many people met Jesus at the end of the road. It is a high role to be a church at the end of the road, "saints and faithful brethren."

—MORE PREACHING VALUES IN THE EPISTLES OF PAUL

"By God's appointment there are in the church . . . powers of organization." (I Cor. 12:28, Weymouth.)

It is worth more than a passing notice that in this classic list of God's gifts to the church, which Paul draws up, the power of organization comes *seventh.* Of course the significance of this ranking must not be pressed too far.

Nevertheless, this is worth reading in an age sorely tempted to exalt organization to the place of first importance. Put this fact in glaring and frankly exaggerated form: We often rank organization first. Paul ranked it *seventh.*

Committees, bureaus, boards, secretaries, budgets, drives, publicity—these are the background and foreground of so much ecclesiastical activity . . . calamity threatens the church; as the machine grows greater and more complex the task of keeping it going grows more and more insistent and engrossing, until the machine itself demands the greater part of the church's energies and the purpose it was designed to serve is obscured or forgotten.

The real source of a church's life and power is not in the engine or boiler room in the basement; it is in the prayer room and sanctuary. It is in lives that have the life of the Master.

"Put affection into your love." (Rom. 12:10, Moffatt.)

The bonds of the church often set loosely and ineffectually because there is not that human grasp of heart to heart pictured here and in Romans 16. Members of the same church are often merely cordial strangers; sometimes even that description is a hope rather than an exact description. And a fellowship of cordial, tolerant strangers will never become that miracle, a church of Jesus Christ. Only where the Christian virtue of love flowers into human affection ardent enough to overcome all repellent rough edges can there be generated the vehement flame which will fuse humanity into a brotherhood.

"But they were discussing something with one another." (Matt. 16:7, Goodspeed.)

And, of course, they missed the point which Jesus was making. They did not hear him at all. Jesus had just given the disciples a solemn warning against becoming like the Pharisees. It was a truth he wished desperately to get into their minds. But they were discussing something and missed it. They were arguing about the lunch.

How often in all the long centuries since that day have Jesus' disciples been discussing something as trivial as the contents of a lunch basket, and missed the message he had for them!

Only a few hundred years later, before the Christian church in North Africa, there unrolled the opportunity to win a whole continent for Christ. Not often in history, before or since, had conditions seemed to conspire so as to make possible the swift extension of Christianity over so vast an area. But they were "discussing something." All their energies were being spent in acrimonious doctrinal controversies. They were so busy slaughtering each other's arguments, and finally each other, that they had no strength or desire to unite against the paganism. Jesus was saying to them—"Go ye into all of Africa," and "Lo, I am with you alway." But they were too busy with their epithets and arguments.

Look at our own time. Think of the momentous issues of this postwar world—a broken world, a world with so much disillusion, with old hatreds not put out but only banked, a world still armed to the teeth, with industrial and race conflicts present or impending—yet with a wistful searching for a better way of life. What a time for bringing to all these great human needs Christ's message of life! Yet how many have been in these years "discussing something"—and, like the disciples of old, have missed what Jesus has been saying! Not discussing lunch exactly but things as far removed from the world's needs—competitive ecclesiastical rivalries, denominational peculiarities, fratricidal warfare over details of science, all making such a frenzied clamor that the still small voice of God was drowned.

—PREACHING VALUES IN NEW TRANSLATIONS OF THE NEW TESTAMENT

"Crispus, the ruler of the synagogue, believed in the Lord with all his house." (Acts 18:8.)

Here is real news—a member of the official board converted! The title translated "ruler of the synagogue" does not imply that Crispus was the head of the synagogue, but rather that he was one of the prominent men. In present-day Protestant terms, he was a "ruling elder," a "chief deacon," a "leading trustee."

Many a parish today would experience a revolution if certain of its most influential trustees believed in the Lord, measured life by his valuations, called great the things that Jesus called great and small the things he called small. All too often the board of directors of the local church, the trustees or vestry men, have a property complex which inhibits daring devotion to the Christian idea when that idea assumes concrete form; they share all the blind spots of local groups about them.

The conversion of Crispus made a deep impression on Paul, for later he mentions it (I Cor. 1:14). In many instances the conversion of the official board would make a deep impression.

Yet here, for our encouragement, is the record that it happened.

> "*And Paul and Barnabas spake out boldly, and said, 'It was necessary that the word of God should first be spoken to you. Seeing ye thrust it from you, . . . lo, we turn to the Gentiles.*" *(Acts 13:46.)*

We must make the church open its doors so wide that each new expression of Christ's spirit can enter in. New political experiments which honestly seek the more abundant life for men should find a sympathetic attitude in the church, however much they may violate traditions. New endeavors to bring the Christian spirit into industry, into business relations, into international contacts should find a cordial welcome, even though they outrage our economic prejudice and alter the course of the stream of profits.

One way of salvation is to escape from the habit of thinking in institutional terms. Religion necessarily gets a leverage on society through institutions. That is its means of influence. But the institutional habit of thought thus generated is a peril which tends to lead to identification of the institution with God. Thus, because the church in Spain has backed the rebels, multitudes of Roman Catholics and others have jumped to the conclusion that God is on the side of Franco. Because Russian Communism rejects theism, multitudes of churchmen have decided that all socialism is antireligious.

If we are to avoid the pitfalls of this sort of institutional thinking, our religion must continually be translated from a passing dialect into a universal language.

—THE ACTS OF THE APOSTLES IN PRESENT-DAY PREACHING. VOL. II

"If salt becomes insipid, what can make it salt again?" (Matt. 5:13, Moffatt.)

This word "insipid," which Dr. Moffatt uses for salt which has lost its savor, is a new window through which to view an old landscape. The word speaks with great vividness to our time. It represents the peculiar danger to a church. The greatest danger which confronts the church is not that it may die. The church will not die. The ever-present danger which always lurks before a church is that it may become *insipid*—that it may stand for nothing in particular. Jesus was giving expression to his fear that his truth and his cause might be committed to those who would lose the bitingly Christian flavor which characterized his way of life.

When does a person become insipid? The dictionary tells us that an insipid thing is something "without tang." That word "tang" is hard to define, but what intensely real pictures, tastes, feelings it suggests! The crisp air of a spring morning, the blue smoke of burning wood, the taste of a russet apple—all these things have *tang*. You can remember them thirty years without any effort.

In one of the most beautiful of all his poems Rupert Brooke has listed with vividness a few of the concrete things of earth which have this individual tang. The words take form and leap out of the printed page:

These I have loved:
White plates and cups, clean-gleaming,
Ringed with blue lines; and feathery, faery dust,
Wet roofs, beneath the lamplight; the strong crust
Of friendly bread; and many-tasting food;
Rainbows; and the blue bitter smoke of wood;
And radiant raindrops couching in cool flowers;
. . . .
blue-massing clouds; the keen
Unpassioned beauty of a great machine;
The benison of hot water; furs to touch.

Jesus was looking for people with tang; for those who had a penetrating, peculiar flavor in act, in viewpoint, and in spirit. Jesus' way of life was both a criticism of the life around him and a redeeming agency to lift it up. If we lose our tang, if we become insipid, what good are we, as far as Jesus' purpose in the world is concerned?

When the church's message loses its piercingly Christian flavor it becomes a thin broth. We have far more respect for a thing we hate than for a thing so insipid that we need not dignify it even by anger. A man was recently saying of another, "He's as insipid as"—and then he paused, hunting for an appropriate simile—"as insipid as the white of an egg," he concluded. The simile was well chosen. Most people would probably admit that there is nothing which excites them less than the white of an egg. Yet the gospel of Jesus has frequently been denatured into such a neutral dish.

How many slippery ways there are of becoming insipid! "We have bleached all the color out of Jesus," declares Dr. W. R. Maltby, describing the way in which the rugged concreteness of the Master has been blurred. Jesus had a coat of many colors, blazingly bright positives. What a tragedy when they are toned down into thin pastels of platitude or the dull gray of generalities, as vague as a Newfoundland fog! Surely we have not so learned Christ. Philip Guedalla reports the French statesman Thiers' conjecture that the morning prayer of Napoleon III was, "Give us, this day, O Lord, our daily platitude." Does it not seem sometimes also to the daily prayer of the preacher whose eloquence exhausts itself on bromidic generalities which have long since lost their power to arrest or pierce?

We can sidestep live questions or delve into antiquarian researches which are eminently safe. We can, and frequently do, straddle controversial issues and flee to the safety zone of the fervent reiteration of obvious platitudes. Or we can occupy ourselves with the mere cranking of ecclesiastical machinery and shrink from the more dangerous business of prophetic leadership. But, as Jesus asked long since, "If we become insipid, what good are we?"

John Kelman says: "It is not for the mere sake of adventure that the preacher of today must often go upon 'the dangerous edge of things.' It is for the souls of men and the love of Christ."

The Church of Christ started in the world with a cutting edge to its truth. It came into the Roman life of the first century with a message so peculiarly different from the standards of life then current that it literally turned the world upside down. Then as it grew it became more reasonable, more sane, more strategic—in a word, insipid. The glory and the radiance had departed. So today if the church has nothing to give but a weak sevenfold "Amen" of blessing on the standards of the world, if it has no shrill reveille of alarm against the forces which prey on human life, it is a mere bankrupt. If it has nothing piercingly Christian to say about the issues of the day, if it merely echoes in resonant, pious tones the safe generalities to be heard everywhere throughout the land, what good is it?

"*Insipid*"—a good word to look at, with the question in our hearts, "Lord, is it I?"

—PREACHING VALUES IN NEW TRANSLATIONS OF THE NEW TESTAMENT

9

Happiness and Discipline—Expositions on the Christian Home and Family

"Happy is he who has thy discipline." (Ps. 94:12, Moffatt.)

TWO VERY PRACTICAL OBSERVATIONS MAY BE PERTINENT. ONE IS CONCERNING the crime against childhood so common today in robbing it of its rightful heritage of discipline as an indispensable foundation for happiness. Fond mothers have an enlightened fear of "rickets," the softening of bones due to undernourishment. They have no such fear of the softening of the whole personality till it has no robust quality. A confused and weakened control by parents has helped to make an indiscriminate freedom a major characteristic of the present environment of childhood. All necessity for struggle is eliminated as far as possible, little realizing that a carefully prepared damnation for the child is thus achieved.

—PREACHING VALUES IN THE OLD TESTAMENT IN THE MODERN TRANSLATIONS

"Whoever receives one such child receives me." (Mark 9:36-37.)

The child set in the midst by Jesus is the symbol of the truth that the final test of a society is what it does to children. How fares the child in our land? There is the hazard of war, preventable disease, social conditions breeding delinquency, inadequate education, spiritual neglect. A few years ago, through a mistake on the roll in Houston, Texas, a child two years old was summoned for jury duty. That was a divinely inspired mistake. For the child is the final jury before whom our civilization must be tried.

"And she went out, and said to her mother,
'What shall I ask?'" (Mark 6:24.)

This question put by the girl to her mother is, in a real though different sense, a vital part of every mother-and-daughter relationship. Every daughter somehow, sometimes says: "What shall I ask of life? What is it you want me most to do and to be? I'll take my cue from you." And she does.

Herodias had no concern for her daughter. Her daughter was not an end in herself, but just a means, an instrument for gratifying her own hatred. Apparently without flicking an eyelid she made her daughter into a guilty accessory to murder.

Many a mother has played a part scarcely less criminal. When the whole growing mind and personality of the daughter asks, "What do you want me to be and do?" the mother has often answered with a callousness resembling that of Herodias: "Why, I want you to be a social success, my dear. What else is there to be? I want you to minister to my own pride and prestige. I don't care about what you really are. I want you to be rich, to be complimented, to be envied." So the daughter takes the fatal cue, and one more life is mangled.

Of course these things are rarely said in so many words. But children have terribly penetrating eyes. No matter how fair or pious the disguise, they see what a parent really cares for most. They know when dancing lessons are more important than Bible lessons. They know when the furnishings of the house are more important than the spiritual climate of the home, when position is more important than character, when the food on the dining-room table is more important than the symbols on the Communion table, when the right hairdo is more important than the thoughts that go on under the permanent wave.

So, perversely but emphatically, it was Mother's Day at the fortress of Machaerus. There is high tragedy in the concluding line of this narrative of Salome. A soldier brought the head of John the Baptist, "and the girl gave it to her mother." She is saying, "Here, mother, is a present for you. This is what you wanted most of all." It is not hard to imagine a daughter who might well have been a great personality, rich in sympathy, generous in spirit, strong in Christian character, bringing to her mother a stunted life and saying, "This is what you wanted, mother." It is a critical hour when another looks to us and says, "What shall I ask?" Pray God for mercy and grace in that hour.

"Whoever does the will of God is my brother, and sister, and mother." (Mark 3:31-35.)

One of life's hardest battles is not that against hate but that against love. It is a battle against the mistaken enclosures which sometimes make family barricades a hazard to a life's service. True family affection should be an incentive and support of service in the larger realm, and not a substitute for it. A family should be a harbor from which the ship leaves to sail the seas, and not a dock where it ties up and rots. Jesus' action and words picture God's compelling priorities—the wider family, the fellowship of the doers of his will. The great values of home, of love, and of community must be carried out into the larger, complete circle.

—Exposition of Mark in THE INTERPRETER'S BIBLE

"*You* hinder me, *for you do not side with God, but with men!" (Matt. 16:23, Goodspeed.)*

This answer of Jesus makes clear that the most formidable hindrances which can shackle any life are the hindrances of love. They are the forces which crowd a person or an organization of persons into the easiest way; which pull them down from the heights of achievement by well-meaning fears.

Friends often hinder each other, till a mistaken love's harping on safety and comfort becomes just what Jesus called it, the very voice of the devil.

The blind, smothering care of parents sends children into the world maimed, as far as the possible powers of their spirits are concerned. We shudder at the story of the slaughter of the innocents in the Gospel of Matthew. But a slaughter of innocents goes on in our comfort-loving day, when the main drive of parents is so often to prepare children for conformity and the material success to which it leads. Every precious individual difference, giving promise of individuality, every spontaneous emotion which might lead to original independent personality is carefully snapped off, as a Japanese gardener binds back and cuts off branches in the training of a stunted tree. Thus they are hindered from ever achieving that self-forgetful enthusiasm which is the very core of Christianity. Soul binding is a far deeper hurt than foot binding.

—PREACHING VALUES IN NEW TRANSLATIONS OF THE NEW TESTAMENT

"Come and lay your hands on her, so that she may be made well and live." (Mark 5:23.)

Even upon sorrow, trouble, affliction, Christ has laid his hand, and instead of bringing death, they have lived to bless. That is an outstanding truth of all Christian history, dark and mysterious, but as true and inescapable as sunlight. . . . The supreme example, of course, is Jesus himself. He laid his hands on an evil thing, a cross. And it lived. . . .

Jairus begged Jesus to lay his hands on a child. Can Christian parents make the same prayer unreservedly? All too often there is a trace of fear lest Christ lay his hands too closely on a young life; lest the youth take him too seriously, and follow him into unusual paths, perhaps dangerous ones; lest the young life be not stamped with the familiar pattern of a social set. The future of Christianity depends in a real way on the number of parents who will say to Christ, "Lay thy hands upon this child."

"And they laughed at him." (Mark 5:40.)

It all comes down to the tremendous doctrine of the Incarnation. If Jesus was just a poetic soul who taught a vague and foggy theism and recommended kindness and goodwill, then a laugh might be excused. But if God was in Christ, reconciling the world to himself, then the last word is with him.

The disciple is not above his Master. The ears of the sensitive disciple will always hear somebody's laughter. It will stretch the whole octave from the deep-throated scorn of power and pride, to the shrill, obscene giggle of frivolity. Jesus heard it—and went on with his saving work.

—Exposition of Mark in THE INTERPRETER'S BIBLE

10

Breaking Bread—Expositions on the Sacraments

"When he had given thanks he gave it to them." (Mark 14:23.)
"Until that day when I drink it new in the kingdom of God." (Mark 14:25.)

DEATH WAS JUST OUTSIDE THE DOOR; YET JESUS TWICE GAVE THANKS. HE could do it in serenity. Death might be just outside the door, but God was inside the door. Jesus' reliance on his Father was so complete that there was no occasion which did not call for thanksgiving. Where trust like his prevails, one can be thankful in any amazement. The Lord's Supper is a joyful affair—not a looking backward to tragedy, but a looking forward to victory and the consummation of a kingdom.

—Exposition of Mark in THE INTERPRETER'S BIBLE

"And they continued steadfastly in the breaking of bread." (Acts 2:42.)

On these words F. J. Foakes-Jackson comments: "Even apart from the Lord's Supper, the breaking of the loaf had a peculiar significance for the disciples of Jesus and a common meal, in which they believed themselves to be closely united to the Master, was partaken of by the Christian community from the first."

These words open to us a glimpse of one of the greater possible advances of Christianity in the next hundred years. That advance is nothing less than the extension into the common life of the conception of the sacramental nature of bread. It is to surround and permeate the whole complex business of breadmaking, bread-winning, and bread-distributing with the spirit of brotherhood. It is to grasp more deeply and largely the social message of the communion service, so that that service shall be a moving symbol of the mutuality of all breaking of bread, as a process of brotherhood in the spirit of Christ. . . .

In this connection Dr. L. P. Jacks has said startling words. "Bread-winning and soul saving are not two independent operations," he says. "A civilization saves its soul by the way it wins its daily bread." And looking about us in many places we may well add, "A civilization damns its soul by the way it forces its members to win their bread." . . .

The communion service should be a symbol of the sanctification of agriculture and industry, a pledge that all meals which the millions eat of the bounty of God on this planet are holy meals. The processes of breadmaking and bread-sharing may be a true means of communion with God, if engaged in in the spirit of Jesus Christ.

—THE ACTS OF THE APOSTLES IN PRESENT-DAY PREACHING. VOL. I

"This is my blood." (Mark 14:24.)

Several years ago a missionary just returned from Borneo, attended a meeting of the executive committee of the board of foreign missions under which he had served in the South Seas. He presented the board a Communion cup. The members were grateful for the gift and expressed their thanks, but did not think too much about it, as they were often given objects brought back by missionaries from fields overseas. Then the missionary went on to explain that this Communion cup had been used by Christian church members who, a few years earlier, had been cannibals. To them the words of the Communion service, this is my blood, had a stark, literal meaning. They had been in the habit of drinking the blood of people they had killed. That cup was a vivid and striking symbol of the power of the gospel to redeem people from savagery. We all too often forget the power of the gospel to lift up from the depths. A church congregation would be greatly surprised if some morning the minister should say, "I have a special message this morning for those who have killed someone this past week." But that is what the missionary could say, and did say, to cannibals.

Christ has a special message to all who are in the grip of sin—any sin.

The righteousness of God is not merely that of a judge condemning sin. It is also his gift of Christ, through whom in faith, men may be forgiven and given power to live according to his will and love.

A man in San Francisco watched with amazement the loading of a ship by means of a magnet. This powerful magnet lifted up a load of pig iron and deposited it on the ship. As this man looked at that demonstration of lifting by an invisible force, the words of Jesus in the Gospel of John came to mind, "I, if I be lifted up . . . will draw all men unto me." The two aspects of the righteousness and justice of God are presented in the prayer known as the General Confession. It confesses that "we have erred and strayed." There is the condemnation of sin by God, but it goes on to pray that "we may lead a godly, righteous, and sober life." There is the other aspect of the righteousness of God, the gift of power through Christ to live a godly life. Will we take that power for our lives?

—NEW CENTURY LEADER

"He broke the loaves and gave them to the disciples to set before the people." (Mark 6:41.)

Jesus has always given back what was given to him, enlarged and multiplied. Mothers brought their children, and he took them, and handed them back dearer than ever before, because he had blessed them. Men brought him a Roman coin, and he handed it back, a larger thing, a symbol of man's relationship to God and the state. Some brought him their lives, responding to his call "Follow me," and he handed those lives back, multiplied in power and possibility. Others brought him a cross, and he took it and handed it back to the world, transformed and enlarged, no longer a thing of shame, but a symbol of God's redeeming love. Whatever we give him he will enlarge for the service of human need.

—Exposition of Mark in THE INTERPRETER'S BIBLE

11

If Christ Had Not Been Raised—Expositions on the Resurrection

"If Christ has not been raised, then our preaching is in vain and your faith is in vain." (I Cor. 15:14.)

THESE WORDS ARE, AMONG OTHER THINGS, EVIDENCE OF THE CENTRAL place of the Resurrection in the earliest message, the Kerygma of the Christian church. It was not an ethical culture society which made its way through the Greek and Roman world. There were plenty of those. Good ones too. It was the story of a man who lived, taught, died, and rose again which won converts by the multitudes. The essential message was that of Jesus and the Resurrection.

That basic conviction grows in importance in our day when the main grasp of the truth of the Resurrection and life eternal is slackening among large parts of Christian people.

Take away that faith in Christ rising from the dead—and much remains. Jesus remains, the teacher remains, the Master remains. But the Savior is gone! There is little foundation for faith in a redeemed world. Such a faith must cover more time than Wednesday afternoon, or time itself. There is no hope for a redeemed world if there is nothing that transcends this earth and time itself.

Things often get so bad that only eternity can heal them. If Christ was not raised from the dead, there is no healing. John Masefield has expressed this powerfully in a dramatic scene from his poem *The Widow in the Bye Street*. A widow is present at the execution of her son. She is moved to pray, and in her prayer for her son, she refers to the hope of eternal life as "a rest for broken things too broke to mend." There was no mending anything on earth for her son. Only the Eternal God can deal with things "too broke to mend."

This is to be held close in the mind to another truth about eternal life. Eternal life means the *quality* of life rather than its length. As one has said, "Easter is not a passport to another world, but a quality of life for this one."

—PREACHING VALUES IN THE EPISTLES OF PAUL

"He is not here; see the place where they laid him." (Mark 16:6.)

The words of this invitation to see the place where Jesus had been buried quicken the imagination. We think of that tomb, and then we think of others in which Jesus has been buried and from which he has burst forth. They have laid him away times without number in tombs so strong, so heavily sealed, that it looked as though he could never again emerge as a disturbing force; only to find once more, in the language of the Easter hymn, that "Christ has burst his prison."

Come, see some of the places "where they laid him." Sometimes he has been interred in the church and in its creeds. Christianity in its official presentation has often been a smothered religion. The face of the Master has been so frequently wrapped around with the winding sheets of philosophy and metaphysics that it has been hard for plain people to recognize him. Theological statements have been substituted for a living experience. Jesus has been imprisoned in stained-glass windows, a figure rich in color but remote from life. He has been buried in a Book, venerated at a distance. He has been shut up in an organization. Mistaken minds have said: "The little area of life in this enclosure is religion. Let Jesus and his ideas stay there, and not get loose in the world, where they would be sure to make trouble." So men have tried to bury him, as the authorities in Jerusalem tried to put him away in a tomb, where he could not interfere with the profits of the temple traffic, or be a threat to their power.

But Jesus breaks out of every man-made tomb. Now and then on the bulletin boards of post offices we see pictured the face of a man who has escaped from jail, with this warning, "Dangerous man at large." That is, in very truth, the message of the Resurrection. "The most dangerous Man in the world is at large. Jesus Christ has broken jail."

"And when the Sabbath was past, Mary Magdalene, and Mary the Mother of James, and Salome, bought spices." (Mark 16:1.)

These women who figure so notably in the resurrection stories portray powerfully the love that does not end with death. They loved Jesus beyond the end. They sought to pay the last reverence that could be paid. But on their sad journey of faithfulness they ran into a surprise. Faithfulness has a way of running into surprises. When one goes faithfully on with duty, doing in times of darkness, disappointment, or defeat, what is often the little that can be done in devotion to Christ one meets the unexpected. The thing beyond one's own power and wit happens. New strength; the comfort of the fortified heart; the fresh awareness of a Burden-bearer, walking alongside; the way opened through seemingly insuperable obstacles—all these surprises of God have been encountered along the road of faithfulness.

—Exposition of Mark in THE INTERPRETER'S BIBLE

"Many of the saints who had fallen asleep rose." (Matt. 27:52, Goodspeed.)

Considered as a symbolic picture, the truth of this miracle has been attested through all the centuries. We have here the statement that, at the supreme moment of the sacrifice of Jesus on Calvary, the dead arose. It is profoundly true that whenever the spirit which Jesus manifested on Calvary finds expression in life it shocks men into life. "Saints who have fallen asleep" arise. There is nothing which has proved so powerful an awakener as Jesus' spirit of sacrificial love incarnate in a personality. It plays havoc with cemeteries, whether in the church or out of it!

—PREACHING VALUES IN NEW TRANSLATIONS OF THE NEW TESTAMENT

"Continued steadfastly in prayer . . . with Mary, the mother of Jesus." (Acts 1:14.)

Here is a fleeting glimpse of a chapter in Mary's life which has been almost totally obscured in the reverence with which she has been covered. (Instead of "covered" one almost writes "smothered.")

After the high days of that last week at Jerusalem; after the supreme experiences of the arrest, trial, crucifixion, and resurrection of Jesus; after drama, tragedy, and grief, Mary takes her place as one of the number forming the Christian fellowship and church.

At first glance this might seem a strange anticlimax. For a chief figure in so momentous a chapter in history, one who had borne such a burden of grief, to become numbered as one among many, quietly taking a place in the ranks of those bent on a new undertaking, might well seem a descent into plain, pedestrian prose.

It was, however, a real climax. Mary's action channeled great experiences into the ongoing purposes of life. And that is always a great climax. It is the great achievement of picking life up again after tumult and catastrophe and making it new. It is the renouncing of what might have been regarded as a claim of exemption due to personal position or grief and taking one's place in the ranks for daily service and fellowship. Mary showed a victorious way of dealing with grief—by transcending it through turning its great emotion into steady power. So often grief is made an excuse for nonparticipation in associated effort. Grief frequently results in a paralyzing fixation of personality and character. The procession of life is definitely halted at the point in experience where the great loss occurred. And over such a life is often written the epitaph in *Hamlet*, "The rest is silence." Mary showed a more excellent way.

The presence of the name of Mary, mother of Jesus, in the list of the makers of the church throws light on another great problem in the management of life, that of making great inspirations available for the plainest labor. These should not be kept locked away from "human nature's daily need." A beautiful picture of the relationship which should hold between great experience and daily work is given by Mrs. Thirkell, the granddaughter of Burne-Jones the painter, in her reminiscences. She says that Burne-Jones put one of his beautiful windows with the Holy Grail over the sink where the scullery maid washed up. Mary put great memories into a place in her life where they might be a power for ongoing tasks.

—The Acts of the Apostles in Present-Day Preaching. Vol. I

> *"It is no longer I who live, but Christ who lives in me; and the life I now live in the flesh I live by faith in the Son of God, who loved me and gave himself for me."* (Gal. 2:20, R.S.V.)

Here is the beating heart of the gospel. Here is the good news to all people. In Christ a man can be a new creature. Christ lives in him. That is the great charter of the Christian faith. The good news of the gospel is not "Try real hard to be good." That is laudable advice, but there is no saving gospel in it. A living power comes into life, making a change in the personality. It is no longer the old "I," but Christ on the throne of a life, directing and empowering it.

Man needs the entrance of a new power into his life. There is a moving portrait which acquires the quality of a symbol in Hermann Hagedorn's biography of Edwin Arlington Robinson, that strangely repressed personality. Hagedorn describes Robinson's lonely years in New York, in his room on the fourth floor back. "Seeing him in his narrow room, sitting with his back to the window, facing the door, it seemed that Robinson was waiting for someone to come in by that door, someone who would change everything." When Christ comes in by the open door of our life, he changes everything. "No longer I." The wonder is described in Revelation, "Behold, I stand at the door and knock; if any one hears my voice and opens the door, I will come in to him and eat with him, and he with me" (3:20). It is the glory of the Christian faith that Christ does come in.

The words "in Christ" must be given a concrete and not a metaphorical meaning. Christ must be enthroned if he is to live in us. It is not enough to make him merely one of a number of interests, and very often not even first. If it is to be "Christ liveth in me," he must be elevated above all.

Notice that preceding the words "Christ liveth in me" are other words, "I am crucified with Christ" (K.J.V.). Remember that that is both the preface and the conclusion of Christ living with us. There are two aspects of being "crucified with Christ." It means participating in all the gifts of God in Christ—forgiveness, sonship, and reconciliation. It means also a tremendous thing, to share the motives and the purposes of Christ, and the way of life that led Jesus to the cross. That is part of the cost of being crucified with Christ. Its high reward is to have Christ live in us.

—MORE PREACHING VALUES IN THE EPISTLES OF PAUL

"The former treatise." (Acts 1:1.)

The Christian message must always take on some of the qualities of a newspaper. The evangel is literally new every morning, with the authentic additions of yesterday's experience and history. All through history there has been the conflict between the Files and Today's Edition. It is not an exaggeration to say that two guilds have been at work in the Christian church, the embalmers and the creators. The embalmers are those who feel that all wisdom and history worth noting are entombed in the back files of yesterday. The creators are those who think of their religion as a living, flowing, dynamic, many-sided experience. In their conception, any "former treatise" is always fulfilled in a new "extra."

The tragedy of conceiving our religion as a closed book is well, though unintentionally, pictured in a religious newspaper's report of a sunrise Easter service: "Easter dawn service began at five-thirty and was over just after the dawn." Too many Christian undertakings have been "over just after the dawn," prematurely embalmed in the back files. —THE ACTS OF THE APOSTLES IN PRESENT-DAY PREACHING. VOL. I

"For we know that if the earthly tent we live in is destroyed, we have a building from God, a house not made with hands, eternal in the heavens." (II Cor. 5:1.)

We're tenting tonight
On the old camp ground.

That bit of an old Civil War song seems like a crude remembrance to associate in any way with Paul's sublime declaration of the Christian faith.

Yet it is true to some of its meaning. We *are* in a *war*, "for we are not contending against flesh and blood, but against the principalities, against the powers, against the world rulers of this present darkness" (Eph. 6:12). And we *are* in a tent, a temporary habitation. We look forward to moving day, to a permanent home, to a house not made with hands. Moffatt's rendering strongly suggests moving day: "If this earthly tent of mine is taken down, I get a home from God." There is an old gospel song, not part of the twaddle which sounded out with such clamor, but true:

> I'm but a stranger here;
> Heaven is my home.

Often it even seems a flapping tent. But do not despise the tent. That has been frequently done, with dire results. Francis Thompson, the poet, at one time in his life despised the earthly tent. He called it "vile corruption." His life was crippled and shortened by his thoughtless abuse of the tent. Our earthly tent is a gift of God to be held in honor. It is a temple of God.

But it is a tent compared to the house prepared for us. When we think of these words, "tent" and "eternal habitation," we are amazed at the amount of decoration that some people put on the tent. They spend a lifetime amassing decorations and hangings for the earthly tent—it becomes their whole concern—but never a thought to the permanent house not made by hands but by God.

What an idiot's folly, a curious show place for the crowd, it would be if a man had fitted out a little tent on the back part of his estate and hung it with priceless hangings and put million-dollar paintings on the sides, and left a great home empty except for dust and echoes. Yet exactly that is a common sight. The point of it all is in Phillips' translation, "We want our transitory life to be absorbed in the life that is eternal" (II Cor. 5:4).

We look over death. Elizabeth Barrett Browning tells how, at the death of little Joe Story, the playmate of her boy, Pen, she was so much overcome that she almost fell off the seat of the carriage. She sat beside the bereaved mother and she wrote her, "I can't look on the earthward side of death. I flinch from corpses and graves. When I look deathwards, I look over death upwards." Over death—upwards! Tent and house!

The tent is God's gift. Cherish it. But don't forget Moving Day.

—MORE PREACHING VALUES IN THE EPISTLES OF PAUL

IV

Commentator

Into this section have gone the letters of Simeon Stylites and parts of chapters from a number of books in which Luccock spoke primarily as commentator and prophet. Hard as this field is to define precisely within its broadest limits he did more of his published writing than in any other area. The weekly column in *The Christian Century* gave him for more than twelve years a forum from which to comment on the passing scene. His subjects ranged all the way from a dim and despairing view of TV commercials and status seekers (whether the social or ecclesiastical variety), to praise for the church choir and encouragement for the "late bloomers." The selections gathered here are those which best express his satire and his humor, his impatience with pomp and cant.

Had he been a baseball pitcher one of his best pitches would surely have been a reverse curve. He put many maxims into reverse and came up with profound truth. He was fascinated by words; he made them his vehicles for probing far reaches of truth.

The titles of the divisions within this section have been lifted up by the editor from a single piece that generally covers an area of interest or concern. In some cases they only vaguely describe the purpose in the author's mind when he wrote the other selections that have been grouped with the title piece. No selection here except the two letters on humor and religion bears any definitive relationship to any other.

Slightly less than 10 per cent of all the letters of Simeon Stylites are represented here. It was a policy rarely violated to include *whole* selections rather than scraps and snippets of pieces. The letters of Simeon are more autobiographical of the author's mind than any other writing he did. The pastor of St. John's-by-the-Gas Station is Halford Luccock's alter ego.

Nearly two thirds of these selections in the Treasury have not appeared previously in book form.

1

"Grace Notes" and Other Notes for Living

Grace Notes

SIR: I LIKE TO WRITE ABOUT MUSIC. MY STYLE IS NOT CRAMPED BY ANY hampering knowledge of that subject, so I have complete freedom. This is known as freedom of the press. This time I am concerned with "grace notes." I can't tell the difference between a flock of grace notes in flight and a herd of counterpoint. To me grace notes are a bevy of little flags and dots dancing with abandon all over the page—unnecessary flourishes to a piece of music. They are not essential to the harmony or melody but they do add a lively sort of rock and roll to the serious business of the opus. In short, they are embellishments. Vive l'embellishment!

Now of course you cannot make a great piece of music out of embellishments, just as you cannot make a full meal out of parsley; you have to have something solid to embellish. But they look nice, and they add enormously to the music.

Grace notes in living are things that are not really necessary to the running of the house or the business or whatever—the flourishes that add immeasurably to the joy of life. Indeed, it is often the flourishes that make life endurable. Someone once said of a friend that he could make the opening of a can of sardines a festival. That is what totally superfluous flounces will do for sardines. Something of the festive quality that is possible in life is indicated in the tribute, "When he came into a room, it was as though another candle had been lighted." We live by admiration, hope, and love—and also by the things that are unnecessary. Without these grace notes life is like a long solo on the bass drum, and the feeling of the last weary mile comes very soon. All too often Duty, that stern daughter of the voice of God, has no grace notes. That is why doing one's duty often seems like taking a cold shower bath at six in the morning. A good mother sometimes has to do her duty with a paddle christened "The Board of Education" (if there is no paddle handy, a hairbrush will do very well), but if she is wise she softens the music of the paddle with grace notes.

Take marriage. (Go ahead and take it, if you don't already have it; you might like it.) A marriage without grace notes is a bleak journey. There is a fine phrase about husband and wife being "joint heirs of the grace of life." To become such they must scatter about a good supply of tuneful notes that are, in the strict bond, superfluous.

The pity is that the unexpected kindness and the tribute that comes like a bolt out of the blue are hard for some awkward husbands to manage. They feel like an elephant picking daisies. But daisies make lovely bouquets! After all, Christopher Morley's definition is right: "The plural of spouse is spice." Spice is a piquant seasoning. Many a wife looking back over the years does not think so much of food or shelter or even of sterling character as of a few words that were said at moments of remembrance—grace notes in the symphony of life.

The decline of conversation is partly due to the scarcity of its own kind of grace notes, lively embellishments to talk. W. S. Gilbert sagely said, "It is not what is on the table that counts, but what is on the chairs." When conversation at home, for instance, degenerates mainly into "What channel does *Manslaughter* come on?" there is an urgent need for life-saving grace notes.

Yours,
SIMEON STYLITES
—THE CHRISTIAN CENTURY

Consider the Corncrake

SIR: I try to learn something new every year. I do not always make it, but this year I have already learned something, and the year is not yet half over. I have learned what a corncrake is. I always thought it was some sort of harvesting machine that went up and down the rows of corn and picked off the ears. Now I have learned that it is a bird. The dictionary calls it "a European rail" and adds that it is a bird common in grain fields.

I began my researches on the corncrake through coming across a tribute to its noble qualities paid about a century ago by Dean Liddon of St. Paul's Cathedral in London. The dean's friend Dr. T. B. Strong, bishop of Oxford, tells us about it:

We were walking in the fields and heard a corncrake croaking in the grass. "I like that bird," Liddon said. I said I thought I had heard birds that sang better.

"Oh, it's not that," said Liddon. "To me it represents moral earnestness. It goes on saying what it knows to be unpalatable."

That is a rare kind of courage—"moral earnestness to keep on saying what it knows to be unpalatable." We need in the United States today the croaking of the corncrake rather than the screaming of the American eagle.

Of course there is no virtue in constantly serving up the unpalatable just for the sake of causing wry faces and sour stomachs. Mere pugnacity gives a stimulation like that of whisky, and is just as deceptive. A single-minded devotion to unpopular truth may be a form of exhibitionism—the only way one can get attention. The English poet Samuel Rogers, who is remembered far more for his breakfast parties than for his poetry, once confessed, "I have a weak voice and unless I say something nasty no one will pay any attention to me."

Nevertheless, the moral earnestness of the corncrake is needed, on the street, in the school, in the legislative halls, and in the pulpit. Truth which has any saving power in a world rushing down a steep place is bound to be unpalatable to large numbers of people and to strongly entrenched interests. Mr. Dooley is a good guide for any public figure. He said, "It is my business to comfort the afflicted and to afflict the comfortable." That, by the way, is a good book on preaching in thirteen words.

We read in the Song of Solomon that "the voice of the turtle (dove) is heard in the land." That is a sign of spring. But internationally and in almost every other way it is still deep winter, and the voice of the corncrake is far more in order than the song of the turtle dove.

The nation needs to hear unpalatable things about our foreign policy. More and more we tend to approach the whole question of world survival with the mind of a drill sergeant. In his introduction to *Androcles and the Lion* George Bernard Shaw wrote: "The world is largely governed by considerations which occur to stockbrokers in the first five minutes." We are worse off than that. We seem to be governed, in fateful hours, by considerations that occur to generals in the first two minutes, and by little else. One encouraging note is that there has been a decidedly corncrake quality in recent statements by many religious bodies on this danger. Talk about civil liberties is very unpalatable in many places. The one counsel is, "For heaven's sake, drop it." There is need for the continuous, even if raucous, song of the corncrake.

I see I have become quite an ornithologist. Yet I have never seen or heard a corncrake. Will someone please tell me whether it thrives and croaks in the U.S.A.?

Yours,
SIMEON STYLITES
—LIVING WITHOUT GLOVES

Total Recall

SIR: I do not know who invented the affliction known to psychologists as "total recall"—whether it was Freud, Jung, or merely Mrs. Whosis—but it is really quite something when you hear it in action. It may not be as dangerous to life as the new brands of virus, so popular this year, but it has twinges of its own. As done in its best form it means exactly what the name says: the ability—and eagerness—to recall everything, which means *everything*.

The commonest variety of sufferer is the person who takes the words of greeting "How are you?" not as a salutation but as an invitation to report on clinical research, and he recalls the total situation of lungs, lights, and liver.

Or take another species. The conversation is moving along—nothing momentous, but it *is* moving—when he is struck with total recall, like a sudden attack of apoplexy. He—in my experience it is usually she—tunes up. Someone has, unfortunately, mentioned Los Angeles. That does it! The total recall is on. Her visit to the place is unrolled all the way from the "unusual" rain to the plots, if any, of all the broadcasts to which she got free tickets—including the biography of the man who gave the tickets, who turned out, this will kill you, to be a nephew of Minnie Wilkins, you know, who used to teach school at Seneca Falls, New York. It is the nearest thing to perpetual motion yet devised.

A special case, or an aggravated one, is a wife's total recall. That puts the husband on the hot seat for an hour or so. Something snaps, and the living wife goes into a complete remembrance of every bonehead act poor Jim ever pulled off, beginning with the forgotten railroad tickets on the wedding journey and coming up by uneasy stages to the time he got arrested for telling off a traffic policeman, with a detour—ten minutes—about the upset canoe. This makes poor Jim, who is thus portrayed as a candidate for a mental hospital, think longingly of the fine old judicial decision of English law that it was permitted to hit your wife with a "reasonable instrument." (Is a nice soft towel soaked with chloroform a "reasonable instrument"?)

Total recall, on the platform or in the pulpit, is the world's best cure for insomnia. Robert Louis Stevenson said that if he knew how to omit he could make an *Iliad* out of a daily newspaper. The total recallers can create a forty-eight-page Sunday supplement out of an obscure footnote. There is so much detail in the background that the foreground goes underground.

What can be done about it? Nothing, I suppose, except resignation to the will of God. However, here is a four-point program to work on:

1. Try to forget one thing a day. That is slow, but concentrate! There is the time you had to walk down the Eiffel Tower. It is a gorgeous conversation piece, like one of the old Paine's fireworks. Forget it!
2. Try tying up your jaws with an old stocking. Do it by degrees, five minutes at first, then up to an hour. Practice makes perfect.
3. Give your ears, instead of your jaws, a workout for a change.
4. Enroll in a memory course. That will paralyze your memory, trying to remember the clue techniques.

I can't recall anything else.

Yours,
Simeon Stylites

Late Bloomers

SIR: I have not been officially authorized by the Amalgamated Youth of America to award a Distinguished Service Medal with Crossed Palms to President Charles W. Cole of Amherst College. But I was never one to stand on formalities; I will volunteer. In his address at an anniversary meeting of the College Entrance Examination Board, Dr. Cole rendered distinguished service to a lot of frustrated youngsters. As a result, history will doubtless take a new turn.

All the downtrodden kids whose lives have been blighted by flunking college board examinations will yell themselves hoarse over the belated appearance of a champion for their case against fate. They always knew there was something wrong with the college boards, and here comes an LL.D. saying, "Boys and girls, you were right. There *is* something rotten in the state of Denmark, New York, Illinois, Texas, and Hollywood." He said that the students who receive mediocre or poor grades very often later become distinguished leaders. He said that the college admission system has put a premium on precocity, favoring those who mature early. He also suggested (oh happy thought!) that many of the geniuses who come through with an average of 96.7 per cent have frequently shot their whole intellectual wad and will never fire again. The colleges, he said, should pay more attention to the "late bloomers" who get a slow start in the spring but before snow falls proliferate into roses the size of sunflowers. (Free translation.)

Sweet music! Play it again! If I had only heard about the "late bloomers" in my misspent high-school days! Then, when I had to face the report that I got 62 in English, 57 in French, and 45 in algebra, I would have had a snappy comeback. I would have said, squaring my shoulders and looking her straight in the face, "Miss Minerva, you are all wet. Your educational theory is behind the times. I am not a moron, as you ignorantly insist. I am one of the late bloomers, and President Cole says we are the white hope of civilization."

What a shot in the arm this news will be to a great host of mothers and fathers! With what agonizing concern they have followed the little craft of Tommie and Jane as it was tossed about in the educational whirlpool, far more turbulent than the Niagara River below the falls. They might pose for a picture of Hope, like the one by Watts, with only one string left on the harp; troubled by every report card, yet not distressed; perplexed, but not in despair; cast down, but not destroyed. Now they can lift up their hearts with the discovery that nature goes in for late bloomers. Teacher's verdict of "lunkhead" on Tommie is premature. The returns are not all in yet. So they can twang that one string again and make music out of it.

In fact, there is a higher authority for late bloomers than even President Cole. It says: "Be not weary . . . for in due season ye shall reap, if ye faint not." Also, in my new translation of the New Testament (everyone is taking a whack at it; why shouldn't I?) it says, "If the vision of Tommie and Jane as topflight performers tarry, wait for it."

Yours,

SIMEON STYLITES

—LIKE A MIGHTY ARMY

In Orbit

SIR: The phrase "in orbit" has been leaping out at us from the front page every day of the winter and spring. Even now it bobs up daily on pages 3 to 14 of the newspaper. Perhaps by the time you get this letter another new little satellite will be "orbiting." As the idea filters through to my dim mind, when a satellite gets high enough up out of the atmosphere it begins to go around and around. I hope no reader writes to me to explain it. That would be like explaining analytical geometry to Rin Tin Tin or Trigger. Perhaps Lassie could understand it. But such things are too high for me. I cannot attain them.

However, seeing the words so often has reminded me that the principal trouble with lots of people is that they do not get "in orbit." Men and women are made for motion but a great many of them never get going in a circle that takes in other people and the rest of the world. They get stuck on themselves. Not "stuck on themselves" in conceit—they may be as humble as a bashful turtle—but stuck on themselves as a fly is stuck on a piece of flypaper. The only Scripture they know is the blessed words "steadfast, immovable." There they stand, like St. George before the Dragon, always charging but never advancing.

Of these immovable saints it is often said in tribute, "You always know where to find him." Now that may be a real accolade of honor. It means that you always know you will find him under a load to be carried or in the front line of battle. But it has another meaning too—that you will find him hiding from a responsibility. When there is a vote for taxes to build a new high school in town, or a house-to-house canvass for the Red Cross or the Polio Fund, you always know where to find him—down in the cellar, sitting on his piggy bank.

> The king was in the countinghouse,
> Counting out his money.

You always knew where to find him!

But why pick on the men? Women can be just as immovable, without any more orbit than the figures on a Grecian urn. For, as the immortal poem records, truly,

> The queen was in the parlor,
> Eating bread and honey.

You always knew where to find her! Or, if the supply of honey is short, you will find her down at the High Calories Restaurant, eating Pie à la Mode with Whipped Cream on the side.

Like some other duds, at Cape Carnival and elsewhere, these people never get high enough off themselves to swing into orbit.

The value of an orbit does not depend on its dimension. St. Paul took a big orbit, the biggest. He wrote of "Whensoever I go to Spain." That was the jumping-off place. But there was a woman who got in orbit also—not around the world but just around the block; but she went round and round, and any case of needed clothes got her attention. Her name was Dorcas. She had a lot of societies named after her.

There is a good text for all this, in case anyone wants a text. It is, "He went about doing good." Jesus was in orbit. A small one. You can cover his whole orbit in two hours' driving. But it counted.

Ready for the countdown—three, two, one, zero! You're in orbit. Happy sailing!

Yours,
SIMEON STYLITES

Consider the Dodo

SIR: I'll bet you one thin dime that you didn't know that the Dodo family is mentioned in the Bible. If you won't take my word for it, look it up in your concordance under "Dodo"; it's there!

We so often use the word "Dodo" to describe an outdated relic that we are mildly shocked when we discover that two men named Dodo actually existed. They never got into any Hall of Fame themselves, but they deserve some recognition as progenitors of some notable characters. The first Dodo (see Judg. 10:1) was the grandfather of Tola, one of the Judges of Israel; the second (II Sam. 23:9) was the father of one of the three mighty men of David.

A pun is not a great spiritual weapon, granted, but even the Bible has a few—and perhaps I can be forgiven just one. As we read about these men named Dodo we cannot help thinking what a perfect name it would be for lots of folks who still walk our streets (and for some who sit in Congress). "Dodo" has come to mean "an obsolete relic of a day that is past." Mr. Noah Webster, always a source of wisdom, says that a Dodo was a large, heavy, flightless bird, now extinct. Our trouble is that so many of the members of the Dodo family are *not* extinct. They are obsolete, but they still go on.

I recall a newspaper story a few years ago which recounted the fact that while excavating for the new library at Princeton, workmen dug up a fossil 175,000 years old. Now you might expect some bigoted men from Harvard or Yale to say that it was quite natural to find fossils at Princeton. But away with such slanders! Too many fossils, unfortunately, are not underground; they are in seats of power. Today's Dodos are those dangerous people who wish to apply to the life of today procedures that were evolved in an earlier and different day and which are no longer fitting or effective—just as back in the early days of the horseless carriages the cars were equipped with, of all things, whip sockets—a senseless carry-over from horse-and-buggy days (a case of what sociologists call "cultural lag").

The Dodo today is an exponent of super-patriotism and one-upmanship in an era in which competition in atomic armaments and threats to use such weapons may lead to global war and total annihilation. Mr. Dodo also still accepts obsolete theories of race superiority which have no standing in science whatever (a fact which bothers him not at all). Large numbers of ministers and laymen in The Methodist Church have recently been deeply concerned by the report of a committee appointed to report on the continuation of the segregated Central Jurisdiction—a report which declares that The Methodist Church should remain a segregated church. Somehow this reminds some of us of the achievements of the illustrious Dodo family.

When Jesus encountered people who live in the past he rebuked them, saying: "Ye have heard it said of old . . . But I say unto you . . ."

Yours,
Simeon Stylites

No Down Payment

SIR: I do not wish to alarm you, but there is a new and virulent disease spreading among us. It is not Asiatic flu—the doctors and care by the people will have that under control. The disease I refer to is one that we are enticed to all over the nation, in advertisements flaunting the seductive words, "No Down Payment!"

That alluring message accompanies advertisements of automobiles with tail lights as high as the second story, or deep freezes that you can crawl into on hot days. So millions get infected, with ultimate symptoms of flushed face and holes in the pocketbook. But on with the dance! They do not look at the number of installments—just at the happy thought of "No Down Payment" and only $49 a month (through all eternity).

Think of what would have happened to Methuselah if he had been taken in by the "No Down Payment" racket. Suppose he had bought a 4004 B.C. model camel for racing purposes. Now, assuming that he bought the racer when he was a gay young blade about town, at the age of 21, he would have had to pay $49 a month for 948 years. Let's see, that makes 948 years times twelve months times $49—it makes me dizzy. It would have made Methuselah dizzy. It makes many modern travelers dizzy, too.

The worst of this sickness is that it spreads to other realms, apparently by contagion. Is not one trouble with modern marriage—a trouble that packs the divorce courts—the illusion of No Down Payment? Not the down payments on the carpets and the furniture (though they are heavy enough), but the failure to make the real down payment for a successful marriage: the patience, the suppression of self, the love up "to the level of each day's most quiet need." That is a high level; in fact, the top.

And, come to think of it—and I hope you will—does not much of the difficulty in making any real advance in church unity arise from the insistence of some church leaders and members that there shall be no down payment? They will talk about church unity, they will write books about it (and occasionally even read them), they will go to conferences and sing about it to the skies:

> We are not divided, all one body we,
> One in hope and doctrine, one in charity.

But no down payment, no concession in any of their practices, no change in a single tittle or jot in their procedures. These are to be kept as the laws of the Medes and Persians. But the fact is that anything good on earth, including the kingdom of God and a united church, demands a down payment.

The same holds in national life. For instance, it is time for a down payment on integration in the public schools. Stalwarts who refuse to admit that there is a United States of America, governed by law and not by anarchy, will have to be made to see that. Integration is, of course, a long installment affair of social change. It calls for understanding and sympathy by all concerned for long years. But there is a down payment due now, in concrete act.

However, let's keep the proportions right. The biggest thing on the horizon in many difficult spots is that down payments of effort and successful practice are being made daily.

Yours,
SIMEON STYLITES

How To

SIR: Seated one day at the card catalogue of the public library I was weary and ill at ease, and my fingers wandered idly over the cards. Then I struck a chord of excitement: I came across the section listing the books beginning with today's magic words in America, "How To." I measured them. There were more than 250 entries. I asked the lady at the desk whether that was all and she said there were cases more, in the attic and in the cellar and down the drain. Apparently it has not entered into the mind of man—or woman—to conceive of a subject for which there is not a complete set of directions on "How to Do It."

There are guides to the whole blooming world. Consider, for example, that useful and fascinating volume *How to Tell Your Friends from the Apes.* These books have an amazing range—*How to Get Rich in Washington* (perhaps the late Senator Albert Fall read that one), *How to Afford That College Education, How to Sell Your Way into the Big Money.* Some of them show a deplorable trace of frivolity, such as *How to Run a Bassoon Factory* (this one from England) and *How to Lie with Statistics.* The themes vary from the highly complicated, such as *How to Train a Young Dog,* to the elementary and simple, *How to Be Happy.*

There must be some great moral to this How-To library, but it keeps eluding me. One thing that is clear is that we are living in a How-To culture. We are more intent on how to do things, anything, than on *what* to do. We are more keen on how to build missiles, guided and unguided, than on how to make missiles obsolete. It is quite a contagious and deadly disease that we have caught—being more interested in means than in ends. This is the conclusion of a man who has studied the subject extensively—William H. Whyte, Jr., who reports in *The Organization Man* that less than a third of our college students "are now majoring in anything that could be called a fundamental discipline—in the liberal arts *or* in the sciences." Content to take society as it is, they "table the subject of ends, and concentrate instead on means." To these college young people strong opinions about social injustices are "old hat"; so they are more and more interested in methodology.

On the large national scale that attitude shows up in a greater interest in how to build atomic submarines than in what to put into civilization to make it worth preserving. Lord Elton, the chief executive officer of the Rhodes scholarship trust, recently delivered a sharp blow when he said, "Education in the space age faces the danger of trying to turn out technologists rather than to provide an education." Speaking of his own university he added: "I regard as the great pride of Oxford its ability to present an entirely 'useless' training in that it does not concentrate on technical know-how."

A present danger is that the How To infection is invading education. The silliest thing I have ever heard on TV—and that covers a wide, wide stretch—is the impassioned utterance of Admiral Rickover to a congressional committee this spring. He said that we should "get education out of the hands of the educators." Three cheers! The admiral did not say who should replace the educators. Perhaps admirals could take over and swab the decks clear of any nonsense about liberal education.

How about giving "How" a bit of a rest? It has been working awfully hard. We might learn "What" and "Why." Could be.

Yours,
SIMEON STYLITES

Adapting the Play

SIR: This is a round trip, free, so all aboard for Japan. But prepare to end up at the church down the street or in your own house. The trip to Japan is conducted by James A. Michener, writing in *Holiday* magazine about the Japanese theater:

> Since a complete historical play of eleven full acts takes more than a day, a *kabuki* program is made up of choice bits of many plays, whose stories are impossible to follow. I once boned up on a play whose synopsis read, "Two men meet in a lonely gorge and are about to kill one another when from a distance a strange man cries, 'Wait a minute,' and tells them how foolish they are to fight." I went to the play, but it wasn't a lonely gorge; it was a luxurious palace. It wasn't two lonely men; it was three bullies, each with

eight retainers. They weren't stopped by a man; it was a woman. And she didn't preach peace, but killed eighteen servants. I went back to the synopsis, and read in the fine print, "Sometimes local companies adapt this play to their own actors."

The punch line, of course, is the last one: "Sometimes local companies adapt this play to their own actors." That happens outside the Japanese theater too. We can set that line down in church history, past and present. We can also set it down in a chair in our own living room and let it look at us. How tragically often local companies have adapted the drama of the gospel to suit the limitations of their own actors! The drama is entitled *God Is Love*, but it has been revised until it suits the talents of actors who turn it into the Inquisition, the torture chamber, the fires of Smithfield, and the whipping of Quakers. God and Love have both disappeared from the script, but otherwise it is good copy. The result in all centuries, alas, has been like the musical compositions we have all heard—"Variations on a Theme by Haydn," or some other composer—so varied that one wonders what the original theme might have been.

But we do not have to go back to the Middle Ages to find striking "adaptations" of the gospel script. We can see them in our own day. Consider the adaptations of the gospel drama made by local companies that are dedicated to sanctifying the practice of segregation. In the original script—admittedly a difficult one to produce—there were great lines such as "And he made from one every nation of men to live on the face of the earth." Since these are quite beyond the talents of some local companies adaptations were made, such as "Suffer the little white children to come unto me." Much easier, and the result is quite an agreeable little farce.

Again, the original script of the gospel had some great scenes, such as "Take up your cross and follow me." But that one did not fit in with what some local companies want to produce—a restful little play of serenity and relaxation. So all the stern demands and all the tragic sense of life are eliminated and the script is filled with happy thoughts and spiritual chaise longues. The theme of the adapted play is "Take it easy, everybody. Just wish your troubles away." Much easier to put on.

However, the original script, when produced by living actors, is a thriller!

Yours,
SIMEON STYLITES

Emergency Brake

SIR: Will you please stop whatever you are doing, put on your emergency brake, and listen to some words of caution about—you guessed it—the emergency brake. The subject recently bobbed up in a traffic court report. A woman who had been involved in a minor accident was closely questioned about how it happened. Asked if her brake was on, she replied with some heat that she was careful always to drive with the emergency brake on, so that in case an emergency arose she would be ready. Another bit of history, of earlier vintage, is the clever work of a freight train brakeman. On his very first run the train came to a steep grade which the engineer had difficulty negotiating. Upon reaching the summit, the engineer turned to his new brakeman and said, "We had a hard climb, didn't we?" "We sure did," said the brakeman, "and if I hadn't put on the brake we would've slipped back!"

A good many people seem to drive with the brake on. They never let themselves go. To them enthusiasm is a most dangerous fuel, one which if freely used will cause a disastrous runaway. So in their friendships, for instance, they drive with the emergency on. Friendship for them never becomes a free-for-all romp. They seem to measure themselves out with a medicine dropper; they seem to say to others, "I guess this little thimbleful of my concern will be enough for you."

Back in those dear dead days beyond recall, Bishop Robert McIntyre of The Methodist Church had one lecture which he gave all over the country. Its title: "Buttoned-Up People." I heard it at a tender age and can remember only its two oratorical high spots—the account of the Chicago fire, and the story of a farm boy going down to the springhouse, getting himself a dish of strawberries, and letting the cream run down over the berries like a glacier. It makes my mouth water yet! The lecture was a grand three-decker frigate which could sail any sea and take any audience into helpless captivity. It was a long, long shot, better than the drivel that is so often served up nowadays on TV (such as bang-bang soufflé).

Bishop McIntyre's point was well taken. The world has quite a number of "buttoned-up" people who drive with the emergency brake on, whose riches of personality are under such perfect control that you might say that *rigor mortis* had set in.

Perhaps even more people drive with the emergency brake on in regard to any kind of financial undertaking in the church or community. Thoreau said that we never know our neighbors until we pass a subscription paper among them. Of course, in these days of community campaigns for every one of the five hundred diseases that humanity is afflicted with, perhaps some kind of brake (or break) is called for. If we give a minimum gift of $5 to every one of the 500, the $2,500 total might make a dent even in *your* salary. Still, this is no excuse for always driving with the brake on. It causes total paralysis of the heart and pocketbook and permits no tingling "Let's go!"

Suppose the early church had been composed of a Brotherhood of Brakemen. Take off the emergency!

Yours,
SIMEON STYLITES

Holy Fog

SIR: How do you like the new Hymnbook? I do not mean one published by a church nor even an unofficial hymnbook for the saints, nor a songbook for the not-so-saintly teen-agers. I mean the entirely unofficial and growing collection of songs supposedly religious in nature which are wailed out from juke boxes or moaned on any occasion for lifting the voice in tune. They are all hymns of a very popular sect of so-called religion, which consists of a vague sort of blurred feeling without any specific belief indicated—just a comfortable kind of Holy Fog.

One popular expression of this cloudy faith is that veteran of many outbursts of harmony, "True Love." The singer declares that he has "a guardian angel on high" who has nothing to do but give him true love. That presents a very uplifting picture of an Unemployed God and a troop of not-so-busy angels. Nothing to do but look after their little Teacher's Pet! A very happy thought, on the same level as the remark of the girl who recommended prayer because she had once got a bicycle by praying.

Another popular anthem of this murky religion is the beautiful song from *Carousel*, "You'll Never Walk Alone." It is a fine melody, and the assurance ought to be welcome. But when one looks at the words the assurance dissolves into the advice to keep a stiff upper lip, throw your chin out, and keep walking, and as a result "you'll never walk alone." To keep your chin up and keep going is good advice at all times, but the song gives no specific reason for its assertion about not walking alone. It makes no suggestion of an Unseen Companion, though when one does not walk alone the reason is usually that someone walks with one. But the song presents no trace of any specific belief. It is just a fine fog blowing in from the unknown.

Another song popular in the services of this undefined religion is the older one entitled "I Believe." This consists of a fine collection of affirmations, either complete nonsense or innocuous commonplaces. This song has even been sung at funerals—God save the mark—as though it had a distant relationship to "I believe in God the Father." It has a wonderful feeling, like a happy period under an ether cone—no duties suggested, no need to disturb the mind. It is like "sleeping on a cloud."

Then there is the hymn to a blind fatalism—still trotted out when the other records have been played—which declares "What will be, will be." This profound idea is put into some language resembling Choctaw: "Kay sa daw sa daw" ("Que Sera, Sera" according to the label). It is another substitution of a somewhat Holy Fog for an articulate faith. Its nebulosity reminds us of the old story of an atheist on his deathbed. A friend encouraged him to "Hold on to it, Tom!" Tom would have liked to, but could only say, sadly, "There is nothing to hold on to."

We read in an old book, "The entrance of Thy word giveth light." It doesn't mention Holy Fog, no matter how melodious. For that is just another form of "Holy Smoke!"

Yours,

SIMEON STYLITES

—THE CHRISTIAN CENTURY

Don't Cut Off the Buttons

SIR: You won't believe this, but I will swear to it on the Revised Standard Version.

One of my neighbors, a woman like Dorcas, "full of good works," has taken vigorous part in several drives to collect clothing for Korea. She reports that on several occasions women's coats have come in with all the buttons cut off. Evidently the big-hearted, generous givers thought the buttons were quite good and could be used again, so they took the scissors and went to work, the whole gift spoiled by a nasty snip. If, as Lowell tells us, "the gift without the giver is bare," a coat without any buttons leaves the receiver very bare, too.

The moral of this mournful story is: Don't cut off the buttons! So many gifts are spoiled and soured by some little twist that keeps them from being openhearted. So there is no kindness deluxe about them.

You remember the farmer's wife who asked her husband as he came in from the barn, "How much milk did the cow give?" He answered grimly, "Nine quarts and a kick." That did it. The kick knocked over the nine quarts and somewhat spoiled the total effect of the gift.

Some gifts are made with an air of patronage, a handing down from a greater height with a feeling of "Oh, did the Lord make you too?" That snips all the buttons off, no matter what the gift. Such an air in giving would make the Hope diamond look like Woolworth's second best.

A different form of cutting off the buttons, as far as the effect is concerned, is that achieved by people who call such attention to their generosity that it becomes hateful. As has been said, "When some people discharge an obligation you can hear the report for miles around."

Other gifts are like coats without buttons, they are just half done. Such half-done, slap-dash affairs are like giving your wife one earring, or giving one roller skate to a child, or passing off one glove for which you cannot find the mate, so you let it go anyhow. The extra touch with a gift, the care that says in unmistakable language, "This is a Class A event. Giving this brings me some real joy"—this is leaving the buttons on.

Many people giving to colleges and other institutions hedge the gift about with so many limitations that it is just about worthless. Like giving a college badly in the red $100,000 to erect a statue of the donor, or to endow a yearly lectureship on Patagonian wild birds.

Real adepts with the shears spoil their gifts by pouring on honeyed words, such as these that accompanied the gift of a hat by one woman to another: "My dear, I saw this lovely new hat and just couldn't resist getting it for you. We are all so tired of that ugly rag you have been wearing for five years." Snip, snip, snip, go the buttons.

Compared to this shabby stuff, the Good Samaritan rated the Nobel prize for giving. He left all the buttons on his gift coat—even sent along an extra one or two, just in case. "He took out two denarii and gave them to the innkeeper." He didn't measure himself out with a medicine dropper. He tossed himself about in large chunks.

Yours,
SIMEON STYLITES
—LIVING WITHOUT GLOVES

Discomfort Index

SIR: The Weather Bureau has slipped something over on us—a Discomfort Index. Now the predictions can be something more than the usual "sunny day, except for showers and a probable hurricane." Now they include a Discomfort Index, showing exactly how uncomfortable we will feel. Most of us can generally do that without any instruments. We know we will be slightly uncomfortable at zero and will feel very lousy at 90 degrees. Not being a scientist I am not able to say how the Discomfort Index is fixed. It seems to be the result of some hocus-pocus with two thermometers, one wet and one dry. Seventy degrees is regarded as a high index.

But there are a lot of things besides the thermometer that send my Discomfort Index shooting up. There is the idiot who is always right behind my car climbing up on my trunk and threatening to mash the lunch basket. He goes on blaring his horn no matter what might have made me slow up. It might be a five-car accident, but he blares right on. It might be—this is just a fantasy, for it rarely happens—that I have slowed up as a courtesy to a car that wants to cross our line of cars. Still he blares. My index rises to my collar, then to the top of my head, where it registers 110. And then I swear with my horn. You think an automobile horn cannot swear? Come along with me sometime.

I still get a high Discomfort Index from many television announcers, particularly those who yell with imbecile eagerness and earnestness about cigarettes and beer. These are the twin curses of television, a couple of Old Men of the Sea that the industry has to carry. These advertising curses never give you any information that might make the blah-blah more endurable. They just keep yelling that Cornsilk cigarettes and Sloppy Suds beer are the best there are. A friend of mine who is a Yankee fan (I associate freely with the lower classes) has given up television baseball entirely because he cannot take the Discomfort Index caused by the insufferable chatter between innings.

Then there is our choir's soprano. She is a lovely girl, and great will be the joy of the man who finally persuades her to do her singing over the kitchen stove. Great also will be her reward in heaven. But often she picks out pieces so full of high C's that Lily Pons couldn't make them all. It says in the Good Book to "make a joyful noise unto the Lord," but her singing brings a strain that sends up the index while I grip the side of the pew and pray, "O Lord, give her a push. Help her make it this time. Let her reach the heights and not stay in the flat."

My Discomfort Index still rises too over "the Rev. Smith." Not only newspapers, whose copyreaders ought to know better, but churches use it a great deal, the latter's bulletin announcing that "Rev. Smith will preach." A fifty-year campaign against such mayhem on the language has not made a dent. I am having my congressman introduce a bill next term making it a felony to print "Rev. Smith" and imposing on offenders a thirty-day stay in the county jail and a fine of fifty dollars.

My Discomfort Index has gone down a bit since getting these gripes off my chest. I still have others, but I'm feeling better.

Yours,
Simeon Stylites

Humor and Religion—I

SIR: May I discuss with you a really serious subject for a change? The subject I have in mind is humor. To say that there is a true relation between humor and religion does not mean that religion shouldn't be taken with deadly seriousness—a blunder which many have made. For that matter, humor is to be taken seriously too, though without solemnity. When a man doesn't recognize the difference between seriousness and solemnity he turns into a stuffed shirt. Religion and humor are related at their roots; both are rooted in humility. Humor is not to be taken as synonymous with wit, for wit can be cruel. Humor leads one to a sense of proportion, just as true religion does. Ethel Barrymore once said that "you grow up when you get your first laugh at yourself." Humor enables us to look at ourselves without illusions; it reveals the gap between pretensions and actuality. That is why we laugh when a pompous soul gets his top hat knocked off by a snowball.

Both religion and humor give a sense of perspective. Religion provides perspective before the greatness of God; humor provides perspective about ourselves and about others. Humor, like religion, has a way of cutting a pompous strutter down to size. Cannon Streeter in his book *Adventure* illustrates this with a story about an aristocrat who, as he leaves his London club, throwing his cape over his shoulder with a flourish, comes upon a long line of cabs. The first of the cabmen says to him, "Cab, sir?" The man does not deign to answer. Then the first cabbie turns to the second and asks, "Bill, did you ever hear of God?" Bill nods. Then the first man says, "That is Archibald, his brother." Perspective restored! Humor is a moral banana skin dedicated to the discomfiture of all who take themselves too solemnly.

Humor is also an affirmation of the human spirit, as one critic has pointed out:

Great comedy is no evasion of the knowledge of the suffering and evil of life, but as true a victory over evil as the exalted acceptance of tragedy. Without ever denying or falsifying the dark realities, comedy rises triumphantly over them in a glorious flood of laughter. Evil is neither subdued nor destroyed, yet somehow it is by the sheer ringing affirmation of the human spirit transcended and thereby conquered.

Thus humor keeps the flag flying. It gives evidence of something that is good to know: The fact that "our flag is still there." A noble flag raising was celebrated a few years ago when a generous trio of instrumentalists, in observance of Music Appreciation Week, visited a ward of a large hospital. One man had a bull fiddle, one a drum and one a saxophone. They played many well-loved hymns such as "I've Been Working on the Railroad" and "Seeing Nellie Home." The patients reveled in it; the nurses gathered from all corridors and all sang with devotion. One man in a cast from neck to foot joined in with the only thing he could join in with—his big toe, which he wagged joyfully. Once again, humor kept the flag flying in the midst of battle. You keep it waving, too.

Yours,
SIMEON STYLITES

Humor and Religion—II

SIR: Humor and religion have something in common in that both are evidences of security. Religious faith is evidence of the highest security, treasure laid up in heaven where neither rust nor moth consumes and where thieves do not break in and steal. Humor likewise gives evidence of security. You can joke about things that are secure; you cannot joke about things that are doubtful. If a man is happily married you can say to him, "Is your wife still living with you? How does she stand it?" But if a marriage is on or near the rocks, you can't joke about it. Better stick to the weather.

People sometimes asked, "Did Jesus have a sense of humor?" Of course some sobersides would regard the question as blasphemous. But we ought to remember that when we hear the words of Jesus we simply hear words; we are unable to see the look his eyes had when he spoke them. Some of Jesus' words contain humorous exaggeration. Another question sometimes asked, solemnly, is "What did Jesus mean when he said that it is easier for a camel to go through the eye of a needle than for a rich man to enter the kindom of heaven?" The true answer is that he meant exactly what he said. He was making a humorous comparison. Similarly with Jesus' other reproof involving a camel: "You blind guides, straining out a gnat, and swallowing a camel!" If a man cannot smile at the mental picture of a big, hairy camel going down the throat—well, surely God himself will give him up! Does God have a sense of humor? We have it on good authority that "He that sitteth in the heavens shall laugh." When one man asked another, "Does God have a sense of humor?" he got this answer: "Well, he made you and me. That must be evidence of *something!*"

Frederick W. Harvey has a lovely poem about a duck affirming that God made comical animals just in case the minds of men should stiffen and become dull, humorless, and glum. The poem declares that when God made the duck he must have smiled—and "He's probably laughing still at the sound that came out of his bill." (The duck's bill, that is.)

Humor can be effectively used in the service of religion. G. K. Chesterton was a past master at this. I recall his terribly serious argument to the effect that in man there is a spark of the divine to which one can appeal. In support of that faith he said, "You can say to a man taking his tenth whiskey, 'Stop! Be a man!'—but you cannot effectively say to a crocodile eating his tenth missionary, 'Stop! Be a crocodile!' " Chesterton answered the common slur to the effect that religion was created by priests by saying that that has just as much sense as the statement that sex was created by jewelers in order to promote the sale of wedding rings.

Yours,

Simeon Stylites

—The Christian Century

Forget It!

How many thousand times we have heard the words! Sometimes good-naturedly, spoken with a laugh. We thank a man for something he has done for us and he says, "Forget it!" But at other times it is jerked out with an ill-natured snarl. "Aw, forget it!" a man says, when his attention is called to a thing. There is a world of difference in the way a thing is said.

I want to repeat those old words good-naturedly today and say, "Forget it!" There are a great many things which it is a good plan to forget. It doesn't do any good to keep dangling them before your eyes all the time. There are some people who never seem able to forget the mistakes a fellow has made at one time or other. They hate to give a man a chance with a clean slate. If you say to them, "Jones seems to be a pretty good sort of chap," they will say, "Yes, but—" and then they will tell you of some trouble Jones had about five years ago and half the time they have got it wrong or else added a lot of things to it that are not so. Here are some verses I read the other day that put the thing very well:

> If you see a tall fellow ahead of the crowd,
> A leader of music, marching fearless and proud,
> And you know of a tale whose mere telling aloud
> Would cause his proud head to in anguish be bowed,
> It's a pretty good plan to forget it.
>
> . . . .
>
> If you know of a thing that will darken the joy
> Of a man or a woman, a girl or a boy,
> That will wipe out a smile or the least way annoy
> A fellow, or cause any gladness to cloy,
> It's a pretty good plan to forget it.

There is good sense as well as kindness to it. Suppose a fellow did slip up on something. Why not forget it and give him a chance to "come back"? Don't you know that the world would be a much better place if a few more hammers were laid aside and some things forgotten which it does not help anyone to keep harping on? Our little part of the world in particular would be much better, at any rate.

It is a pretty good plan to forget something else, too—whatever a man may have in the way of a grudge or "bad feeling" which is waiting for a chance to "get even." The reason is a very simple one: It costs too much to remember it. A feeling of bitterness which a man has against someone else is a very expensive thing; it is bound to spoil and embitter and make sour a great deal of his time, and he himself loses more even when his chance to "get even" comes. It will spread a feeling of discontent and unhappiness over our days that would otherwise be lighthearted. I know a man who lost a good job five years ago through untrue stories that were told about him by another man in the shop. It was a mean, cowardly trick. The man who was injured got another place, which eventually proved a better one. But he never forgot for a day the wrong done him or gave up for a moment his intention to "get back" at the other man in some way. He has been glum and miserable ever since. He has suffered ten times as much unhappiness from his feeling of hatred and revenge as he did from the loss of the job. He would have been a much happier man if he had forgotten it.

Of course it isn't easy to forget things like that. There is only one way we can do it—think of something else. Here is a good plan of a man who was full of good ideas, a man named Paul:

"Finally, brethren, whatsoever things are true, whatsoever things are honest, whatsoever things are just, whatsoever things are pure, whatsoever things are lovely, and if there be any virtue, and if there be any praise—think on these things."

And we may add, Forget the rest.

Some Nominations from the Observation Ward

A friend of mine was telling me the other day about a visit he had paid to a very interesting place, the observation ward of the Bellevue Hospital. This ward is the part of the hospital to which they send people about whom they are not quite sure whether they are sane or not. They put them in there for a few days and watch them to find out, if they can. From this observation ward a great many people are released. Others, however, are passed on to the asylum as being actually insane.

Especially in summer the observation ward is crowded. People who do things out of the ordinary, or eccentric, are frequently sent there for watching when they are perfectly sane. It is a strange collection of people. Some of the folks my friend saw and told me about have been very interesting and started some thoughts I am going to pass on to you. The people he mentioned were all there because they were doing "queer" things. The thought that always came into my mind was that I could nominate some people I knew to be sent to the observation ward for doing things just as queer, or much more so. And yet no one ever sends them to the hospital to be observed.

Think it over with me in two or three cases.

There was one man there, sent by his relatives because he had started down the street in which he lived in Brooklyn, after taking a pocket full of change from the cash drawer of the store which he owned, and gave a quarter to every person he met. You can imagine there was something a good deal like a riot before he got very far. A good many people were anxious to meet him two or three times, and as the crowd grew, he was taken by the police to be "observed" for insanity. I agree perfectly that that was the best thing to do. A man who tries to give twenty-five cents to everyone he meets is certainly out of his senses and belongs in the observation ward. But I submit this: If we are going to send up there the man who gives something to everybody, then the man who *never* gives *anything* to anybody belongs there too. The man who *never* carelessly gives a quarter away is just as likely a candidate for the insane asylum as the fellow who tried to give one to everyone. The miser, the close-fisted, downright "mean" person, has about as feebleminded an idea of how to get the most out of life in the way of well-being and happiness, and all the things that sane men value, such as self-respect, and the good opinion of associates, as the most hopeless case in the asylum.

There was a good-natured, harmless sort of a man there, who had been sent in from the country because he was walking along the country roads all the time and was never able to give a very clear account of himself or of where he was going or why. He seemed quite satisfied just to walk along the road looking, so he was picked up for a vagrant and sent to be watched to determine his sanity. I have no criticism to make of that. What I do insist on is that someone else is just as fit for the observation ward, and that is the man who *never* cares to walk along a country road, who is quite blind to the beauty of the fields and trees. He is just as lacking on one side as the simple-minded vagrant who just shifts from place to place is on the other, and the man who has lost his love for nature as seen in the fields, forests, and streams; who has lost in one way or another the capacity to enjoy simple things, such as the sights of the country or park or the plain, simple pleasures which children bring, is, in the literal meaning of the word, "insane." The word "insane" means "not whole" and certainly such a man does not have in good condition all the faculties which God has given to him.

Another man had been sent to the observation ward for trying to count the stars. It was a kind of mania which had settled upon him, not permanent, the doctor said, but the only way to quiet him was to allow him to go to a window and look up in the sky, so that he could go on with his counting. He was well up into the hundred thousands when he was taken to the hospital, although of course there are only a few thousand stars visible to the naked eye. It was a pitiable case—always looking up in the sky. But if we are going to doubt a man's sanity for that, how about the man who *never* looks up to the sky—who never really sees a star, and who is never moved with wonder, or awe, or reverence, as the thought of the immensity and mystery of the universe comes over him? The man who looks up into the heavens all the time is not a whit more insane than the man who never looks up in wonder and reverence. Back in the ancient days men felt the same wonder and humility they feel today when they realize how large creation is and how small they are. As one of them wrote: "When I consider Thy heavens . . . what is man that Thou art mindful of him?" Later another, greater Man looked up into the same sky and said, "Our Father." It is a great experience when, with wonder and yet with faith, we can say the same words.

We use the word "half-witted" a good deal. There is a sense in which many men are really half-witted. And it is a poor way to be. Their wits are busy with the small half of this world they can see and touch, the here and now. For the rest, for the future, and for that great power above, which Jesus taught us to call Father, they have no wits at all. They are all busy elsewhere. A man who does this all his life, giving his mind to his little corner alone when there is so much above to stir him to wonder, really belongs in the observation ward.

—FIVE-MINUTE SHOP-TALKS

The Funeral March of a Marionette

That haunting little melody of Gounod's, "The Funeral March of a Marionette," was fixed in my memory at the age of twelve, as eternally as the tunes set in the teeth of a barrel organ.

The title of the piece has always remained alluring. Why a funeral march for a marionette? What tragedy befell the quaint little fellow pulled by strings? How did he come to his sudden end? Surely a lively dance would be much more fitting to bear the name of such an agile creature!

Then the picturesque significance of the title leaps out on us, if we loose the checkrein of our imagination a bit. For a marionette always moves to a funeral march. When the forces which move a person are strings pulled from the outside rather than the self-willed and directed movement of his own mind and heart, he is parading in a funeral march, however nimble and prodigious his pirouettings may be. To the human doll pulled about by strings in other fingers than his own, life is a doll's funeral march, even though the tempo be lively and fast.

When we have a whole nation of marionettes the national anthem is a funeral march. The end is in sight. The vital problem in America today is that of preserving a thinking democracy. A thinking minority, perhaps, is all that we can hope for. But it must be large and strong enough to keep great aims and ideals active in the life of the nation. These are the days of quantity production of ideas as well as of machines, and such quantity production of programs and opinions is a great machinelike force for the making of thoughtless human dolls. The line of least resistance when we feel the squeeze of the crowd is to conform to the popular molds of near-thought.

On the island of Saint Lucie there was just one coat among the whole population, and the natives used to wear it in turn as they made their appearance before the king. That successive appearance of the solitary coat is a picture of what goes on in much more civilized communities when we all borrow our neighbors' opinions in which to make our public appearance. There is a haunting expression frequently used, "The cry of the lost soul." We have often tired to imagine what it must be like. Usually the expression suggests the lone, weird howl of a coyote on a cold night. But in reality the cry of a lost soul may be a giggle, a laugh, a hurrah, a sigh of content—any vocal sign of the surrender of self-determination.

There is in nearly every church gathering an efficient corps of ecclesiastical dentists who pull the teeth of resolutions, until they are as harmless as a baby kitten. A little boy once watched a minister in one of the old-fashioned enclosed pulpits waxing eloquent at the top of his voice and shaking his fists. "Oh, mother," cried he, "what if he should get out!" That is just the tragedy of it. So frequently he never gets out. Or if he does, he is as tame as a lamb.

The Church of Christ is today entering on the most tremendous battle of all its long history. It has seen some hard fighting, against slavery, against liquor, but today, as in the first quarter of this century, it ranges itself against the evil of war and the injustices of the present social orders; it turns from a war against pygmies to a war against giants. That struggle will not be a puppet show but a Hundred Years' War. That war will never be won by marionettes. It will be won only by men and women who have something of the spirit of the "Lone Dog" portrayed by Irene McLeod:

I'm a lean dog, a keen dog, a wild dog and lone;
I'm a rough dog, a tough dog, hunting on my own:
I'm a bad dog, a mad dog, teasing silly sheep;
I love to sit and bay the moon, to keep fat souls from sleep.

I'll never be a lap dog, licking dirty feet,
A sleek dog, a meek dog, cringing for my meat,
Not for me the fireside, the well-filled plate,
But shut door, and sharp stone, and cuff and kick and hate.

Not for me the other dogs, running by my side.
Some have run a short while, but none of them would bide,
Oh, mine is still the lone trail, the hard trail, the best,
Wild wind and wild stars, and the hunger of the quest.

A Plea for the Conservation of Some Old-Fashioned Diseases

It has been a long time since I have heard of a genuine case of writers' cramp. I do not know whether its extinction is due to the fact that Dr. Carrel has isolated the germ or whether the efforts of Messrs. Remington and Underwood have wrought our deliverance. Perhaps even the free-arm movement of the Spencerian penmanship, with its alluring circles and curves, which we so painfully learned in the third grade and so painlessly forgot ever afterward, may have had something to do with it. At any rate, whatever the causes, few today seek the doctor to be cured of writers' cramp. The present generation writes as easily and unweariedly as it breathes. No matter how, in the rush and stress of the day, our other muscles may grow faint and utterly weary, the muscles of our fingers renew their strength with each bottle of ink emptied or typewriter ribbon worn out. A fitting coat-of-arms for the times might be a fountain pen rampant over Truth dormant, with a devil-fish squirting ink embossed on the shield.

Hence we venture to suggest that science has been pushing the conquest of disease a bit too relentlessly. Would it not be well to conserve at least a few score germs of writers' cramp to be scattered about the community where they will do the greatest good? It is too great a servant of humanity to be allowed to perish from the earth.

Suppose that some morning one of our great daily papers should be forced to make this humiliating announcement on the front page: "Owing to such a large number of our staff being afflicted with writers' cramp we are reluctantly compelled to print nothing but the news in today's issue."

Would it not be an occasion for the long-meter doxology?

While we are speaking of blessings, how can we forget *lockjaw?* What an unmixed boon a judicious and well-timed epidemic of lockjaw in the United States Senate would be! Especially when a budding Daniel comes to judgment and outlines a policy of world relations for the United States, as seen from the coign of vantage of a cracker barrel in the general store at Corntassel Crossing. Or in the House of Representatives on occasion when the Honorable Member from Buncombe thunders "Mr. Speaker," and starts on a three-hour carnival of unnecessary noise for the purpose of impressing home constituents a thousand miles away.

Come to think of it, might not an intelligent epidemic of lockjaw prove a blessing to church conferences and conventions? Carbon dioxide is the most poisonous gas known. An hour's exhalation of it in the form of extemporaneous oratory is usually sufficient to kill any budding promise of useful action deader than an Egyptian mummy which has been embalmed for four thousand years.

One of the many "Develop Your Personality" courses now flourishing has an advertising booklet which tells "How Silent Sims Became a Fluent Talker." That is easy enough. What we need more is someone who can teach the reverse process—how to make many a fluent talker into a "Silent Sims." *Hic labor, hic opus est!*

I would not seem to be guilty of speaking lightly of so dreadful an affliction as *locomotor ataxia,* but only to notice with commendation one aspect of it, that it does keep a person in one place. That much of it, if it could be arranged painlessly and in a homeopathic degree, might prove at times a real boon. For the virtues of "a traveling ministry" may easily be overdone. The climax of a well-constructed drama does not come until the third or fourth act, and too many dramas of kingdom extension suffer by having the curtain rung down in the midst of the first or second act, just as the plot thickens and events begin to move to a conclusion. The scenery is shifted, and the star moves on to begin another engagement elsewhere.

Some ministers, on going to a church, seem to follow the advice of the fire department, printed on theater programs: "Look about now and choose the nearest exit." A church should always be treated as an end, never as a means of advancement for its minister. Some men use a church as a springboard, on which they bounce up down for a year or so until they gain enough momentum to vault them up to some other spot. And the Kingdom suffers from such athletic prowess. A little less mobility would result surely in more of those permanent benefits which take time to nourish and grow in any community.

There is another aspect of the work of the church in which just a tendency toward locomotor ataxia might prove a great blessing. That is the custom of ecclesiastical rearrangement which masquerades under the guise of promotion. As soon as a man demonstrates fine ability in one place he is summarily removed and set to doing something entirely different. How would a baseball team fare if as soon as a man proved to be a star shortstop he were immediately "promoted" to the pitcher's box, while the fellow who dared to make good as a catcher would be dragged away from it and "promoted" to the outfield? "One star differeth from another in glory" on the ball field just as surely as in the heavens, but the manager who produces a winning team keeps the stars where they shine best, instead of indulging a passion for changing the line-up. Yet in the church the theory seems frequently to be, "When a man makes good in any field, stop him right away and put him somewhere else." Is he a strong, competent pastor? Away with such a fellow! Make him a district superintendent! Is he an effective preacher? Stop him—make him an editor! Is he doing great things in a rural charge? Quick! Catch him! Send him traveling around the country! Has he done great service as a board secretary? Ah, we'll soon put an end to that! Make him a bishop! Anything so long as the nice round pegs are pulled out of the round holes and pounded into others, whether square or round!

There is a far better theory of promotion than that, which will yield many fold more results. Tennyson calls it "the glory of going on." Instead of so much of the game of ecclesiastical "stagecoach" where everyone changes chairs, we might try a policy suggested a long time ago—"Stand still and see the salvation of God." We are liable to miss a good deal of it by gadding around.

—SKYLINES

The High Art of Refreshing

"They have refreshed my spirit." (I Cor. 16:18.)

Not all your friends would be readily classed as "refreshments." They may be—and are—people of integrity, straight as a telegraph pole and just about as charming and alluring. Such saints may win many adjectives on their pilgrimage through life. They are given noble adjectives, too, such as "useful," "loyal," and "courageous." Yet one adjective never springs to our lips in this connection, the gorgeous adjective, which Paul used of Stephanas, and Fortunatus, and Achaicus—"refreshing." We would give much to know more about them and in just what ways they were refreshing to Paul. He writes as though it were more than food or drink. They brought refreshing spirits, a much headier drink than any liquid on earth.

What a tribute Paul pays to this trio. Phillips gets great feeling into his translation, "They are a tonic to me." Their very presence brought a bracing invigoration of spirit, so that the whole being tingled with life, even though Paul spent a good deal of his time getting in and out of jails.

This quality of refreshment is hard to analyze just as spring is hard to analyze. It is much better to get down on your knees and thank heaven, fasting, for people who bring refreshment.

Without too much analysis, grapple them to your heart with hoops of steel. Paul had a lot of hoops of that sort, a wonderful collection of refreshing friends. His hoops are on exhibit in this chapter. The last chapter of his first letter to the church at Corinth is short, but even so, seven refreshing spirits pass by. In the last chapter of Romans about thirty appear. Paul was a great friend, as well as a great apostle.

Some marks of a "refresher" appear. A heart at leisure from itself, so that it does not need its pound of advantage or boastful comment. It is a real thrill to find that the person talking to you is not trying to sell you anything. There is no apprehensive danger that the mask of cordiality will fall and the sales talk begin, just as a corner huckster will do a few tricks and then from under the counter draw out bottles of snake oil to sell.

Sometimes one's face is no great refreshment. Yet for anyone a pair of smiling eyes and a few wrinkles around a grin will turn a February face into something suggesting June and make an enchanting invitation.

John Bunyan was never ordained by any church. But he was ordained by the Holy Spirit of God to be a power for refreshment. He felt that seriousness and gaiety had been joined by God and ought not to be put asunder by man.

It is a high role to which to aspire—"He refreshed me." Most of us will not sit on the seats of the mighty, but we can serve God and man mightily on a different level when anyone can say, "He refreshed my spirit."

—Preaching Values in the Epistles of Paul

2

"Fire Drill in Church" and Other Alarms for the Church

Fire Drill in Church

SIR: OUR ATTENTION HAS BEEN CALLED—THAT IS THE PHRASE YOU USE when you wish to tell an editor that you are too high-brow and busy to read his insignificant little sheet, but some busybody has pointed out to you an item in it—as we were saying when we were interrupted, our attention has been called by a dear and non-busy friend to a stirring report about a fire drill which was part of a worship service in the Methodist church at Madison Heights, Michigan. Since we are always on the alert for new advances in worship, we were all interest. We quote from the caption of a photograph of the congregation getting out of church in a hurry (we hope it was not before the morning offering was taken!): "These church-goers practice a fire drill as a part of the safety program undertaken by their Methodist church. It took less than two minutes to evacuate over 100 persons in the drill."

We showed this report to a neighbor of ours who tries to keep our conscience in repair, the pastor of St. John's-by-the-Gas-Station. He gave a snort. "That is nothing," he said disdainfully. "One of my sermons can evacuate four hundred people in less than 30 seconds flat. I've done it again and again." Paying no attention to his irrelevant remarks, let us proceed.

In days long gone every Sunday was a fire drill in some churches. The sermon was a vigorous drill in escaping the flames of hell. But the Madison Heights church has a different kind of "hot gospel." Now we are all for Safety First. We are glad the congregation will be ready for a fire.

There are too few earnest Christians still extant, and we don't want any of them burned up. But we wonder whether this drill may not be some sort of symbol. Are our churches more interested in safety than in adventure? We seem to recall that the marching orders for the first Christians went in pretty strongly for adventure. They were promised lots of tribulations; even a cross was mentioned, and mobs, and being haled before governors and kings.

A sentence in the photo caption sticks in our mind: "Other safety measures have been and will be taken for the protection of those attending church." *What* other measures? For there are many great dangers to those attending church.

There is the danger of being badly cut by the preaching. We read that at the first Christian sermon the hearers were "cut to the quick." There are many words in the Bible which are sharper than a two-edged sword. If the danger of drawing blood is to be avoided, care must be taken with what is read from it.

Then there is often danger (thank God!) of incendiary remarks by the preacher, following the example of the Great Firebrand, who said, "I came to cast fire upon the earth, and would that it were already kindled!"

And there is always danger when the Holy Spirit gets loose in a church. It began that way, you remember—with little tongues of fire descending on the congregation. The Spirit is still inflammatory and the danger is ever present that the blaze might be carried to a whole town. It has happened. If a few people really get on fire with the gospel no board of underwriters can measure the results.

You see, there are lots of dangers in going to church. Hope you meet a few.

Yours,
Simeon Stylites
—The Christian Century

Calamity by Flood

SIR: The many disastrous flash floods in the spring of 1952 caused one catastrophe that has never received the wide attention it deserved. The little town of Meadowbrook in the Dakotas was terribly hard hit. (Meadowbrook is probably not on your gas station road map.) The rains descended and the floods came and great was the fall of the village. The usually placid brook became a young Niagara Falls. All wires went down—telephone, telegraph, and power wires—and railroad tracks were washed away. The whole region was incommunicado for several days.

Among other crises, this made a terrific problem for Grace Church in the town. It was put completely out of touch with any General Headquarters of the denomination. The congregation was entirely without direction from above about what Special Days had been designated for the next two Sundays. That meant nothing less than that they were "on their own"—a situation without pecedent for the past few years.

What could they do? No new Enlistment Day, no Uncles' and Nephews' Day, no Day at all, just a blank Sunday! Of course, a few houses had radios run on batteries. But headquarters did not get on the radio, and no directives were dropped by plane. Came Thursday, then Friday, and still no word from Nashville or Chicago or New York.

But the church faced the disaster with calm courage. After much discussion about what they should do with a Sunday on their own, one simple soul suggested that they worship God. That was a radical solution, but in the absence of anything else it was adopted. On the undesignated Sunday the preacher spoke on the text, "Be still, and know that I am God." No quotas were mentioned and no special cards were passed out.

Strangely enough, the people liked it. The pastor, evidently a sentimentalist, writes that after two whole Sundays of such a strange interlude they returned to the program of assigned Days and Drives with refreshed spirits and renewed vigor.

Yours,
SIMEON STYLITES

Like a Mighty Army

SIR: I met the pastor of St. John's-by-the-Gas-Station last Monday. He was all lit up—not alcoholically but emotionally. I said, "You must have been pretty good yesterday."

"Better than that," he replied, "I had a guest artist take over. And he took everybody over."

"How come?" I asked.

"It was Layman's Sunday. Usually that Sunday brings joy, like a visit to the dentist. A good thing, but better to look back on than forward to. This year I slipped one over on them. You know Jimmy Mitchell, just back from two years in the army in Korea? I figured he would give

Layman's Sunday a shot in the arm, but I didn't reckon on him blowing the place up. He refused at first. Then, with a funny light in his eye, he said he would speak if I had the congregation sing 'Onward, Christian Soldiers' just before he began. So I had them give forth with song, and then Jimmy let loose. He didn't waste any time in shadow-boxing. He waded right in. This is what he said: 'You have been singing

> Like a mighty army
> Moves the church of God.

That might have been all right once. The trouble is now that just about ten million men know exactly how an army moves. And it doesn't move the way a lot of you folks at St. John's do—or do not. Suppose the army accepted the lame excuses that many of you people think are good enough to serve as an alibi for not attending Church Parade.

" 'Imagine this, if you can. Reveille seven a.m. Squads on the parade ground. The sergeant barks out, "Count fours." "One!" "Two!" "Three!" Number Four missing. "Where's Private Smith?"

" ' "Oh," pipes up a chap by the vacant place, "Mr. Smith was too sleepy to get up this morning. He was out late last night and needed the sleep. He said to tell you that he would be with you in spirit."

" ' "That's fine," says the sergeant. "Remember me to him."

" ' "Where's Brown?" asks the sergeant.

" ' "Oh," puts in another chap, "he's out playing golf. He gets only one day a week for recreation, and you know how important that is."

" ' "Sure, sure," is the sergeant's cheerful answer. "Hope he has a good game. Where's Robinson?"

" ' "Robinson," explains a buddy, "is sorry not to greet you in person. But he is entertaining guests today and of course couldn't come. Besides, he was at drill last week."

" ' "Thank you," says the sergeant, smiling. "Tell him he is welcome any time he is able to drop in."

" 'Honest, now, did any conversation like that ever happen in any army? Don't make me laugh. If any G.I. tried to pull that stuff he would get twenty days in the guardhouse. Yet you hear stuff like that every week in the church, and said with a straight face, too.

" 'Like a mighty army! Why, if St. John's really moved like a mighty army, a lot of you folks would be court-martialed!'

"That was the general drift," said the pastor gleefully.

"Too bad the stay-aways didn't hear it," I remarked.

"Don't worry. I have it on a tape recorder, and I am going to spring it on them next Easter, instead of the Second Lesson."

Forward March!

SIMEON STYLITES
—LIKE A MIGHTY ARMY

Salvation by Disturbance

SIR: The pastor of St. John's-by-the-Gas-Station appeared at my door, pencil in one hand and notebook in the other. "I am making a list," he said, "of texts for use by preachers who want to move in a hurry. They are guaranteed to get the man who uses them moved suddenly. I used one of them Sunday. By the way, do you know of any pulpit that is open to a blunderbuss of doubtful reputation?

"It was a good text too," he went on. "Right out of the Good Book, and who ought to kick about that? It was about the Pool of Bethesda, which got disturbed every once in a while, and then the fast worker who beat the gun and jumped in first, got cured of what ailed him. I told them that the main point of that text is often lost. The main point is that salvation comes by disturbance. Just look at it. Only when the pool was disturbed was anyone cured. If there was no disturbance they could sit in the water for six months and nothing would happen. That is always true. I told them that the reason most of them were not saved was that there was no disturbance. Most of the trustees didn't like it too well.

"Disturbance is really a sacrament, in that it does mediate divine grace. If the gospel ever gets loose in the world it always kicks up a big disturbance. The people who first saw it explode called it 'upsetting the world.' I told the saints and sinners at St. John's that too many of them had only three favorite hymns in the whole book—'Peace, perfect peace,' and 'If on a quiet sea toward heaven I calmly sail,' and 'Drop thy still dews of quietness till all our strivings cease.' Great hymns. But what we really need is half a dozen more strivings. And I mean *strivings!*

"Sometimes we seem to get the motto for our church life from the barber shop: 'Once over lightly.' And do we hit it lightly! As a musical composer said, 'No one who plays the piano with a feather duster, instead of driving down for the music that is in the depths, can ever become a concert artist.' That is what too many of us do. Being a member of the church ought to be a very disturbing thing, for it really disturbs absolutely everything about us. But we often make it like joining a country club, with this one difference, it doesn't cost as much. The attitude many of you have to the church, I said, is something like a yawn, and that while listening to me! Imagine!

"Disturbance, and a big one, is the only thing that will save us in a disturbed world. Yet often sitting here comfortably in church is like having a few years under the ether cone. There ought to be a disturbance over Hungary's troubles. That is not only safe, it is fashionable now. But there ought also to be a disturbance over racial discrimination, over the national neglect of education and health. Things do have a way of moving. A new day is on us. Since the bus segregation in Montgomery, Alabama, seems to be on its way to ending without eruption, it may be safe for some highly perched ecclesiastics, from whom we have not heard, to come down and speak in favor of desegregation on buses.

"As I asked you, Do you know any vacant pulpits?"

Hoping to hear from you,

Yours,
Simeon Stylites

Money Changers in the Temple

SIR: A rich friend of mine—I have one, or did have one until the second installment of the income tax came due—calls our attention to a bit of wisdom he found in a financial journal. (The only financial news *I* read is the announcement that chuck roast or hamburger has dropped to 75 cents a pound.) This financial journal, *Barron's*, covers a wide territory. The item in question read, "Since the first coin came from the first mint, men have been divided into two groups: Those who work for money and those who put money to work for them."

So that covers the subject of money. There are only two things you can do with it. You literally pays your money and you takes your choice. According to this journal of busy finance there is no third group made up of people who make their money work for something higher than themselves. Everyone knows that there are people who go through life as though it were a sort of blindman's buff, and, alas, the author of the *Barron's* item appears to be one of that number. He has completely missed the great host of people, whose total estate varies in quantity from $5 to $5 million, who make their money work for human welfare.

The Sterling Silversmiths of America have made a suggestion which has a wider reference than to the matter of silver polishing. They say that the best care one can give his sterling silver flatware is hard use. That goes for coined silver as well. The best care one can give to a part of his silver hoard is to put it to hard use in the service of others. That treatment is a lot more effective than a whole barrel of silver polish.

Let's put a new meaning—at least it is new to me—into the well-known phrase "money changers in the temple." We can all remember our childhood scorn for the money changers who were driven out of the Temple by Jesus. We can remember too the fierce political invective directed at the "money changers" in the Temple of High Finance in more recent days.

But there are other money changers, people who go into the temple and change money into life. They have the will to say of a dollar brought into the church and dropped on the collection plate what Jesus said of Lazarus as he came from the grave: "Loose him and let him go." For people who bring money to the church become money changers deluxe. Through the agency of the church they change money into character. They change disease into health, hunger into well-being, ignorance into education. It is one of the world's greatest miracles. A good trick if you can do it. And everyone can do it every Sunday.

The Book of Ecclesiasticus gives this advice, "Be good money changers." Let's get going.

Yours,
SIMEON STYLITES

Are You Still Alive?

SIR: The state of Ohio has put a neat problem to the churches within its borders: Nothing less than the task of proving that they are still alive! A directive from the secretary of state requires that they file with his department a "statement of continued existence." Churches failing to record that they are still functioning run the danger of having their charters cancelled. And the secretary is complaining that the churches are not complying to any great extent with his request.

Churches had better get on the ball and prove that they are still alive, but some of them may have a bit of trouble proving that very conclusively. Take that word "alive" in its full New Testament sense. How could a church prove that it is still alive? What are the proofs of life in a church?

Some churches might be fairly well content with a report of solvency: "All bills paid and money in the bank." That might satisfy the state department as a report from a nonprofit corporation. But somehow it does not quite seem to echo the New Testament.

There have been times when a person was confronted with the same ticklish problem. For instance, during World War II a young man in Amarillo, Texas, needed a birth certificate when he enlisted in the army. He went to the town clerk, only to be greeted with the startling information. "Why you're dead! Here is the record in black and white that you were dead at your birth!" Just how would you go about proving that you are alive—alive, that is, in the highest sense? A church ought to be able to prove "its continued existence," even by the highest standards. To do so is worth the concern of every church.

Surely one test of life in the New Testament sense of that word is that a church be a distinctly religious fellowship. A lively bingo game every Wednesday evening does not quite meet the requirement. Neither do Gothic arches and stained-glass windows. To be a living church in the fullest sense a church must be a church of the living God. Proof of its continuing existence as a body of Christ must include an outthrust in service to the world. Its door must open outward. Some churches are centripetal. Everything comes inward. But some churches, by the grace of God, are centrifugal. Life moves outward from the center. The words "Go ye into all the world" are no longer Greek to them.

Another sure sign of life in a church that meets the New Testament idea is that it has invested heavily in tomorrow. It is a teaching and a nurturing church. Whether it has an investment in A. T. & T. or General Motors is not really relevant. What counts is that its investments are in the tomorrow of the church, its children and young people—that teaching and training are at the very top of its agenda.

Robert W. Clarke, the secretary of the Student Christian Union in Cleveland, Ohio, who relays the breathless information about the new directive for churches in his state, also records that a short time ago he passed a church in Ohio in front of which was the sign "Church—Danger!" He could see no imminent danger from traffic or any other source. Except an orderly little cemetery! That is the danger that awaits a church, the big danger—the cemetery! You are hereby warned!

Yours,
SIMEON STYLITES

Round Churches

SIR: Ever see a round church? There is something to be said for such a church. In the May *Harper's* reference is made to churches built by the grandfather of Mr. William Bartley: "[He] had constructed many of the 'round churches' in the Pittsburgh area (deliberately built without corners 'so the Devil couldn't get in')." A great idea! A church barricaded against the devil would be a wonder! We wonder how the round churches worked. For the devil certainly gets around. We have a vivid picture of his travels in Job 1:6-7: "Now there was a day when the sons of God came to present themselves before the Lord, and Satan came also among them. [Just like any Sunday morning!] The Lord said to Satan, 'Whence have you come?' Satan answered the Lord, 'From going to and fro on the earth, and from walking up and down on it.'" Perhaps even a round church would not prevent Satan from attending. But it would be worth a try.

There are so many ways for the devil to get into a church. Sometimes he comes by the most public way possible, walking right up the aisle, behind the choir in the processional—the glass of fashion and the mold of form, all set to deliver what he calls "the Word." He gives forth a "charming sound, harmonious to the ear." He is a skillful exodontist too —he pulls the teeth out of the gospel so there is nothing left but the gums, which are not very dangerous. Very painlessly, too. His message is: "Do not get excited about anything. This Christianity is really a very easy thing to practice. Just expel all unpleasant thoughts and you too can be a big success."

Sometimes the devil gets into the congregation by a subtle form of amnesia. He makes people forget that they belong to a fighting and working outfit. They feel instead that they belong prematurely to a Saints' Everlasting Rest—here on earth. Forgotten is their ancestry, a great company of resisters: "Some were tortured, refusing to accept release . . . others suffered mocking and even chains and imprisonment; they were stoned; they were sawn in two, they were killed with the sword . . . of whom the world was not worthy" (Heb. 11:35-38). Even those who weren't sawed in two were a company of workers. Listen to the roll call (Rom. 16): Phoebe, a *helper* of many; Mary, who *worked* hard; Urbanus, our fellow *worker;* Persis, who has *worked* for the Lord; those *workers* Tryphaena and Tryphosa; Timothy, my fellow *worker*. Not a flowery bed of ease in the whole outfit!

The devil does some of his best work without getting into church at all. He insinuates into the minds of the people the thought of some other thing that must come first, so that they do not bother to go to the church service. The modern forms of excuse making by those invited to the feast would be: "I have purchased a new car, and must go to test it on the road." "I have just built a summer cottage and must get to it over the week end." "It isn't the thing to do to go to church in the summer. Pray have me excused." Nice going, Satan!

As a matter of fact, the devil may get in as he did before there was any building at all. He can inject this question, sheer poison to any group: "Who shall be greatest?" That is a virus which will lay low any organization.

Let's build a few round churches. They might help.

Yours,
Simeon Stylites

Confidence Spending

SIR: The Pastor of St. John's-by-the-Gas-Station took a deep breath and went on talking, as he usually does:

"You should have been there Sunday. We had a field day. We raised some money, too. It was Budget Sunday, but it was no Budget Basement affair. The sermon was so deeply moving that I saw even Deacon Close reach for his checkbook. (Unfortunately, he couldn't find it.) The text wasn't in the Bible, but it was within shooting distance of it, and it shot hard and straight. It was a news dispatch from Detroit a few weeks ago, an item about the Recession. A businessman there (honest, this is true) gave each of his fourteen employees an extra five dollars with their paychecks as a 'confidence spending' measure. He explained that the wage earners seemed to be holding back in their expenditures because of lack of confidence. By giving the extra five dollars for four consecutive weeks, he hoped to do his part in stabilizing the national economy. He specified that the money must be spent immediately on something not normally purchased.

"If anyone gave me five dollars," the pastor continued feelingly, "I would have great confidence in his judgment. And I would purchase some upper-bracket items, such as lamb chops.

"Then I rolled up my sleeves and went to work. I put in a rousing plea for confidence spending. It is spending in confidence that the church is the church of the Living God, not just another country club or a bridge club. It is spending in confidence that the church has a gospel of salvation to a world on the dizzy edge of disaster, and that there is none other name but that of her Lord by which the world may be saved from the final explosion. It is spending in confidence that God's kingdom is an everlasting kingdom, and not a here-today-and-gone-tomorrow affair. It is spending in confidence that 'God's truth abideth still' and he must win the battle. I poured it on. Giving in a niggardly fashion, I told them, is a vote of no confidence in God and his church.

"One of our nonelect ladies told a canvasser from the church on the every-member roundup that she would be glad to give what she had given for the past twenty-five years, which was five dollars a year. That was like a red flag to him, and he pawed the earth like an enraged bull. He said: 'Tell that to the man in the shoestore, that you will be glad to pay for a pair of shoes what you paid twenty-five years ago. You can't buy more than a pair of shoe laces for that. Tell the butcher you will be glad to pay for a tenderloin steak what you paid a quarter of a century ago. That wouldn't buy a good bone for your dog.' She didn't like it for some reason.

"I asked them to do some rousing confidence spending and not deserve the wondering exclamation of the Master, 'O ye of little faith!' I asked them to think of the staggering confidence spending that was done by the martyrs in the Coliseum at Rome, who

Let goods and kindred go,
This mortal life also.

That really was spending in confidence!"

The ushers will now wait on the congregation!

Yours,
SIMEON STYLITES

Appointment for the Prophet Amos

SIR: The pastor of St. John's-by-the-Gas-Station was having a morning coffee break at the drugstore across the street. "You are getting to be quite a barfly," I said deferentially, hoping to start a fight. No use; I was beneath notice. Then all of a sudden he asked, "How long will a tape taken by a tape recorder last?" "Longer than you will," I answered. "Perhaps fifty years." "I wish it had been invented some centuries ago," he said. "I would like to have a tape recording of Socrates' speech before taking his last brimming cup of hemlock. I would like to have one of Martin Luther's defiance of the Diet of Worms. And of Lincoln's Second Inaugural address."

Then he went on: "I would also like to have recordings of some things I have heard myself. One I would like most is the recording of an informal speech given at a meeting several years ago by Methodist Bishop Francis J. McConnell. He was called on to sum up the proceedings. He did that—and then he generously wandered off on a fascinating detour as a bonus gift. Believe me, it was a *big* bonus. His subject was what would happen if the prophet Amos came up for appointment at a Methodist annual conference. The bishop really went to town. He staged for our imagination a conference cabinet meeting with the district superintendents facing the question, 'What shall we do for the prophet Amos?' One by one they shed bitter tears, vowing undying admiration for the prophet Amos, and explaining why they could not give him a church in their districts.

"The superintendent of the North district said in a faltering voice (they were all utterly sincere, no doubt about that): 'You all know how I love and admire Brother Amos. He is one of the finest men in the church since John Wesley, one of God's gifts to our time. But he doesn't have enough tact for Grace Church. He just blurts out his ideas with no suavity at all, and Grace Church folks need a lot of suavity. They are in a building campaign. If only Brother Amos would raise fewer controversial issues and more money he would get on better. He went to an anniversary celebration at Grace Church and had no more judgment than to denounce some of the members as being at ease in Zion. So obviously he is not the man for Grace.'

"Then the superintendent of the West district opened up. 'I too have loved Brother Amos,' he said. 'I have been deeply moved by many of his sermons. I would love to put him at Trinity Church. But he is just not eloquent enough. It has been a great preaching place. You remember the crowds that Dr. Demosthenes drew, and Dr. Webster. But Brother Amos is a plain blunt man who speaks straight on. He doesn't have the literary touch or the oratorical lift the people of Trinity are used to. I'm sorry.'

"The superintendent of the South district was perplexed, too. 'I wish that Brother Amos was more interested in matters of organization,' he said. 'I would like to put him at Wesley Memorial. But it has been the leading church in the conference. It is used to men who take places of leadership. Its last three pastors have all gone to General Conference. The church will want a man who takes a sharper interest in leadership and does not spend all his time on his prophecies and on people—some of them, not the outstanding ones.'

"After careful consideration, the superintendents agreed to give the prophet Amos a sabbatical year.

"I wish I had a tape recording. It would be a good one to play at the first session of the cabinet in every annual conference, or at a presbytery or state association."

Yours,
SIMEON STYLITES

Anthem by the Choir

SIR: Take a telegram, please! I would like to send a night letter to all the members of volunteer church choirs in America. It is hard to put into fifty words the congratulations and gratitude of a host of people without number, but I will try. It will cost quite a bit, but charge it to the Fund for the Republic; it is right up their alley. For church choirs have done more for this Republic in sustaining morale in millions of citizens and bringing quickening to their spirits, than can ever be added up.

I feel much as Christopher Morley did on looking at a telephone receiver and thinking of the multitude of folks waiting to hear some news, all the way from those waiting for a life-and-death message to young girls waiting to hear from a squire. He says that he wished he "could call them all, and give some good news to each." That goes for the choir members.

Here is one instance in which a church choir got into history in a big way, just by the faithful performing of its duties. There is a memorable entry in John Wesley's Journal for May 24, 1739, the day of his spiritual experience of having his heart "strangely warmed" at the Aldersgate Chapel. Something else happened that day, something which was a preparation for that warming of the heart and, as a consequence, had a real part in the launching of the Evangelical Revival. John Wesley thus records it: "In the afternoon, I was asked to go to St. Paul's. The anthem was, 'Out of the deep have I called unto Thee, O Lord. O let thine ears consider well the voice of my complaint. If thou, Lord, wilt be extreme to mark what is amiss, who may abide it? For there is mercy with Thee; therefore shalt thou be feared.'" The choir at St. Paul's made a deep impression; Wesley remembered it all. Of course, we must give at least an assist to Handel. But this was not the first time that a choir played an unpretentious part in great events. Nor was it the last.

On a less distinguished historical level springs my own gratitude to church choirs. May the Lord reward them for saving the life of a young boy in church. The anthem by the choir was always a blessed interlude between the "long" prayer (that was the right adjective, all right!) and the sermon. The choir lightened an ordeal which many will remember. Some research genius has computed that the amount of energy devoted to keeping awake at public meetings every week is enough to propel every steamboat on all the seven seas. My boyhood experience leads me to believe it. The choir furnished real excitement. It was a tense moment when the soprano, the pride of First Church (she can top anything in town), came to the place where she was to take the high note. We listened with our hearts in our mouths. It was more exciting than watching the pole vaulter attempt the fifteen-foot mark.

Perhaps the soprano is no Jenny Lind, and the stout gentleman who essays tenor no Caruso, nor even a Nelson Eddy. But they are all givers of great gifts. No doubt they do better when they do not try to sing Opus 163 No. 7 in G-sharp minor. But with something less severe, musically, they make a joyful noise unto the Lord.

As my chances of ever hearing the Heavenly Choir, with harp accompaniment, grow less and less, I value more and more the earthly choir up in the choir loft. For it does more good. The Heavenly Choir sings only to the angels; the choir down here sings to the sinners.

Yours,
Simeon Stylites

Ten-Year Rehearsal

SIR: Some of our public prints have been giving us news of the revival of Confucianism that is going on in Vietnam—a temple rebuilt in Saigon, literary contests flourishing, handbooks on the Chinese sage selling in the Vietnamese equivalent of carload lots. One feature in the reports that catches the eye is the account of the Confucian Ballet of the Imperial City of Hué, which, as *Time* says, "has been rehearsed for ten years, without a public performance." This picture of an endless rehearsal behind closed doors—the tiny tots of ten years ago now cavorting as top-flight ballerinas—makes the imagination jump.

The imagination jumps across fences into other fields. In our down-hearted moments, it seems to us that some churches have had a long, long rehearsal of the script—the Christian gospel—but no public performance. It is a magnificent script, this gospel for all men, irrespective of color or race, breed or clan or boundary. There have been many dress rehearsals, Sunday after Sunday, until the cast is letter-perfect. But no public performance to give the outside world an idea of the beauty and power of the drama, which, emphatically, was made to be produced.

These eternal rehearsals remind us of the words printed at the beginning of Thomas Hardy's tremendous play *The Dynasts*, done in three parts with 19 acts and 130 scenes. The play is prefaced with the caution, "Intended for mental performance only." Some church organizations and institutions seem to think the script of the New Testament is "intended for mental performance only," and that is what they give. White men have devoted years of rehearsal to the great, thrilling lines of the script: "And he made from one every nation of men to live on all the face of the earth." But alas, in so many instances they never put on an actual performance. Nations have done the same thing with the drama written in the script for them: "And they shall beat their swords into plowshares, and their spears into pruning hooks; nation shall not lift up sword against nation, neither shall they learn war any more." Too bad such a terrific drama is taken as "intended for mental performance only"! One of the red-letter days of all history came when Wilberforce and his helpers brought the Christian script against human slavery out of rehearsal into perfectly stunning performance.

One habit that operates to keep the gospel from performance is too much talk. Talk makes a pleasant detour around the job to be done. It has been recognized that the more an author talks about his next book, the less chance there is of its ever being written. Some authors will not speak of their work in process, lest it be drowned in a sea of words.

It may well be that the trouble with the priest going to Jerusalem on the Jericho road, the day the traveler got beaten up, was not that he was a coldhearted monster but that he was on his way to make a rousing speech in Jerusalem, denouncing the civic administration for allowing highwaymen to beat up travelers on the Jericho road. It is one of the perversities of human nature that when a man has made a thumping speech there steals over him the pleasant delusion that he has vanquished the evil, by spraying it with words. *Caveat orator!*

A little girl of seven wanted to get her grandfather to go swimming with her. She was not impressed by either the speed or the grace with which the venerable man got into motion. "Come on, granpa," she said, "let's get the show on the road." The gospel is a great show. Let's get it on the road!

Yours,
SIMEON STYLITES

On Your Own

SIR: I have discovered a little trend (one instance makes a trend big enough to support a massive generalization), and it makes me nervous. For if great oaks from little acorns grow, great disturbances may grow from trends no bigger than a mustard seed. This little trend indicates the dangers that pastors and churches may squirm out of the control of boards, commissions, and all central planning agencies that work out programs for pastors and churches to follow.

What brought this up was a piece of literature sent me by a friend—a year's program for the churches drawn up by the Troy Conference of The Methodist Church's Board of Evangelization. The program is vigorous, detailed, and exhaustive. (Note: exhaustive, not exhausting.) The board is doing a noble work. More power to it. Now that that resounding approval is recorded, let us proceed.

There is one beautiful typographical error. The program for one of the months is announced to be "Our Methodist Beliefs." But the printed sheet came out with "Our Methodist *Reliefs*." Was that a Freudian slip on the part of the typesetters? Did they have a suspicion that some reliefs might be welcome?

But here is the statement that may be setting a dangerous precedent. The program says: "With the beginning of Lent *the pastor is left on his own with no suggested program*" (italics mine). That looks innocent enough. But who can tell what a pastor "left on his own" might do? He might conceivably, in desperation, take up preaching the gospel. It could be! And the laymen, being so impressionable, might like it. And then where would the week-by-week programs and schedules be? It could no longer be said that "without a program spake he not unto them."

All kinds of things might happen if the preacher were left on his own, and for six weeks too! Long ago, at the very beginning, some evangelists were left on their own. And what happened? (I am not making this up. You will find it in a history book, Acts 11:20.) "And some of them were men of Cyprus and Cyrene, which spake unto the Grecians." That was something new. Grecians? Speaking unto them was not on any official program. The evangelists were on their own. You see?

So we call attention to the danger of this little trend's spreading and growing larger. If that goes on too far and too long, we may say, with Mark Anthony, "Mischief, thou art afoot!" For with being left too much on their own, preachers may discover that the most precious asset of the church is the preaching power of its ministers. They may feel, What shall it profit a church to gain a whole world of promotion and lose its own power to seize people by its arresting message? That essential power can be crushed by a multitude of detailed compulsions. As someone has said, "the resurrection did not result in a committee with an executive, but in a fellowship with an experience." One or two people already fear that what many officials desire to carry out the programs is not a preacher but an ecclesiastical bulldozer.

Yours on his own,
SIMEON STYLITES

Forced Ventilation

SIR: John M. Krout, chaplain of Columbia University, has noticed that Simeon has been running down. So he springs to the rescue by sending a stirring piece of information which should be read and inwardly digested, if possible. The communiqué comes from the bulletin of a church in Lake Forest, Illinois, informing the world that the vestry has "voted to install forced ventilation in the church."

Thinking of the churches in which the saints (and sinners) have been slowly asphyxiated, I have been tempted to greet this news as the greatest advance in religion since the Reformation. Especially in those New England churches whose windows have not been opened since the Revolution, and in those churches of much later date whose windows have remained closed since the Civil War.

The devil's secret weapon has been carbon dioxide. Satan has slain his thousands, but unventilated air has slain its tens of thousands. The grace of God has often been no match for lack of ventilation. We can prove this from the Bible itself, for it says that the enemy is the "prince of the power of the air" (Eph. 2:2). That, being interpreted, means the evil prince of bad air. The young man who achieved immortality by going to sleep while St. Paul was preaching was not chloroformed by Paul's arguments, but by lack of ventilation up among the rafters where he was perched. Many times the real struggle of the gospel has been not with the souls of men but with their lungs! So we pray for all churches: "Strength to the pumps that force the ventilation." And to all official boards, vestries and trustees we say: "Do a little pumping yourselves."

This item of news reminds us also that the *ideas* in a church very frequently need forced ventilation. Sometimes there has been no more chance for a new idea to blow into them than for a breeze to blow through a billiard ball. Occasionally the obstruction has been the same—solid ivory. The theme song has been

Our fathers have been churchmen
Nineteen hundred years or so,
And to every new proposal
They have always answered "No!"

Bless their stout little hearts! But ideas do need ventilation, so fresh life can course through them. That often takes a strong pump, one which does not get discouraged easily.

Any organization can get stuffy when not even a gentle zephyr gets inside to freshen the air. Thoreau made this entry in his *Journal:* "I asked Therien this afternoon if he had got a new idea this summer. 'Good Lord,' he said, 'a man who has to work as hard as I do, if he does not forget the ideas he has he will do well.'" That is about all some groups can manage. Thoreau puts this question in *Walden:* "Will you live? Or will you be embalmed? Will you live, though it be astride of a sunbeam, or will you repose safely in the catacombs for a thousand years?" These queries must be faced by every organization, political, social, and religious. When there is little traffic in ideas and no ventilation, the procedures and habits of an organization can become like a whatnot in a corner, displaying a collection of curiosities—things which used to be alive, such as seashells, starfish and little fossils.

When no ventilation gets in from the changing and needy world outside, the message of the church or any other organization reminds us of the reply of a notable jazz performer, Wild Bill Davidson, when a reporter asked him, "Mr. Davidson, when you start on a trumpet solo, what do you think about?" "Man," said Mr. Davidson, "I don't think about nothin'; I just blow." Sometimes it seems as if that were the strategy of an unventilated routine. The members of some organizations don't think about nothin'. They just blow. Without fresh motion in their heads, their declarations are full of what T. E. Lawrence called "passenger words." They do not work. They are just passengers going along for the ride.

To the pumps, men, for a little forced ventilation!

Yours,
SIMEON STYLITES

Cowboys or Shepherds?

SIR: Deep in the heart of Texas, or rather north by northwest, a ministers' retreat was held which turned out to be quite an advance, according to the report of one of our ever alert scouts, the Rev. William R. Stephens of Lubbock, Texas. One speaker launched into quite an oratorical flight and made a deep impression as he unfolded the facts of animal husbandry. He described the difference between a cowboy and a shepherd, with particular reference to ministers and churches. No doubt the difference is well known and considered in cow country, but perhaps the tenderfeet back east and up north, far from the memories of the Chisholm Trail and Dodge City, need to be enlightened.

The speaker put the searching question to the preachers: "Are we cowboys or shepherds?"

Now, as every Texan knows, the cowboys get the cattle together at intervals and count them and brand them. The big thing is to count them, and to make sure that there are more than last year. Often cowboys brand the strays too. Then they are turned loose for a year or so.

That is not too far from some ecclesiastical procedures. By all means count them and put the denominational brand on them. There should be no mavericks loose if by any means the beloved brand can be put on them. In best proselyting fashion, if a stray looks as though he came from a special corral, brand him and save him from a fate worse than death. The theme song becomes, "Git along, little dogies, git along." It is great sport, riding herd!

The shepherd has a name older than that of cowboy. And his chief concern is not arithmetic, not how many do we have this time, not to have the biggest herd in the state, but to follow an old injunction, "Feed my sheep." Being a shepherd is not all a quiet job. It calls for vigor and daring. Charles E. Jefferson once described a part of the shepherd's work that is often overlooked. A shepherd, he said, should lead the sheep gently and carry the lambs in his bosom; but once in a while he comes across a rambunctious old ram, and then he has to take him by the horns and throw him over the fence, for his duty is to protect the sheep. The New Testament pictures the last full measure of a shepherd's devotion: "He layeth down his life for his sheep."

The danger for a church which gets to have an inordinate appetite for numbers is that its eyes will be fixed on the roundup. It grows concerned to have long lariats which can lasso the largest numbers. When the Epistle to the Philippians urges us to think on "things of good report," it probably does not mean that we should concentrate on things of good report to the annual conference or synod or state association *numerically*. The concern is that the sheep may go in and out and find pasture.

The last is a special responsibility in these days when special brands of theological jargon are becoming a staple food. The sheep cannot exist on a diet of thistles. What shall it profit a church to have an erudite young shepherd who has mastered five brands of existentialism if the hungry sheep look up and are not fed?

It is exciting to see cowboys in a rodeo. It is far more wonderful to see a shepherd leading the sheep and feeding them.

Yours,
SIMEON STYLITES
—THE CHRISTIAN CENTURY

The Bullpen

SIR: Now that the baseball season is with us again and the joyous sound of wood against horsehide is heard over the land, I recall one of the high moments of my career. For I have had my moments. I once talked for half an hour with the manager of a major-league baseball team. True, he couldn't get away from me, as he was wedged in on the seat next to the window in a crowded railroad car, and I was on the outside seat.

We talked of curves, knuckle balls, and Texas leaguers, and finally reached the subject of the bullpen. The bullpen, as everyone except possibly Great Aunt Matilda knows, is a space, usually fenced in, in a corner of the outfield, to which reserve pitchers are sent to "warm up" in view of the possible collapse of the pitcher when he can't find the plate or is being hit all over the lot.

I asked the manager what effect it has on a pitcher when he sees another pitcher warming up to take his place. He said that some pitchers get more jittery than ever and begin dealing out bases on balls with generous abandon, while others tighten up and sail the ball over the plate with the deadly aim of an Annie Oakley. It must be a tough place for a pitcher to be in, hearing the thump of the ball in the catcher's mitt out in the bullpen and realizing that any pitch may be his last for that game.

Then I got to thinking what might happen if the bullpen were introduced in other realms than baseball. What effect would it have on a preacher if he knew there was another man warming up out in the Sunday-school room, ready to step into the pulpit and displace him whenever his points got going wide of the congregation? The chances are, I think, that most preachers would not go to pieces, but would pitch with fresh fervor and drive, with speed, curves, and control. A bullpen in a church might be a means of grace.

Or how would an editor feel if he came across the office boy warming up out in the cloakroom, batting out on the old Hammond typewriter an editorial on America's foreign policy to take the place of the one the editor was writing mid toil and tribulation? What effect would it have on a businessman or a teacher if he knew that the next room was a bullpen in which his successor was getting ready to take his place?

Of course, that is just what is happening everywhere. Josephine Lawrence in her novel, *The Sound of Running Feet*, portrayed vividly the feelings of people in an office fearing that any day they might be motioned to the bench and someone else put into their job. The running feet were not those of a Hound of Heaven, but of a Hound of Elsewhere—the feet of someone running to take over their job.

Perhaps the bullpen is responsible for a large part of the good work being done in the world. It keeps us on our toes. We can readily see the disastrous effects that often come from a lifetime tenure of a job. Church history would be very different if there had been no life offices, if all popes and archbishops had been forcibly retired in the seventh inning.

By the way, who is warming up in your office to take the place of

Yours,

SIMEON STYLITES

—LIKE A MIGHTY ARMY

Taken for Grunted

SIR: Our uplifting thought for the week is taken from the conversation of a trim little Private Secretary. She was asked what she thought of her boss, and replied: "He's fine, except when he's dictating. Then you have to take too much for *grunted.*" Too bad the Man in the Gray Flannel Suit whom she was describing could not hear that. Then he could have heard himself as others hear him.

But the boss in the office is not the only person from whom we "have to take too much for grunted." That noblest of the instruments of speech, the English language, as spoken by many people has traded the birthright of Shakespeare, Milton, and Edmund Burke for a mess of grunts. We know what Hamlet thought of the Grunters, for we have it in clear words —the best advice ever given to talkers in private and in public: "Speak the speech, I pray you, as I pronounced it to you, trippingly on the tongue; but if you mouth it, as many of your players do, I had as lief the town-crier spoke my lines." Among the tribe of public speakers there are still a good many mouthers. They get (and deserve) the critical response of Tennyson's Northern Farmer:

> An' I niver knaw'd whot a meän'd, but I thowt a 'ad summut to saäy,
> An' I thowt a said whot a owt to 'a said, an' I coom'd awaäy.

Such is the fate of Grunters. By the time they get going the audience—in attention at least—has "coom'd awaäy."

Sometimes the trouble is dropping the voice at the last part of a sentence, where, presumably, the plot thickens and meaning might emerge; but the voice sounds like an automobile running out of gas. Often, however, the indistinct grunting is something more than a vocal blur: The meaning is grunted away into invisible fog. We read in the Old Testament that "it is the glory of God to conceal a thing." But it is not the glory of man to conceal his meaning. The English have a name for this kind of concealer—a "trimmer." Thus Senator Sorghum, a master of grunting, can make a thrilling tribute to "liberty and justice for all," while from the other side of his mouth he is rousing the rabble to defiance of the law of the land. Out of the same mouth (different sides) come blessing and cursing. In other words, grunts. Such statesmanship brings to mind the request of a man to the typewriter company for a key that could be taken for both "e" and "i," so he would be spared agonies of indecision when he was called on to type such baffling words as "recieve" and "beleive."

In the presentation of Christian teaching likewise too many grunts have been taken for granted. Then the trumpet gives forth an uncertain sound, and nobody prepares for war—just for another nap. It sometimes happens that the message from the pulpit becomes impressionistic, like a fog seen through a cloud. Instead of a signboard saying "This is the way," the pulpiteer holds forth a painting by Picasso. Often the trouble with the church is what Bishop Henry Knox Sherrill diagnosed as "too many great convictions about little things," a calamity of mistaken magnitudes. Or, as a frank apostle recently put it, too many people join the church on "confusion of faith." In short, too many grunts, which confuse the order of the day, which is, emphatically, "Fall in!" Being an accomplished Grunter myself, I should know.

Yours,
SIMEON STYLITES

'The Boneless Wonder'

SIR: "The Monday morning preachers' meeting," said the pastor of St. John's-by-the-Gas-Station over a ham on rye, "had some tough luck yesterday."

"How come?" I asked.

"Well," he said, "the Demosthenes from on high who was to have orated failed to show up. The meeting had to get by on local talent, and before I knew what dirty work was going on I was elected to make a few remarks. So I told them about my travels fro and to in the summer and of the sermons I had heard.

"I mentioned one discourse I heard several times, one that might well be called the 'Boneless Wonder.' There were no bones, no skeleton in this sermon, not even a backbone to hold together the points, if any. It was an interesting thing to watch—like a large jellyfish trying to walk on land and collapsing gelatinously all over the place. You have seen it at the eleven o'clock service.

"Another type of sermon that is popular—particularly among the younger men who have vocabularies full of jargon—is the 'Mammoth Cave Sermon.' The Mammoth Cave is a big, dark place, one of nature's wonders. So is this sermon. It abounds in Stygian darkness. Someone has said that this type of oration is best described in the words of Scripture, 'without form and void, and darkness was upon the face of it.' Listening to it, I told my Monday morning colleagues, was like playing a game of blindman's buff, reaching out for an idea, if haply they might find one. The Mammoth Cave Sermon had several illustrations which helpfully explained the unknown in terms of the unheard-of. The language was so wrapped up around whatever it was wrapped around that a bit of advice was fitting to the speaker: 'Discocoon yourself.'

"A few times this summer I heard an achievement which deserved the name of the 'Emily Post Sermon.' Not that Emily wrote it. But it was done in such 'taste, perfect taste, in all this world of wrong.' It did not involve any noisy cavortings in the pulpit, nothing that might offend some delicate soul. But as a hearer said on one occasion, if man cannot live by bread alone neither can he live by perfect taste alone. There ought to be something to be tasted. But in this Emily Post Sermon there was no meat of the Word, just a bit of skim milk. Think of the terribly poor taste shown at certain lively moments in history—for example, Peter and John telling the High Priest that he was a 'whited sepulcher,' or William Penn calling the Vice-Chancellor of Cambridge University 'You poor mushroom!' There are a lot more lovely bits of English prose that Emily Post could not possibly approve.

"Then there is a sermon of my own, which I have developed to a high point of frustration. I call it the 'Cape Canaveral Sermon.' The reason for the name is that it doesn't get off the ground. The load is too heavy for the power of the blast. Often this model starts off with great preparation, such as a short history of the Hebrews from the Garden of Eden to the Maccabees. There goes the fuse—look out! But alas, it does not get the sermon off the firing platform."

The pastor of St. Johns-by-the-Gas-Station regarded his empty plate and sighed. "That's what I told the preachers," he said. "They haven't asked me back again. They never do."

Yours,
Simeon Stylites
—The Christian Century

The Wife of Sisyphus

SIR: One figure of Greek mythology who has always greatly interested me and drawn my sympathy is Merope, the wife of Sisyphus. Sisyphus was the unlucky chap who, you remember, in the world of the shades, had to roll a huge stone up the hill till it reached the top, only to have it always roll down again to the bottom; an endless, unvarying, heartbreaking job.

I have often wondered just what technique his wife found most effective. Did she say every time the stone rolled down, "Tough break, old top. But up and at 'em again?" The poor old boy might get pretty tired of that. Or did she take another tack: "For Jupiter's sake, forget that silly old stone. Let it alone. You can't win"? The trouble with that would be that rolling up the stone was his job and he couldn't resign.

One modern Sisyphus is the pastor of a church. Every week, with many a huff and puff, he rolls the big stone up to the top on Sunday morning. Every Sunday night it rolls down to the bottom. Even Sunday noon, standing at the door of the church, he often wonders whether he has said anything at all; all the comments are on the weather. Monday morning he starts the long push again. It is an endless hill through the year. All during Lent he is shoving the stone up to the top of Easter morning. Then, plunk! Next morning it is down at the bottom again. No wonder they call the Sunday after Easter Low Sunday. Even at best, the pastor's account of his work is like that of the Australian prize fighter who wired his father after a bout, "Won easily in eighty-four rounds."

What of Merope, the pastor's wife? How should she deal with these unending ups and downs? Sometimes she tries the role of "constructive critic," thus: "Sisyphus, my dear, why don't you try shoving it up on the bias and then giving a little hitch and twist at the top? That would hold it." Some wives even turn on this helpful criticism on Sunday night. That is plainly against Scripture, for the Good Book says, "A broken reed he shall not break." The pastor is a broken reed on many a Sunday night all right. The ram's-horn resonance has gone from his voice and spirit. And even when the helpful criticism is put off for a day, it is not exactly balm in Gilead.

Strangely enough, the best thing that Merope can do for any Sisyphus is to help him forget, for a while, the big stone and the hill. The "ideal" wife, who appears in all the books on the subject and in the dream of many an innocent student, the well-trained associate who is right in there helping all the time, is often a burden too grievous to be borne. She is likely to say, "Now, dear Sisyphus, we can have a nice long evening working out the curriculum for the intermediate grade." Or, "Now we can plan that party for Circle C." The poor man is likely to fall into profanity.

The wisest Merope is more apt to say, "Well, Sis, that old stone will stay there safely overnight. We don't have to watch it. Let's step out and trip the light fantastic." Of course the original Merope didn't say exactly that, for she had not read John Milton, back in those days. But the Greeks had a word for it, I'm sure.

Yours,
SIMEON STYLITES

Delilah on the Hearth

SIR: I wish I could claim to have invented the title above as a description of some wives, but it comes from Holbrook Jackson. He uses it to describe Mrs. Samuel L. Clemens, who spent a good deal of her time giving Mark Twain a literary haircut, shearing the strength from his literary style.

It is, of course, not chivalrous to call any wife a Delilah. That is a fighting word. Yet there have been wives (it is much safer to put it in the past tense) who have played the part of the Lady with the Shears—a Delilah on the hearth cutting away her husband's strength and his native endowment for indiscretion. The modern Delilah's work with the scissors differs greatly in motive from that of the original in Samson's affairs. That one was a siren, up to no good. The wifely Delilah loves her husband dearly—so dearly, in fact, that she wants to keep him from taking any risks to health, wealth, or reputation. In other words, she keeps him from life.

I wish I could read the memoirs of Mrs. Christopher Columbus, if she wrote any. I would not be at all surprised if she frequently wound her loving fingers in his dark locks and said in soothing tones: "Chris, you are foolish to go on that wild voyage to the Indies. Goodness knows what winds may blow up. Your last winter's overcoat isn't heavy enough. You'll get pneumonia. Besides, that little rowboat, the Santa Maria, leaks." She would have kept him at home. Snip, snip, snip. But he got away.

We do know that John Wesley had a Delilah on the hearth. She tried to stop those long, silly horseback rides all over England. But John could say, "My head is bloody, but unshorn." After one of her diatribes he was all the more eager for boot and saddle. I wonder whether John ever preached on "a thorn in the flesh to buffet me." He could have done a honey on that!

A real-life Delilah at the fireside was Mrs. Nathaniel Hawthorne. Her loving watchfulness to keep her husband polite and elegant clipped the curls of his strength as a writer. She changed his writing, substituting "look" for "squint," "pool" for "puddle," "perceived" for "smelt," "sat" for "sprawled." She softened passages describing poverty or sickness. In fact, whenever a word of specific power appeared she clipped it with shears she called "good taste."

Edward A. Steiner once said that often the wife of a preacher will slip a silken B.V.D. under the hair shirt her husband wears, so that the poor dear shall not suffer. Sometimes Delilah is a demon housekeeper; the washing machine and the vacuum cleaner become the sun and the moon. So the prophet is smothered in home economics. His locks are sheared.

Often the wife of a man of great possible usefulness is so concerned for his health that she keeps him from doing anything notable with it. Frances Power Cobbe described the process of the trimming of the hair of strength in these words:

> The higher good of the husband occupies most wives comparatively little; and often a man who starts with a great many lofty and disinterested aspirations deteriorates, year by year, in a deplorable manner under the influence of a well-meaning and personally affectionate wife. She urges her husband to think of himself and his own interests, rather than the people and objects for which he was ready to sacrifice himself. "Do not go on that charitable errand today. You have a cold coming on. Tomorrow will do, or later." "Do not invite that dull old friend." "Do not join that tiresome committee." "Do refrain from confessing your unorthodox opinions."

The girl with the shears at work!

Sometimes when her Samson is about to flex his muscles in real fighting, Delilah puts in a "What will people say?" And the native hue of resolution is sicklied o'er with the pale cast of propriety.

I don't know what to say about Delilah. She is a lovely girl, and it is nice to have her around. Just keep the shears out of her reach—down in the coal cellar, perhaps.

Yours,
SIMEON STYLITES

—LIKE A MIGHTY ARMY

3

A Short Glossary of Words

Blurt

"No cautious man blurts out all that he knows." (Prov. 12:23, Moffatt.)

NOT EVEN IF IT BE TRUE.

Or in a good cause.

Or even if it insures a resounding speech.

That verb "blurt" is a visible index of mind and spirit. Blurting is an art rarely of use in effective persuasion to any good cause. It is the human equivalent of braying.

There is one good test of the efficacy of a resonant "blurt" of all one knows (or thinks he knows), exploding without any disciplined adjustment to other people or a given situation. Ask yourself whether you can "blurt out" love. As has been well said, it is so much easier to give a person a piece of your mind than the whole of your heart.

—PREACHING VALUES IN THE OLD TESTAMENT IN THE MODERN TRANSLATIONS

Grumble

"Do all things without grumbling." (Phil. 2:14.)

This plea to avoid grumbling comes at the conclusion of the great hymn in the preceding verses describing the acts of Christ. Coming so close, the words indicate that grumbling is a major calamity, that the freedom of grumbling is one of the consequences of the ransomed and redeemed life.

Grumbling is more than a peccadillo, a somewhat unfortunate trait of personality. The habit of grumbling is a major sin, judged by what it does to character. It can spoil the whole climate of a life.

To allow oneself to become a pathological and habitual grumbler is a major affliction, for such a one easily slides down the steep descent to the state where nothing is right, something is the matter with everything. Someone said, when he heard of the death of Matthew Arnold, "Poor Matthew, he won't like God." That was certainly unfair, but it does describe the critical, often scolding attitude of Matthew Arnold.

Living with a grumbler is like living in a room with all the window shutters banging in the wind. The tragedy, too, is that the grumbler hears the banging all the time.

Grumbling also drives the spirit of service out of a life. How can a person think of others with any ongoing love if he is always concerned with his sore toe? How can his world open out to human need if it is full of his own complaints and bewailing? The constant clang of the riveting machine of his own dissatisfaction shuts out the still small voice of God and the still gay music of humanity.

But the grumbler can be saved by the Savior. Christ proclaimed that he came to bring deliverance to the captive. The captive to the habit of grumbling can be delivered. When the mind is focused on what God has done, when one really sees as the great landscape of life the grace wherein we stand, the bars of a one-celled imprisonment are broken and a soul is freed.

—MORE PREACHING VALUES IN THE EPISTLES OF PAUL

Nevertheless

When Henrik Ibsen, the Norwegian dramatist, came to die, his last word was "Nevertheless." He was a great critic of the society in which he lived, a great objector and debater. It was fitting that this should be his last word. Just as he started to say something in rebuttal to what had been said, he got out the word, "Nevertheless," and then death struck suddenly.

A good word for the last word, "Nevertheless." In a very real way that is what Christian faith is all about. It takes an honest look at all the evil in the world. It faces all of life's confusions, its frustrations, its suffering, its disaster, and says, "Nevertheless." It was true in the very beginning of Christian history. In the Crucifixion of Jesus, all the agents of evil had done their utmost—Judas, Caiaphas, Pilate, and the mob. "Nevertheless," on the first day of the week, "as it began to dawn. . . ." There is a beautiful picture of that in an Edinburgh cemetery, at the grave of the little daughter of Sir James Simpson, the discoverer of chloroform. On her tombstone are carved her name and the words "*Nevertheless I Live.*"

We find the word used in a connection similar to the plight of our world today, the feeling that disaster was imminent. We read in II Pet. 3:10: "The heavens will pass away with a loud noise, and the elements will be dissolved with fire, and the earth and the works that are upon it will be burned up." Doesn't that sound exactly like a description of the effect of a hydrogen bomb? Yet in the face of that we read on: "*Nevertheless* we look for a new heaven and a new earth." That was Christian faith in the first century. It must be our faith in the twentieth.

—UNFINISHED BUSINESS

Therefore

"Therefore, my beloved brethren, be steadfast, immovable, always abounding in the work of the Lord, knowing that in the Lord your labor is not in vain." (I Cor. 15:58.)

Here is the grand conclusion of the Resurrection, the motive power which it brings to life. You can almost hear it rushing by, like a swollen river in spring when a dam has broken. "The victory through our Lord Jesus Christ"; then, with hardly a stop for breath, "*therefore.*" That is apostolic logic. It is God's logic. "Death is swallowed up"—therefore! Bring this power to bear on life. The knowledge that your labor is not vain in the Lord brings endless energy and propulsion.

It answers one of life's questions which sometimes stares us down. This is how William E. Henley framed it:

O how shall summer's homey breath hold out
Against the wrackful siege of battering days!

What a description of life—"siege of battering days!" Yet, some days do batter, do they not? It is eternal life realized here and now which conquers the battering. Henley's own "I am the captain of my soul" can't do it.

It is a gloriously irrational faith. Faith in the Resurrection does not come at the end of a syllogism. It does come at the end of life lived in the power of the Son of God.

Yet the irrational eternal world does find rational guideposts pointing in its direction. Here is a pointing post erected by a great physicist, Dr. Arthur H. Compton. He protests against incredible waste:

> It takes a whole lifetime to build the character of a noble man. The exercise of the discipline of youth, the pains and pleasures of reality, the loneliness and tranquility of age. These make up the fire through which we must press to bring out the gold in the soul. Having thus been perfected, what shall nature do with him? Annihilate him? What infinite waste!

—PREACHING VALUES IN THE EPISTLES OF PAUL

Meanwhile

"They therefore returned to Jerusalem and preached the gospel to many villages of the Samaritans." (Acts 8:25.)

"But Philip was found at Azotus: and passing through he preached the gospel to all the cities, till he came to Caesarea." (Acts 8:40.)

Twice in the eighth chapter of Acts, as well as many other times in the book, we find it recorded that the apostles or other evangelists preached in certain places while making a journey to another place. They had a habit of making the most of incidental wayside opportunities for spreading the good news. Such preaching was not their immediate aim at the time. They were on their way to larger and more important destinations. But meanwhile, without departing from the main direction, they came upon something unplanned, an incidental opportunity. And they seized it, picking it up, as it were, in their stride. . . .

We are on the way to Jerusalem; right now, however, we are in Samaria.

—THE ACTS OF THE APOSTLES IN PRESENT-DAY PREACHING. VOL. I

But

"Struck down, but not destroyed." (II Cor. 4:9.)

It would sound like a strange thing to say that the conjunction "but" is one of the most glorious words in the New Testament. But look at the manner in which the word is used four times in the eighth and ninth verses of this chapter. Each time the word says, in effect, "We may be at the very end of our rope, but God." This passage proclaims that God has the last word.

There is an expressive line of Strickland Gillilan's verse which really says something pertinent about the Holy Spirit:

> I think God kept on talking when
> His book had gone to press.

The style is colloquial, but the truth is profound. So, God keeps on talking after the world has said its worst, after it has passed all its sentences and ordered its executions. Drop into your imagination the supreme example of God's use of the conjunction "but." In the crucifixion of Jesus, Pilate and Caiaphas, Herod and Judas, had done their worst. It was all over. Pilate had said, "Make it as sure as you can." The soldiers made it sure. They rolled up an "immovable" stone against the grave, "*but* on the first day of the week, at early dawn." It was all over, except that God had another chapter to add! Surely as that word appears in the resurrection story (Luke 24:1) it is a glorious word!

Now

"Now is the day of salvation." (II Cor. 6:2.)

The word "now" is a tremendous word in the New Testament. We never get away from it. There is no dream world of procrastination. The New Testament moves to the drumbeat of now. That drum plays us up into the line of action.

Among the Hebrews up till the advent of Jesus, two principal words were "yesterday" and "tomorrow." The first recorded word of Jesus' ministry, his address at the synagogue at Nazareth, was the word "today." After reading from Isaiah he said, "Today this scripture has been fulfilled in your hearing" (Luke 4:21).

Those same two words which bulked so largely in the thought and speech of the Hebrews may be our pitfalls today. We may dwell in the confines of the word "yesterday," which may be like prison walls to us. Yesterday may have for us not the propelling power of a great tradition but a crippling kind of nostalgia. Ours may be merely a bondage to the details of a past. Jaures, the Frenchman, warned against that when he said, "We should take from the past its fires, not its ashes."

Or we may live chiefly in the world of tomorrow. We can feel "disregard today, dream of tomorrow." That becomes a spiritual obituary. Great hosts of people have died of tomorrow, as far as any spiritual life is concerned.

The word "now" not only marks the day of salvation. It is a *word* of salvation. *Now* is the time to receive the grace of God. *Now* is the time to enlist in his service. *Now* is the time to live life to its fullest possibilities. There is a memorable word in Thornton Wilder's play *Our Town*, which pictures the common failing to reach the limit of the possibilities of *now* as life rushes by. A young woman, dead at a very early age, returns from the cemetery to her birthday party of years ago and can be seen by her parents only as she was. As she leaves them she wonders whether people "ever realize life while they live it, every minute." She cries out, "Why don't we look at each other?" Robert Louis Stevenson wrote that "the obscurest epoch is today." That is true in many senses, especially whenever the imperative of the *now* drops out of life. The hour in which we are now living is the magic hour in the truest sense, for now is the day of salvation.

—MORE PREACHING VALUES IN THE EPISTLES OF PAUL

Watch

"Take heed, watch and pray; for you do not know when the time will come." (Mark 13:33.)

The word "watch" reaches into the whole spread of life. Someone has said that the worst "ism" in the world is not Fascism or Communism but Somnambulism. There are so many forms of sleepwalking—the glazed eyes which never notice that one's ideals are being whittled away, one's purposes being pared down; never notice the evil forces in the world, gaining strength. *Watch and pray* against the sin that so easily trips us up, the compromise with wrong, so reasonable in the beginning, so deadly in the end. *Watch,* lest we neglect the renewal of life in communion with God, lest our sympathies harden! *Watch,* lest the great opportunities for service to God's kingdom come and pass by, unseen and unseized.

—Exposition of Mark in The Interpreter's Bible

And

Paul . . . and our brother Sosthenes. (I Cor. 1:1.)

The word "and" is one of the greatest and most beautiful words in the language. Before we say "nonsense" to that extravagant statement, reflect on it. Here, as in many other places in Paul's letters, and in millions of places in life, it represents the fortifying power of friendship and companionship. In the opening sentence of five of Paul's letters, we read "Paul and"—somebody else. That represents a sustaining fellowship. It was not just Paul, but Paul plus—Paul plus the reserve force of love in a yokefellow. The words "and someone" do not indicate a joint authorship, but a joint moral and spiritual strength.

Trace that golden word "and" through Paul's letters. "And our brother Sosthenes" (I Cor. 1:1); "and Timothy" (II Cor. 1:1); "and all the brethren who are with me" (Gal. 1:1); "and Timothy our brother" (Col. 1:1); "Silvanus and Timothy" (I Thess. 1:1 and II Thess. 1:1).

We do not know about Sosthenes. Probably a convert, he perhaps wrote the letter from Paul's dictation. The inclusion of these names in the salutations is an evidence of Paul's fine courtesy. But more, it is an evidence of friendship. His strength was as the strength of two or three, those who were beside him, with lifting power to his heart and mind.

What a field of service these salutations offer to the imagination and dedication. People, included after the word, very rarely get into an encyclopedia or even a Who's Who. But they are enrolled in God's Book of Life. Those who stand by a friend have an inseparable part of his achievement and service. This word "and" is part of the very genius of the

Christian life and fellowship. We do not walk alone. It is Christ *and* his disciples; Paul *and* Sosthenes.

Often on the brightest pages of history it is written, "John Smith *and wife.*" Burma saw the heroic drama of Adoniram Judson, *and* wife, Ann. It was beautifully and truly said of Canon Barnett and his wife that their two lives burned as "a single flaming candle" in the darkness of East London. Often it has been written in extra-illuminated letters, a man or woman, and mother. Think of St. Augustine *and mother*, or John Wesley *and mother!*

The word pictures memorably the high office of friend. Such sustaining friends, even though inarticulate so far as the world is concerned, do not die with all their music in them. It comes out melodiously in other lives. Such sustaining friends are God's "reinforcements." Many a battle has been won by reinforcements.

—PREACHING VALUES IN THE EPISTLES OF PAUL

Klunk!

SIR: If Lord Dunsany were not already a Lord he should have been knighted for a few warm words he exploded not long ago in London. He was paying his respects, if that is the proper word, to the pretentious lunatic fringe of ultramodern poetry. He was not afraid of being called by that nasty name, "traditionalist." He admitted that our age may be chaotic but, he added, "it does not want chaotic messages. If you are lost in a fog, you do not want a foggy answer."

But what we are giving him a laurel crown for here is his gift of an expressive word "klunk." He said that many modern poems are bells of lead; "they should tinkle melodiously, but usually they just klunk."

A grand word for speeches; they do go "klunk." Listen and you can hear them now! A metallic thud indicating that all is lost. At the last annual meeting of the P.T.A. Simeon made a speech that was a complete klunk.

What makes a speech go "klunk"?

Sometimes it is language. No gritty detail, which, like sand on a slippery road up a hill, will give traction for the mind. There are speakers who talk like this: "Regardless of their pigmentation or coloration under normal illumination, felines of all species, it has been learned authoritatively, have been found to be cinereous when the earth becomes enveloped in tenebrosity." What they mean is "All cats are gray at night." But they would lose caste if they said it that way.

This may sound exaggerated, but if it does you have not heard as many sermons on existentialism as I have.

Now, behold, I show you a mystery. Why is it that so many speeches and sermons on ecumenicity and the ecumenical church go "klunk!" and become as soporific as laudanum? It is the most wonderful subject in the world, but it will sink most any oratorical craft.

We have known magnificent speakers, who ordinarily move with all the agility and deadly effectiveness of a destroyer, but when they take the subject of ecumenicity they give a gurgle, and the ship goes down forty fathoms deep. The reason is, in large part, that there is no detail, nothing for the eye to follow, all a struggle for definition and talk of generalities.

Many speeches go "klunk!" because of a lack of narrative. That is part of the unfailing power of the parables of Jesus. Narrative has kept Aesop very much alive for many centuries. Take that most gifted speaker of all times, the Ancient Mariner. Notice how he begins a speech: "There was a ship, quoth he." That gave him a half-nelson on his audience. He did not begin, "Now let us consider the principles of navigation." He knew a trick worth two of that. He held his audience by narrative. Look at the record:

> He holds him with his glittering eye,
> The wedding guest stood still,
> And listens like a three years' child,
> The Mariner hath his will.

Go thou and do likewise.

Yours,
SIMEON STYLITES
—LIKE A MIGHTY ARMY

4

"Whoops! It's Christmas"

Whoops! It's Christmas

In which the old order of seating changeth

The other day I bumped into Santa Claus. A good bump it was, too! I ought to have been arrested, for there is no open season on Santa Claus. But sometimes a first-class collision is an exciting thing. It will knock the wind out of you, and it may knock an idea into your head. True, this Santa Claus did not have white cotton whiskers or a red coat, but she was the real thing all right! Santa Claus in the flesh and plenty of it.

A lady, who looked like an animated Christmas tree with packages dangling from every limb, and I bumped and spilled. As I was trying to pick up the packages she gasped out, "Oh, I hate Christmas, anyhow! It turns everything upside down."

I said, "That is just what it was made for." But this lofty sentiment did not stop her dirty looks at all. But it *is* the big thing about Christmas!

Christmas is a story about a baby, and that is a baby's chief business, turning things upside down. It is gross slander on babies that their chief passion is food. It is rearrangement! Every orthodox baby rearranges everything he sees, or can get his little hooks into, from the order of who's important in the family, to the dishes on the table. A baby in a family divides time into two eras, just as Christmas does. There is B.C., which means "before child," and A.D., which means "after deluge."

The central core of truth is that Christmas turns everything upside down, the upside of heaven come down to earth. The Christmas story puts a new value on every man. He is not a thing to be used, not a chemical accident, not an educated ape. Every man is a V.I.P., because he has divine worth. That was revealed when "Love came down at Christmas." A scientist said, making a plea for exchange scholarships between nations, "The best way to send an idea is to wrap it up in a person." That was what happened at Christmas. The idea of divine love was wrapped up in a person.

Christmas is good news in a world of bad news. This was so on the first Christmas and on Christmas, 1959. During the blackout of London in the Second World War, a newspaper correspondent wrote, "The night was so dark that even the cats ran into each other." That *would* be a dark night! We are often tempted today to think that of our world. But Christmas brings hope in a dark world.

Christmas puts down the mighty things in a man's mind, such as place, rights, power, and exalts the things of low degree, humility, simplicity, and trust. Charles Lamb set high praise on All Fools' Day. He wrote, "All Fools' Day says to a man, 'You look wise; pray correct that error.'" Christmas says to each of us, "You look great; pray correct that error."

Christmas turns things inside out, and under the spell of the Christmas story the locked-up treasures of kindliness and sympathy come from the inside of the heart to the outside world of actual deed. The danger that we all run is that when we keep the kindness locked inside, our biography can be written in one sentence: "This little pig went to market." The symbol of Christmas is a gift.

A big point to remember about Christmas giving, which we often forget, is: Don't, when you are out shopping, make a break for the necktie counter or the lace handkerchiefs. Give an inappropriate gift. Yes, we mean it! Give something as silly as that Christmas gift which people have sung about for several hundred years, "A partridge in a pear tree." That calls for imagination. That makes something to sing about. Would folks have sung about a floor mop (highly appropriate for housework), or a teakettle, or a foot warmer? Not much! So don't get grandma another lace cap or a pair of mittens. She hates the things. Get her a bottle of Chanel No. 5, or a set of lipsticks, or dancing slippers. That makes her feel she is still alive, and it will give a big boost to her morale. As you reach for a present for your beloved physician, that monumental *History of Medicine,* stop! Go to the next counter and get *The New Yorker Book of Cartoons.* There will be several tangy cartoons by Peter Arno that will enable him to step out of character for a while, and that's a lot of fun. And for father, don't get him pajamas; he has some. Get him an electric train. (Kids stay away!) The best Christmas gifts are those that show a lovely lack of common sense. Honest!

And Christmas turns things tail end foremost. The day and the spirit of Christmas rearrange the world parade. As the world arranges it, usually there come first in importance—leading the parade with a big blare of a band—the Big Shots. Frequently they are also the Stuffed

Shirts. That's the first of the parade. Then at the tail end, as of little importance, trudge the weary, the poor, the lame, the halt, and the blind. But in the Christmas spirit the procession is turned around. Those at the tail end are put first in the arrangement of the Child of Christmas.

Christmas calls for haste to meet the world's need. In the Christmas story in Luke we read how the shepherds "came with haste." Evidently the Christmas rush started early! The first response to the good news was speed, hurry, haste, rush. We have a different kind of Christmas rush. Masefield's line, "Life's a long headache in a noisy street," was not written about Christmas but it is a fair description of the shopping rush. One of the ironies of our time is that the celebration of Christmas has become the most frantic convulsion of commercialism. In many places the loudest Christmas bell is the one attached to the cash register. For a few days before Christmas we sing "God rest ye merry, gentlemen," but there is little rest. We sing "Silent Night, Holy Night . . . sleep in heavenly peace," but there is little peace. There is, however, a real rush in which we should join to bring peace and help to a needy world.

We need a new arrangement of the human parade which passes before our eyes. Here is the order of seating in an old New England church: "First, dignity of descent; Second, place of public office; Third, pious disposition; Fourth, estate; Last, peculiar serviceableness of any kind." Christmas comes along and knocks that arrangement into a cocked hat. Yet often we unconsciously arrange our acquaintances, or possible acquaintances, in the order of what advantage they may be to us. That scheme belongs on the junk pile! "The last shall be first."

Let old man Scrooge have the last word. At the end of his travels, which were started by the ghost of Jacob Marley, who "was dead to begin with," after giving his years to what he thought was his business he discovered this: "Mankind was my business. Human need was my business." A good idea to bump into!

So, deck the halls with holly!

—ABBOTT CHRISTMAS BOOK, 1959

A Partridge in a Pear Tree

SIR: With Christmas coming up, may I remind you that there is no carol that offers more fun for a few people singing together, whether they can sing or not, than the old stand-by "The Twelve Days of

Christmas." There is a fine lilt to it, and the fascination that children of all ages find in a cumulative song on the model of "The house that Jack built," where the list of things to be remembered and repeated gets longer with each stanza, and you get all out of breath and have a grand time.

It is an old and universal carol, in celebration of the twelve days from Christmas to Epiphany. You know it—

On the first day of Christmas
My true love gave to me
A partridge in a pear tree.

Then it goes on with a list of the most riotously inappropriate and ludicrous gifts—two turtledoves, three French hens, six geese laying, seven swans singing, eight maids milking, ending with twelve drummers drumming.

Nonsense? Not by a jugful of wassail. It is a profound philosophy of giving. It celebrates the high wisdom of completely inappropriate and largely useless gifts. And a good thing to remember just before Christmas. A partridge in a pear tree—what on earth could one do with that? That's the beauty of it! That makes it something to sing about! And folks have been singing about it for several hundred years. Would they have sung about a floor mop (highly appropriate for housecleaning) or a teakettle or a foot warmer? Not much!

So take a suggestion for your shopping list. Give your true love an inappropriate gift. Don't get grandma another lace cap or pair of woolen mittens. She has plenty already, and besides she hates the things. Get her a little bottle of Chanel No. 5 or a set of lipsticks or a pair of dancing slippers. That will boost her morale, make her feel she is still alive. As you reach for that fine book for your beloved pastor, the learned tome *Archaeology and the Bible*, stay your hand. Reach over to the next counter and get him *The New Yorker Book of Cartoons*. There will be several cartoons by Peter Arno, highly inappropriate for the clergy. That's the idea. There are few joys greater than that of stepping out of character for a time. And I'll bet it will do a lot more for his sermons too. And father—lay off the neckties and the conservative scarf. Get him an electric train, appropriate for age nine. (All his own; Junior keep away!) Dad has always had a yen for one. And for your wife—well, that has me stumped, as usual. How about a—er—ah—Oh well, how about a partridge in a pear tree? It would be a surprise.

The best gifts of love are those which show a lovely lack of common sense. Flowers (they fade, don't they?), a bracelet (invariably a nuisance). It is usually on the twenty-fifth anniversary that a husband gives a vacuum cleaner or a Mix Master.

There is high precedent for all this. The first Christmas gift was highly inappropriate—a Baby in a barn. Who wanted that? No one clapped his hands and said, "Goody, goody, just what I wanted!" That is, no one except a few souls who could really see—Simeon and Anna in the Temple, some shepherds, his mother.

They were all looking for a king
To slay their foes and lift them high.
Thou cam'st a little baby thing
To make a woman cry.

Yours with a sprig of holly,
SIMEON STYLITES

Wise Men From the West

SIR: I heard the words being read, "In the days of Herod the King, behold, Wise Men from the East came to Jerusalem. . . ." Then my mind, never very strong at sticking to the point, trailed off. Suppose, I thought, suppose that the Wise Men had come from the West rather than from the East. Suppose, too, that they shared and expressed some of the main, dominant ideas and drives of our Western civilization and world. What would have happened if it had been Wise Men from the West journeying eastward toward a star? The extracanonical scriptures might have read like this:

The First Wise Man, being a top ruler in the Western world, was a merchant prince, a big industrialist, ever alert to the opportunity of bigger and better sales. At the start of the journey he said to himself: "We are going to be traveling through large, untapped markets. I can follow the star and at the same time open up new outlets for the Caspar Manufacturing Company and triple our exports." So he diligently called on all the tradesmen along the way. He amassed a big sheaf of orders. But it all took time and delayed him greatly, so that the star faded and he never got to Bethlehem at all.

The Second Wise Man had a true Western feeling for military power and defense. He said to himself: "We will be traveling through foreign nations and strange peoples. The gifts we bear will need armed protection. I must recruit a strong force and arm them well. Otherwise we will never get to Jerusalem." But the recruiting and problems of logistics took time, and his soldiers were always getting into brawls with the soldiers of the nations through which they passed. Rome refused to allow such a menacing task force to pass through Italy. So they did not get any farther than Gaul, where they went into winter quarters.

The Third Wise Man was very different from the other two, in everything except his vision of the star and the desire to find the King. But he too was a true man of Western culture and aims. He had been called many harsh things by rivals, but no one had ever called him a shrinking violet. He had a high position—no less than president of Melchior, Melchior, Melchior & Melchior, Advertising and Public Relations Consultants. He said to himself: "This finding of a new King will be a tremendously big thing. It has great publicity possibilities and must be handled in a big way. We will be marching right into history and the whole world must get the full story." So he was much engaged in giving out press releases at every town at which they stopped, and entertaining local journalists. For the sake of complete coverage he made a detour into Egypt, which took three months. But by that time the King of the Jews had been born at Bethlehem, and he never got to see the King at all or to present his gifts.

Perhaps it is just as well that the Wise Men came from the East. Perhaps the West, with all its power and skill, still misses the way to the Star and the Babe in Swaddling Clothes.

Yours,
SIMEON STYLITES
—LIKE A MIGHTY ARMY

"She'll Be Comin' Round the Mountain"

SIR: A crowd of youngsters in a church parlor were having a Christmas "sing" around a briskly burning fire on the hearth. One lad with a lovely whisky tenor started the old song "She'll be comin' round the mountain when she comes." The leader—in this case a "leaderess"—was shocked. "No, no!" she cried. "That is *not* a Christmas carol." And all melody stopped short.

But one observer, all set to burst into barbershop chords, said to himself: "You're all wrong, sister! That emphatically *is* a Christmas carol, and a good one." For "She'll be comin' round the mountain when she comes" is a forecast of hope, in a world where hope is in very short supply. It is the business of Christmas to bring hope. It began that way—"to give light to them that sit in darkness and in the shadow of death." And that is right where we sit today, "in the shadow of death."

We are in a mountain country. If there is to be any real hope for the world, think of the mountains we must get around. Mountains of prejudice that loom like Everest, mountains of ignorance, of ancestral blindness, of entrenched privilege, of inertia, which block the road to a better world like a range of the Rockies.

So the news that "she'll be comin' round the mountain" is "good news which shall be to all people." This is not only hope; it is history. For a "great day coming" *has* come around great mountains. Think of the power of the slave trade in England in the eighteenth century. *There* was a mountain that sat on top of trade, of government, and, yes, of the church. But change did come around it.

We read in the letter to the Corinthians of "faith to remove mountains." But if the mountains of evil don't move—and a lot of them seem to be set pretty solidly—we can come around them. There are mountains that we cannot blast away or tunnel through. Christmas hope and faith sings that "she'll be comin' round the mountains" that block the way.

Thus, Christmas saves us from the ultimate despair, such as that of the dying H. G. Wells, who wrote in his last years: "It now seems to me that the whole universe is utterly bored by the whole species of mankind. I can see the human race sweeping along the stream of fate to defeat, degradation and final defeat." That seems to cover it! No program ahead except that of Richard II:

> For God's sake, let us sit upon the ground
> And tell sad stories of the death of kings.

There is another line of action. We can all rise and instead of intoning that dirge we can sing a different tune: "He shall reign forever and ever."

We are told that Christmas is this and Christmas is that. As a matter of fact Christmas is a whistle, proclaiming that something is coming round the mountain. It may be away off, but she'll be comin', sure. So get up on tiptoe and listen. Can't you hear it? There it is: "The dayspring from on high hath visited us . . . And thou, Child, shalt go before the face of the Lord to prepare his ways, and. . . . guide our feet into the way of peace."

So deck the halls with holly!

Yours,
SIMEON STYLITES

Christmas Roses

SIR: There they are. There is no doubt about it. Incredible, but true. Christmas roses, blooming in a bed of snow! Ever-green leaves and ever-blooming flowers—white, shaped like a wild rose. People going by stop and gaze with wide-eyed astonishment. The roses have absolutely no business to be there! But they are no optical illusion. Astonishing!

That astonishment of people stopped on the sidewalk is a symbol of one of the great gifts of Christmas: Its quickening of the capacity for astonishment. That is a gift desperately needed in a world where the capacity for amazement is becoming more and more depleted. The decline of the ability to wonder, to be astonished, is partly the result of the tragedy of growing up, of losing much of that rich fund of curiosity with which the child is endowed.

A. A. Milne pictured alluringly the child's inheritance of wonder when he wrote of a boy's reeling off a list of amazing things he could see while out for a walk: sun on river and hill; the sound of the sea "if you stand quite still"; new puppies at a near-by farm; most awe-inspiring of all, an old sailor with an empty sleeve. But—there were the grownups standing quite still instead of jumping with joy, able only to admonish: "Run along, run along."

Oldsters can so easily become a Society for the Suppression of Astonishment. The vision splendid in the child's eye so often fades into the light of very common day. So it is fitting that Christmas, the festival of the Child, should bring the gift of astonishment restored.

The Christmas story began with wonder. The shepherds were "sore afraid." That is, they were stunned with astonishment. The whole affair was fantastic. Chesterton sensed the very genius of the Day: "the things that cannot be and are."

And how sorely we need an increased ability to wonder! Ours is a world surfeited with facts and information and entertainment, but deficient in wonder. We have an unceasing parade of novelties, but a "rapidity of things going stale." It is one of the strange paradoxes of our time that a world full of wonders has lost the sense of wonder. The two are quite different. We gape at a bewildering succession of marvelous machines, but there is little of the deep amazement felt on the Judean hills so long ago: "When I consider the heavens, the work of thy fingers, the moon and the stars which thou hast ordained." One reason religion to so many becomes stale, flat, and wearisome is that the sheer wonder is left out.

Increasingly we live in a push-button world—no surprises, no fantastic wonders, just common sense, which gets to be as stale as the "remainder biscuit after a voyage." But Christmas knocks a routine world of order topsy-turvy. Everything is gloriously out of place—a song in the sky, a baby in a barn. That out-of-placeness brings astonishment to lives needing badly the thrill of wonder. For life is truly measured not by the number of breaths taken, but by the number not taken, the occasions when breath is stopped in amazement. This is the breathtaking astonishment of Christmas.

Christmas roses—a root out of dry ground, the Day-spring from on high—that is enough astonishment for one day, and for all days.

And many of them to you,

SIMEON STYLITES

—LIVING WITHOUT GLOVES

Star in the Sky

SIR: The year 1957 has been a year of stars, strange new stars in the sky—stars out of a fantastic dream, Sputniks I and II chasing each other across the firmament at 18,000 miles an hour. These little stars seem like portents such as the Roman augurs used to discern in the heavens, terrifying signs of a red doom on the way. Hilltops have been crowded with people straining their eyes to catch a glimpse of these new stars disturbing the sky, man-made stars, satellites.

But Christmas brings a reminder greatly needed at this hour that there was once another group of people on a hillside looking up at the sky.

In the bleak midwinter
Frosty wind made moan,
Earth stood hard as iron
Water like a stone.

A new star appeared then also. "And lo, a star . . . stood over where the young child was"—a new star and a strange one.

Amid the stars a stranger,
It beams above a manger.

But it was not a star of threatening, but of promise and hope. "Star of wonder, star of light." The first words of the Christmas message from the sky were, "Fear not!" "Fear not"—those are good first words for this day of jittery apprehension. Christmas proclaims that "God has not given us a spirit of fear." Christmas brings hope. It ought to turn our minds away from fantastic and fearsome speculations about space and back to earth. Our minds are full of space. Indeed to hear some people talk you might think that there is nothing in their minds but space, empty space. The most important bit of space is the ground we stand on. "Emanuel" means "God with us," on the earth.

Men ask eagerly, "Will we get to the moon?" The prior question is, "Will we get to the earth in time to forestall the final explosion and bonfire?" Our big problem is not on the moon but here on earth. It is to continue to weave the fabric of peace, against every obstacle, and to give to that undertaking every energy of mind and heart and sinew.

One of the most direct and passionate pleas for this first concern of the world was made two days after the first appearance of the satellite—not by an evangelistic preacher, but in the columns of the *New York Times*. Here it is:

> The creature who descended from a tree or crawled out of a cave is now on the eve of incredible journeys. Yet it is not these journeys which chiefly matter. Will we be happier for seeing the other side of the moon, or strolling in the meadows of Mars? The greatest adventure of all is not to go to the moon or to explore the rings of Saturn. It is rather to understand the heart and soul of man, and to turn away from wrath and destruction toward creativeness and brotherly love.

A clear echo of an old song which comes across the valley of the centuries: "Peace among men of good will."

> There's a song in the air,
> There's a star in the sky.

And many of them!

Yours,
Simeon Stylites
—The Christian Century

VII

From the Workshop

In this final section the purpose is to show something of the way Halford Luccock worked. Material in three stages of development is reproduced. First are transcriptions of what was on a sampling of cards in his study card file. Here were thousands of cards on which he pasted clippings from papers and journals, wrote ideas which had come to him along the way, copied excerpts from books he was reading. Usually he added brief comments of his own. These cards later became sermon themes, illustrations, raw material to go into lectures, addresses, articles. The few which are printed here were selected altogether at random to demonstrate how he began much of the creative process. He did not leave much material that had not been "worked." The cards chosen for "exhibit" in this *Treasury* are some which to the editor's knowledge had not been used, at least in any prominent way.

Ideas in Development are what the ideas look like in a second stage. Many of these excerpts are from short expositions of church-school lessons. He has already worked on the "raw material" and brought it into use for teaching. Usually just the central idea is developed at this stage. Around it a full sermon may later be built. Or the idea may find its way into exposition or interpretation of some passage or theme that does not now appear.

Springboards for Sermons are sermons condensed to such capsules for printing in *The Pulpit Digest* to which he contributed a monthly department for fifteen years. They are essentially thrusts by which a preacher gets his sermon into orbit. They are not illustrations in the conventional sense, nor are they intended as bright detours around the difficult hills of preaching from scripture. To use an image of the space age, a springboard is a booster by which a truth is put in orbit in the listeners' mind and imagination. But the truth for Luccock was always the Word of God.

1

From His Card File

If You Were a Fisherman

A MAN ONCE WROTE: "LONG AGO, WHEN I WAS STAYING IN CORNWALL, A boy from St. Ives came down to my cottage with fish. A heavy sea was crashing on the rocks below, and I admired the beautiful spectacle. The boy looked grave. 'If your people were fishermen,' he said, 'you wouldn't say that. Our boats are out today.' "

"God Be with You"—or words to that effect

In two or three minutes Mr. Roosevelt came through. "Mr. President, what's this about Japan?" "It's quite true," he replied. "They have attacked us at Pearl Harbour. We are all in the same boat now." I put Winant on to the line and some interchanges took place, the Ambassador at first saying, "Good," "Good"—and then, apparently graver, "Ah!" I got on again and said, "This certainly simplifies things. God be with you," or words to that effect.

—From Winston Churchill, *The Grand Alliance*

There *are no* "words to that effect." Saying "Good luck" is not words to the effect of saying "God be with you." We cannot truly say, "the Lord God Omnipotent reigneth—or words to that effect." Or, "underneath are the everlasting arms—or words to that effect." There are no words to that effect. There are no words to the effect that God was in Christ, reconciling the world to himself, although prodigious efforts have been made to find equivalent words.

The Premature Assurance

"Have you understood these things? They say unto him, 'Yea.'" (Matt. 13:51.)

They were sadly mistaken. They *did not* understand. The Gospels are full of the misunderstandings of Jesus. Here was a particularly involved parable. The disciples responded with a quiet confident "*Yea,*" altogether too quickly.

How many times this has happened through the centuries!

On how many occasions does it happen today?

The preventative? Awe, humility.

A dangerous word—*Yea.*

Not in Stock

A sign in a hardware store window in Grand Central Terminal, New York read: "Not everything displayed in the window is in stock."

So with many of our Christian professions—often in the window, but not always in stock.

American Heritage—Or American Way

Esau traded his heritage for a mess of pottage. We do the same when we trade our American heritage for the American way of life.

Warning of an Invasion

During the Second World War the church bells in England were reserved to be used as a warning of an invasion. A report says that they did ring one September day in 1940 on the mistaken word that invasion had begun.

Church bells should always warn of an invasion—sub-Christian and anti-Christian ideas and forces. They should warn, also, of the invasion of our will by God.

We Improve Where We Are Criticized

Donatello left Padua where he was happy and well treated. But he said his art could never *improve* at Padua where all men praised him; he must, for art's sake, return to Florence where all men criticized all.

—From Will Durant, *The Renaissance*

New and Old

The deepest realities of life are not new but old. A minister was called one night to visit a man who had just lost a son. The telephone over which the message came was new. The automobile in which he drove to the man's home was new. The apartment house in which the man lived was new. The automatic elevator that took him to the man's front door was new. There he met a man in his grief. That was not new. That was old.

"Absalom, my son, my son, would that I had died for thee."

The Long Trail of Prophecy

"Thou must prophesy again before many peoples and nations and tongues and kings." (Rev. 10:11.)

The long, long trail that winds into court and prison—into danger—endless prophecy. How delightful it would be to settle down! But what are the things these days—peoples, tongues, kings, and nations before which we must still prophesy? The glib jargon, kings, popular opinion, peoples.

Three Kinds of Silence

"Don't you hear me keeping still?" (Attributed to Samuel Goldwyn)

There are three kinds of silence: A loud silence, a shameful silence, a noble silence.

Race Prejudice—Polynesian Style

Isobel Field tells of hearing a Samoan reprove a Polynesian child for teasing a Negro: "You must not despise him," the Samoan said, "because his skin is black. His soul is as brown as yours and mine."

The Face Shines Through

Saint Sophia in Istanbul is a symbol of one truth about Christianity. The building is an intermixture of Christian and heathen elements. A Christian ground plan overlaid with a Mohammedan mosque. Building materials from Roman and Greek heathenism. But the Christian symbols are not entirely obliterated; the face of Christ in the dome still shines forth dimly but with real radiance. The Christian Evangel has been overlaid with heathen elements, compromised with materialism, militarism, caste, and idolatry, but the faith shines through.

"Mr. Wordsworth Is Never Interrupted"

During one visit to Wordsworth, the sage was making some weighty pronouncements to Keats on poetry. Keats, in full agreement with what he was saying, was about to make an assenting remark. He had scarcely opened his mouth before Mrs. Wordsworth, that sedulous acolyte, had put her hand on his arm, saying, "Mr. Wordsworth is never interrupted."

—From Dorothy Hewlett, *Adonais*

So he learned little or nothing in his later years!

Powder Keg of the Christian View of Man

The really radical and revolutionary way of life does not lie in the East at all, but in the West. The ideas and aspirations of Western man are still the most startling thing that has ever happened to the human race. Stalin's views of man and society are, by comparison, mortally static and archaic. In fact, the world today presents the astonishing spectacle of Western man sleeping unaware on the powder keg of his own revolutionary philosophy and the Stalinists leaping up and down proclaiming as a new revolution a view of man and society which was old when the Pyramids were built."

—From Barbara Ward, *Policy for the West*

An Old Heart Goes A-Journeying

Title of a book by Hans Fallada. A grand ideal of life.

Nine Days' "Wonder"

The sense of wonder is the most precious, maybe the most exhausting of mortal emotions. It doesn't last long; man, the coward, prefers to wallow in the familiar and the habitual. There is always wisdom in the old catchword—"Nine days' wonder." True, for about the tenth day one begins to adapt, to osmose. By then you have lost the fine bouquet of surprise. You no longer gape at Britain's unchangeable habits, not even at her explanatory interpolation, "D'you see?" at every pause of narrative. By the tenth day you have given up trying to get a glass of water at meals, or preventing the waiter from pouring coffee and hot milk simultaneously into your cup (spoiling them both).

—From Christopher Morley, "Notes on an Island," *The Ironing Board*

Watch out for the tenth day—when the "wonder" fades into the light of common day.

The phrase "a nine days' wonder" has a terrible suggestion—that a thing may be a "wonder" for nine days then it fades into something dull and unburnished. That may be true of the Gospel—O the wonder of the Father's love that we should be called the children of God—"And so we are."

But, there is no warning more deeply needed than this—to all Christians, "Watch out for the tenth day, when it all goes." What happens on the tenth day?

Understatement

"When will some shrewd manager be shrewd enough to perceive that in a world full of dull shrieking the still, small voice, the boast foregone, the falsehood dispensed with, the absurdity renounced, the fact understated, or stated with demurely delicate precision, have power to pique and almost to startle?"

—From C. E. Montague, *A Writer's Notes on His Trade*

Edna St. Vincent Millay perceived this in her poem "The Unshouted Thing."

Swiss Tunes

They say there is a tune which is forbidden to be played in the European armies because it makes the Swiss desert, since it reminds them so forcibly of their hills and home. I have heard many *Swiss tunes* played in college. Balancing between getting and not getting a hard lesson, a breath of fragrant air from the fields coming in at the window would serve as a Swiss tune and make me desert to the glens from which it came. Nor is that vagabond inclination wholly gone yet. And many a sultry afternoon, last summer, I left my Latin and my English to go with my gun and see the rabbits and squirrels and robins in the woods. Goodby, Sir. Stop a moment. I have heard a clergyman of Maine say that in his Parish are the Penobscot Indians, and that when any one of them in summer has been absent for some weeks a-hunting, he comes back among them a different person and altogether unlike any of the rest with an eagle's eye, a wild look, and commanding carriage and gesture; but after a few weeks it wears off again into the indolent dronelike apathy which all exhibit. Goodday, Sir.

—From BLISS PERRY, *The Heart of Emerson's Journals*

For an Easier Key

Hymn No. 377 in the hymnal, *Christian Worship and Praise*, is "O Mind of God." At the top of the score the note "For an easier key see 337." How nice to find an easier key for the mind of God.

Evocation in Preaching

A great, difficult, and necessary art. The dictionary defines the word, *evoke:* "The act of calling forth, as from seclusion or the grave or of summoning a spirit by incantation." Preaching must call people forth from the seclusion of preoccupation or the grave of indifference. It must *evoke.*

Theology—Preaching

Theology will be saved by preaching, just as much as preaching will be saved by theology.

Throwing Curves

Preachers have said to me, "After you have been in a church fifteen years what kind of curve can you throw that the congregation does not know?" I couldn't tell them that my knowledge of back-breaking curves and screwballs is sadly limited. But: If preaching the Gospel is a matter of throwing new curves, we are, of all men, most miserable! It is hard to imagine such a verse as this: "And seeing the multitude he went up on a hill to teach them and thought to himself, 'What kind of curve can I throw that these people have not seen?' "

Theme in a Sentence

The record shows that Mr. van Druten has come pretty close to turning out a play a year since he left a London law office to be a full-time dramatist, after the production of "Young Woodley" in 1925. Like every pro, he has had his flops along with his hits, but his percentage of success is still impressive. His own long-tested routine of composition is a simple one. Write only of what you really know. Never write unless you feel. Keep your theme fluid until the last possible moment, but frame it in a single declarative sentence before you put a word on paper. Insist that your characters make your plot, even if you must give them their heads completely. Above all, never be afraid to experiment.

—From James McBride, a review of *Playwright At Work,* by John van Druten, the *New York Times*

"Put your theme in a single declarative sentence."

Approach of a Novelist

One gain which the preacher can make from literature is the discovery and employment of the approach of the novelist, rather than the immediate assumption of the role of a *didactic moralizer.*

Spoiling the Show by Setting Up too Many Rings

Sermons are often so spoiled!

When an Airplane Leaves the Ground

A mystical, magical quality of motion when a plane leaves the ground. So the same thrilling moment ought to come in a sermon, an argument, or a speech: For example, the sermons of Wesley and Whitefield. Also in every dramatic performance in a life, in the ministry of the Church there ought to come a mystical, magical quality when it "leaves the ground."

Doctrinal Preaching

Doctrinal preaching might very well be like doctrine in Paul's letters. Paul "only took to writing when he had to answer quite definite questions or to overcome practical difficulties, and never for the purpose of giving a connected account of his teaching."

—From Hans Leitzman *Beginnings of the Christian Church*

Away from the People

His work is full of imaginative penetration into Shakespeare's thinking. . . . Yet in his later writings one may detect a tendency toward the bookshelves and away not from the stage itself, but from the auditorium. The Quarto texts loom larger and larger and the faces looking down from the second balcony recede into a dim and darkened background.

A commentary on Granville Barker, by Webster.

It can happen to a preacher. It has happened!

Away From the People—To the Bookshelves

What a Bright Boy Mr. Shaw Is

Irwin Shaw's "Gunners' Passage" got second prize (in the *O'Henry Memorial Award Prize Stories of 1945*), and if really slick writing were all, it should have had first. It's deft and precise and technically perfect, but the reader finishes it thinking what a bright boy Mr. Shaw is, rather than thinking anything much about the gunners of whom he writes.

—From Marion Sturges-Jones, book review in the *New York Herald-Tribune*

How often could it be said of our sermons: What a bright boy the preacher is!

A Squeeze of the Lemon

It was once reported that Principal Selbie, of Mansfield College, Oxford, spoke at a meeting, mingling the note of hope and confidence with his old inimitable sub-acid touch—what Lord Morley used to call "a squeeze of the lemon."

Without a "squeeze of the lemon" our preaching can become unbearably bland.

Looking at Mrs. Butler

In the afternoon to Henry the Seventh's chapel, where I heard a sermon and spent (God forgive me) most of my time in looking upon Mrs. Butler.

—From Samuel Pepys, *Diary*

This has been the fate of many sermons!

A Cartoon to Hang in the Preacher's Study

A cartoon shows two men traveling in Europe. One of them says, "Let's look around a bit before we write our books."

Protest No Substitute for Workmanship

Marjorie Faber, a literary critic, has pointed to a common editorial bias which tolerates bad writing in the name of "progress."

A preacher, concerned for the social gospel, must always look out for making his protest a substitute for workmanship.

Pigeonholed

Noel Coward's genius for light comedy has pigeonholed him.

How about the preacher?

Three Qualities of Preaching

J. Donald Adams, writing in the *New York Times*, pays tribute to Barrett Wendell's *English Composition*, a textbook much valued in his day at Harvard, a book which stressed that the three qualities most to be admired in a writer are clarity, force, and elegance.

These might well be considered three qualities of preaching.

Patient Died on the Table

Dr. Cuticle, the surgeon in Melville's *White Jacket*, who, in his concern to demonstrate his own skill, did not observe that the patient had died on the table.

—From Van Wyck Brooks, *Writer in America*

Many preachers, in similar concern for their own skill, have failed to see that their sermons have died on the pulpit.

Ideas Need Landing Fields

An airplane circling a city in heavy fog sometimes can find no opportunity to land and must go back hundreds of miles to another city. The same problem confronts the preacher, for ideas need landing fields as well as wings.

Pharaoh and Simon Legree

Every preacher who would be worthy of the name, must be his own Pharaoh and Simon Legree in keeping himself at work.

A Love Affair with Your Subject

Emil Ludwig's first message to America on his arrival was this expression of his ideals of biography:

> You cannot write about a great man in the cool, dispassionate manner of the average scholar. You have got to have a love affair, not just a marriage with the person you are describing. You have got to be with him constantly; you must have him in your thoughts all the time. Without a little passionate, furious, mad relationship to your subject you will not be able to make him live in your writings.

So must the preacher with the Christ whom he proclaims.

"Today I start my new novel. Who's got a good idea?"

Reprinted by permission of *Saturday Review* and Garrett Price.

"Guess I'll read this one. Everybody I recommended it to says it's good."

Reprinted by permission of *Saturday Review* and A. John Kaunus.

"Have you got something that won't give me cow-like complacency about the world . . . I want to be concerned, stimulated, stirred, worried . . ."

(1955, The Register and Tribune Syndicate)

THROUGH HISTORY WITH J. WESLEY SMITH

"And on the seventh day I rested."

Reprinted by permission of *Saturday Review* and Burr Shafer.

"I just loved your autobiography—I hope you'll write another."

Reprinted by permission of *Saturday Review* and W. P. Trent.

"It's a little late for that now, Kraufmeyer."

Drawing by Alain; Copyright © 1941 The New Yorker Magazine, Inc.

2

Ideas in Development

The Second Chance

Some of the finest stories of Abraham Lincoln have to do with his mercy and clemency in pardoning soldiers.

A certain Roswell McIntyre deserted the Union Army during the Civil War. Such an offense was punishable by death, and McIntyre was tried and condemned to die. He admitted his guilt, made no excuse, but made the plea that if he were given a second chance he would be loyal. In pity for the boy, and touched by his promise, President Lincoln pardoned him. Mr. Lincoln wrote out a pass for him to return to his regiment.

Executive Mansion
October 4, 1864

Upon condition that Roswell McIntyre of Co. E, Sixth Regiment of New York Calvary, returns to his regiment and faithfully serves out his term, making up for lost time or until otherwise discharged, he is fully pardoned for any supposed desertion, and this paper is his pass to go to his regiment.

A. Lincoln

In the government records in Washington this paper is preserved, with this notation written across the outside, "Taken from the body of R. McIntyre at the battle of Five Forks, Virginia, 1865."

McIntyre made good on his second chance!

John Mark had much the same history. He was given a second chance and made good. Paul even wrote to the effect that Mark was useful for the gospel!

Two things come from these stories.

1. Don't give up on account of failure.
2. Give other people a chance to make good.

Pushing Back the Horizon

Undoubtedly not one of a thousand persons in the United States ever heard of Mr. LeBar of Mexico. Mr. LeBar taught the eight million people in New York City one of the most effective lessons they ever had set before them.

Mr. LeBar was a Mexican importer who, in 1947, journeyed to New York City with a fatal smallpox infection. He produced a panic in the great city by spreading the disease and almost creating an epidemic. That was averted only by vaccinating nearly six million New Yorkers in a hurry. We can say truly that he preached a tremendous sermon on the text, "We are members one of another."

More Than Money

A collection was being taken. It was at a missionary rally during a Methodist Conference in Mississippi in the early 1850's. A new teacher from New York was in the audience and was moved deeply by the picturing of the world's need of the gospel of Christ. When the collection plate was passed to her, she put on it a five dollar bill and a note which read, "I give five dollars and myself. Mary I. McClellan."

The gift of five dollars was a large one for a young schoolteacher; the gift of herself infinitely larger. A few years later this young teacher married a young pioneer missionary to China, James W. Lambuth. The son of this couple, Walter R. Lambuth, later Bishop of the Methodist Episcopal Church, South, physician, and missionary, became one of the great Christian statesmen of his time.

This is something to think about when the collection plate is passed to us. We put money on it, but do we ever put ourselves on it? That is what God wants—to translate into actual living the words of Paul, "I beseech you, therefore, brethren, by the mercies of God, that you present your bodies a living sacrifice."

We should put on God's collection plate three things:

1. *A busy body.* Not the unpleasant "busybody." But the separate words which mean something entirely different, a living sacrifice unto God.
2. *A busy heart.*
3. *A busy mind.*

After Christmas—What?

A minister was speaking at an evening meeting at a rescue mission. Before him were a company of men among whom were many derelicts; men who, temporarily at least, were "down and out." Some had been for years sad and familiar sights along "Skid Row." Hoping to bring them some inspiration, he sought to appeal to the will and determination of his audience by reciting the familiar poem, "If," by Rudyard Kipling. It begins: "If you can keep your head when all about you . . ." and ends with the following lines:

> If you can fill the unforgiving minute
> With sixty seconds' worth of distance run.

When he had finished a man in the back of the hall called out, "What if you can't?"

Christianity has an answer to that question! It brings a power which makes possible what man cannot do by his own efforts. "As many as received him, to them gave he power to become the sons of God" (John 1:12).

Something to Lean Against

"When does she want it delivered?" asked a store manager of a clerk who had just sold a large amount of furniture to a woman.

"She wants it delivered yesterday afternoon!" said the exasperated clerk.

Those words picture the trouble with a great many people in our time. They are in a hurry. Consequently the teaching of Jesus on slow steady growth, is very much in date.

On the Witness Stand

Many years ago a rash but determined young preacher began his sermon to a wondering congregation with these words: "I am preaching this morning on the whole of the 29th chapter of Acts. It is one of the greatest and most stirring chapters in the New Testament."

Many in the congregation nodded their heads gravely as though they were perfectly familiar with the wonderful 29th chapter of Acts. When they settled back comfortably to await the sermon, he startled them by explaining that there was no 29th chapter of Acts. There are only twenty-eight chapters in the book. Then he added that they themselves were the 29th chapter of Acts, for the Book of Acts of the Apostles is never finished. It is a continued story, and we are all adding new chapters every day. We are in the unbroken line of witnesses to Jesus. The question that he put that morning is one that comes close to all of us: "How does the 29th chapter of the Book of Acts, which we are writing in our lives, compare with the 28th chapter of the original book?"

Sunset or Sunrise?

A young woman was preparing to show some Kodachrome films on a projector. A few of the films bothered her. "It is hard to tell whether these are pictures of sunsets or sunrises. They look just about the same," she explained.

In those words she said something profound about many of life's experiences. So many things seem to be "sunsets." That is, they look as though night were closing in, as though there were no more hope. Then these "sunsets" turn out to be "sunrises"; they usher in a new day with new beginnings. It is God's overruling providence which so often turns sunsets into sunrises.

Our Prayers Must Match Our Lives

When Michael Faraday, the great scientist, was a small boy he earned his living by selling newspapers. In his biography there is a very interesting story of an experience during his early days. He was once waiting outside the building where the newspapers were printed, so that he could get a supply to sell. He put his head and arms through the railings of an iron gate. Then, being a thoughtful lad, he began to wonder which side of the gate he was on. He said, "My head and my hands are on one side and my heart and my body are on the other." He gave a big pull, which was very painful, but it got his head loose. Then he made a good observation to the effect that head and heart should be on the same side.

Reliving Great Discoveries

When Professor Samuel E. Morrison of Harvard began to write his life of Columbus, *Admiral of the Ocean Sea*, he concluded that the best preparation would be to go over the course of the actual voyages of Columbus, in a sailing ship just about the size of the Santa Maria, so that he would see everything exactly as Columbus saw it. He said, "I set out to relive the discoveries of the great discoverer."

That is a noble phrase—"to relive the discoveries of the great discoverer." Jesus was the Great Discoverer. He made known to men the truth about God and the way of life. We learn the profound truth that he revealed only by living it.

There Were Two Ships

Along the Maine coast, a traveler going along Route U.S. 1 can notice two ships in striking contrast, within ten miles of each other.

One is tied to the dock of an iron works at Bath, Maine—a Navy destroyer, which has just been built, commissioned, and launched. Ten miles east at Wiscasset, Maine, there is an old sailing ship, which has been tied to the dock for fifteen years, a rotting hulk. It has no commission, no future but to continue rotting.

With those ships in mind, consider two lives, which can be found near each other in any town in America. One is a "commissioned life." It is always ready for an assignment. It is literally "sent," for that is the root meaning for the word "commissioned." The other life is like the abandoned hulk. It is chained up to its own small interests. It responds to no orders from outside itself.

—NEW CENTURY LEADER

3

Springboards for Sermons

A Date With the Gulf Stream

A FEW YEARS AGO A LITTLE SHIP PUT OUT FROM A PORT ON THE GULF OF Mexico, headed for a port on the northeastern coast of the United States. The ship was not only small and much the worse for wear; it looked like something left over from Admiral Farragut's attack on New Orleans in the Civil War. Quite a crowd of friends of the skipper, and a chorus who came to jeer, gathered for the embarkation. They had a lot of sport.

"You won't get anywhere in that tub," was the cheering send-off.

"Oh, yes, I will," confidently replied the skipper.

"What makes you think so?" he was asked by many of the bystanders.

"I've got a date," he replied. "I've got a date with the Gulf Stream." And he had!

The skipper was a mariner, first class. He knew his winds and water. He had a definite date with a power greater than himself or his little craft. He was not sailing under his own wit or the momentum of his engines alone. He had a date with a power not of himself that made for marine "righteousness."

The fortification the skipper found in the confidence in his "date with the Gulf Stream" comes, I think, close to the experience of every one of us. It is certainly true, is it not, that our first and deepest need is for the renewal of the sense that, however uncharted the sea or land on which we travel, we have a date with the "Gulf Stream," a date with God.

Consider the experience of a man who, like Abraham, went out, not knowing whither he went.

Paul had seen a vision of a man needing help, as many men have seen it. He sailed from Troas to Philippi. On arriving he had to face the disappointment of what must have seemed an anticlimax. He found no multitude waiting at the port. There were just a few women holding a prayer meeting. A pretty slim beginning for the evangelization of a continent! But, also, God was at the dock to meet him.

As it was in the beginning—so now. You have a date with a God who will meet you on any landing beach. If men can go into action of any sort with that assurance as the deepest thing in their minds and hearts, they go in force.

—UNFINISHED BUSINESS

The Prevented Christ

On the walk to Emmaus taken by two disciples after the resurrection, Jesus joined them and "expounded unto them in all the scriptures the things concerning himself." Then we read in Luke 24:28: "And they drew nigh unto the village, whither they went: and he made as though he would have gone further."

With the words, "He would have gone further," before our imagination, we can readily think of many times when Jesus would have gone further with his disciples. In true humility we can think of the times when Jesus would have gone further with us.

In that sense, we can think of Jesus as "the prevented Christ." We ourselves many times have prevented him from going further in discipleship.

He would have gone further so often *in our religious life.*

Jesus would have gone further in *human contacts for us.*

Jesus would have gone further *in the service of the Church.*

Some years ago Dean Willard Sperry published a book entitled *Jesus, Then and Now.* Someone sent in an order to the publishers for the book as *Jesus, Now and Then.* That is what the Christian religion amounts to with some church members: "Jesus, now and then." That is all he gets. He would have gone further than that!

Doors Opening Outward

When William James, the American philosopher, was a child, he wrote to a friend about a summer home in New Hampshire which his family had acquired. He was quite excited about it. He wrote: "It is a wonderful house, with all the doors opening outward."

This is a great way to live—with all the doors of the heart and mind opening outward! It is the way the heart and mind should open.

Our minds should open outward.
Our hearts should open outward.
Our interests should open outward.
Church doors should open outward.

"Drowns All Music But Its Own"

Crown Him with many crowns
The Lamb upon the throne.
Hark! how the heavenly anthem drowns
All music but its own!

There is thrill to these words as well as the familiar music. The words are profoundly true to the experience of multitudes. The heavenly anthem of God's revelation in Christ has silenced all other music. It was so with Paul: "I count everything as loss because of the surpassing worth of knowing Christ Jesus my Lord." That anthem drowned out all other music in David Livingstone. He said: "I hold everything I have in relationship to God and His Kingdom."

But, unfortunately, that is not the only thing that drowns out all other music. Lower preoccupations can make men deaf to the music of faith. Suppose that Heifitz were playing Beethoven's Violin Concerto, accompanied by a big bass drum, on which the drummer pounded with all his might. The exquisite music of the violin would be drowned out by the "boom, boom" of the bass drum.

That is exactly what has happened in many lives, and may happen in any life.

A complaining disposition can drown out all music but its own. The habit of mournful self-pity and bitter complaint can drown out the notes of Christian joy as effectively as a drum can drown out the soft notes of a flute.

All too often the clink of coins can drown out all music but its own in a life. We read that at the end of the Last Supper, "after they had sung a hymn they went out." Judas did not hear the hymn. He heard other noises, the clink of thirty pieces of silver.

There is only one resource. It is to allow God to "open our ear" day by day to the song of Moses and the Lamb.

Catching Up to Jesus

There is a much quoted remark of D. H. Lawrence, written in a letter to Katherine Mansfield: "Cheer up, Kate, Jesus is a back number!" Just what cheer that might bring to a young woman dying of tuberculosis does not appear! But let that pass.

What we cannot let pass is the assertion: "Jesus is a back number." So much in our present world contradicts it. The daily newspapers, to say nothing of books, print news that demonstrates that, in many very real ways, history is a process of overtaking the insights and teachings of Jesus.

Many people, particularly some of the scholars, scientists, and philosophers, seem to throw the gospels away and quote from memory. Bertrand Russell is a good example of this. Several years ago, looking around on the shambles that man has made out of his world, he came up with the conclusion that what was necessary was "to diminish the instincts that center around possession." A profound observation! The only trouble was that it was made 1900 years before Mr. Russell discovered it. It was made by Jesus, more succinctly and deeply, when he said: "He that loseth his life shall find it." Another "discovery" that Mr. Russell reported two years ago was very remarkable. In an address at Columbia University, it was rather amusing to see and hear the apologies and hesitations with which he made his announcement that Christian love was the world's greatest need. Here it is, with all the apologies left in:

> The root of the matter (if we want a stable world) is a very simple and old fashioned thing, so simple that I am almost ashamed to mention it for fear of the derisive smile with which wise cynics will greet my words. The thing I mean is love, Christian love, or compassion. If you feel this you have a motive for existence, a reason for courage, an imperative necessity for intellectual honesty.

Two more recent examples of getting abreast of Jesus have appeared. Dr. William C. Menninger, the distinguished psychiatrist, said in Philadelphia, May 17: "If we could love our neighbors as ourselves we could have Utopia. In fact, the hope of the world rests on our capacity to love, because it is the only way to neutralize the hate within us that comes from the deepest layers of our personality."

Let's see. Didn't Jesus say: "A new commandment I give unto you, that you love one another"?

A few weeks later Dr. Clarence P. Oberndorf, professor of psychiatry at Columbia University, told a convention of psychologists that "mental health depends upon the extent of awareness that a person has attained in his relation with his fellow beings."

That sounds familiar, doesn't it? Jesus is the "great contemporary."

Keeping Mad in a Sane World

A man on an auto trip through the country was deeply impressed by a sermon topic which he saw announced on a church bulletin board. It was "Keeping Sane in a Mad World." He thought "I wish I could hear the sermon. It is a timely and big topic." Then, as he continued thinking of it, he concluded that the topic would be just as true and timely in reverse: "Keeping Mad in a Sane World."

That is not just fantastic. For in a very true sense one of the troubles of our imperiled world is just its *sanity*. For, to many people, sanity means going on just as the world has been going. Wisdom is regarded as keeping things just as usual.

We should remember that both Paul and Jesus were accused of being mad. A Roman official shouted at Paul: "Paul, you are mad!" Some people listened to Jesus and because he did not say just what they had always been accustomed to hear, they said he was "beside himself," meaning that he was crazy.

We need that kind of Christian madness. If we really believe in the possibility of a Christian world deeply enough to work for it, many will call us "mad." But that will be the way of escape from the deadly "sanity" of those who are content to keep our world just as it is. One of the wisest words ever spoken, and very timely today, is the remark of a French soldier, when someone told him that Joan of Arc was "mad": "We could do with a few mad men," he said, "look where the sane ones have landed us." Even so, the case for Christianity can be expressed in two lines by Christopher Morley:

> O cautious men who get us into trouble!
> And reckless dreamers have to get us out.

Christ is the "reckless dreamer" who can lead the world out of its trouble. We need the madness of believing in the reality of God as Jesus did, and of following the more excellent way of love.

Book Value and Market Value

A widow was left many shares of stock in a gold mine, worth, it read on the certificate, $100 a share! The lawyer smiled sadly, saying, "This stock isn't worth thirty cents."

The Trustees of a religious institution recently reported: "The book value of all stocks and bonds including government ones at maturity prices, as of February 28, was $1,300,581.34, while the market value of the securities on the same date was $1,385,736."

In that case, the market value was greater than the book value. But so often the scales tip the other way!

How does the market value of our Christian faith, as visible in our lives, compare to the book value? The "book value" as expressed in the New Testament is high, very high. Here are some evaluations: "I am strong for all things through him who strengtheneth me. . . . If any man is in Christ, he is a new creature. . . . It is no longer I that live but Christ who liveth in me."

What is the "market value" of this spiritual wealth in actual life? "Strong for all things?" Well, not exactly! Many people who profess this tremendous faith are completely bowled over by trouble or care, just as those who do not have the faith. The book value of the faith is 100 per cent. The market value, alas, is often about 22 per cent! So, many may say the words, with genuine sincerity: "Christ liveth in me." And yet there are other forces and desires which live in them strongly—self-gratification and financial frenzy.

In the epistle to Titus this matter of difference between the faith and the conduct of those who profess it is put sharply. The author pleads: "Show yourself in all respects a model of good deeds . . . so that an opponent may be put to shame, having nothing evil to say against us." (Tit. 2:8.) In more modern words, bring the market value up to the book value.

The theme of the sermon will be to give suggestions on how this may be done.

I Know How to Abound

A very sad, striking, and disturbing story has lately been retold. It raised questions that we should ask ourselves. It is the story of a family named Danks, and it goes something like this:

In 1874 Mr. and Mrs. Danks with their little family were devoted to each other and made a happy home. They were poor. Mr. Danks was a songwriter, which was a very precarious business, up one day and down the next. But their poverty seemed to draw them closer together. Mr. Danks was so strongly impressed with this affection that he wrote a song which everyone knows, "Silver Threads Among the Gold."

That brought him both fame and fortune. But it brought also discord and unhappiness. The home was broken up, and in 1903 Mr. and Mrs. Danks were separated. Some years later Mr. Danks was found dead, kneeling beside his bed in a cheap boarding house in Philadelphia. On the bed beside him lay an old copy of his song "Silver Threads Among the Gold," with these words written across it: "It is hard to grow old alone."

The preacher can take it from there.

Prosperity is a harder moral and spiritual test than adversity. Paul wrote that he knew how to be abased and how to abound. There is no slightest doubt that the second is the hardest.

Get off the Earth

The phrase "get off the earth," is a common one, usually spoken in disdain or derision. But today it has entered the realm of reality. This phrase brings other pictures to the imagination in addition to voyages to the moon. For one thing, man's inventions, used for human obliteration, as they are now being prepared for use, may well say to the whole race of man, "Get off the earth." We now have in view the possibility of collective suicide of the human race.

But, in a deeper sense, we must get off the earth in our thinking and acting if life is to be saved. That is, we must take our directions and compulsions not from the prudences of earth, but from another world, from heaven, from the will of God. That is the high meaning of the petitions in the Lord's Prayer: "Thy kingdom come; Thy will be done." We must get off the earth into the law of heaven, into the law of love. Brotherhood is no longer a lovely extracurricular activity of men. It is a condition of survival.

As He Did Aforetime

The phrase above is found in the story of Daniel in the lions' den, in the sixth chapter of Daniel. It is a stirring phrase which has timeliness and relevance to the life of every Christian in these days of crisis and uncertainty.

Read the story in Daniel again. A decree had gone out from King Darius that no one should be worshiped except himself. This put the young Hebrew servant of the King, Daniel, in a difficult spot. He had been in the habit of praying to his God. That was forbidden now. What should he do? Risk his life for just a habit? Here is what happened, as you remember: "Now when Daniel knew that the writing was signed, he went to his house; and his windows being open in his chamber toward Jerusalem, he kneeled on his knees three times a day, and gave thanks before his God, *as he did aforetime.*"

Those last five words are glorious words. They picture vividly the steadiness and continuity of faith in a day of change. Daniel's whole world had been changed greatly for the worse by this cruel decree, punishing the worship of Jehovah by death. But he went on, *as he did aforetime.*

By his action he showed that he was conscious of the things that had not changed. God had not changed. He was still the same God he had been before the decree of Darius. God's love had not changed. The world had not passed out of God's hands.

So, Daniel did not change his faith. He went on "as aforetime." He is a great example for any time of change and crisis.

Epigoni

The word is an unusual one, but we come across it often enough to cause us to stop, look, and listen.

The word comes from the Greek, from the word for "offspring." The meaning came from Greek legend. The epigoni were the sons and successors of the Seven against Thebes. Ten years after their fathers died at Thebes, they conquered Thebes, but gave the kingdom away. The meaning is that the successors were not as great as the fathers. Thus the word, "epigoni," comes to stand for the successors of fathers when they have degenerated and are not as great as the fathers.

John Chamberlain wrote in the *New York Herald Tribune* on May 22, 1960: "A time dominated by the epigoni can never be a time for heroes."

Let us bring this home to ourselves.

We are the epigoni, or successors, of the early Christians. We love to sing of many of them:

> They climbed the steep ascent of heaven
> Through peril, toil, and pain.

How are we doing as their successors?

Again, we are the successors of those who planted the Christian churches in New England. What kind of successors are we? May we not be degenerate sons and daughters! May we be those who say sincerely and earnestly:

> O God, to us may grace be given
> To follow in their train.

Before the Drag Takes Over

In these days of space travel and reaching for the moon, there has come a suggestion for life on the same old planet on which we have lived. This suggestion, entirely unintended, occurs in the midst of a speculation on journeying to the other planets.

Here it is (including one perfect jawbreaker of a scientific word):

> Mathematics must enter a new dimension of magnetohydrodynamics [that's the jawbreaker] to bring the voyagers safely home. The tables drawn up by tomorrow's astronomers will have to tell where the pull of the earth's gravity ends, how far out a man can go before the drag of the moon takes over, at what point Jupiter makes itself felt.

The words to be studied are: "how far out a man can go before the drag of another world takes over."

This should be a major theme of the preacher in discerning and warning men and women, "how far out" people can go from the pull of God and Christian faith before the various other kinds of "pulls" take over. The sermon will be on the various kinds of situations and actions in which the pull away from God begins to prevail.

—PULPIT DIGEST

Greatest Bridge in the World

The late Bishop of London, Dr. Winnington-Ingraham, when walking on a holiday, fell into step with a shepherd leading his flock. The bishop said to the shepherd, "I am a kind of shepherd too." No answer. But after a while the shepherd asked, "How many sheep do you have?" Thinking of his enormous diocese in London the bishop replied, "About a million." A long stretch of silence. Then the shepherd asked, "What do you do at lambing time?" A good, tough question for any church. "What do you do at lambing time?" What do you do about the great stream of young life that flows into your church and often out of it?

SIMEON STYLITES
—THE CHRISTIAN CENTURY

No Faith in the Future

While a company of people were having dinner together, one man in the party, who had spent many summers in Maine, fascinated his companions by telling of his experiences with a little town named Flagstaff in the months before it was to be flooded as part of a large lake for which a dam was being built. All improvements and repairs in the whole town were stopped. What was the use of painting a house if it were to be covered with water in six months? Why repair anything when the whole village was to be wiped out? So, week by week, the whole town became more and more bedraggled, more gone to seed, more woebegone. Then he added by way of explanation: "Where there is no faith in the future, there is no power in the present."

That word is a profound one and has a far wider application than merely to the flooding of a town. Of course, it applied with crystal clearness to that little town of Flagstaff. The people of Flagstaff had no faith in the future and, of course, had no power in the present.

It applies to our world right now. So many people are very close to despair over the possibility of a third world war and of wiping the human race off the planet. There are some couples who are even refusing to have children, because they fear they would just be blown to bits. A dire consequence of this is a lack of power in the present. This is a completely unchristian state of mind and heart. It practically says that God is dead, or will not be a factor in the world from now on. We should not minimize the seriousness of the hour or pretend that it is not dangerous. But if we are Christians we must not leave God out of our world. For the final question is not what Russia is going to do, but what *God* is going to do. Our world has not slipped out of God's pocket. It is still in his shaping hands. We need that deep faith if we are to confront our world today with anything other than despair. Otherwise we have no power in the present with which to arm ourselves for action to make God's will prevail.

The same is true of our attitude to the Church. There are some within the Church, perhaps a large number, who do not have a stout faith in its future. They think and act as though it were a losing venture. They look at the obstacles, and there are many and staggering ones: The collapse of China, the disregard of religion in such large parts of Europe, the frequent lack of drive and devotion among church people in the United States, the slow movement toward church unity. That distrust is one reason for the lack of power in the present. We need a faith that God never gets down to his last nickel, that his Church is the Body of Christ and will not be left without his power and direction. Faith in God's tomorrow will bring strength to our action in God's today. Vachel Lindsay has put the questions, and the answer, in noble poetry:

What is the final ending?
The issue, who can know?
Will Christ outlive Mohammed?
Will Kali's altars go?

This is our faith tremendous—
Our wild hope, who shall scorn—
That in the name of Jesus
The world shall be reborn!

—UNFINISHED BUSINESS

Get Christmas Out of the Stocking

About thirty years ago Gerald Stanley Lee wrote some words about Christmas which are always in order. His plea was to keep Christmas to its original size. Here was the original size of Christmas: "Behold, I bring you good tidings of great joy, *which shall be to all people.*" It was for *all people*—it was Christmas Unlimited. Mr. Lee put it in this arresting way:

> Why should Christmas—that stern, imperious moment in the world when with a child's cry and a woman's smile, God turned the world over, and began all in a minute a new human race—why should Christmas be tucked away in men's minds as a feebly pretty country sentiment, a woman's holiday, a baby's frolic, the sublimest event on earth thrust playfully into the bottom of a stocking?

There is danger that the very loveliness of Christmas as a home festival may imprison it within the home, and thus men may forget that it is a *world* festival, celebrating the truth that God so loved the world—all of it —"that he gave his only begotten son." Christmas must be pulled out of a stocking and carried to the dispossessed, the defrauded, to the whole globe, as well as to America.

Jesus deliberately widened the family ties to include the brotherhood of all mankind. "Whosoever shall do the will of God, the same is my brother, and my sister, and my mother." (Mark 3:33-34.)

The danger of living in too small a world is a danger that Christmas ought to overcome.

Jesus—Disturber of Loyalties

There is a verse in the gospel, a statement by Jesus, which pictures Jesus in a role which many people find hard to accept. Here it is: "For I am come to set a man at variance against his father, and the daughter-in-law against her mother-in-law." (Matt. 10:35.) These words give the conception of Jesus as the Great Disturber of Loyalties.

True, Jesus did say, "My peace I give unto thee." But the peace which Jesus brings is not quietness in the face of evil or agreement with a lesser loyalty. Jesus seeks to disturb unworthy loyalties which prevent the great and highest loyalty.

Canon E. C. Raven of England writes, "To rest content with less than the best, to set up as our ideal a loyalty that is deliberately selfish, second-rate, is to be guilty of idolatry."

Here are some of the loyalties which compete with a loyalty to Christ and his teachings, as given by William B. Spofford:

> We are often urged to be loyal and our loyalty must be to institutions and authorities rather than to facts. Forsooth! Loyalty to muddled thinking; loyalty to ecclesiastical arrogance, against which Jesus fought his way to Calvary; loyalty to superstitions which obscure the kingdom of God; loyalty to the closed mind . . . loyalty to those who tithe mint, anise, and cumin, and neglect the weightier matters of the law.

There is the danger of loyalty to a *tradition,* which has been followed for a long time, and which we now follow just because it has been in force, and yet, it may not fit today's need at all.

There is loyalty to a *prejudice,* which very often prevents genuine loyalty to the purposes of God as disclosed in Christ.

Partial loyalties must be gathered up into the all-comprehending loyalty to Christ and to all our brothers in Christ.

Terrestrial Magnetism

The *New Yorker* once printed the report of a visit by a reporter to a strange place, the "Department of Terrestrial Magnetism" of the Carnegie Institute in Washington, D.C. This department is deeply concerned with all the properties of the earth's crust, including its magnetism, of which it seems to have plenty. This power of earth magnetism is manifested in many ways.

It is a title to ponder, "Terrestrial Magnetism." Turn the imagination on it. It may run loose, but it is a good thing to give the imagination a canter. As a rule, it does not get enough exercise.

It is not stretching the truth at all to consider this title as picturing a chief danger to the Christian life. There is a pull of the world on every one of us. A perfect picture of the disaster which the lure of the world may bring about is in the sorrowful record in Paul's letter to Timothy: "For Demas, in love with this present world, has deserted me" (II Tim. 4:10).

The terrestrial magnetism of the city was too much for Demas. He could not resist the pull of the giddy life of glamorous cities. There was too much magnetism. We read in the story of the temptation of Jesus that Satan tried the magnetism of the earth: "The devil took him to a very high mountain and showed him the kingdom of the world and the glory of them." (Matt. 4:8.) This was a big magnet! But it had no power over Jesus. He had been exposed to a stronger magnet, for he said: "You shall worship the Lord, your God, and him only shall you serve."

Do not underestimate the enemy. That has been one of the most damaging mistakes of the strategy of the Christian life. There *is* a strong magnetism of the earth. There is the lust of the eye, the pomp and circumstance of power, the magic of money. Let him that thinketh he standeth, take heed lest he fall. Many people put in a life of window-shopping, gazing at things which the world has and which they greatly desire. Do not give your desires for things power over you. Put one desire above all. Get the pearl of great price! And remember that the only way to overcome the magnetism of the world and its prizes is to bring to bear the greater power of the love of God.

The Middle-Age Letdown

The manufacturers of a patent medicine have been frantically advertising their product as a cure for what they call "Middle-age letdown." The deathless prose of the advertisements pictures wearied strugglers battling the ills of exhaustion and weary bones. Just to read about the symptoms gives anyone who has entered the "middle years" a bad backache.

Yet the phrase "middle-age letdown" is very provocative when we think of something other than physical weariness. It calls to mind a striking verse in Psalms: "the destruction that wasteth at noonday" (91:16). There is, truly, a great danger and hazard in middle age, not that of physical tiredness, but of a spiritual letdown. There is a risk of a loss of zest and of uprightness and energy of character.

There is the danger of the generous ardor of youth and the unselfish devotion to great causes for human welfare giving way to a listless lack of interest in what does not make for one's advantage.

The person in middle age becomes one of whom it is said, "He used to. . . ." He used to be active in the church, he used to be a dependable leader in civic causes. His case is worse than "tired blood"—whatever that may be. It is the tragedy of a "tired mind and heart."

There is often a letdown in inner character.

This collapse of the spiritual and moral life can be averted only by a renewal of the mind and heart. Paul points the way: "Be ye transformed by the renewal of your mind."

Reflected Light and Direct Encounter

Some years ago a family had a summer home on Lake Champlain. Although they were on the eastern shore of the lake, their home was situated on a peninsula in such a way that they still faced eastward. Every evening, when the sun was setting in burning splendor over the Adirondack Mountains, they were rhapsodic in telling their more prosperous friends, who watched the sunsets from homes high on the cliffs looking westward across the lake, about the glories of the eastern afterglow. But their tributes never quite convinced their friends or themselves. It remained that they had only the dying reflection—the real glory was in the west!

So it is with a church! We can live on in the reflected glory of remote experiences, but the real glory of the Lord comes in immediate, direct encounter with God. A wise man of our day has made this sharp observation: "The decline of the power of an institution is in direct ratio to its distance to the experience out of which it grows." The diminution of the power of a church will be in direct ratio to its distance from the personal experience of Pentecost.

Downsittings

There is a verse in the Psalms which comes very close to many actions and moods of our lives. It is that in the Ps. 139:2: "Thou knowest my downsitting."

How varied and frequent are our downsittings! How they express the many moods of discouragement! And many of our faults and failings are found in our downsittings!

On this there is a quaint word by Jeremy Taylor, the seventeenth-century minister and author. He wrote: "Some people collect a bunch of thorns and sit down on them." We often do that. And today, as in Taylor's time, some people do it constantly. They select the disagreeable things about a situation and dwell on those to the exclusion of anything pleasant or hopeful.

We all know the "downsittings" caused by grief. George Eliot, the novelist, once wrote: "My Address is Grief Castle, Melancholia Street." We can understand that. Then, far less excusable, are the downsittings which come from pure laziness. We are like the son in the parable of Jesus, who, when his father sent him out to work, said with alacrity, "I go, Sir"; but he went not!

God deals with our downsittings, from every cause. Among the Bible's frequent words of God to man is, "Arise." He lifts people to their feet. Faith in the goodness of God, and fidelity to his word, lifts us from the downsitting in grief, and in indolence, and in despair.

Gifts for Casual Living

Many people recently received in the mail a large, illustrated booklet, in technicolor, entitled "Gifts for Casual Living." Looking through it was like taking a personally conducted tour through Ali Baba's treasure cave. There were some things which almost anyone would like to have; there were also about a hundred things which, one would judge, no one in his right mind would want even in the trash can. Most of them were too terribly casual for any rational use!

There was a set of "Watermelon Zombie Glasses." You can work that one out for yourself. Then there was also a "Pink Bird Larabo." Perhaps you can get along without that!

As we think it over, we feel that one thing the matter with our distressed world is *too much casual living.* Too many of us take living too casually, have too little sense of responsibility, *too little committed and dedicated living.* We seem to have elevated the parting greeting we give to each other, "Take it easy," into a high wisdom for living.

There are, by the grace of God, *great gifts for serious living* which are available to us all if we will take them. They will enable us for truly Christian living instead of merely casual living.

The Gift of Eyes. Paul writes of "the eyes of your heart." If our eyes have the spirit of Christ directing them, we can see the people who need help. Jesus said: "Lift up your eyes. The fields are white unto harvest." If we are just living casually or carelessly—or both, for the two always go together—we are like men and women stumbling through life blindfolded.

The Gift of Ears. We often say: "You could have heard a pin drop." The ears of Jesus were more sensitive than that. He could hear the unspoken cries of people in need. His sympathy was so quick and his hearing so acute that he was aware of human need when others around him heard nothing. We read in Paul's letters: "We have the mind of Christ." In order to have that, we must have the *ears* of Christ.

The Gift of the Morning Star. In Rev. 2:28, we read, as the supreme gift of God: "I will give him the morning star." This means the gift of God's love in Christ, the day star from on high that has visited us. This gift brings hope in dark places, power when life needs power.

If we take these gifts, life is lifted out of triviality into eternal meaning.

I Forgot the Message

A cartoon in the *Saturday Review* has a frightfully close relationship to the life of the individual Christian and the church, although it had nothing whatever to do, ostensibly, with the subject of religion. In 490 B.C. the Greek army under Miltiades defeated a large Persian army at Marathon, about twenty-five miles from Athens. It was one of the decisive battles of history, for the whole existence of the state of Athens was at stake. A runner, Pheidipides, ran all the way to Athens carrying the news. He gasped out the one word, "Victory," and then dropped dead.

The cartoon in the *Saturday Review* showed a runner with a torch coming swiftly to a group of anxious Athenians and the caption read, "*I forgot the message.*"

No wonder that we smile at that! What a terrific anticlimax that would be. The distraught Athenians waiting to hear the words that meant life or death, and then the confession of a dumb oaf, "I forgot the message."

Let the preacher look at that with heart-searching introspection. A preacher may have powerful equipment for pulpit work—great learning, rare skill, and moving eloquence. But even with these gifts, he might still have to say, if he told the truth, "I forgot the message." In exhibiting his learning and eloquence, he might forget the message of God's love to men, put into language that all can understand. It is a great, continual hazard in preaching against which every preacher must watch and pray.

The cartoon applies to all of us who are not preachers. We *are* messengers. People, often without our knowing it, are looking for some word from God in our lives. Do we say anything more than "I forgot the message"? There will be no message from God through us.

This picture of a man gasping out, "I forgot the message," applies also to a church. A church may have a magnificent Gothic building or Georgian Colonial edifice, or be a modern, functional structure, and, even with all this equipment, still be so spiritually bankrupt that it forgets God's message which all this equipment is designed to serve.

It is not the word, "forget," but a finer word, "remember." "*Remember* the words of the Lord Jesus" (Acts 20:35).

He Allowed His Claim to Lapse

In Mark Twain's novel *Roughing It* there is the story of a heartrending occurrence. It tells of a miner who staked out a rich claim, but lost it because of failure to do the necessary work on it during the required time. After he had allowed his claim to lapse, it proved to be immensely valuable. But the miner got nothing from it, for it was his no longer.

Think of that phrase used by Mark Twain, "Allowed his claim to lapse." Christopher Morley wrote that "there is nothing easier than not to read a book!" Agreed! When a person reads nothing worthwhile he allows his claim to be a citizen of the world of ideas to lapse. When a person does nothing about his religious life he allows his claim to be a citizen of the kingdom of heaven to lapse. Look at some of the causes for losing our riches of the Christian life.

1. The same cause as the one in the story by Mark Twain accounts for the failure of many people to keep their religious life as their possession; that is, "*failure to do the necessary work on it.*"

2. Our religious life fades away *if our purposes and dedications are not renewed.*

3. Religious life dwindles to nothing *when we do not feed the mind.*

Her Tasks Unequal to Her Strength

The closing hymn was "Rise up, O men of God." The congregation sang lustily, as that hymn should be sung. One man joined heartily in the singing, but he noticed that in one place he got some words in the wrong order. The mistake occurred in the lines about the Church:

> Her strength unequal to her task
> Rise up, and make her great!

The man found himself singing, "Her tasks unequal to her *strength.*"

The words of his mistake kept rolling around in his mind. He thought: "That often happens in the life of a church; the tasks which it undertakes are unequal to the strength which the church has."

So often a church could do many times more the work it is doing, could lift loads many times heavier than the easy loads it elects to lift.

"Dick" Sheppard, the beloved rector of St. Martin's-in-the-Fields in London, once described the situation of tasks unequal to strength by saying that many Christians are like a man who would put on a full mountaineering outfit, with pick and spikes on the shoes and fur clothing, all ready for an ascent up the Alps, and then merely walked up Ludgate Hill, an elevation of only a few feet.

Often a church which has the resources in men and women, and in brains and experience, might do great things in social conditions in the community—such as juvenile delinquency, or vice conditions—but it does nothing much more than put a new carpet in the church parlor.

Often we are like a person who, when a heavy sofa is to be moved into a house, calls out, "I will carry the pillow!" Do we carry pillows when there are heavy loads to lift? Are the tasks we accept at all equal to our strength?

A Bridge Costs a Life

There is a very common superstition about bridges to the effect that every bridge costs a life in the building. It is really more than a superstition, for many bridges have cost lives before they were finished. The same feeling is true of the erection of a skyscraper. Years ago in the early days of building skyscrapers, it did take about one life to a story in the building.

The idea of a bridge costing a life does picture the truth that throwing bridges across the tragic chasms which separate group from group, race from race, and nation from nation, is a costly undertaking into which life must be put. We read in the Bible that "without the shedding of blood there is no forgiveness of sins." It is true that without the shedding of blood there is no great and lasting accomplishment for the welfare of mankind. Think of the missionaries who have put their lives into the building of bridges of understanding and friendship between Asia and the West. How desperately such bridges are needed today! Think of the cruel discrimination against the black people in South Africa. Yet, thank God, there can be set against that the fact which looms big in the eyes of many Africans: Dr. Schweitzer in his hospital, is a white man as are hundreds of others who are giving their lives for the redemption of Africa.

Bridges of fellowship and brotherhood are needed in all our contacts. Bridge builders are peacemakers.

—PULPIT DIGEST

Man Is an Island

One of the quotations from literature most widely used in recent years is that from John Donne that declares that "no man is an island." This was made popular by Ernest Hemingway when he took the title for his novel, *For Whom the Bell Tolls*, from this quotation. The sentences from John Donne run: "No man is an island entire . . . Do not send to ask for whom the bell tolls . . . It tolls for thee."

That is deeply true. We are bound together in one bundle of life. We are, as John Donne goes on to say, "diminished" when someone dies. We are debtor to all.

Yet there is the reverse side of this truth which ought not to be forgotten. Man *is* an island. He lives in solitary confinement in the sense that he has a personal, individual life, which is his alone.

Of course, there is a bad sense in which some people are islands. The German writer Novalis said that "every Englishman is an island." That was not a compliment, but a criticism. He meant that Englishmen are reserved, withdrawn, hard to get acquainted with. However that may be, it is true that a person can make himself an island, an island on which he lives like a lonesome Robinson Crusoe, wrapped up in himself, like an island off from the mainland of human need and fellowship.

But there is a real sense in which every man *is* an island. Someone has called man the "Isle of Man." Each one has an inner life that is not a social affair, but an individual concern in the sight of God. The Spanish philosopher Ortega y Gasset in his last book has pictured this solitary nature of man's life. He writes: "Each man is an island in that he lives and dies in the solitude of his own consciousness." This private world, Ortega rightly says, is all important, and he thinks it is a tragic loss when that private world is lost in the pressure of "usages" about us. There is a very somber aspect to this, pictured in the solemn words of Kipling's poem, "Tomlinson":

> The sin that you do by two and two
> You pay for one by one.

It is true of some people that the reason they are so afraid of death is that it will be the first thing that they have ever done *alone!*

We live in days when the social quality of our culture is emphasized. This is a thing of great value. But we need, on that very account, to stress to this generation the personal responsibility of each person. The question is often asked and discussed: "If you were on a desert island, what books would you wish to have with you?" This question skips the point. In some ways, as we have been exploring, we *are* on a desert island where we have our personal life, shut away from the outside world. And the best book for the desert island on which each of us lives is the Bible.

It is well to carry in our mind that, just as each of us has his own personal responsibility, which we cannot unload on others or on "society," we also have the personal and eternal value of one soul, in the mind and heart of God. In that remembrance we know that our personal island is a blessed island, for "I know my sheep by *name.*"

Never Do Today . . .

Here is a loaded text. Go easy on it! *Never do today what you can put off till tomorrow.* Upon the truth of the familiar words one hardly need dwell. Their truth is obvious.

But there is another side to it. There are a lot of things which a person ought to leave open to the new data which will be supplied by further experience. It is a real tragedy to make up your mind too soon on matters where there is insufficient evidence. You don't have to make up your mind finally and completely. Put it off till tomorrow.

The whole thorny matter of prejudice comes in here. Prejudice means literally "judging too soon"; anti-race feeling directed against the Negro, for instance, is all too often caused by people unthinkingly accepting, without examination, popular slanders against a people or a race. They have not put off till tomorrow what could be put off, the final idea that is to guide them. Consequently their minds are not made up by thinking, but by gulping old prejudices that are not founded on real knowledge. You don't have to make up your mind now. Leave it open to larger experience. Put it off until tomorrow!

So with religion. All too many people have made up their minds, as they call it, before the real evidence from experience has begun to come in. Some people have shut themselves out of all the richness and power that might have come into life through Christian faith and discipleship, simply because they have closed the door early in life to any further consideration of religion. It is like a boy making up his mind about geometry while he is in the fourth grade, arriving at the profound conclusion that "there is nothing in it." Put it off! Jesus said, "He that doeth the will of God, shall know of the doctrine." Out of the doing will come an understanding that is based on experience.

So it is often, about our ideas about people. We make snap judgments, and never give them a chance. We make up our minds too soon, and too finally.

The same advice is true in connection with ideas about the welfare of the country in the political and economic realm. Science begins when the observation of facts is substituted for the repetition of traditions. When we cease to mouth over old slogans and really begin to open our eyes on the actual facts of the situation at present we are on our way to real thinking.

—THE CHAPLAIN

Talk Is *Not* Cheap

Hardly any popular saying is repeated more often, usually with scorn, than the words: "Talk is cheap." Of course, in the sense in which these words are usually said, it is *true* that talk is cheap. When mere talk, which costs nothing but a few breaths, is substituted for action, it is very cheap, a shabby, shamefully tawdry thing. Jesus gave his verdict on that kind of talk for all time when he said that the persons whom he accepted were not those who said "Lord, Lord!" but those who did the things that he said. That judgment falls on a church if it confines its attention to saying "Lord, Lord" every Sunday morning, but does not do sacrificially the things of love that he said all of his disciples should do.

There is a sense, however, and we had better remember it, in which talk is *not* cheap. That is, the right kind of talk.

In the days of the persecution of Christians under the Roman empire, the question was asked of a member of the Christian fellowship which met in the catacombs: "Are you a Christian?" If a man or woman answered with a firm "I am," that talk was not cheap. It cost a life! So, today, when we are asked to be included in some tough enterprise of the Church and the kingdom of God, and we say, "Yes, you can include me in it," that kind of talk is *not* cheap. All too frequently, when people are asked to be included in a hazardous and difficult undertaking, they respond with what was reported to have been the phrase of Sam Goldwyn, the movie producer: "Include me out."

Another kind of talk is not cheap—genuine talk to God in prayer. Some folks may be surprised at this. We have heard so much about the comfort of prayer. And it *is* a comfort! We have heard people speak and write about the privilege of prayer. And it *is* a privilege! But whoever says that genuine prayer is easy does not know what he is talking about. Prayer has its high costs. We must have humility, and that does not come easily. We must have honesty, and it is not easy for us always to stand without evasion. We must have repentance, and it is not always easy to say with conviction, "I was wrong. Forgive me." Someone has said that the three hardest words in the language to pronounce are "I was wrong." But if we will pay the price, the "talk" of prayer will be beyond all other words in its richness and benefit.

Put a silencer on the "cheap talk." Praise God with the costly talk.

Words Speak Louder Than Actions

The words above surely look like a printer's mistake! There is no proverb more deeply implanted within us than the reverse of the sentence above: "Actions speak louder than words." This, of course, is true. Often words, frequently swelling, windy words, are spoken when actions are needed to prove good faith, and such words are worth nothing as substitute for deeds. Jesus repeatedly emphasized this. He said: "By their fruits ye shall know them." Jesus' scorn for mere words is shown in his parable of the servant who, on being given an order by his master, said briskly, "I go, sir," and then did not go at all.

Yet, as often happens, the reverse is true in certain respects. Dr. J. A. Findlay, the British biblical scholar, has pointed out with truth that "quite half the things we do every day are done mechanically and would tell an observer nothing about our characters. On the other hand, nothing that we say offhand but reveals in one way or another the kind of person we are."

Think of this in terms of actual experience. How often there is no personal word to people recommending Christianity or inviting them to share in the worship of the church. It is all very well to put on a church bulletin board or in a newspaper advertisement, "Everyone welcome." But there is a world of difference between that formal statement, which often is only half true, and a personal word to an individual: "Will *you* come with *me* next Sunday?"

Think, in this connection, of the first verse of the Gospel of John: "In the beginning was the Word." In the beginning of every effective testimony of the church, or outreach to its community, is the Word. Christianity in the beginning was not spread by a company of mutes. It will not spread that way today, or ever. The early disciples went everywhere speaking the gospel.

Will you take these words, not as just a piece of writing, but as an earnest plea for putting God's invitation in our words to people? Will you hear the call: "Let the redeemed of the Lord say so"?

The Best Things in Life Are Not Free

An idea which by means of popular songs and endless repetition has worked its way into many minds is that "the best things of life are free." A few years ago there was a phonograph record in a juke box which kept moaning out this misinformation. That, of course, is true in the sense that

God's gifts of sky and sea and air are *gifts*. This is the truth expressed in Lowell's fine lines:

> 'Tis heaven alone that is given away
> 'Tis only God may be had for the asking.

The trouble begins when that feeling of the free gifts of God is spread over the whole of life, and thus blots out the deep truth that the best things of life cost heavily in time, effort, and devoted work. That is easily overlooked by people who are seeking something free. The goal of multitudes of people is expressed in the title of a recent book, *1001 Valuable Things You Can Get Free*. People prowl through the "give-aways" of life!

The old song affirmed that "love" is free. *Love and a happy home are not a free accident.* They cost heavily and continually. The high cost of a home is not in furniture or the refrigerator or the house, though those come high. The real cost of a happy home is greater. It is the denial of self, the demand for patience, the creating of a spiritual climate in the home. There is no bargain basement in the building of a true home.

The joy of the Lord is not free. An old song used to declare: "I'm glad salvation's free." Those words are misleading. Of course, we cannot buy the joy of the Lord with cash. But we find it only through following the way of loving self-giving after the manner of Jesus, "who for the joy that was set before him, endured the cross, despising the shame." That is never "free!" *Friendship is not free.* The only way to have a friend is to be one, and that involves thinking of others before one's self. And *a world of peace is never free.* It does not come from wishing. It demands a costly devotion to the things that make for peace among the nations. It demands courage to stand up for the things that make for peace against the clamor of groups that can see no policy in world affairs other than brute force.

The cost of such "best things" as these is great. But the value of them is beyond all measure!

—PULPIT DIGEST

Epilogue

"Now Go On With the Story"

It is a very common experience to pick up a magazine in which an installment of a serial story is printed and find at the beginning a short synopsis of the preceding chapters. That summary of what has gone before frequently ends with the words, "Now go on with the story."

Christianity is a serial story. It has been published in great installments. The next installment must be written by the minds and hearts, the life and work, of this generation. We may hear the commanding words, "Now go on with the story!"

The story from its earliest days has been a story about *God*. Bishop Kenneth Kirk, of Oxford, has said that in every time of upheaval people have asked the same question, "What is the world coming to?" They were asking it in the first century A.D. The Christians said that the world was asking the wrong question. The real question was not, "What is the world coming to?" but "*What has come to the world?*" The Christians were convinced that they had the answer to that query, that God has come to the world in Christ and that the things which Jesus Christ taught and for which he lived and died are the very center of the universe. That is our story. Go on with that story.

—Endless Line of Splendor

Index of Persons, Subjects, and Titles

Index of Scripture